Ruben E. Reina is chairman of the Anthropology Department at the University of Pennsylvania and curator of Latin American ethnology at the University Museum. He has published widely in the field of cultural anthropology. His most recent book is *The Law of the Saints: A Pokomam Pueblo and Its Community Culture* (1967).

PARANA
Social Boundaries in an Argentine City

Latin American Monographs, No. 31
Institute of Latin American Studies
The University of Texas at Austin

PARANA
Social Boundaries in an Argentine City

By RUBEN E. REINA

PUBLISHED FOR THE INSTITUTE OF LATIN AMERICAN STUDIES
BY THE UNIVERSITY OF TEXAS PRESS, AUSTIN AND LONDON

HN
270
P28
R4

Library of Congress Cataloging in Publication Data

Reina, Ruben E
　　Paraná; social boundaries in an Argentine city.

　　(Latin American monographs, no. 31)
　　Bibliography: p.
　　1. Paraná, Argentine Republic.—Social conditions.
　　2. Social classes—Paraná. Argentine Republic.
　　3. Social structure.　I. Title.　II. Series:
Latin American monographs (Austin, Tex.) no. 31.
HN270.P28R44　　　　301.4′00982′2　　　　72-8265
ISBN 0-292-76408-1

Copyright © 1973 by Ruben E. Reina
All Rights Reserved
Printed in the United States of America

Composition by G&S Typesetters, Austin
Printing by The University of Texas Printing Division, Austin
Binding by Universal Bookbindery, Inc., San Antonio

To

my parents, who continue to enjoy Argentina;
my wife and three sons, who graciously learned the Argentine ways;
my Paranaense friends;
and my friend Mark van Aken, who introduced me to
anthropology in 1946 while he was visiting Argentina.

CONTENTS

Acknowledgments xiii

Introduction xv

I. Paraná in History
    1. From Village to City 3
    2. The City and Its People 39

II. The Setting for Social Relations
    3. The Space for Social Relations: The *Vecindad* . . 85
    4. The *Vecindad* Style of Life: An Urban Paradox . . 111
    5. *Vecindad* and Beyond: Voluntary Associations . . 138

III. Principles of Social Organization
    6. Social Class: The Basic Model for Social Organization 171
    7. Social Classes: Manifestations and Dynamics . . 217

IV. Growing Up: To Live Is to Conquer
    Introduction 259
    8. Finding Social Boundaries 263
    9. Alone in School 278
    10. The Argentine Paranaense 313

V. Images of the City
    11. The Diversity of Social Images: An Inventory
        of Paranaense Views 339

Epilogue 367

Works Cited 377

Index 383

ILLUSTRATIONS

Plates

Following page 168

Entre Ríos: From the Country to the City
   Entre Ríos Countryside; Approaching Paraná
   Entering the City; A Tobacco Farmer beside His Home
   A Russian-German Farmer; Farmyard of a Russian-German Family
   The Country and the City; The City Seen from across the River

The City: From the Plaza to the Barrios
   La Plaza Central; The Cathedral
   City Hall and the Normal School; The Public Library
   Second-Floor Residence of a Socially Prominent Family; Club Social
   Traditional Residences in the Central Part of the City
   "Modern Style" Residences Overlooking the Paraná River
   Asociación Español; Residences of Early Basque Immigrants
   Residences Farther Away from the Plaza
   Modest Middle-Class Homes; *Rancho* Homes of the *Clase Baja*
   Barricada of *Rancho* Homes; Fisherman's Home along the River

Vecindad Life
   A Middle-Class *Vecindad*; Retailing Soda Water House-to-House
   Green-Vegetable Seller; Milk Delivery; Carnival Water-Throwing Game

Public Celebrations
   Carnival Pageantry
   Funeral Procession Leaving the Cathedral
   Celebration of the Mass at the Statue of Justo José de Urquiza
   Observance of a National Holiday

Following page 344

Social Classes in Paraná
   A Woman of the *Clase Tradicional*; Country People; *Vecinos*

Illustrations   xi

A Paraná River Fisherman and His Family
La Tradición Criolla; *La Curandera*; Shoeshine Boy

Private and Public Schools
The Traditional Public-School White Uniform
Private-School Boys; Public-School Football Team

Burial by Social Class
The Cemetery
Individual Mausoleums of Upper-Class Families
Mausoleum for Members of the Italian Society
Graves in the Walls of the Cemetery
Individual Tombs
Modest Graves
Grave Marker

FIGURES

1.	Argentina	5
2.	Distribution by Age and Sex: Total Population (1824)	11
3.	Distribution by Age and Sex: Whites (1824)	12
4.	Distribution by Age and Sex: Pardos (1824)	12
5.	Distribution by Age and Sex: Indians (1824)	13
6.	Distribution by Age and Sex: Negroes (1824)	13
7.	Entre Ríos Province: Rural Land Use	22
8.	Cross Section of Street Ecology	27
9.	Plan of the City of Paraná, 1890	34
10.	Growth of Paraná	36
11.	City of Paraná, 1965	41
12.	Social *Ambiente* of Paraná	49
13.	Distribution of Social Institutions	54
14.	Floor Plan of a Traditional Upper-Class Home	57
15.	Sources of Street Names	67
16.	Percentage of Argentines in the Grandparents' Generation	72
17.	An Informant's Social Map of Paraná	77
18.	City Clubs in Paraná	139
19.	Informant's Social Class Model	200
20.	Map of the Cemetery	218
21.	Stratification Model through Time	253

TABLES

1.	Household Composition: Case I	17
2.	Household Composition: Case II	17
3.	Distribution of Male Occupations by Ethnic Categories	18
4.	Comparative Census Figures	24
5.	Distribution of Population in the Four City Quarters, 1890	35
6.	Marriage by Ethnic Background	74
7.	Distribution of Paranaenses of Foreign Descent	75
8.	Distribution of Argentine Paranaenses by Place of Birth	76
9.	Paranaense Students	292

ACKNOWLEDGMENTS

In the course of the field work, hundreds of individuals were observed and thousands of telephone calls made and received. But much credit must go to a group of informants, representing all social levels, who were most cooperative in my undertaking. The informants' statements, combined with observations, my early experiences as an Argentine, and the literature available provided an overwhelming amount of information. In the labyrinth of data, however, I have uncovered explanations and derived interpretations. I consciously reimmersed myself in the Argentine city way of life, and I am grateful to the people of Paraná who allowed me to be in familiar territory as a stranger. They did this patiently, with curiosity and elegant courtesy. The list of people that I would thank is just too long, but each one knows the degree of my personal appreciation. I cannot, however, bypass this opportunity to mention three gentlemen who met with me for hours during my revisit in September 1967 to listen to the content of each chapter and to comment upon my interpretations. To Professor Filberto Reula, Professor Marcos Rosenberg, and Enrique Etchemendigaray, my warm thanks. Also, this study would not have been possible without the enthusiasm of Dr. Jorge Hardoy, now affiliated with the Instituto Torcuato Di Tella and director of the city planning program.

I am especially grateful to two graduate students in anthropology at the University of Pennsylvania, Henry Schwarz III and Sandra Hurlong Karawalla, who took the opportunity to further their anthropological training by assisting me in the field work. Their cooperation, enthusiasm, and friendship made the field situation a pleasant learning experience for everyone.

My thanks go as well to Virginia Greene, also a graduate student in the Anthropology Department at the University of Pennsylvania, who prepared the maps and drawings; to Joel Sherzer and Malcah Yeager, graduate students in the Linguistics Department of the University of Pennsylvania, who assisted me with the analysis of the linguistic data; to Edward O'Flaherty, S.J., graduate student in anthropology at the University of Pennsylvania, who, as first reader, made helpful comments; to Ronald Hicks for his editorial advice at an early stage of the manuscript; to Virginia Lathbury, my research assistant in anthropology at the University of Pennsylvania, for her helpful editorial comments; to Mrs. Lee Ann Crawford for her fine typing of the final manuscript; and to Ruth M. and Alfred G. Zantzinger for sponsoring the publication of photographs and illustrations. I am indebted to each of these persons for his or her special contribution.

I particularly appreciate the teaching of Dr. Horace Miner of the University of Michigan, who in 1948 introduced me to the study of cities through his work in Timbuctoo. My special thanks also to my University of Pennsylvania colleagues, Dr. Richard Beeman of the History Department and Drs. Robert Dyson and Igor Kopytoff of the Anthropology Department, and to Dr. James Scobie of the History Department at Indiana University, for their suggestions and the exchange of ideas while I was preparing the manuscript. In the course of interacting with colleagues and students, I gained further insight into the nature of the phenomena studied.

I am deeply indebted to Miss Roma Skoczylas, who worked for me as research assistant. Miss Skoczylas undertook the administration of the work, went through each page of the manuscript making valuable suggestions for improving the text, and contributed to the presentation of the study. For her fine assistance over a period of two years and her dedication to the task of helping me to complete the work at an earlier date than would have been otherwise possible, I am sincerely grateful.

Under the sponsorship of the Overseas Latin American Program of the Ford Foundation, I spent a year (1964–1965) in Argentina. My gratitude for the cooperation of Mr. Harry Wilhelm of the Ford Foundation and the financial support of this institution can hardly be expressed with a simple word of thanks. Views and interpretations do not necessarily represent the opinion of those who assisted me or made the research work possible; for that aspect of the work, I assume full responsibility.

INTRODUCTION

In Argentina, modern cities are fascinating centers in which rural Argentines strongly aspire to become urbanites. Cities dominate the *ambiente* of the nation, and nowadays much of the people's behavior may be understood in relation to the strong desire to be a city resident. To them, this means being modern, progressive, and cosmopolitan. This book explores the ways of an Argentine city. Daily events and personalities are a major source of information, making this study of Paraná an intimate social portrait of the life of the present population. The study is specific and actual, and it portrays the basic cultural and social profiles of its people.

The general reader may find the work to be a departure from the traditional anthropological studies of contemporary primitives.[1] Relatively recently, however, there has been a shift of attention from primitive, nonliterate societies to peasants, to rural people, to the urbanites of modern states.[2] The study of our complex civilization presents a promising new intellectual endeavor for anthropologists; life in complex and industrialized societies can be expected to bring fresh insights and the development of further conceptual perspectives.[3]

Paraná, with a population of over 100,000, contains many—if not

[1] Early anthropologists did not address themselves to the study of contemporary states or nations, and American anthropology in particular, linked as it has been to European scholarship, was "built on detailed studies of the living behavior, the buried remnants of earlier periods, the vanishing complicated languages, and the remembered customs of the American Indians" (Mead and Bunzel 1960:1). For further treatment of the history of anthropology, the following works are recommended: Lowie 1937; Penniman 1952; C. Erasmus 1953; Mead and Bunzel 1960; De Laguna 1960; Hallowell 1960.

[2] For an extended discussion of early anthropology, see also Powdermaker 1966: chapter 2.

[3] For further information on "the problems arising out of the application of the methods and approaches developed in social anthropology to the study of more complex societies—whether 'historical' or modern societies or parts thereof," see Eisenstadt 1961.

all—of the basic Argentine national elements. It is, however, a city of less urban sophistication than the industrialized cities of Buenos Aires or Córdoba. Paraná in 1965 was an administrative center, capital of the province of Entre Ríos. If Paraná is representative of Argentina in some ways, it is not in many others.

What makes Paraná ideal for anthropological research? Historically, Paraná participated in the consolidation and development of the nation, particularly when in 1852 it led the Confederación of several provinces of the interior. It became the provisional seat of the Confederación, and in that role the city social structure was modified. For a period of almost ten years there was social agitation in the city because of the addition of people of distinction. Social differentiations were sharpened as diplomats and politicians were added to a local aristocracy that had developed in previous years with land as the basis of its wealth and social standing. Dating from 1730, the small settlement along the shores of the Paraná River grew in population and political importance until it formally became a city in 1826 and the capital of its province in 1883. Local and national events during this period helped to harden the lines of social structure in the city in ways that parallel those of Buenos Aires, the capital and model of Argentine culture.

Many Argentine social features must be related to an era of European colonization between 1853 and 1895. Paraná is the product of much immigration. Italians, Russians, Germans, British, Swiss, and Middle Easterners came to Paraná and surrounding towns, and without a doubt these newcomers behaved, consciously or unconsciously, according to patterns prevalent in the countries of their origin. No doubt they introduced new models into the developing community culture. The process of social coagulation that resulted from the arrival in the "promised land" of these many human elements with their variety of cultural traditions constitutes an intimate aspect of Paraná development.

Paraná was finally selected for study above other possible choices because neither recent urban development and industrial expansion nor political revolution has changed it radically, although Paraná is in the current of twentieth-century Argentina. The absence of severe

Introduction   xvii

breakdowns has resulted in a minimum of outside interference, and the city contains many unadulterated elements of earlier periods of Argentine culture. The culture of this city, which originated as a village and grew with the development of the nation, has—in comparison with other Argentine cities—retained many of the early elements, and early families now form the core of the traditional elite group. There is also a strong criollo element—natives of Spanish ancestry. The situation seemed therefore most appropriate for an attempt to ascertain the basic model of the society and to explore questions related to the fundamental nature of the Paranaenses' interpersonal relations, social principles, and cultural trends.

The present study has as its main objective the description of the way of life of people in a *city*. The nature of the urban way of life and of the urban world view has become known to anthropologists primarily through the efforts of other disciplines. The assumption of an urban life style as a unique cultural consequence of the city has been given wide theoretical treatment. However, the disassociation of urban life from cities has begun to evolve from the empirical material as a significant theoretical proposition. Some studies[4] support the cautious statement made by Louis Wirth that "urbanism as a way of life [is] not exclusively found in settlements which are cities in the physical and demographic sense."[5] Many questions about the city and about urbanism remain unanswered. I personally hope that, as a contemporary city study, this work will not only give a new dimension to our understanding of Paraná society, to Argentine culture, and to those Latin American cities that are products of Spanish conquest and European colonization, but also a clearer theoretical understanding of the city as a social entity.

Specific Approach

Culture is a central anthropological concept, one that has played a vital and basic role in every anthropologist's research. One's conception of culture becomes central to the perspective of one's analysis.[6]

---
[4] E.g., Reina 1964.
[5] Wirth 1938:7.
[6] Kroeber and Kluckhohn 1952.

Culture is defined here as the accumulation of human events through *time*, directly *experienced* by members of a specific social group, from which the living members derive *assumptions* and create *principles*[7] to guide their thinking and behavior. Culture is then an ever-moving phenomenon with a high degree of constancy that, while uninterrupted, may continue to move and to build upon its own components and dynamics. As the members of a society procreate and new generations move through time (history), they cannot escape confrontation with new events. These cause the testing and reevaluation of the principles formulated earlier that underlie the culture. The assumptions made about these principles and the dynamics of their interrelations may be thus summarized:

1. The principles form a philosophical system—closed and tightly woven, or partially and loosely interwoven.
2. Through time, single principles and clusters of functionally related ones may remain unchanged, be modified, or simply pass to an inactive level and perhaps be forgotten as events in history demand their reevaluation.
3. Periods of strenuous and competitive contact are the crucial moments for reflection, critical analysis, and evaluation of these principles.
4. The principles are directly related to bringing about a satisfactory form of human existence, variously viewed with optimism or skepticism as the holders and active practitioners are experiencing comforts under normal conditions or stress during crisis.
5. In this theoretical context, material traits, by their symbolic meaning, assume an integral relationship to the principles and thus to culture.
6. In sum, human activities become culturally relevant because they are governed by the socially bounded system of principles. This system, when recognized and widely shared, serves to activate the forces of social history.

The stage (ecology), the actors (people), and the action (activi-

---

[7] Taken in the sense of a governing law of conduct.

Introduction

ties) represent the overall features of a basic social setting, a setting that can be observed in the present, cannot be divorced from the roots of its past, and has all the potential for surviving into the future. The anthropologist, therefore, immerses himself in the setting of the present to observe and to participate in this historically created phenomenon called *culture*.

Other scientists have verbalized the principles of a society through other procedures or derived them subjectively, and it is the anthropologist's task to verify and to amplify these other statements. The role of the anthropologist requires more than mere participation and observation in a society at a single point in time; rather, like a historian, it is by association with the society through time that depth can be achieved. In this fashion, the anthropologist will be able to derive and test what is culturally relevant in a society. Such studies will show *when* and *how* principles acquire the philosophical importance and strength that guide the relationships of people with each other, with their environment, and with their universe, both in the present and in the future.

To study culture in complex societies can indeed be an overwhelming task, particularly since the methodology and theory compel one to search through time for the meaning of events and their relationship to principles and to observed behavior. Through this intellectual process, anthropology seeks an empirically based statement of the principles underlying human behavior for the organization of data.

In Paraná, the middle class served as the focal point for the study of city culture. But as a consequence of the holistic anthropological approach, other social levels were also surveyed; one cannot treat one social level without reference to the others. Since Paraná has only a very small group of non-middle-class families, the numerical factor forced one to be in constant touch with persons of the *clase media*. For certain social interactions the city has its ideal and real class distinctions, but the majority of Paranaenses consider themselves middle class. Among this middle class one finds social and economic life of the city continuing at a rapid pace of development and mobility, and the concomitant ambitions and aspirations are above the real means of the people. Furthermore, the people of the middle class were responsible for significant political changes following 1890,[8] and in their hands today rests much of the destiny of the nation. Social scientists and historians have published studies about the end result of the public and personal actions of the middle class, and it seems especially appropriate to begin with them and then to branch out to the *clase aristocrática* and to the *clase humilde*.

In 1948 Carl C. Taylor interpreted "the cultural status, participation and behavior of the Argentine farmers." In his discussion, the national class differentiation was needed to classify the people. He states: "Farm operators and their families are the real *middle class*. . . . Peons, especially transient farm laborors, are the *lower class*. Owners of great tracts of land, often absentee owners, are the *upper class*."[9]

If the concept of social class is central to understanding the rural situation, the same principle is basic to understanding the total situation of Paraná. The emphasis in this work is on the relationships between individuals and between groups and the tensions experienced in the course of the development of a distinct way of life. An important aspect of this ethnography is, then, to show the differentiation, the structural separation, and the interconnection between classes in the city.

The differentiation of Paranaenses into classes is not based solely on economic status, occupation, or educational criteria. Along with the structure of classes, a strong awareness or consciousness of being in a distinctive social category is fundamental. Each level possesses significant stylistic differences, yet these are not sufficient to consider each level a separate subculture. The complexity of the middle class alone, not to mention the classes above or below it, presents innumerable problems of analysis. Since a really thorough ethnographic study would provide material for several volumes, I have chosen to focus on the interrelationships of individuals within each of the social categories that are acknowledged by the whole population. The social

---

[8] Scobie 1964a:195.
[9] Taylor 1948:419, emphasis added. For another treatment on the subject, see Strickon 1962.

structure of Paraná allows for the movement of people between the classes, and such socially marginal individuals, who are in the process of changing their social affiliation, provide data on the interrelationship between the three classes in Paraná.

In preparing this work I have therefore consciously presented an ethnography in which I allow the facts and the informants to speak for themselves. The general reader can become well informed about life in an Argentine city while teachers and students may feel stimulated to apply to the data classical theoretical models that have contributed to the understanding of the organization of society. Discussion of economic development or formal political life of the city as specific and separate categories has not been included. Nor have I included direct discussions of Paraná social organization in the context of theories on urbanization or social class.[10] The point of view of the informants has prevailed, and their interpretations have dictated much of the composition of the work. The reader may be left with the task of piecing together some facts and undeveloped ideas. But central to the study is the attempt to document the premises underlying public behavior and to focus on the social elements that hold the city culture together. This has been the author's task.

The Problem of Participation

The study of a technologically modern group of people residing in a city that is the head of a *municipio* and the capital of a province has constituted a challenge, especially for learning about the culture of an urban environment in a Latin American nation. My personal experiences in Argentina and North America—education in Argentine primary and secondary schools, my professional training in North Ameri-

---

[10] The literature dealing with the social phenomenon of social class and urbanization and urbanism as a way of life is voluminous, but each is a topic in its own right, not to be discussed directly in this study. One significant contribution on urbanization in Latin America is Morse 1965. Another excellent historical treatment of urbanization, with an emphasis upon failure of social historians to undertake the study of urbanization as a social process, can be found in Lampard 1961.

For a review of "Differentiation and Variation in Social Structures," see Parsons, Shils, Naegele, and Pitts 1962: vol. 1, part 2, especially pp. 517–573 on stratification and mobility.

can universities, the years of field work among the Maya of Guatemala, the study of entrepreneurship in Argentina, and my acquaintance with Spain—all stand as the background for this study. However, although on familiar ground in studying an Argentine social group, I purposely attempted to maintain a detached curiosity for the phenomena at hand, just as I had done among the Guatemalans of Mayan descent. Because Argentina presented a familiar context, I was able to bypass the period of cultural disorientation, and the problem became the further penetration into the adult world that I had missed. I decided to organize the data relevant to the theoretical context of cultural anthropology, but this process was not simple. Perhaps the hardest part for an anthropologist is to immerse himself in the study of a culture of which he has been a part.

For methodological purposes, the work bespeaks its usefulness and its limitations. That the findings have been secured in only certain segments of the city society could not have been avoided. This, in fact, has been the inevitable result of most anthropological studies, although it is assumed that one misses fewer aspects of the way of life when the settlement is small. By ordering my findings and by searching for explanations through the use of (1) traditional concepts that were found to be active social guidelines for that society and (2) concepts from the general social sciences, particularly those concerned with the phenomena of social organizations and culture, it is hoped that a satisfactory contribution to the understanding of urban life can be made. It is my special concern, however, to begin to understand those fundamental aspects of Argentine culture that condition those born in Argentina.

"To enter into the minds of the people," to look at individuals and, through them, at their world, was fundamental to the approach of this study; and much was gained by playing a consciously detached role among familiar things and by not becoming "renativized." The approach to the study of Paraná was not different from that used in my study of a pueblo of Mayan Indians in Guatemala.[11] If among the people of Chinautla I was stimulated by the many theoretical issues regarding the nature of culture and the nature of existence in that

[11] Reina 1966.

milieu, my curiosity was even greater about the phenomenon of life in a city. Of course, subduing this curiosity presented a task far more difficult than the Guatemalan case; the difference in size alone was overwhelming. Fortunately, Argentines are generous informants. They are people who value and cultivate the art of verbal interaction; but, by the same token perhaps, they are more sensitive than other persons to observation. One other obstacle to my inquiry was their high degree of awareness of social differentiation. My field experience in Argentina was different from that among the Mayan people because, after all, it was within another type of society—one composed of highly literate and socially sensitive individuals struggling with the uncertainties provoked by national and international politics and dealing with other, secondary problems characteristic of our modern world.

Following completion of the field-work period, the analysis and interpretation of the data was a stimulating intellectual process. Presentation of the material was guided by the basic assumption that life is not lived compartmentally but integrally, and that it is my task "to grasp what integration [one] can perceive,"[12] for it is assumed that "it is this integration that meets the needs of a people, as it also guides their needs; and [the anthropologist] is aware of the adaptive qualities of these links, their resistance to change, the wider ramification in the lives of people when they are broken."[13]

In sum, this work does not claim to be more than an exploratory study, both for its methodology and for its ethnographic description. If a theoretical contribution is expected, it should derive from the specific emphasis on the social organization of the city and on the ways in which the elements of culture and the present national political and economic situation affect the behavior of the residents.

During the 37th Congress of Americanists in September 1966, scholars interested in urbanization in America felt that there had been a lack of interest among specialists in the field of contemporary urbanization.[14] Perhaps this study of a modern Argentine city may be con-

---

[12] Wolf 1964:93.
[13] Ibid.
[14] Hardoy 1967:84.

sidered a step forward in this vacant area and may be the basis for future comparisons. Further, it is hoped that the work may answer some of the questions raised by Argentines themselves concerning the many perplexing aspects of their society and culture, particularly questions related to changes, reforms, development, and culture continuity.

I. Paraṇā in History

1. FROM VILLAGE TO CITY

It is the story of how these villagers, leaders and followers, made up their minds to do something and then did it. The unity of the history lies in the central fact of the conspicuous collective effort of these people to make their community the progressive chief community of their region. This is a small history with a central theme: a purpose of a people and its outcome.[1]

Early Settlements

The delta region of the Río de la Plata was discovered by the Spanish in 1516, and later was visited many times by explorers. In search of an easy access to Peru, they traveled upstream on the Paraná River and established the town of Asunción del Paraguay in 1537. The first attempt to settle and develop Buenos Aires was not successful, and Asunción became a place of importance in the southern hemisphere. No easy passage was found to Peru, but much territory was discovered and mapped, and other cities besides Asunción were founded, including Tucumán (1565), Córdoba (1573), Santiago del Estero (1582), Salta (1582), La Rioja (1591), and Jujuy (1592)—a line of cities linking Peru on the Pacific with the Atlantic coast. Another series of cities was established following a westerly course to Chile; it

---

[1] Redfield 1958:101–102.

included Mendoza (1561), San Juan (1562), and San Luis (1596). These are testimony to the assertion that, in their strenuous effort to dominate the southern portion of South America, the Spaniards—who were not "frontiersmen or farmers, but rather soldiers, administrators, and masters"—relied on the "institution of the city, so deeply rooted in their own history, for the means to settle and control these new lands and peoples."[2]

The geographic region within which these historical events took place is generally known today as the Mesopotamia of Argentina (fig. 1). It is an area located between two large and navigable rivers, the Paraná-Paraguay system and the Uruguay. In this region, more specifically along the margin of the Paraná River, colonizer and Indian dramatically came into contact, each in his own way seeking to maintain hegemony.

Several groups of Indians inhabited the entire area of the Chaco, Mesopotamia, and Pampa regions. The native Indian population of Argentina was not large (about 300,000). In some instances the Indians were taken under Spanish authority; in others a chief (cacique) with a handful of families requested that they be settled in a town with a religious leader. Many Indians died, some from fighting the white men and others from European diseases, especially smallpox. As a result of such conditions, Argentina presents a different picture from that of Mexico, Guatemala, or Peru, where many thousands of Indians were subjugated and acculturated. The history of Argentina is filled with examples of times in which the Spanish and criollos were not conquering natives with the same enthusiasm with which they were acquiring land.[3] In this part of the New World, the Spanish

[2] Scobie 1964a:36.
[3] The word "criollo" originally distinguished Spanish descendants born in the new lands under the Spanish crown from the Spanish born on the Iberian Peninsula. This definition remains today, with the addition that it may sometimes include others of European descent born in Argentina. It has also acquired in some regions a social connotation of another tenor. A criollo could be a person who follows a pseudo-gaucho way of life, is poor, and lives in the peripheral and socially marginal areas of the city or in the country. A *criollito* or *criollita* can mean an uneducated native person of humble origin, very likely someone who performs domestic service. In these cases the concept is even stronger when the physical characteristic of dark skin is present. Criollo in this sense is used interchangeably with *negro*.

Fig. 1. Argentina

from different parts of Spain, holders of different Spanish regional traditions, faced a new territory with a new project. They were settlers, and thus the situation represents a different conceptual problem. The process in the southern part of the hemisphere appears to have been a strong instance of cultural transplantation rather than one of grafting.

In this case, the anthropologist does not have to deal with two traditions in a situation of acculturation, as in other regions of South and Central America. Rather, he simply needs to concentrate on the "culture of conquest," that is, what was discarded, added, adjusted, and screened as territorial expansion occurred in a new environment.[4] It might seem in this new situation that many ideals of the old Spanish culture could have been more sharply defined in response to the exciting challenge of turning social chaos into order. It must be remembered, however, that these patterns were ideal for the homeland but were not practicable here.

The real problem faced by the colonists was the Spanish cultural plurality that no longer remained spatially separated as it had been in the motherland. The variety of Spanish regional cultures was dramatically represented within one settlement, and Andalusians, Basques, Galicians, Castilians, and others had to learn to share the locale and its administration and to compromise in their high aspirations of acquiring wealth, social status, and political power. So the years of the conquest were decades of many decisions, a formative period when new adjustments were necessary.

Ortega y Gasset, analyzing the Spanish colonization of America, indicates that this was the work of the pueblo, of the common people. The problems of colonization were of a social nature, because the common people, "without conscious design, without directors, without deliberate tactics, engendered other peoples . . . but they did not give what they did not have—discipline, a live culture, a progressive civilization."[5] He indicates, again rather pessimistically, the absence of qualified people during the colonization which prevented the colonies

---

[4] Cf. Foster 1960:12.
[5] Ortega y Gasset 1937:84–85.

from developing like some other nations. "The masses," he writes, are unable "to distinguish the best man from the worst"[6] and destroy the good men when they have them.

But if the masses came without the proper background to govern well, the exigencies of the New World were sufficient impetus for them to develop, to achieve status and establish an elite in each locale, and to accumulate wealth from natural resources and from public administration. If it was the commoners who came and translated the wishes of the Crown into reality, if it was the commoners who, when experiencing a new sense of freedom, found possible the realization of their aspirations and the exercising of their egos, it was also the commoners who attempted to create a new society, a modification of what they knew; and the criollos, their descendants, found even more justification for politically independent society. It became their task, although probably without awareness of the goals, to create a vertebrated society in the New World, rather than to perpetuate the social and political problems of an "invertebrated Spain."[7]

The settlements of the Mesopotamian region of Argentina and, more directly, of Santa Fé and Paraná share many fundamental features of conquest-colonization with other areas of Hispano America. The Paraná case allows us to see some of the sociocultural processes from the outset, but it is only a limited case. Paraná is unique in that it was not settled with the thought that it would become a leading city; it was also a latecomer in the list of colonial settlements, having been founded to facilitate communication and commerce with Tucumán and Peru.

Of more importance during the sixteenth century was Santa Fé, a good port established on the western bank of the Paraná River in 1573 by the conquistador Juan de Garay, who also founded Buenos Aires in 1580. (In both of Garay's expeditions, the number of criollo settlers exceeded that of the Spaniards.) The history of Santa Fé for a period of 150 years is filled with accounts of attacks by marauding Indians who plundered in search of merchandise, and who so debilitated the community that at times its survival was in question.

[6] Ibid., p. 86.
[7] General theme of Ortega y Gasset.

The *reducciones* organized by the Jesuits did not halt the Indian attacks, though they perhaps facilitated the occupation of large expanses of land by the settlers. Still, it was nearly two centuries before the Indians retreated north and west and the frontiers of this region became safe for the founding of other pueblos. And while Santa Fé was defending itself against the Indians, other communities such as Córdoba were enjoying relative peace and were able to develop without the threat of Indian attacks.

Survival was in question. The Spanish conquerors felt that even should the Indians be subdued they could never become truly "civilized." But if they regarded the Indians in this manner, they actually felt no more secure about the criollos, who were considered untrustworthy. And mestizos were believed to be even less reliable.

While Santa Fé was trying to forestall assaults by the Indians, colonists were moving to the fertile land along the Paraná River. The available land was at first divided into long parallel tracts perpendicular to the eastern bank of the river. A large part of the region between the Paraná and the Uruguay rivers, which is now the province of Entre Ríos, was owned by one man, don Hernando Arias de Saavedra of Santa Fé, who in 1607 headed an expedition and took for himself twenty leagues of land along the eastern bank of the Paraná, extending eastward to the Uruguay River, a total of one thousand square leagues. By 1648, much of the territory between the two rivers had been settled by administrators and leaders of Santa Fé and by the Jesuit order.

It was in 1671 that the officials of Santa Fé decided to establish an encomienda for Maestro de Campo Francisco Arias de Saavedra, in whose trust were placed the Indians of the land. The settlement was called La Bajada de Paraná and was located four leagues from Santa Fé, across the river. The first settlers came from Santa Fé, and from this beginning the city of Paraná grew.[8]

During the first fifty years of its existence, La Bajada de Paraná was producing most of the food for Santa Fé. Indian raiders frequently

[8] Cervera 1907.

terrorized the newer settlement, seeing its prosperity as an easy means to satisfy their needs. In addition to the Indians, the area around La Bajada attracted unwanted displaced persons, including vagrants (*vagos*), vicious men (*viciosos*), and outlaws (*alzados*). The activities of these social outcasts, as well as those of the Indian marauders, filled the reports transmitted from the mayor of La Bajada to the officials in Santa Fé.

Toward the end of the eighteenth century, La Bajada became the largest town between the Paraná and Uruguay rivers. Ecclesiastically, it was a *parroquia* (parish) under the protection of the Virgin of Rosario, and was serviced by one priest. Politically, it was still administered from Santa Fé. But progress was in the minds of its inhabitants; records provide evidence that the people of La Bajada entertained the idea of separating themselves from the administration of Santa Fé. With communication across the river not always easy and with increasing pressure from the politically unorganized interior, separation from Santa Fé became the political issue of the day.

Santa Fé did not approve of such an action, but a petition received by the viceroy prompted him to commission the assistant mayor, don Tomás de Rocamora, to look into the situation. Rocamora favored the separation and argued that the fertility of the soil around Paraná and the robust character of its people would be positive factors. Its men, he stated in his report, could serve in the military and help to protect the area from vagrants or from foreigners who could easily navigate the river.

Even though the viceroy approved the recommendation, relations between Santa Fé and La Bajada de Paraná grew very tense. Rocamora now had military and political power in his hands, and he continued to apply pressure toward separation by not accepting the nomination of a mayor (*alcalde de hermandad*) proposed by Santa Fé. Only after several years of political uncertainty did La Bajada de Paraná become a *villa* in 1801, though without the formal approval of the higher colonial authorities. Viceroy Cisneros visited Paraná in 1809, when the question of declaring La Bajada a *villa* was discussed formally, and finally in 1810, Paraná was given this status by the General Assembly.

The *villa* continued under the protection of the Virgin of Rosario, although she was not declared patroness until 1825. Paraná could now form its own *cabildo* (town administration), composed of an *alcalde ordinario*, a *corregidor decano*, an *alguacil mayor*, a *regidor defensor de pobres*, *regidor defensor de menores*, and a *síndico personero de la villa*.

The territory became known as Entre Ríos; the people became active in commercial and clandestine dealings with Brazil and La Banda Oriental del Uruguay. Terrain with heavy vegetation provided safe places for covert activities and hideouts for outlaws. The population of the interior, socially outcast and ethnically mixed, became known for its shrewdness and bravado, though at the same time it was acknowledged that these persons led lawless and seditious lives. These people, later called the *gauchos entrerrianos*, actively participated in the civil disturbances under the leadership of strongmen (caudillos).

The aim of total separation from Santa Fé and of creation of a new province remained an important public issue on which steady progress was made. Following Argentina's independence from Spain in 1816, the Congress of Tucumán drafted a central constitution; this the Entrerrianos rejected, instead proclaiming themselves the Republic of Entre Ríos, a creation that was soon dissolved, however. In 1822, Paraná became the capital of the province of Entre Ríos, but the seat of the provincial government was shortly transferred to Concepción del Uruguay, a town on the banks of the Uruguay River.

In 1826 both Paraná and Concepción del Uruguay were elevated to city status, and their political and economic roles divided the province into two spheres of influence. By this time, the province was under the control of citizens of Entre Ríos, criollos who became the public administrators active in the political, social, and economic existence of the area. They were to become prominent, to hold much land in the province, and to form the social aristocracy of the region. The economic and political domination of the province by criollos became evident; they held the important positions in the administration, the clergy, and the military, while Indians and Negroes were given no place in government and depended for their livelihood upon employment as domestic servants.

DISTRIBUTION BY AGE AND SEX: TOTAL POPULATION
3,643 INDIVIDUALS

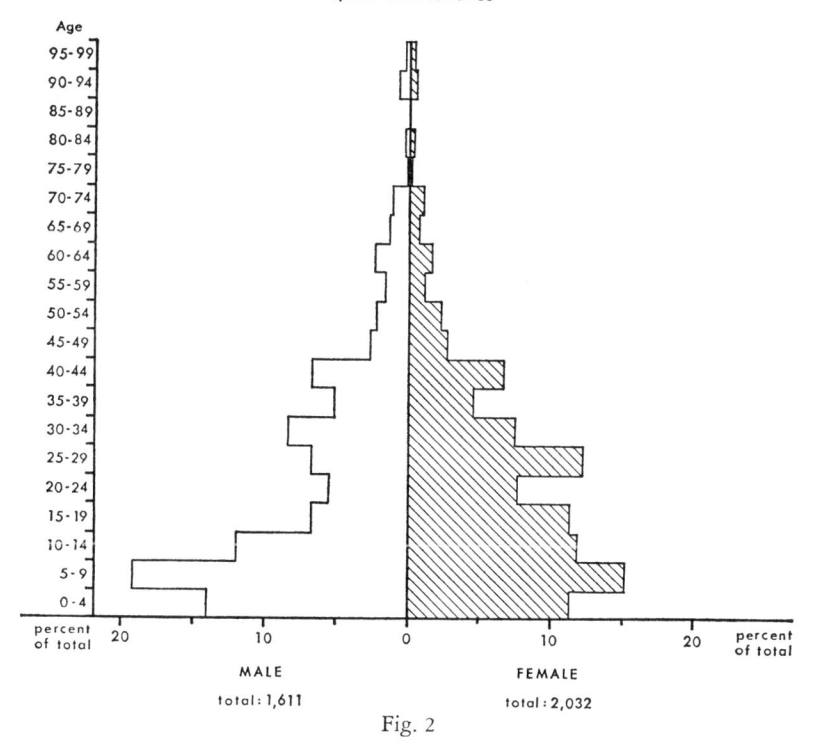

Fig. 2

Sociological Profile of the Village

By 1820, Paraná had begun to acquire its own social physiognomy and to offer the services of a stable settlement. In 1824, the local authorities conducted a census. This record, now in the provincial archives in Paraná, provides information about every household in that year by listing each resident and giving his status (husband, wife, child, servant, slave, peon, or resident employee), birthplace, age, race, and occupation. Thus, an analysis of this document offers a broad picture of the village's demographic and social composition; it shows, for example, that Paraná then contained 3,643 inhabitants—1,611 males and 2,032 females—and that the majority of individuals were white (67.6 percent), while 16.1 percent were Pardo, 12.0 percent were Indian, and 4.3 percent Negro (figs. 2–6).[9]

[9] The statistics in figures 2–6 are from the 1824 census.

DISTRIBUTION BY AGE AND SEX: WHITES
2,466 INDIVIDUALS

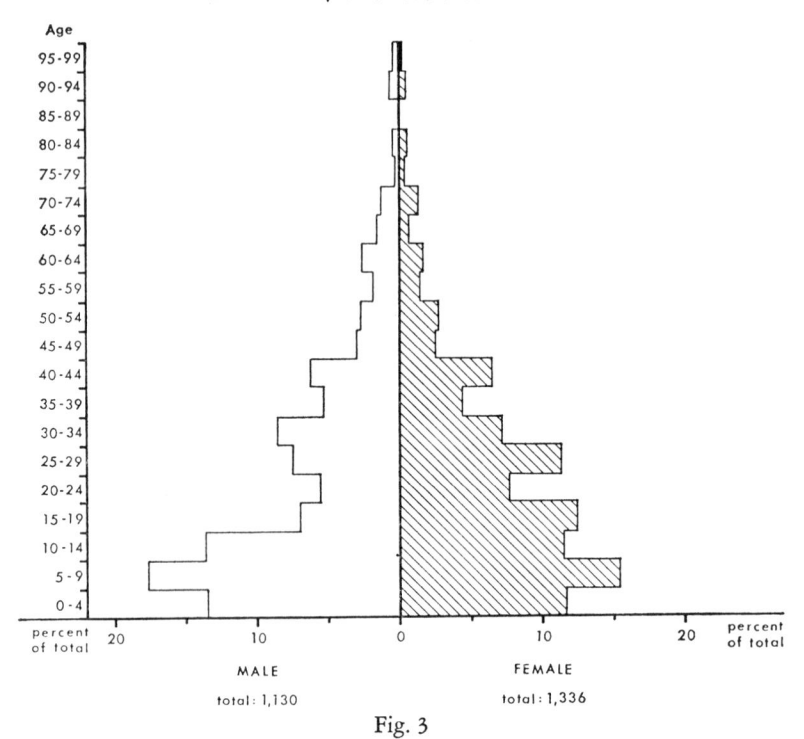

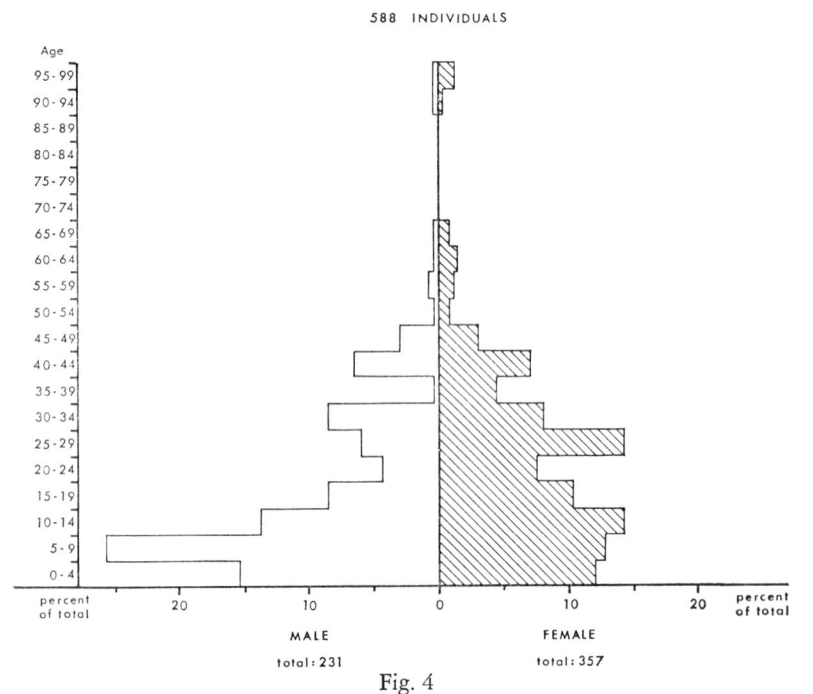

Fig. 3

DISTRIBUTION BY AGE AND SEX: PARDOS
588 INDIVIDUALS

Fig. 4

DISTRIBUTION BY AGE AND SEX: INDIANS
418 INDIVIDUALS

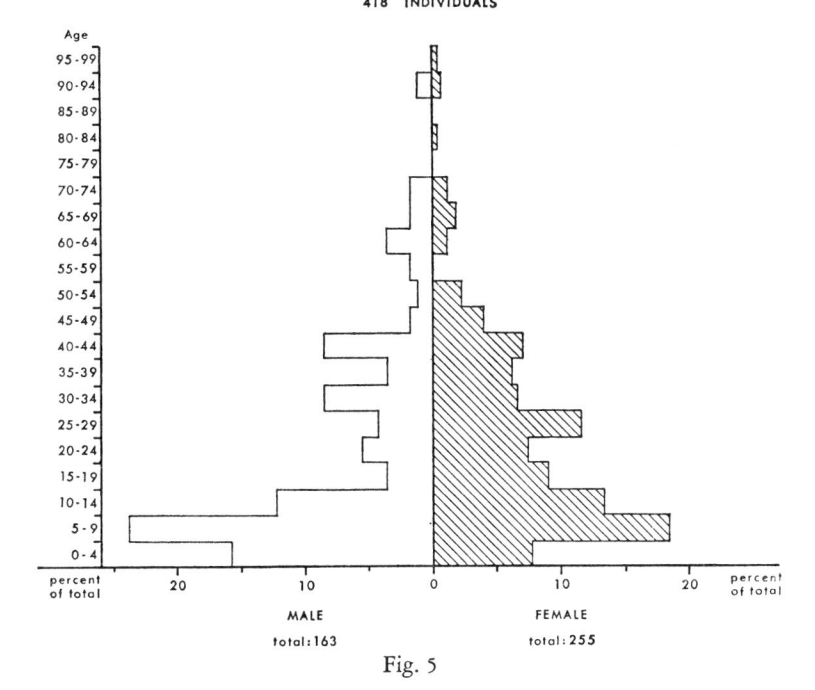

Fig. 5

DISTRIBUTION BY AGE AND SEX: NEGROES
171 INDIVIDUALS

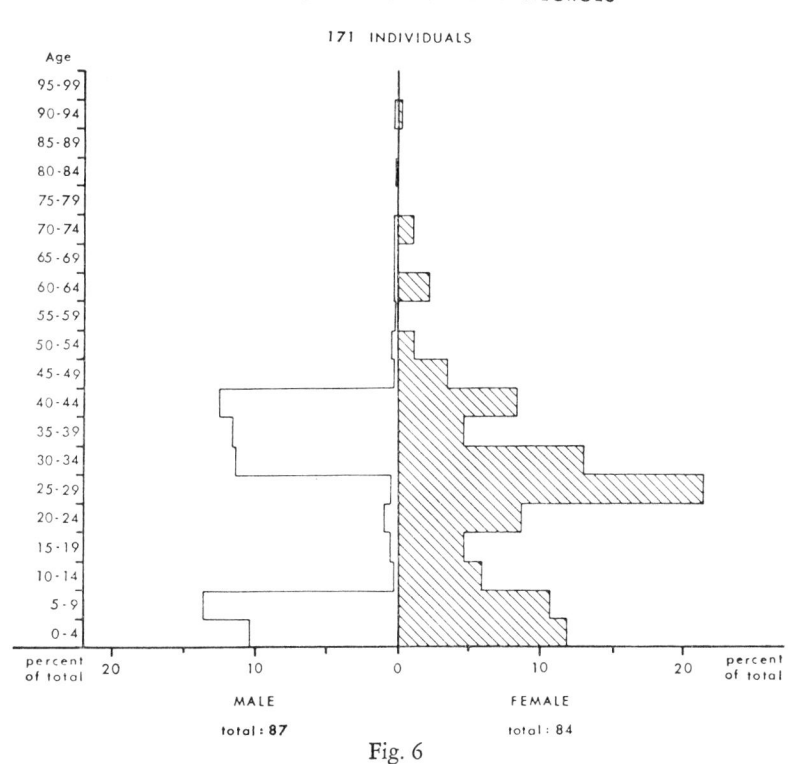

Fig. 6

The 1824 census, in its information on ethnicity and place of birth and marriage, provides some insight into the social dynamics of its time. It indicates, for example, that the majority of marriages in Paraná (375 out of 400) were not mixed, although the population was ethnically diverse. It also shows that the preponderance of intragroup marriages was among whites, while the other ethnic groups were less rigid. There were 276 cases of whites marrying whites; twenty-three of Pardos marrying Pardos; twenty-two of Indians marrying Indians; and nine of Negroes marrying Negroes. The following distribution of mixed marriages is recorded:

White and Indian	14
White and Pardo	18
White and Negro	3
Pardo and Negro	1
Pardo and Indian	7
Indian and Negro	2
Total	45

The significance of racial identity, however, is evident on all social levels, as the classification of children of mixed marriages shows. The following table lists the possible combinations of the four categories in marriage, indicating which cases occurred according to the census and how the offspring were classified.

Husband	Wife	Offspring
White	Pardo	Pardo
White	Indian	Indian
White	Negro	No case with children listed
Pardo	White	White
Pardo	Indian	Indian
Pardo	Negro	No case listed in census
Indian	White	White
Indian	Pardo	Pardo
Indian	Negro	No case listed in census
Negro	White	No case listed in census
Negro	Pardo	No case listed in census
Negro	Indian	No case listed in census

From Village to City

The rule seems to be that the racial classification of the mother becomes that of the children of her marriage. The absence of some of the possible combinations, however, does not allow us to state a matrilineal rule with complete certainty. The question of the origin of the Pardos still remains. Extensive attempts have been made to clarify the definition of Pardo. The great amount of regional variation in South America makes one reluctant to generalize from other areas, and specific data in the census reinforce this limitation. According to Charles Gibson (1964:603), a Pardo in Mexico is a person of mixed white and Negro or Indian and Negro parents. Our census offers no definitions of its terminology, and for the specific combinations mentioned by Gibson, no offspring are listed. If, in Paraná, the rule holds that the mother gives the child racial identity, the definition of Pardo as used in Mexico (mixing of white and Negro or Indian and Negro) cannot be applied. It has been suggested that any mixed marriage with a Negro mother would produce Pardo offspring. This would explain the origin of Pardos, but negate the matrilineal rule. All persons classified as Negro were born in Africa and were slaves; almost all of the Pardos were born in Argentina or Paraguay and were free (*libres*). These facts may indicate that Negroes born in America could have received the classification of Pardo, particularly if their mothers and fathers were African Negroes. The analogous situation is that of criollos, Spanish born in America.

Perhaps the accuracy of the 1824 census may be questioned in some respects, particularly on the age distribution, and perhaps even on the classification of the mixed ethnic groups. But in general it provides reasonable indications of certain patterns. It shows, for example, a shortage of men among the various ethnic sectors of the population. Comparison of the distribution of people by age and sex clearly reveals that there was a scarcity of men between the ages of fifteen and thirty (among the Negro men this reduction was over the longer period between 10 and 35), while the women of Paraná appear not only to have been more numerous but also to have had a more normal age distribution. The statistical pattern among the males may be in part attributed to migration, but the more direct causes were the constant wars and the pre- and post-independence regional civil strife.

One can also visualize some of the social aspects of Paraná in 1824 by considering the ethnic and occupational distribution provided by the census data. Negroes, Pardos, and Indians constituted 32.4 percent of the total population; all of them were in the lower economic and occupational brackets. There were eighteen men and thirty-four women listed as slaves; they had arrived before the slave traffic was prohibited in the province in 1820. Thus, the social stratigraphy of Paraná in 1824 presents us with the dramatic extremes of the *estancieros*, the white men of European descent (mainly Spanish) holding substantial amounts of land, and the slaves brought from Africa. Intermediate on the social scale were Indians, Pardos, and free Negroes—servants, peons, or unskilled laborers. There were, then, the *estanciero*, the businessman, and the government official toward one end of the socioeconomic continuum of Paraná, slave and servant at the other; the small entrepreneur, the semiskilled laborer, and the small farmer (*chacarero*) were in the lower-middle part of the spectrum.

In addition, around this time, a distinction between the people of the town and those of the countryside became apparent. The degree of importance that should be attached to the differentiation at this time is difficult to evaluate. No doubt it grew more noticeable as the village acquired greater political and economic importance and concomitantly assumed a social dominance. The classification of individuals by socially defined categories, the definition of these categories, and the use of stereotypes doubtless emanated from the "urban" center.

A perusal of the 1824 census shows that most of the white families had either slaves or servants. Those whose economic condition was good had many servants and peons attached to their households; furthermore, some of these workers (but not the peons) took the name of the master's family, as the configuration of a prominent household shows (table 1). In another segment of the social scale, there were ethnic origins: it reflects a town involved in the administration of its own political and social destiny, one beginning to benefit economically from the development of both rural and urban styles of life. As the Spaniards utilized the rural area more and expanded the frontier, the village grew in importance and gave opportunities to semiskilled and

From Village to City 17

skilled labor. The population of Paraná showed a more rapid economic households with a simpler social configuration (table 2).

Table 3 represents the distribution of male occupations according to progress than that of the surrounding rural areas. Its criollo merchant group was numerically larger than any other, and competition with individuals of foreign origin, particularly Spanish, was presumably acute. Nothing could be learned from the census about the attitude of

Table 1. Household Composition: Case I

	Name	Birthplace	Age	Marital Status	Race	Occupation
Husband:	don Franco La Puente	Montanas, Spain	44	M	White	Lime factory
Wife:	doña Josefa Los Santos	Santa Fé	40	M	White	
Children:	Dolores La Puente	Santa Fé	17	S	White	
	Margarita La Puente	Paraná	12	S	White	
	Saturnina La Puente	Paraná	11	S	White	
	Josefa La Puente	Paraná	9	S	White	
	Francisco La Puente	Paraná	5	S	White	
	Luis La Puente	Paraná	1	S	White	
Servants:	Manuel La Puente	Angola	60	M	Negro	Slave
	María La Puente	Angola	40	M	Negro	Slave
	Matias La Puente	Angola	90	S	Negro	Slave
	José María La Puente	Congo	40	S	Negro	Slave
	Andrés La Puente	Moro	32	S	Negro	Slave
	Felipa La Puente	Paraná	13	S	Pardo	Slave

Table 2. Household Composition: Case II

	Name	Birthplace	Age	Marital Status	Race
Husband:	don Victoriano Freviedo	Galicia	52	M	White
Wife:	doña Ana Pereyra	Santa Fé	56	M	White
In-law:	don Juan Pereyra	Santa Fé	60	Widower	White
Servant:	Victoria Pereyra	Paraná	24	S	Parda
Children:	Roque Pereyra	Paraná	5	S	Pardo
	María Antonia Pereyra	Paraná	3	S	Parda
Orphan:	Geniveva Pereyra	Paraná	7	S	Negro

Table 3. Distribution of Male Occupations by Ethnic Categories

	White				Non-white		
Occupation	Argentine Criollos	Spanish	European: Portugal Britain France	South American: Paraguay Uruguay Peru Bolivia	Negro Africans	Pardo Argentines	Indian Argentines
Farmer	46	9	7	2	0	1	1
Peon	38	1	4	8	1	1	5
Vagrant	24	1	1	4	2	0	4
Carpenter	23	2	1	4	1	1	0
Shoemaker	22	1	3	3	1	3	3
Merchant	20	17	3	1	0	0	0
Tailor	20	2	1	1	0	0	0
Herdsman	16	2	2	0	0	0	0
Butcher	16	0	0	1	0	1	1
Carter	14	9	5	2	2	0	1
Bartender	11	10	5	1	0	0	1
Military	10	0	0	1	0	0	0
Tanner	10	1	4	1	0	1	3
Fisherman	10	0	1	0	0	0	0
Lime producer	9	2	0	1	0	1	0
Brickmason	9	3	1	1	1	1	0
Horticulturalist	8	3	4	1	1	0	0
Government officials	7	1	0	0	0	1	0
Harnessmaker	6	0	0	0	0	0	0
Silversmith	5	0	0	1	0	0	0
Roofer	5	0	0	0	0	0	0
Postboy	5	0	0	0	0	1	0
Hatmaker	4	0	4	1	0	0	0
Tobacco	4	0	0	0	0	0	0
Baker	4	3	0	0	0	0	0
Storekeeper	4	2	0	0	0	0	0
Woodcutter	4	0	0	0	0	1	0
Boatman	4	0	2	0	0	0	0
Badge maker	3	2	0	0	1	0	0
Comb maker	2	0	2	1	0	0	0
Sailor	2	5	1	0	0	0	0
Restaurant	2	0	0	0	0	0	0
Blacksmith	2	0	0	1	0	0	1
Clerk	1	0	0	0	0	0	0
Barber	1	2	0	1	0	1	0

Estanciero	1	0	0	0	0	0	0
Pharmacist	1	0	0	0	0	0	0
Retired	1	0	0	0	0	0	0
Medical doctor	1	0	0	0	0	0	0
Caretaker of sanctuary	1	0	0	0	0	0	0
Midwife	1	0	0	0	0	0	0
Chairmaker	1	0	0	0	0	0	0
Musician	1	0	0	1	0	0	0
Candlemaker	1	0	0	0	0	0	0
Cartback	1	0	0	0	0	0	0
Soapmaker	0	2	0	0	0	0	0
Estancia manager	0	1	0	0	0	0	0
Slave	0	0	0	0	26	4	0
Schoolteacher	0	1	0	0	0	0	0
Miller	0	1	0	0	0	0	0
Servant	0	0	0	0	0	0	5
Farmhand	0	0	0	0	0	0	4
Foreman	0	1	0	0	0	0	0

criollos toward the other ethnic groups and their enterprises, though it is clear that foreigners were active participants in the business circle. It is, in this regard, interesting that European immigrants were already involved in business and that, while twenty-four criollos were classified as vagrant, only six Europeans were in this category.

The expanding frontier and the easily navigated Paraná River linked the village to Buenos Aires and thus allowed rivalry with Santa Fé and encouraged the development of local resources. There arose great opportunities for individuals who were interested in business and in small manufacturing enterprises such as limemaking, harnessmaking, shoemaking, blacksmithing, and tailoring. There developed, as well, an apprenticeship system that supplied the town with the necessary skilled labor. Although professional people were few, they nonetheless pioneered a social style that remains basic to features of life today.

Of the families listed in the Census of 1824, thirty-eight had names still known to an elderly resident of Paraná in 1965. Fifteen of these became prominent families that participated in the local government's acquisitions of large tracts of land or became noted for their intellectual and political activities. Presently these constitute the core of the patrician households and of the local aristocracy. Others of these listed in the census left Paraná and settled in Santa Fé, in reaction to the continual provincial and interprovincial strife under the rule of the political bosses known as caudillos. In the social situation of the village, white people held positions of high distinction; they were the officials, the military, and the clergy. There were also entrepreneurs, artisans, and farmers, and the successful entrepreneurs and new *estancieros* quickly ascended the social scale. Among the latter, the *estanciero* was at the peak. Very likely he was a direct descendant of a conquistador who, besides his duties as official and as military man, acquired vast expanses of land and *peones* (gauchos) who cared for the livestock.[10]

This cultural plurality of the past, its strands linked by an independent political framework instituted later, is socially significant for the present and is sketched here as a background for the culture of the province of Entre Ríos and its capital, Paraná.

Economy

The economy is primarily based on cereal crop farming and livestock. Agricultural activities have been on the increase since the turn of the century. In 1869, 457 farmers were reported; by 1914 the number had increased to 30,000. As the number of individual farmers increased, the large landholders (*estancieros*) for the same period decreased from 8,138 to 4,454.

The province of Entre Ríos shares a good many economic features with the provinces of the Pampa region: Buenos Aires, the eastern part of Córdoba, and particularly Santa Fé. Currently, they form one of the most active and well-developed farming areas of the country, in which flax, wheat, corn, barley, and alfalfa are among the leading crops.

Early in the century the province developed cooperative programs,

---

[10] Many of the basic features of the gaucho tradition, the psychology of the people and their world view, have been skillfully portrayed in the epic *El Gaucho Martín Fierro*, by José Hernández (new edition by EUDEBA, 1962). The horse, guitar, meat, *mate*, *boleadoras*, and particularly the style of clothing constitute the basic material traits of the gaucho. He is associated with *estancia* life, with livestock not agriculture.

and by 1934 there was in operation a federation of cooperatives known as La Federación Entrerriana de Cooperativas Agrícolas de la Provincia. The Entre Ríos development generally paralleled trends in the Pampa provinces, although at a slower pace. Figure 7 shows the proportional uses of land for 1962 (Instituto de Planeamiento, 1963, vol. 2, map 9).

Livestock has also played an important part in the economy of the province and the nation, particularly the preparation of meat for export. In the area circling Paraná, dairy farming is an important activity, and in areas where European settlement was heavy (particularly Swiss immigrants), creameries and cheese factories have been established. So far, however, most of the Entre Ríos produce is exported unprocessed. It has only been in recent years that some factories have been established, such as flour mills and canneries.

As the city grew, building material came into great demand, creating the need for extensive development of nearby lime quarries and clay pits, and the city of Paraná has cement as well as brick and tile works. The exploitation of wood for charcoal has also been important as a source of income in the northern parts of Entre Ríos.

The economy of Paraná has, therefore, been greatly affected by land use in the region, converting the city into an administrative center for all these activities, including transportation. Most of the communications networks converge on the city, from which, by ferry, truck, railroad, and boat, products are shipped to other parts of the country. A tunnel under the Paraná River was under construction at the time of the field work, a much-needed link to overcome the many hours of delay caused by the ferry service to Santa Fé.

In the city, there are people employed by national and provincial government, by private, provincial, and national banks, by the few large chains of businesses or stores, and by large national transport companies. Furthermore, the situation has lent itself very well to the development of small businesses specializing in either city or country services.

As one approaches the city from the east, along the road are many stores and businesses displaying farm products and machinery, as well

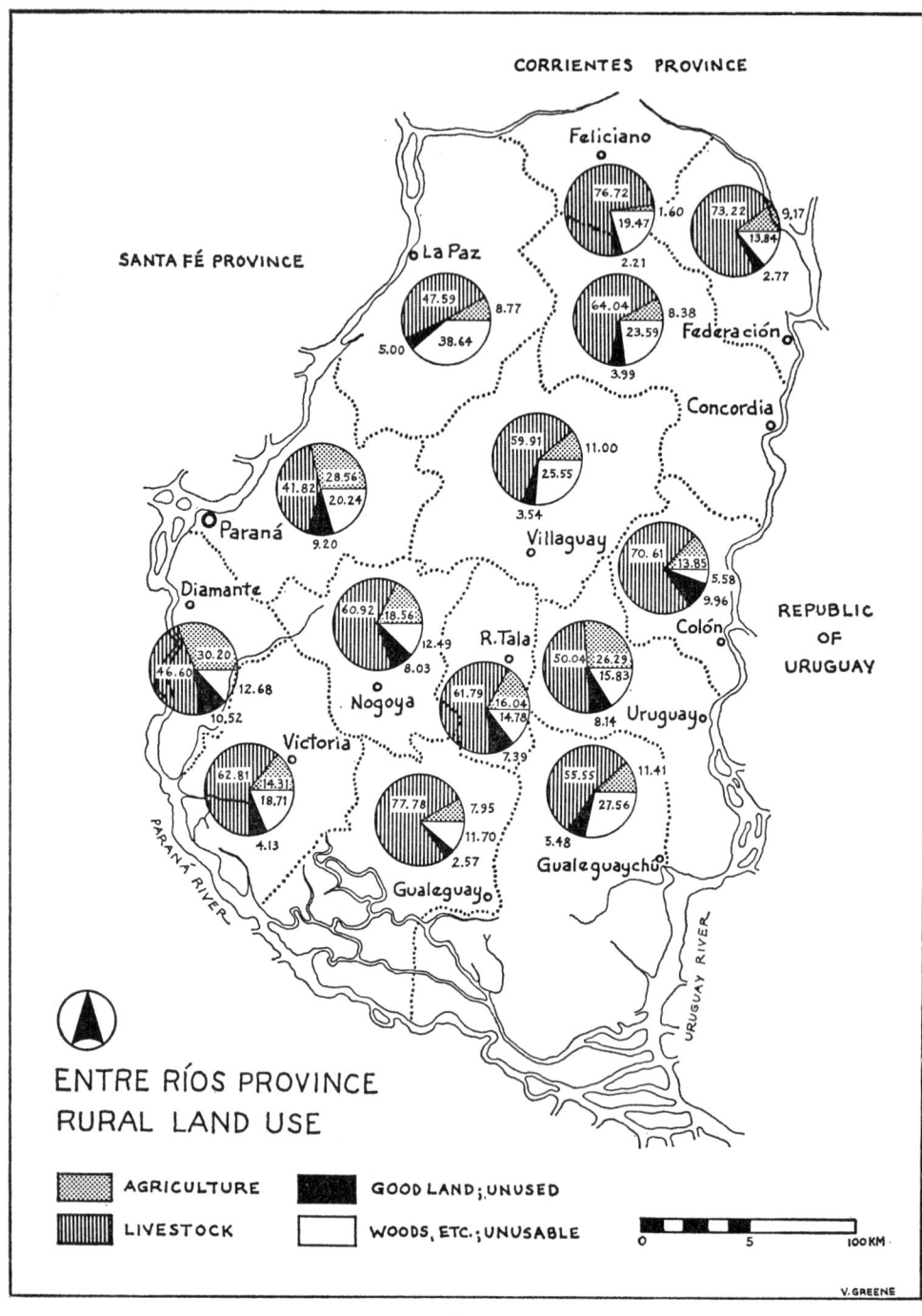

Fig. 7

as repair shops and warehouses for the storage of crops. By the time one reaches the central plaza, the change to city stores and institutional services marks the difference between rural and city life and people.

It is the combination of strong rural activity surrounding the city together with the variety of local, provincial, and national administrative services that provides economic opportunity for all Paranaenses. Industrial development has been the hope of the middle class and the worry and preoccupation of the upper class. Paraná is not, however, an industrial center, and consequently the general pace of life is still slow and personal. The city is at present an administrative entity, depending a great deal on activities of the rural areas of the province.

Urban Growth

To understand culture, and more precisely the community culture of a city, it is helpful to acquire an intimate knowledge of the past events experienced by the people. Although thorough ethnohistoric study of private and public documents is beyond the scope of this work, it is to our advantage to bring into focus some events and experiences faced by the leaders and the people who, together, were involved in creating a new Paraná.

The early years of the city's history were filled with problems of health, morality, immigration, social identity, and physical urban development. Officials were forced by circumstances to solve these problems rapidly. They were expected to reach firm decisions, decisions that had to be based on sound, recognizable principles. Study of early documents allows us to see the formation and use of basic principles as leaders and people experienced great tension formulating city policies for which there was no direct precedent.[11]

The four thousand inhabitants of the village of La Bajada de Paraná and people from other villages along the Paraná River experienced radical political change, control passing in 1824 from the Spanish crown to a new and independent nation. This transition was clouded by much internal political strife under the strong hands of caudillos. For some time civil wars stifled the growth of the population, and life in the town was interrupted by fighting or by rumors of invasions.

[11] Reula 1963:vol. 1.

The plaza at such times was covered with military trenches. A relatively short period of peaceful resettlement and progress came after 1852.

Paraná, a city since 1826, had grown to a population of seven thousand by 1860, most of whom resided in the central part of the town in white houses surrounded by poorly arranged gardens and frequently provided with cisterns for collecting rain water for domestic use (see table 4). It was also evident that in the social situation of the town,

Table 4. Comparative Census Figures

Year	Dept. of Paraná	Paraná City	Entre Ríos Province
1700	300		
1743	920		
1797	3,000		
1820		4,292	
1824		3,276	
1862	18,649	9,832	134,271
1895	51,221	19,228	292,019
1914	71,848	36,089	425,373
1947	148,106	83,824	787,363
1956	128,630		959,401
1960	174,272	111,272	803,805

white people held a status above the Indians, Negroes, or persons of mixed race. There appears to have been a merging, however, of many traditions. The Spanish attempted to practice and to impose on the social landscape pure or modified Iberian cultural forms. The criollos took customs from their Spanish ancestors but were adapting to the society what they had learned from their fathers, giving these elements a new identity. The rural gauchos, who were of mixed ethnic descent (Indian-criollo, Indian-Spanish, or Indian-Negro), began to adjust to the economic development of the period, while preserving cultural aspects of the local native patterns.

It was in 1873, under the national administration of President Domingo Faustino Sarmiento, that Paraná and the surrounding region became consolidated into a single administrative unit, a *municipalidad*, which constituted an independent political entity with a government elected by the people. This had as its responsibility the security of the area, education, health, justice at the local level, and whatever else concerned the land and people under its jurisdiction. In general, the *municipalidad* had sufficient freedom from other levels of the governmental structure to operate independently. It was free to establish the rate of taxation and to administer the revenues, being responsible to the judicial authorities only for abuses. Officers were elected for a period of two years, and people of foreign birth could participate in the municipal government if properly elected. The administration of the city was headed by the president of the *municipalidad* (sometimes referred to as the *intendente-mayor*), whose term of office was also two years. When the population had reached the size of a city, the *consejo deliberante* (council) was composed of eight members, and additional representatives were elected after a stipulated increase in the population. The *consejo deliberante* sanctioned orders as well as gave orders that the president and other municipal employees were expected to put into effect. Through the municipal government, the Paranaenses of both Argentine and foreign origin had now acquired sufficient control and power to dictate some of their domestic policies.

From the initiation of autonomous local government in 1873 until 1900, accounts of aspects of public life were incorporated into the minutes of meetings held by the councilmen, a valuable source of information for understanding the social and cultural development of the city. During the first ten years, the council considered the problem of urban expansion and planning. There was interest in moving the city limits in order to accommodate the steady migrations from Europe and from the rural areas. In 1876 the boundaries of the city were determined. The barrancas (cliffs) overlooking the Paraná River and the Arroyo Antoñico were the two natural north and west boundaries for the area of four hundred square blocks established by law for the "urban shell." The eastern line was parallel to the north-south magnetic line, and the southern line was perpendicular to it.

Typical of the planning of Central and South American cities, Paraná was divided into four *cuarteles* (quarters) by two major streets intersecting at the main plaza. This constituted the *zona de ciudad* (city zone). The city was encircled by the *zona de quinta* (the zone of small truck farms), each *quinta* containing two *manzanas* (each equal to the area of a city block). In turn the *zona de quinta* was encircled by the *zona de chacras* (farms), each *chacra* containing four *manzanas* (four square blocks). This was not only a territorial division but also a definite foundation for future social differences. The basic distinction between urban and rural people took form: those in the *cuarteles* were urban by definition, those in the *quintas* were marginal, and those in the *chacras* were definitely rural. The distinction was based on economic services and specialization. The *chacareros* raised livestock and cereal; the *quinteros* raised vegetables, chickens, rabbits, and provided dairy products for the city markets. Both of these groups benefited from the administrative and commercial services of the city. The functional and economic interdependency of the three ecological areas during the years before 1900 was intense.

One of the early issues confronting the municipal council was the provision and improvement of city facilities. There was much official concern with such matters as the construction of bridges across Arroyo Antoñico, extension of roads to the *quinta* area, the naming of streets, the numbering of each house in the city, and the specification of building rules. The rules dealt with the type of construction—such as prohibiting houses with straw roofs near the center of the city—and also with the inspection and approval of the location of new houses so that the gridiron pattern would be maintained. Regulations, however, brought about litigation among neighbors and between neighbors and officials; records indicate that the city council was constantly involved in disagreements about the nature of "urban progress."

The building of sidewalks and walls around each property was considered part of the city's beautification program. The walls enclosing every household separated and isolated each family from others (fig. 8). The river and the horizon disappeared from the view of the housewife as she went about her domestic duties. Family activities became hidden; neighbors were no longer in sight of each other, and only voices and domestic sounds could be overheard through the physical barriers. In order to be with a neighbor or to see people other than those in one's own family, one had to pass through corridors, vestibules, and rooms to reach the sidewalk in front of one's own house. This was considered part of the urbanization process: the social boundaries were made real by means of physical divisions; individuality, iso-

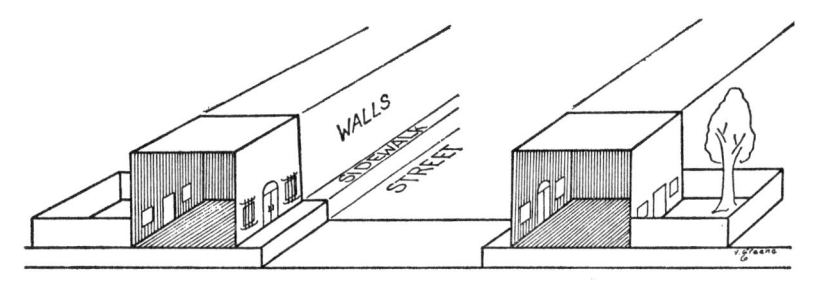

A CROSS SECTION OF STREET ECOLOGY
Fig. 8

lation, and social differentiation became strong trends. The open lots around the main plaza rapidly disappeared as urban development continued. Each street became framed by parallel sidewalks of a variety of materials and quality, dependent on the taste and economic position of each resident. The material chosen for the front of the house demonstrated the family's individuality and engendered social competition between neighbors.

The strongest impulse to development came when Paraná became the capital of the province in 1883. Though there had been many urban improvements, Paraná had remained a frontier city. The "beautification of the city" was for many years a topic for discussion among the councilmen, who pondered such problems as street drainage and lighting, planting trees and planning public gardens, and building and maintaining statues in the public plazas. Committees from the council were also involved in the study of long-term problems, but limited technical advice resulted in decisions not entirely suitable to the sound development of the city.

In the early period, residents had offered labor and money for public improvements, but as the city grew in size and importance, and with increased need for improvements and administrative activities— even before it became the provincial capital—taxes were higher and well institutionalized, and straightforward petitions were made requesting that the municipality undertake the urban development. The council had to cope with public sentiment that stressed the municipality's rather than the citizens' responsibilities. More and more of the financial responsibility for the public services fell to all inhabitants, rich and poor alike. While progressive elements of the city population demanded services, others felt that they could get along without them in a semirural style of life. And as urban growth continued, the financial resources of the municipality remained insufficient to meet the demands and expectations of the public. No definitive tax system had been worked out, and it was difficult for the municipality to undertake physical projects in the city or to make an equitable distribution of financial obligations among the rich, the active merchants using public services, and the poor. Though funds in the municipal treasury dropped to a critically low level, necessitating a cutback in services and delays in meeting obligations, yet when the *municipalidad* tried to enforce ordinances or collect taxes it met with much resistance from the pueblo.

Owing to the precarious economic state of the *municipalidad*, the councilmen faced severe criticism from the people.[12] It was necessary to approve petitions of exoneration from many in the poor classes who could not afford to pay the taxes and dues, and, because of increased efforts to assure the collection of all revenues, some people felt that they were being dealt with unfairly. By 1876 the integrity of the city government was questioned and accusations of favoritism were made.[13] But the major criticism by the people was that the municipality had been charging for services that were not properly provided. In reaction to the accusations, some councilmen chose to resign to register their objection to this and to defend their dignity. In the name of good citizenship and public decorum, and because of the rights of the state to require public support and service from its citizens for the benefit of the pueblo, resignations were seldom accepted. Sensitive individuals with little practical ambition began to avoid city public office, and this led to the emergence of professional politicians.

[12] *Actas* 1874. Much of the data for this chapter was secured from the *Actas Municipales 1873–1900* at the municipal archives. The document pages are not numbered; thus, citations will refer only to the year of the book.

[13] A newspaper, *El Argentino*, published a series of editorials castigating the mayor and indirectly the municipal government. The council debated what action should be taken so that the editor would cease accusing the municipal corporation. It was agreed that the editor had manifested low moral character, and it was proposed that the incident be overlooked. *Actas* 1876.

Colonization Problems

By the middle of the nineteenth century, Basque, French, Italian, Irish, and English immigrants had arrived in the municipality of Paraná.[14] Land owned by the municipality was allotted to immigrants who settled in the city proper or on the *quintas* and *chacras*. As they developed the land and became "good citizens," they began to fit well into the local program of economic development. In 1877 the council voted to sponsor colonization by Russian-Germans and reported to the central government that land from the *ejido municipal* would be available for this purpose. A total of five thousand Russian-Germans (twenty-four complete villages) arrived en masse. Officials of the municipality felt that the immigrants should not become "Argentinized," but rather that they should retain their customs, their cooperative spirit, and their good work habits. All these factors would constitute a beautiful opportunity for the development of the city and the province of Entre Ríos, one which should not be overlooked.[15]

After much negotiation, the Russian-Germans settled in sections of land bordering Paraná. Because they established themselves outside the jurisdiction of the municipality, they did not pose as much of a problem to the councilmen as did the Italians and the Swiss sent to reside in Paraná proper. Interestingly enough, the rural Russian-Germans next to Paraná opened up good economic opportunities for the Germans and the Jews of the city.

The coming of the colonists was looked upon as a matter of business, potential progress, and economic benefit to the region. The experiences with the immigrant families, however, brought about serious social reactions from the people, particularly Argentines. It was generally felt that while officials were very tolerant of the colonists, they were very severe with Argentines. For instance, heated public argu-

[14] By 1861 the population of Paraná had increased to 7,000 and a year later to 9,832; by 1895 the number of inhabitants was 19,228 (of which 9,249 were male and 9,979 were female). Of the total number of persons listed for 1890, 14,897 were classified as Argentine and 4,331 as foreigners, with a total of 3,062 houses. There were in that year 400 businesses and 167 centers where some kind of elementary processing of raw material took place (Zanio 1926).

[15] *Actas* 1877.

ments erupted over the case of a "son of the land" who requested rights to a piece of land he had been cultivating for many years. According to the law, he did not qualify. Similar cases were the basis for much jealousy and protest. Argentines, particularly the criollo group, became suspicious of immigrants who could afford the trip from Europe to America but claimed complete poverty soon after arrival. Furthermore, those who had been settled with the financial aid of the *municipalidad* claimed constant poverty due to crop failure. The public felt, however, that this became an excuse in order to pay the *municipalidad* the very least amount or nothing.[16] In general, Paranaenses became disenchanted with the first immigrant groups because the majority were "undesirables" from European cities and most were uneducated. Public opinion was divided, and while some politicians wanted to continue bringing in more colonists under any conditions, others were interested only in colonists who had their own resources and education.

The general situation was difficult and public relations tense. The Argentines' attitude toward colonists clearly indicated the general stereotype created was rather negative; it was symptomatic of an unpremeditated social division: the criollo, the *extranjero* (foreigner), the *colonos* (colonists).[17]

The Council's Role in Regulating Values

The municipality, in defining its role and duties, felt responsible for the city public morals. Councilmen intended to formulate policy according to specified or unspecified but generally accepted definitions, and to agree on the way of life (culture) for the inhabitants of the city. They were concerned with a culture in formation, with many aspects inherited from various European sources. Culture or "tradition" was to be consciously manipulated, and in their hands, therefore, was the difficult task of culture change or, more accurately, of culture creation.

---

[16] *Actas* 1880.

[17] *Extranjeros* were all foreigners, including Spanish, who came to America on their own or assisted by relatives. *Colonos* were those in the colonization program of this period.

At the end of the nineteenth century, for instance, councilmen became concerned with the "great conglomeration of beggars" on the streets and considered that the practice of begging should be regulated.[18] A complete program to obliterate begging was not introduced, and it continued to be very much in evidence in public, both in the plazas and from door to door. It was possible for individuals to request permission from the municipality to approach people on the streets or to go from door to door begging for money because of old age or illness, or for a specific need, such as a trip to Buenos Aires with the family to accept a job promised in a letter from a relative.

From municipal records it appears also that delinquency was a serious local problem during these early years. Large numbers of children were in the streets frequenting houses of entertainment, handball courts, billiard halls, lotteries, and cock fights. As a consequence, many were not attending school as required by law, and their parents were apparently unconcerned. On such occasions the city police were ordered to take the children into custody for a period of time until parents claimed them and paid a fine.

Gambling activity provided a source of revenue, although some on the council felt that gambling was morally wrong and should be prohibited. The president of the council agreed with those who felt it was morally wrong, but because of the critical financial needs of the municipality, he did not think it would be possible to suspend such activity totally. Between 1880 and 1890, debates on this issue continued, but the revenue from gambling was apparently too significant to regulate.

Public performances required the permission of the president of the municipality. It was declared that a presentation must not "offend the morality and good habits of the pueblo and that such a public spectacle should not upset the public order."[19] The hours of all public performances were also set; they were required to begin at 8:00 P.M. and end not later than midnight in the winter and 1:00 A.M. in the summer. Public behavior was regulated; spontaneous outbursts of noise, use of

[18] *Actas* 1870.
[19] *Actas* 1880–1890.

offensive language, lack of respect for performers or patrons of the theater, and interruption of the show were considered offenses; those involved were asked to leave and fined a sum of four pesos.

Houses of prostitution were regulated by the municipality. Requests were received by the Committee of Public Morality asking permission to establish houses of prostitution. But from time to time, petitions were also received in the municipality from housewives requesting that action be taken to remove "certain women of bad living" from their particular neighborhood.

By 1877 some of the councilmen felt that the increase in public and legal prostitution had created a social problem and that a well-planned study had to be made in order to regulate such activities properly. By 1891 discussion recorded in the documents indicated that houses of prostitution were considered a natural and logical phenomenon of society. There appeared to be no opposition to them nor any suggestion to eliminate them. Consequently, the council established rules governing their location and operations. Fines were to be imposed on all those not complying with such rules and regulations, which were the most encompassing of any found in the municipal records.[20]

Carnaval (celebrated prior to the beginning of the Lenten season) was also under the jurisdiction of the Committee of Public Morality. It was, and still is, considered the *fiesta de los pobres* (poor people's celebration). Each year, after a new group took office, the first order of business for the committee was a discussion of the nature and extent of the Carnaval celebration. They allowed it some years but not in others. Those in authority considered the festivity to be somewhat immoral, and from year to year the people waited anxiously for the authorities to take their position and publish their ordinances.

The municipality was asked to spend more and more on the Carnaval festivities.[21] Every year Carnaval remained a political issue. Councilmen constantly argued over the moral implications of the public celebration; some felt that the people should not be left without their

---

[20] Houses of prostitution were abolished after 1945, during the regime of Juan Perón.
[21] *Actas* 1876.

celebration or without proper lighting and decorations for the festivity. Fines were imposed on those whose songs, speeches, manners, or dances were considered indecent or insulting. The tradition of Carnaval had been well implanted, but its relation to the social classes was a constant public issue. Although individuals of the middle and upper classes always participated through their own clubs, the celebration in the streets was considered the fiesta of and for the poor people. They felt free at that time to walk to the center of the city with no self-consciousness, assured that they were enjoying their rights and privileges.

In general the council felt that their duties, besides the problems of urban growth, included insuring a high level of public morality and *cultura*.[22] Here their concern was with group public behavior and with social problems, particularly those due to poverty and ignorance.

Ordering Cultural Diversity

During the stage of development in which the population lived as villagers, the community was a small social unit, a place in which inhabitants shared equal social standing. The plaza, the church, the market, and the cemetery brought the people together with no regard for social standing. There was a local elite, but the social distance that they maintained from those referred to as *el pueblo* was largely a matter of qualities inherited from ancestors; it was then a natural and quiet social distinction. Theoretically, it would seem that in the early days to be a "Christian," and therefore a "human being," was basic to achieving social unity.

As the century advanced, the village of Paraná was rapidly transformed both economically and numerically into a pueblo (town) and then into a city. By 1850 the single-town ecology had been altered. The unity of the past was lost with the division of the city into four quadrants; but the social unit was to some extent retained by the construction of secondary plazas in each of the four quarters.

The chessboard pattern continued to be central to the physical

---

[22] The possession or lack of *cultura* is frequently used to describe an individual or a group. *Cultura* translates as culture, but in this work the word "culture" is used to mean the way of life of a people. *Cultura* is used here to mean refinement, enlightenment, and politeness—with connotations of urbanity.

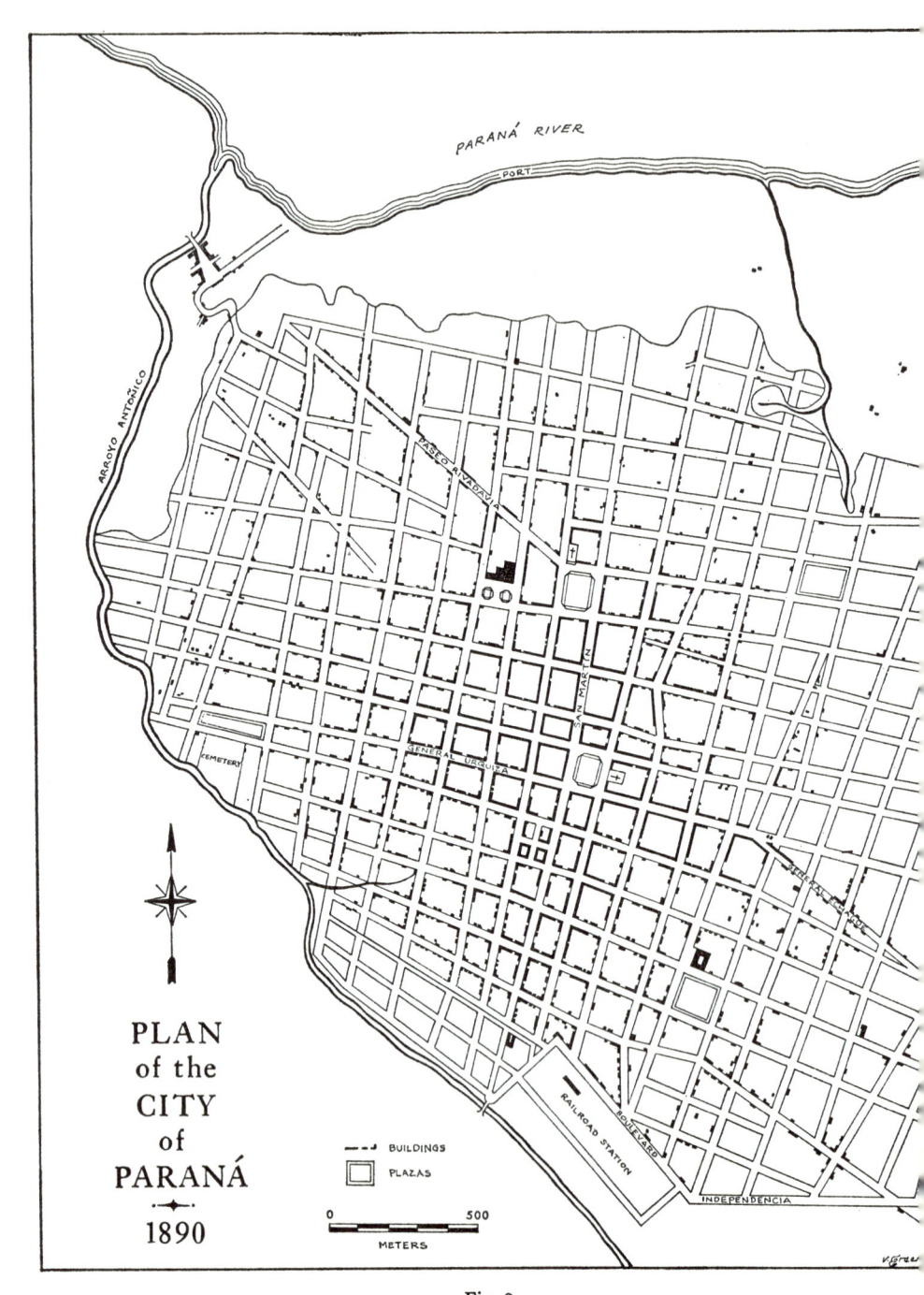

Fig. 9

planning of the town and guided the social distribution of people. There emerged a social grouping not only within the four quarters of the city but also within block areas of each quarter. Increasing immigration led to a distribution of population based on particular life styles. The city thus became divided socially as well as physically to the extent that each major division acquired distinctiveness (see table 5). The concept of neighborhood (*vecindad*) acquired force and played an important part during this period.

The ideal model of social structure was modified as the reality of life changed, although the principle of human equality and the democratic way of life remained essential parts of the model. Demographic pressures and diversity in ethnic backgrounds imposed social distinctions. Social relations were greatly influenced by these opposing concepts. Categorization of people and their neighborhoods guided the social relations in the city.

Areas of the city became clearly distinguished into first and second social standing, referred to respectively as *primera categoría* and *segundia categoría*. Even the cemetery has places of first and second social category. The cathedral, in contrast to other churches, is of the first category, and, although by definition publicly and socially neutral, it is the place for the prominent people of *primera categoría*, the city elite. The large groups of European immigrants arriving in Argentina resulted in the development of specific and socially significant terms to distinguish between people born in the country and the newcomers. Criollo referred to those of the land; gringos was the popular name for immigrants. To be a city person or to be from a rural area had social implications with respect to the above as well as to the concepts of *cultura* and *civilización*. The coincidence of groupings by the

Table 5. Distribution of Population in the Four City Quarters, 1890

Cuartel	Population		Population	
	Argentine	Foreign	Male	Female
1	4,053	1,251	2,511	2,793
2	2,808	822	1,722	1,908
3	3,111	869	1,861	2,119
4	4,509	1,170	2,717	2,962

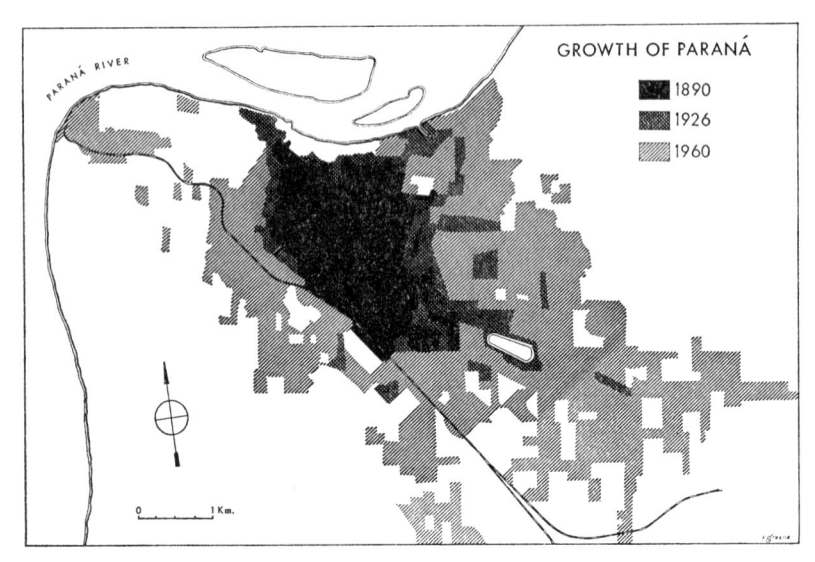

Fig. 10

several systems of categorizing provided additional force in many cases. For example, to be rural implied isolation, a lack of both education and general *cultura*; where the rural classification coincided with that of gringo, it reinforced existing negative characteristics.

People were cast in two oppositional molds: the popular and common, and the outstanding. Thus: men vs. cultured men, men vs. civilized men, women vs. respectable women (*matronas respetables*), *vecinos* vs. respectable *vecinos*, people vs. respectable people (*gente despetable*).

Furthermore, individuals could be classified in terms of economic, social, and political significance: poor vs. rich, peon vs. *patrón*, people vs. authority, person of bad reputation (*persona mal vivir*) vs. person of good reputation (*persona decente*), exploiters vs. decent persons (*persona decente*), person of the street (*persona de la calle*) vs. family person (*persona de su hogar*).

The significant fact relates to the dynamics of all classifications. For example, if one is *persona decente*, he is no longer viewed as an individual who is a decent person, but merely as *persona decente*. A significant depersonalization emerges along with a strong collective representation for each major group. This grew more forceful as the city continued to expand.

There is no doubt that at this juncture in the social history of the city, just as in the nation, there was a basic underlying assumption that Argentine society was to have social classes. Social stratification based on inequality became natural and expected in Paraná and elsewhere in Argentina. Everyone differed culturally, and because this diversity of cultural heritages existed, differentiation in social rights was inevitable. There was already prestige in being Argentine, with lineage traced from the colonial patriots who made history. In addition, prestige demanded the public display of precise social manners referred to as *lo apropriado*, "appropriateness." Across social classes there was no single prestige scale based upon similar principles, but there was a single model of social stratification accepted by all. Each group followed its own patterns of behavior dictated by the group's value system.

The public rituals of the Carnaval festivities developed an interesting projection of the ideal nature of the social model. At this time of the year, the city center belonged to everyone, and the ideal of social equality could be portrayed through masquerades. Behind the many masks, the daily identity could be hidden, and thus the aristocrat could become a nobleman or a king, or he could be simply a person; the gringo could be a gaucho; the poor could be rich; the rich could be the poorest; the civilized could be uncivilized (Indian or Negro); the uncivilized could be civilized; the prostitute could be a lady (*matrona*) of distinction; a man could be a woman; a woman could be a man. It was a social moment when rules of respect and acknowledgment of social superiority could be suspended, when water could be thrown on any bystander without personal insult even though personal annoyance might be felt.

During the early years of the twentieth century, Paranaenses experienced economic progress due to the rapid national economic development. Under this condition fundamental social principles, at one time useful to all, were questioned. Social mobility became desirable to those who aspired to social distinction, and the degree of social openness was constantly being tested. It was a time when opposite social poles were being separated by the group known as the *clase media* (middle class). With the emergence of this middle class, the old social model burst at the seams and there came into existence three social levels with a seemingly infinite variety of social and economic models to be recombined.

2. THE CITY AND ITS PEOPLE

> The city is not built for one person, but for great numbers of people, of widely varying backgrounds, temperaments, occupations, and class.[1]

To understand the city, the guiding concern should be the answers to questions such as how residents conceive of their environment, which points in the city are central, where the whole of the city begins, who are the residents, and what are their cultural backgrounds. This chapter will deal with general aspects of city ecology; the reader, however, should not be surprised to find variations from the usual manner of approaching this subject. Anthropologists have studied group activities and ideas of primitive or peasant people centered around specific landmarks (bush, water holes, milpa agriculture, etc.). On this basis Redfield states, "In primitive communities we find it possible to describe concurrent regularities of man and nature in such a way as to include much of the life of the people and to describe the unique character of that people."[2]

The strong interdependent relationship with nature constitutes a forceful organizing principle among peasant, primitive, or rural people. In highly urbanized situations, this relationship is replaced by the relationship of people to the urban environment. Hence, the study of a

[1] Lynch 1960:110.
[2] Redfield 1955:29.

city "becomes a study of the spatial and temporal orders of settlement and of institutions without reference" to the natural landmarks and elements of nature.[3] In place of natural landmarks, one finds buildings that are central to the social, economic, and political life of the city. These physical elements, or artificial landmarks, and one's relationship with and attitudes toward them are important in the study of a city. Consequently, the first part of this chapter will introduce the reader to an understanding of the people's mental organization of the urban environment; more specifically, we deal here with how the informants see, evaluate, and classify their surroundings. In turn, the relationship of these elements, when clustered, brings out "natural" divisions of areas; they are primarily formed by localization of sentiment and history and provide the formula for everyday existence. The implications for interpersonal relations, type of interactions, and communication become evident.

The second part of the chapter includes a general description of the formal political divisions of the city: the four *cuarteles*, as part of the settlement pattern established in the early days, and the barrios resulting from the city's later growth. At this point, it is interesting to survey the naming of public places as possibly another reflection of the Paranaenses' cognitive system. A complete demographic study of the city for the years 1964–1965 is not the aim of this chapter; this would warrant a study in its own right. The purpose here is to select through a random sample certain blocks to illustrate partially the background of the population. Familiarity with the background of the present population is, after all, important for our understanding of the city and its social organization.

In summary, our present interest is to understand the mutual relations between people and their environment. In this general sense we are dealing with an artificially created ecological system on which urbanites depend for their social and psychological existence.

Conceptualizing the City's Social Ambiente: El Centro and Plaza Primero de Mayo

The city, with all its complexity of buildings, markets, plazas, and

[3] Ibid.

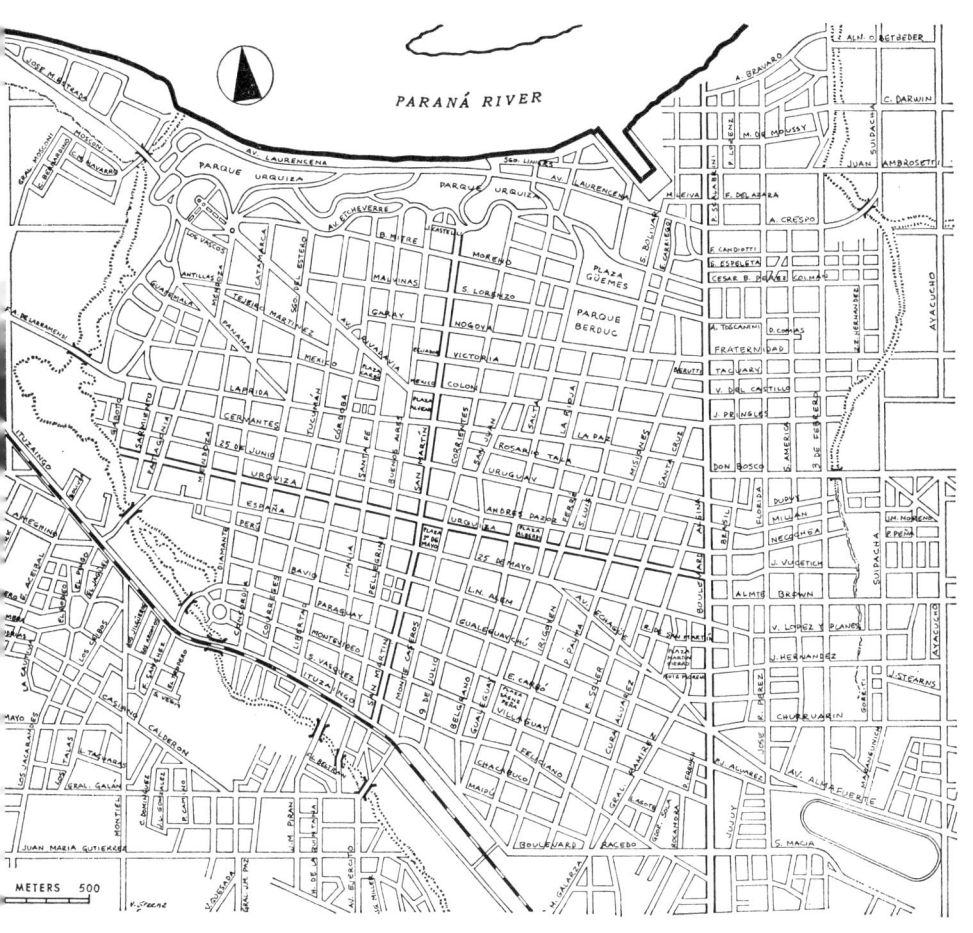

Fig. 11. City of Paraná, 1965

variety of institutions caring for and giving service to more than 100,000 inhabitants, is not conceived by its people as an impersonal and phlegmatic thing. The city is an extension of one's self and is strongly imbued with one's own psychological experiences. It is a further extension of one's household; it is the "shell" in which one must not only reside but also exist as in one's own household. The city, in other words, is not a means to an end but an end in itself. This differs from the viewpoint that the city is a material entity, separate from one's most personal cognitive structure.

Physically, the city of Paraná, referred to by the people as *la ciudad*, is contained in a square area (see fig. 11) truncated by a creek on the southwest. Alsina Boulevard marks the eastern boundary, while the northern boundary is naturally set by the Paraná River. Between these boundaries lies the city proper. It is immediately evident to the visitor that the central plaza and its surroundings constitute the oldest part of the city as seen by the ostentatious residences of the traditional families, the city's public buildings, and the cathedral. This central section is known as El Centro. It is generally assumed that in El Centro, which includes the plaza and approximately five city blocks surrounding it, one will find *los dueños de la ciudad*, the "owners of the city," as one informant suggested. The very heart of the city was within the city boundary in 1890. Even with the expansion of the last few decades, much of the political power structure of the city and the province may be found residing in this "historical" section of the city. It is of interest to note that the plaza is located on one of the highest geographical points of the area, reinforcing by spatial relationship the perception of its role in the city and its history. It is around the central plaza that people live in a truly "citified fashion."

Immigrants to the city who took up residence around the center came to be known as the people of the city (*las gentes de la ciudad*); those taking residence farther out, as those of the outskirts (*los de los alrededores*). Beyond this area, until very recently, lay the zone of the *quintas*, small tracts of land used for horticultural activities in most cases and for weekend homes of city residents occasionally. Most of these *quintas* have been rezoned for residences and housing projects. One frequently hears individuals from the center of the city refer to the outskirts as the *zona de los barrios* and to the inhabitants as *las gentes de barrios*. Each grouping of houses is recognized by specific names such as Barrio San Agustín, Barrio Sarmiento, and Barrio Antoñico.

As mentioned earlier, the city is divided into four *cuarteles*; the two main streets (San Martín and Urquiza) also serve as lines for the changing of street names. At the intersection of San Martín and Urquiza stands the Plaza Primero de Mayo, not only a symbol of patriotic events but also the central point of reference for Paranaenses and outsiders. This is literally the "plaza of the city" and contrasts with the "plazas of the barrios."

Individuals from other towns may find first-class hotels near the Plaza Mayo, along with fine department stores (Gath and Chaves, Guipur, and Casa Rosa). Banking services are provided by the National Bank and the Bank of the Province of Entre Ríos. The post office is located here, as are bars, coffee shops, and movie houses. Two of the largest schools stand on Urquiza Street at the plaza—the Normal School for training primary-school teachers and a private Catholic school for girls. Municipal offices are here, including tax and administrative offices. And here one finds the main social club of the elite, the Club Social, and the Cathedral, La Catedral de la Ciudad. Above the business quarters are a few private residences of socially and historically well-known local families. Recently built modern apartment houses several stories high have brought new residents into the plaza area.

The plaza plays an important role in the orientation and surely in the world view of the city population, in their economic activities, and in the public social life. With the cathedral at the main plaza, all major religious processions take place around the plaza. On such occasions, many inhabitants of each *cuartel* who only occasionally come to the Centro converge upon the plaza through the major thoroughfares of the city. From the corner of the plaza selected for their entry, one can deduce the section from which the person has come. The social standing and even the approximate place of residence of the people within the *cuartels* can be pointed out on the basis of the person's appearance, language and gestures, and manner of walk. After the procession, the plaza rapidly empties as people leave by way of the main streets, San Martín and Urquiza, and head toward their homes. Only those who frequent the plaza regularly remain in the area or linger at coffee shops and *confiterías*. These individuals are not from the barrios; they are in the latest fashion and conduct themselves as citified and modern individuals.

Seldom does a day pass that a businessman does not appear in the plaza either for banking or leisure. For outsiders, the plaza is an orientation center. It is neutral ground in the sense that countrymen, townsmen, and city men all may be seen there, each carrying on his own economic or social activities at the proper time of the day.[4] It is in the plaza that the poor newspaper boy and the wealthy man may be seen; and it is here that the businessmen, those less occupied, and the retired men may congregate. Each, regardless of his social condition, feels that he has a right to be there, as all human beings have a right to a space in the city.

Perhaps the best manner of conveying a real understanding of the plaza and what it means in the context of the social life of the city is through the words of an informant who said:

> The social center of Paraná is the Plaza Mayo. This is not because of those who happen to reside there, but it is in the thinking of the Paranaense; he knows that the Plaza Mayo dominates all the social aspects of the city. People are drawn into the plaza not just for commercial and business activities, but simply for social reasons. Each one of us feels that the plaza is something central, with a touch of sophistication. It is a focus of political, economic, and social activities. One can go as far as to say that Paraná *is* Plaza Mayo, the center—it is the compass of the city.

The plaza is, then, a separate unit; it is a place where one can experience a sense of personal freedom during business hours; yet outside business hours, there is a sense of social limitation.

To move upward socially one should reside near the center of the city, being attracted by the sophistication the plaza provides. For everyone, both poor and rich, both lower and upper social classes, the plaza is a point of reference. Although there are plazas in other parts of the city (see fig. 13), and they are old, they are conceived of as little parks and are not central in the mind of all the people in the city. These secondary plazas, with smaller churches, are physical entities conceived of as residential areas only. The central plaza is viewed as something of superior status, particularly for the *gente inferior*. It is seen as a

---

[4] Urquiza Park, covering portions of Cuarteles 1 and 4, may be considered another neutral area of the city, though it is generally viewed as an appendix of Cuartel 4. There is a free public bathing area known as the Balneario Municipal; those individuals who are not members of private clubs may use these facilities, though most of the area along the river is under the administration of the "clubs of the city."

symbol of urban sophistication, so much so that seldom does one see country people in its vicinity. The country people consider the plaza as something complex and luxurious, and therefore those from the small pueblos (*pueblitos*) and the country feel out of place there.

Until 1945 the Plaza Mayo was an important place for courtship. It was the place for *la vuelta del perro* (literally, the round of the dogs). At night, hundreds of young people converged on the plaza, and while women went around the plaza clockwise, men went around counterclockwise. On weekends at certain hours, it became difficult to find space on the sidewalks. The courting pattern now has changed to some extent, but encounters still take place in and around the main plaza. Those who can afford an automobile visit the plaza at some time during their car "promenades" through the city. In years past, when separation of the sexes was strict, the plaza was a place where boys and girls could come together and see each other while moving around the plaza. It was here that one learned to express feelings through gestures, looks, and elegant words as one passed by the young person for whom one had taken a strong liking. It was here that romance was initiated, where even with the strict rhythm of plaza life a boy could see "his girl" and eventually make the preliminary arrangements for a short meeting (chaperoned by friends) outside the plaza.

The plaza arrangement and the sex restrictions were closely related to the notion that a girl had to be conquered (*conquistar*). One's own social image was expressed by the quality of dress and behavior in public. When a meeting was finally arranged, the day of the week and the hour of the evening were selected. The choice of chaperon and the color and style of dress for the occasion indicated one's social standing. Thus one could recognize the other's social level, and with equality established, the process of *conquista* could begin.

All that is socially and politically important to the city is embodied in the Plaza Mayo. The buildings of the municipal government cluster in the area, but those of the provincial government are centered in another part of Paraná, around a small plaza with no particular social attraction. The *confiterías* and coffee shops of the Plaza Mayo bring together city and out-of-city businessmen, and in the open areas of the plaza retired men sit on benches on sunny days discussing their problems, complaining about government decisions, and offering solutions to local and world problems.

From the plaza one can gain much insight into the city life. Through constant observation one learns the daily rhythm of life adopted by the inhabitants. In Paraná people like to see and to be seen—*nos gusta estar viendo*; hence, the social success of many of the *confiterías* around the plaza. It is quite common for people to go much out of their way to reach their destination; to pass by the plaza constitutes a basic social need. People like to see other people, to know who is with whom and to gather information for conversations with others. By the same token, one cannot help but be very conscious of oneself in the plaza surroundings. But for anyone who needs to feel the pulse of the city, the plaza is the place. One knows through the years who are one's friends and who avoids whom because of animosity or personal, social, or political incompatibility. "At a distance" one learns much about those who adopt the plaza as their arena for social action. This information is often projected into the future and their degree of social success is predicted.

People in general welcome city street noises. An informant expressed many people's view by saying "we basically like urban noises —*bullicio y movimiento*. We like to appear where people gather. In our city the plaza attracts the people. Other large cities cordon off a street for several blocks, forbidding traffic during certain hours of the day so that people may congregate and use it for promenades." It was implied that with sharp social separation the need to be together increases proportionally. It is a manner of being with el pueblo (people) and in the pueblo (town). "There is a need to see one another even though one is not on speaking terms or directly acquainted with each other; but one finds familiar faces, and this we like." Thus, through the years, hundreds of people become familiar, and each evaluates and keeps up with the other's progress by their outward appearance. Biographies are kept alive and the versions, as may be expected, are innumerable. "One sometimes learns to greet someone because for years one has seen the person in the street and one feels happy to see the person continuously. Such is the case with neighbors where social contact is nil, but it is indeed fulfilling to greet the person every morning on the way to work. One knows that he is there, and that is all one needs to know."

It is interesting to note that when an individual has done some wrong and he and his family are socially embarrassed, the most noticeable thing is his disappearance from the plaza. With the trend toward social aggressiveness and changes in moral standards, some such people might soon appear again, but before long they will be given a nickname, and they feel the public sanction deeply, even though they try to dismiss it. There are also individuals known as *personas de baja vida* —people of low moral life—who do not frequent the plaza. "They impose on themselves a self-control and do not openly operate in the central plaza." Although ideally the plaza is an open and neutral ground for all, the poor conscientiously avoid it; if they appear there, they have a feeling of social insecurity that is quite noticeable. The very poor, unless begging professionally, tend to remain in their own neighborhoods; they consider the central plaza a place for the rich. But regardless of the amount of time anyone spends there, everyone thinks of the plaza as "the heart of the city," the focal point, and the place for and of everybody. It is, however, the most neutral place, and the stage for the most significant aspects of public living.

The city begins at the central plaza, and from here public life emanates. This is also the center of the living history and the symbol of a powerful past, mixed with elements of progress. An imaginary ring around the center, enclosing the plaza and three or four blocks surrounding it, would delineate the most highly rated area, commonly referred to as the *primera categoría*. From this point outward one perceives a gradation of sophistication from elaborate to modest to humble residences. The gradation is a meaningful model, but if too rigidly conceived would not do justice to the many exceptions that in reality exist. Such exceptions, however, generally disappear with modernization.

From the Plaza to the Barrios with an Informant: Introducing the City

Having seen the role of the plaza as a centralizing power in public life, now we are ready to proceed with a general survey of the city.

This will be accomplished through the eyes of a Paranaense who sees himself as a person of middle social class and recognizes that he has incorporated in his views a historical dimension generally associated with the elite.

It is not surprising that the informant began in the plaza when attempting to orient a stranger in his city. It is, after all, the point where the Paranaenses' "world" begins. A walk in a straight line in any direction is sufficient to recognize the ecological areas of the city, or, in native terminology, the *ambientes* of the city (fig. 12). As one moves in any direction from the plaza, he will find a similar change in architectural style and social background of residents. The direction chosen by the informant was northwestward; from his point of view, any other route would serve as well.

In showing the city to strangers, the informant projected a model of his orientation, his conceptualization of the city as a whole. His Paranaense upbringing by Spanish paternal grandparents gave him the basis for selecting, distinguishing, and classifying the elements he observed. These elements were put into a historical context by his own personal experiences in the city. He pointed out houses up to three blocks from the plaza and, without hesitation, said of the owners, "They are mostly *gente bien*" (literally, well-off people). Further inquiry revealed that *gente bien* does not necessarily denote people of wealth but rather a group that supports the distinctive social trait of good upbringing. In some cases the residents were and still are wealthy, but this consideration was not basic in the conceptualization of the informant. He pointed to the bronze door plaques at the entrance to many of these homes that indicate the professional rank (medical doctor, lawyer, court clerk, lawyer's clerk, piano professor) of a member of the household. Homes without door plaques are owned by men who are either bank employees with high rank, teachers in first-category schools, journalists, or others with education—*gente con educación*—who tend to reside in the central area of the city around the plaza.

At the termination of the area that the informant described as "El Centro" (approximately within a four-block radius of the plaza), he indicated that one could expect to find people of the middle economic

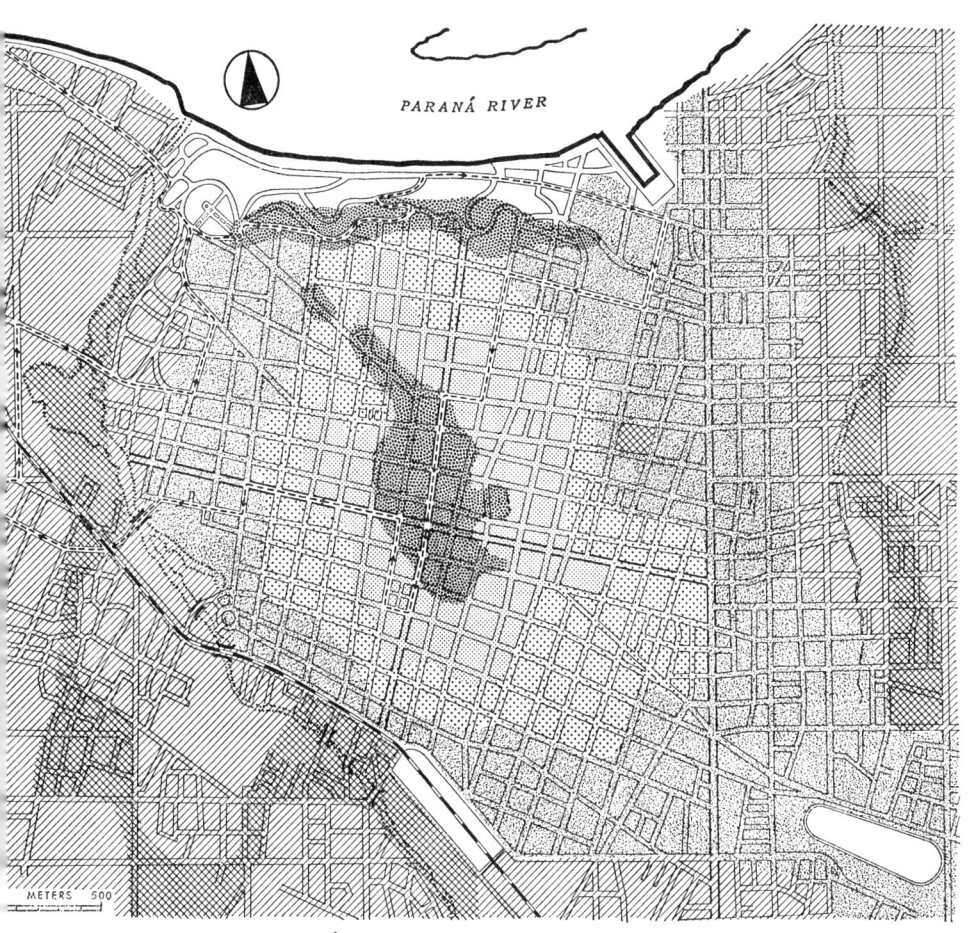

SOCIAL AMBIENTE OF PARANÁ

→ — — Route Introducing the City

ATEGORÍA

- PRIMERA (GENTE BIEN)
- CLASE MEDIA BIEN
- CLASE MEDIA
- GENTE MODESTA
- GENTE HUMILDE
- GENTE DE RANCHOS

Fig. 12

category, *"las familias de la clase media bien"* as he expressed it. He first pointed out that many more residents in this section of the city rent their homes because the devaluation of the peso, inflation, and rent-freezing legislation have created an advantageous economic position for the renter and an extremely disadvantageous one for the landlords.

As one moves further away from the central plaza and the nearby central market, there appear more corner stores—*almacenes de barrio* —which supply the neighborhoods with staple products other than meat and vegetables. Vegetable vendors, shouting their produce, tour such areas with their horses and carts.

Seven blocks from the main plaza, the informant pointed to the true *clase media*. To him this meant that the houses were modest in appearance, and any luxury of style was an exception. Even though there was generally more "modesty" and an absence of bronze plaques at the doors, indicating the lack of professionals, there were well-employed individuals. On the whole, one feels a definite decrease in the level of education. In this area emphasis is on completion of primary school; only those with a relatively good income will provide secondary education for their children, and fewer yet a university education. There may be many in the parents' generation who have been unable to complete even the primary level, *gente modesta*.

In moving farther westward from the plaza, now about ten blocks, the informant indicated that the inhabitants of this area were *gente humilde*—humble people. Wealthy families and those of social distinction (*de categoría*) were entirely absent from this locality. For all social purposes this area, which is beyond the cemetery, is where Paraná, the city, ends. The informant jovially stated that everyone, regardless of social category, will end there in the cemetery. The walls of the cemetery house everyone and inside "everyone finds his social place just like in the city."[5]

To the outsider it is not apparent that once he leaves the cemetery the city should end. The concept from the past that the cemetery lies outside the city still remains strong in the orientation of the people.

---

[5] The cemetery as a social replica of the city will be discussed in chapter 7.

The City and Its People

In 1890 the cemetery was in the zone of the *quintas*, a good distance away from the population center. But the expansion of the city has placed the cemetery totally within the city proper. It remains, however, a social landmark, so residents and *vecindades* beyond it are assigned a lower social category. Antoñico Creek, bordering the cemetery, reinforces the popular conception that once it is crossed, one approaches an *ambiente* outside the city—almost a rural one. The main streets linking this area with the city are flanked by houses with empty lots at intervals, occasionally fenced for gardening or enclosing domestic animals, such as chickens, horses, or dogs. Side streets are not paved. All this indicates poverty and uncomfortable existence, especially during rainy days, for the *gente humildes* residing in modest houses.

As we moved even farther away from the city, the informant reflected:

This is a zone of *ranchos* [huts]; it is uneven terrain with barrancas [ravines]. These people have lived here since who knows when. They were born here, live here, and die here, and who can move them? We just passed the *humilde* zone [the zone of poor people], but now we come to an area of the *gente humildísima* [the poorest people], *gente de ranchos* [people of the huts]. Most of the land belongs to the city. One sector of this area looks different because it is a housing development built in 1943 for these people. Those living in the development are employees of the municipal or the provincial government. But most of these homes are *ranchos* [huts]. Generally the residents are fishermen or peons in some government department. The *gente de ranchos* do not want to spend their money in improving their living quarters and they enjoy staying here without paying rent, buying property, or planning to move. They like this type of *rancho*, typically *entrerriano*, sometimes more than a regular house. Some of them are well made, clean, and nice. The *gente de ranchos* work as peons or in the local tile factory. They are poor, but there is no starvation. They have their own diet and cannot live without their *asado* [barbecued meat], *mate* [herb tea], wine, and bread. Many of these people have come from the countryside.

As one moves northward along Antoñico Creek, one notices *ranchos* distinguished by their red tile roofs. These contrast with the thatched roofs typical of the area and indicate a better economic standing. The owner probably works steadily at the local tile factory and has bought defective tiles at a reduced price. But he is still too poor to own land, and his hut—like almost all the *ranchos*—may stand on municipal land.

Upon reentering the city with the informant, we passed by the dock, a historical landmark. The informant stated that the first Basque immigrants (*los primitivos vascos*) had resided here. The houses are now dilapidated, but show the large European construction brought to Paraná. The point of central interest is a squash court (*cancha de pelota a la pared*), which is no longer used but was a great attraction to the Basques. Many Basques or their descendants, the informant remarked, are now wealthy and part of the *primera categoría*. Their marrying into long-established Paranaenses families aided their rise. Some now own large expanses of land or highly valued property in the city proper; others are professionals, often lawyers or medical doctors active in political life, having distinguished themselves at various levels since their grandparents arrived in Argentina. One descendant of a combination of patrician and Basque families has purchased one of these early houses, renovated it, and created a residence of outstanding local interest.

Moving toward the Parque Urquiza, the informant pointed to sophisticated chalet homes—"American style"—owned or rented by professional people: engineers, doctors, lawyers. These were considered by the informant to be families of very good economic standing, late-comers, and somewhat socially prominent. The residential park area is a development of the past three decades, regarded by the majority of the city's residents with envy and pride.

According to the informant, most of these residents of Parque Urquiza are descendants of European immigrants. More here are of Italian descent than Spanish. They are progressive in their view and style of life: their children attend secondary school and go to universities in other provinces. They seek opportunity to travel abroad, and many have done so. Education is very important in their lives, and they are very critical of the lack of higher education in their province. This area is presented to the outsider as the symbol of progress, an area one can compare with Europeanized areas of Buenos

Aires and residential areas of the United States or Northern Europe. An old building in this area represents something of the past and is an annoyance; it is quite common for people to state that such a building should be eliminated and replaced by something modern. Modernization and progress are the social marks of this ecological niche of the city.

Continuing on Laurencena Avenue, one passes the ferry landing at the Puerto Nuevo (new port) where passenger services for crossing the river to Santa Fé are available. Here one enters an area of the city inhabited by a class of less-affluent people, again the *clase media*.

The informant's sketch presented above was accepted by many other Paranaenses. In one social *ambiente* may appear material items typical of another, but these are exceptions to the concentric model. However, this is expected in a changing world, remarked the informant.

The City: Social Ambiente of Each Section

Early in its history Paraná was divided into four administrative sections known as *cuarteles*, each of which was further subdivided into square blocks known as *manzanas* (100 square meters, or 119.6 square yards). The gridiron pattern established by the Spanish when founding the village has been not only a physical arrangement of the land, but also a structure in the mind. The physical ordering of space, things, and people has become an important social orientation.

Each *cuartel* touches the central plaza. Cuartel 1 is to the northeast, Cuartel 4 to the northwest; Cuarteles 2 and 3 are south of Cuarteles 1 and 4 respectively. Each is known for its peculiar social characteristics and specialized services; each, however, shares equally in the total history of the city. Although the gridiron pattern determines people's physical orientation, the social orientation comes from the superimposition of imaginary concentric circles over the layout of squares with the plaza at the center, as we described in the preceding section. Each circle contains similar architectural styles and family social backgrounds. The circular layout of the social zones remained until the 1930's when Rivadavia Avenue in Cuartel 4 acquired a reputation equal to that of the central plaza. Thereafter everything

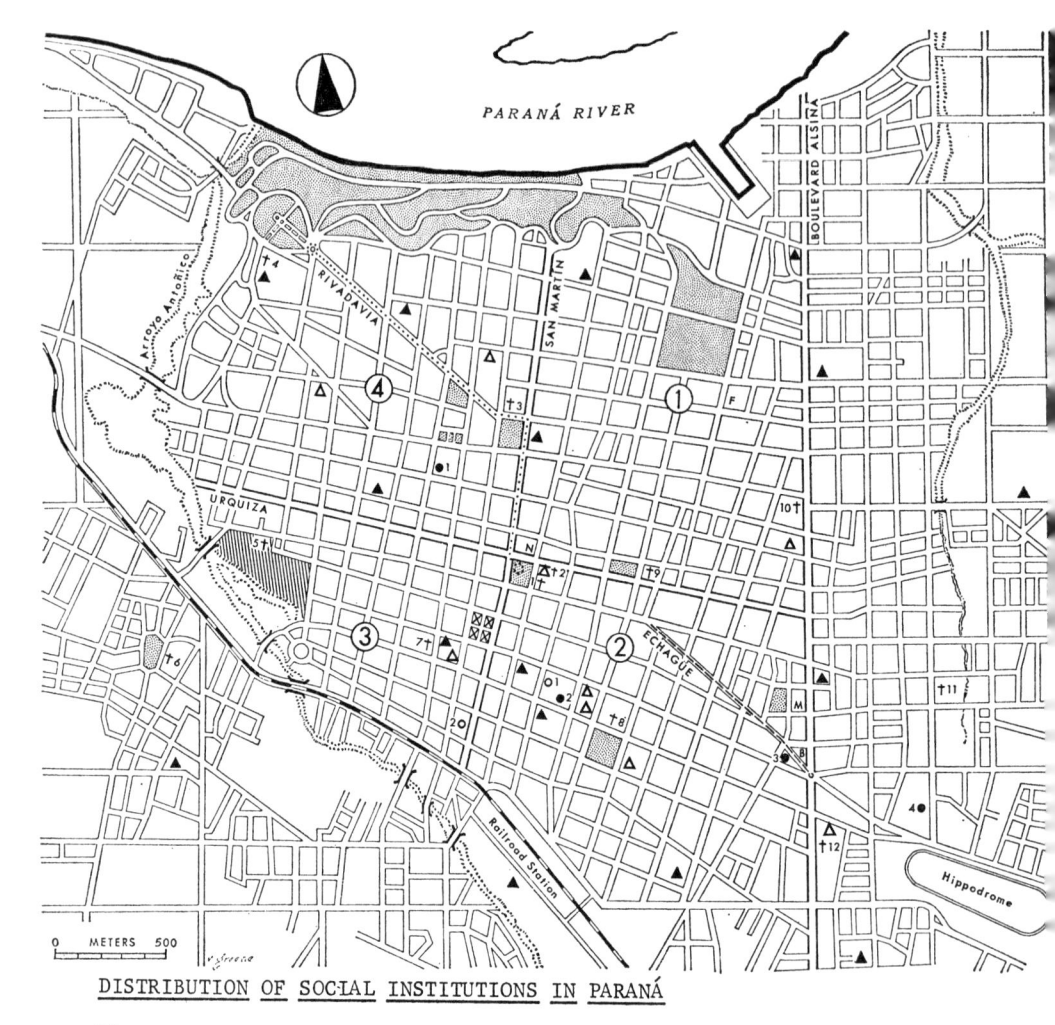

DISTRIBUTION OF SOCIAL INSTITUTIONS IN PARANÁ

① CUARTELES

PARKS AND PLAZAS

CEMETERY

✝ ROMAN CATHOLIC CHURCHES
    1 CATEDRAL
    2 NUESTRA SEÑORA DEL HUERTO
    3 PARROQUIA SAN MIGUEL
    4 PARROQUIA NUESTRA SEÑORA DEL CARMEN
    5 CEMENTERIO
    6 PARROQUIA SAN AGUSTIN
    7 SAN ANTONIO
    8 PARROQUIA SAGRADO CORAZÓN
    9 NUESTRA SEÑORA DE LORETO
   10 DON BOSCO
   11 PARROQUIA SANTA TERESA
   12 CRISTO REDENTOR

● PROTESTANT CHURCHES
    1 SEVENTH-DAY ADVENTIST
    2 METHODIST
    3 BAPTIST
    4 LUTHERAN

○ SYNAGOGUES
    1 ASHKENAZIC
    2 SEPHARDIC

▲ ESCUELA FISCAL (PROVINCIAL PRIMARY SCHOOL)

△ ESCUELA PARTICULAR (PRIVATE PRIMARY SCHOOL)

N ESCUELA NORMAL (NATIONAL NORMAL SCHOOL)

⊠⊠
⊠⊠ CENTRAL MARKET

M WHOLESALE MARKET

F FARMERS' MARKET

B BUS TERMINAL

•••••• PARADE ROUTE FOR PATRIOTIC CELEBRATIONS

— — — ROUTE OF CORSO (CARNAVAL)

Fig. 13

of the *primera categoría* expanded in this direction while the remainder of the city maintained the aforementioned pattern of concentric rings.

There is a direct relationship between the *cuarteles*, specific types of city events, and the social type of the population. It seems to follow that the concept of "appropriateness" is superimposed upon the city ecology; the concept serves as an organizing guidepost for decisions of city officials and residents alike. Through a discussion of each *cuartel*, a fuller understanding of the city may be obtained.

Cuartel 1

Some of the most elegant old homes in Cuartel 1 have now been rented to small hotels or government agencies. Their elegance is indicative of an ostentatious formative social period. Portions of some of the streets still have their original cobblestones, and the rails of the first street cars are mute testimony of an earlier means of public transportation. The architecture of the houses, the bronze plaques at the entrances displaying the profession of the residents, and the family names constitute a combination of variables that publicly portray the old social standing of many families.

Within Cuartel 1 is the port for river transportation, where the line servicing Buenos Aires, Asunción, and intermediary points along the Paraná River makes a stop. Also the passenger and ferry service to Santa Fé departs from here each hour. The activity in this section is intense and constant. Further away from the plaza, businesses (*tiendas* and *almacenes*) located at corners of blocks increase in number. A farmers' market has been opened in the district, and some permanent stalls give daily service to the neighborhood.

As in all districts of equal distance from the main plaza, in this *cuartel* and others, the pattern of the front wall of the houses facing the sidewalks is socially significant. The house fronts—sometimes trimmed with marble at the entrances, wrought-iron balconies, heavy carved doors, and relief decoration on the walls—are vivid symbols of an active social past. These house walls on each side of the street hide elaborate residences of Italian and Spanish styles adapted to the New

World. The backs of the houses were designed for servants' quarters and gardens.

The study of each residential unit reveals relevant historical information. Each house has been an individual and personal undertaking, and is in a sense a public monument to the accomplishment of the

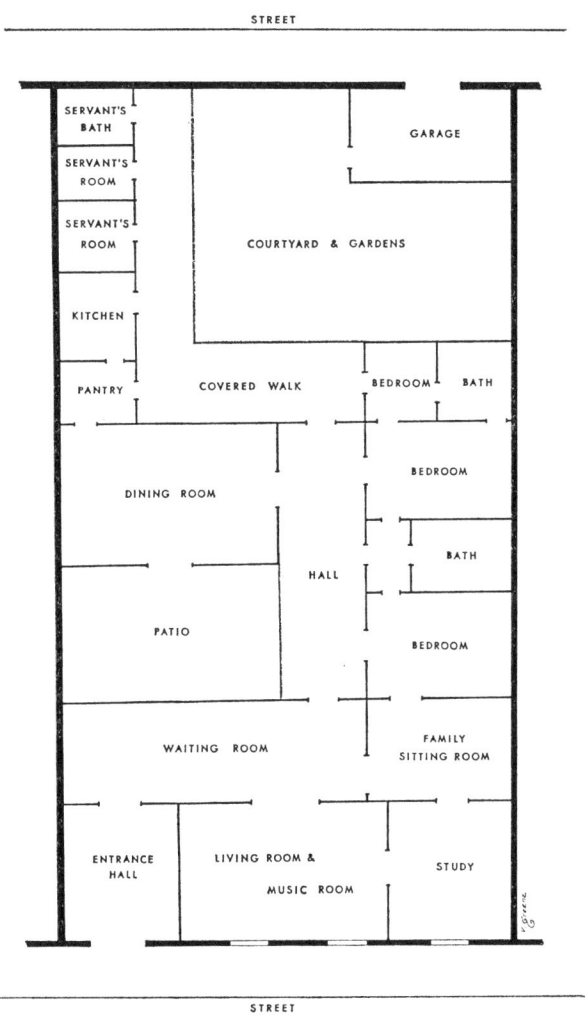

Fig. 14. Floor Plan of a Traditional Upper-Class Home

family. In time the residence signifies a public commitment to what the family is and will continue to be through the succeeding generations. Everyone in Paraná looks upon the residence as a mark of social standing, and any discrepancy between the social traits of the family and its economic power becomes the basis for public ridicule of the lack of appropriateness.

The residences within the central circle are conspicuous, with the exaggerated height of the one-story houses, the service and main entrances, the front rooms that are opened only on special occasions, the way in which rooms are heavily decorated with fine European items, and the frequency with which rooms face primary and secondary interconnected patios. In sections farther away from the plaza there are lower houses (if they are tall, they tend to have more than one floor). Still farther away, the urban pattern of the two facing walls is broken with the appearance of small flower gardens in front of the houses or a combination of garden and garage entrance through which a portion of the interior of the domestic grounds may be seen. Walls surrounding the property continue to separate each house. A high front wall, with a modest wooden door, may hide an empty lot or a series of interconnected rooms opening upon a courtyard. While a modest house usually has brick walls, a more costly one may combine brick with iron bars.

About six blocks to the east of the main plaza in Cuartel 1 is a zone of true *ranchos*, where families of squatters live on municipal land. Houses are constructed with scrap material and roofs are made of straw. Rooms are roughly partitioned, and the huts are fenced with boards and wire. It is a situation of "professional poverty, a primitive existence and a politically exploited situation," commented one informant. The city does not want to evict the squatters, yet municipal growth around the area causes nearby residents to press for measures to remove blight.

Three public schools provide instruction for children of the *cuartel*. In addition, the Catholic private school for girls located on a corner across from the main plaza and the Normal School, on another corner opposite the plaza, which has a teacher training course and a primary school, provide services to all *cuarteles*, according to qualification and public school standing. In addition there is a private school for boys on Alsina Boulevard open to all residents of the city. Since it is quite far from the center of the city, however, it is difficult for residents of Cuarteles 3 and 4 to enroll their sons there. Nevertheless, ambitious families who believe that private school education is superior to that of public schools often make the economic effort to send their sons. Although the standards are indeed good, its distance from center city causes *gente del centro* (the people of the center) to consider this private school to be of lower social standing, inappropriate for themselves.

Cuartel 2

Although Cuartel 2 is a separate political unit, in most ways it is a continuation of Cuartel 1. Around the plaza the buildings bespeak years of prosperity for some of the oldest families of the city, just as in Cuartel 1. This district contains the largest number of educational and religious institutions in the city. There is a secondary plaza with a barrio Catholic church. In this area also are located Methodist and Baptist churches and a synagogue, the Sociedad Israelita "Deguel Jehuda."

Immigrants from rural areas have been settling in this section and have joined an active economic "middle class."[6] Some descendants of rural Italian and Russian-German immigrants have purchased property in this district and have helped younger members of their families to continue their education or to open a business, thus attaining a higher social status.

Since there is no full market in this district, street vendors with horse-drawn vehicles sell green vegetables, bread, milk, and bottled soda; fish vendors walk through the streets carrying two large baskets, one attached to each end of a long pole balanced across the shoulders. Frequently the cries of the vendors may be heard. Occasionally others appear, offering bargains in competition with established vendors on their routes. There are also other door-to-door salesmen who come to

---

[6] The concept of classes will be discussed in a later chapter; the term "middle class," as popularly used, denotes that group between the conspicuous upper class and the lower group.

the doorstep of the busy homemaker and who may be greeted by a *nada hoy* ("nothing today") shouted from inside the house or spoken by a child sent to the door. Now, with the rapid expansion of the city, the municipality has allowed the opening of stalls on the sidewalks of Almafuerte Boulevard and Alsina Boulevard for the retailing of meat and fish.

Gualeguaychú Street, running east and west, is known as the "street of the Jews." Most residents here are of Jewish origin, though there are Italian and Spanish families as well. In many Jewish households the front room has been converted into a store for retailing clothing and sundry articles.

Cuartel 2 is bisected diagonally by Echagüe Avenue, which hosts *corso*, a celebration during the annual Carnaval. When the city was smaller and the upper social classes participated in the public celebration, the *corso* was held in the main plaza, but the increased number of humble and middle-class people in the city has forced the municipal officials to move the Carnaval activities to an avenue of second category. Cuartel 2 has become the host to all people of Paraná, including those from the poorest barrios, who, during Carnaval, feel that they have rights to the center of the city. For the *corso*, the municipality adorns the streets with colored lights and builds *palcos* (stands) for city officials and judges, as thousands of Paranaenses come to watch or join in the masquerade parade.

Five Corners, at Echagüe Avenue, is a second neutral area of the city. While those things surrounding the plaza are considered of *primera categoría*, those around Five Corners are of *segunda categoría*. It is a base of operations for commercial transportation, and the bus station located here is the main route for incoming and outgoing passengers. Traffic moves either toward the river ferry for the crossing to Santa Fé or toward the countryside to several villages in the province, or even beyond; there is also some movement to the railroad station. In addition to an important city wholesale market for fruits and vegetables located on Alsina Boulevard, other businesses at Five Corners include hotels, restaurants, coffee shops, hardware stores, beauty shops—all of second category. The effort to entice the rural population to shop in this area is most evident. Displays of mer-

The City and Its People   61

chandise lack the style and fashionable sophistication of those in the center city. Many merchants put special bargains out on the sidewalks; stores are small and crowded. City people know that these stores have a large variety of trinkets and often visit them when searching for some item whose manufacture has been discontinued. Frequently the merchants are of Jewish or Syrian descent, but all are popularly classified as Turcos.

People do not spend their leisure time at Five Corners as they do in the main plaza. Bus service between Paraná and nearby towns and villages is frequent. People from nearby rural areas come to the city to purchase household needs, to transact business, to visit relatives, or to receive medical services. Teachers and traveling salesmen residing in the city come to the bus terminal to commute to nearby towns. The city people ignore the terminal shops; advertising, by means of a loudspeaker, is to entice rural people to buy. Gypsies come to this area from their tent sites. They frequent the coffee shops, restaurants, and other shops in the bus terminal area, hoping to find customers for their fortune-telling services. It is also here at Five Corners that a man with a snake around his neck or with a monkey on his shoulder performs to a crowd and then sells trinkets or advertises a cause. He knows that rural travelers are easily involved in chance buying, and he exploits this. Aggressive, fast-talking salesmen use public embarrassment in an attempt to sell their wares. By quick verbal manipulation and gestures, a person may be tricked into purchases he had no intention of making.

The shouting of vendors selling pastries (*alfajores*), the constant advertising and music from the loudspeaker, the announcements of arrivals and departures of buses; running passengers, some wearing urban clothing and others still in gaucho outfits; the gypsies; horses and buggies passing by; old buses and the modern "Greyhound" type; old-model trucks, cars, and taxis, and newer ones; the "French style" sidewalk cafe; people embracing and shaking hands—all constitute the panorama of daily activities in this secondary business center. It is here that urban and rural elements meet. This particular area is dominant in the image of urban Paraná held by residents of the surrounding rural areas.

Cuartel 3

Cuartel 3 is primarily a residential area. Along the plaza the homes are large and of an early architectural style. An old part of the city, Cuartel 3 has a variety of styles, each representing the economic ability and the social standing of the original owners. On the slopes of Antoñico Creek, *ranchos* and homes of very modest means mark a significant socioeconomic transition. Two schools, built at the turn of the century, serve this section of the city.

In this *cuartel* are two important centers: (1) the city's retail market, supplying fresh vegetables, meat, fish, and poultry, flanked by other retail businesses—dry goods, hardware, and variety stores; and (2) the cemetery for the entire population of the city. Here the frequent passing of funeral processions may be witnessed. The selling of flowers to those visiting the cemetery is an important family business enterprise in the area. The railroad and Antoñico Creek separate this section of the city from the outlying barrios.

Cuartel 4

Cuartel 4, bounded on the north by the Paraná River, is now considered the "up and coming" social area for residence. The *nouveaux riches*, along with a few traditional families, own elegant homes here. A portion of the area near the river was converted during the depression of the 1930s into an attractive city region; within it now are residences of well-to-do families. Along the river banks social clubs of the city maintain beach areas for summer activities. Cuartel 4 is distinctive in that professional architects have introduced a new chalet style for homes. It is an area of high land values, expensive homes, and distinctive architectural change symbolizing modernization. It is the section of the city for socially aspiring families. These may not be families of patrician distinction, but they are well-known families in the city. A few wealthy patrician families of the last part of the nineteenth century built homes on Rivadavia Avenue, which in most cases their descendants have not been able to maintain. Newer homes tend to have front gardens, elegant garage entrances, and open terraces; the entire house is open to view. It represents a different architectural period known as *americano* or *moderno*. Many attempt to imitate this style, but in more modest proportions, particularly in the recently settled areas toward the outer fringes of each *cuartel*.

West of Santiago del Estero Street there is a sudden change. Houses are close to each other with living quarters facing the street and patios in the rear. The southern section of the *cuartel* is a continuation of Cuartel 3, the transition being evidenced only by the change in street names.

Urquiza Park, near the bank of the Paraná River, was zoned for residences in 1890 but was transformed in the 1930s into a park for Sunday promenades (*paseos*), although the Plaza Mayo still maintains its traditional role. During the day and on weekends, many downtown families come to the park in cars for short outings; but at night, contrary to the pattern of the main plaza, the park is not considered a desirable place—it may be visited only with the proper company of a relative or other adult. At the end of Rivadavia Avenue, near the western end of the bank, is an area dedicated to General Justo José de Urquiza, the provincial *patrón* of Paraná and Entre Ríos whose participation in the national history in the mid-nineteenth century cannot be forgotten and who dominates the area's history in the minds of the residents. A large statue in his memory stands there, and parades on civic holidays, with school children and the army participating, begin at this statue, march down Rivadavia Avenue, and end at the monument to San Martín in the main plaza. All primary and secondary public and private schools participate, the first-category schools fully and others to a decreasing extent as the social category of the school declines. If the holiday calls for a Mass in the cathedral, then the route of the parade is reversed, ending at the statue of Urquiza. On such occasions poetic speeches, ornate flower arrangements, and striking bronze plaques all pay homage to Urquiza; thus local residents come to feel the historical significance of this Entrerriano governor who influenced the history of *la patria* (the country) by leading an open rebellion against Juan Manuel de Rosas, an absolute ruler for two decades.

Cuartel 4, therefore, provides the stage for the celebration of national events. The arousal of patriotic sentiments seems most appropriate here, where landmarks and streets bear the names of the most important national symbols and where well-known families and provincial and national officials reside. This section of the city has the monument to "Mother." Flowers are placed at the foot of this statue on Mother's Day.

The Barrios

The areas surrounding the four *cuarteles*, heavily populated by rural immigrants, are known as barrios. One of the oldest is Barrio San Agustín, linked to the city by two bridges across Antoñico Creek. City residents associate this barrio with the lower classes, *"los negros."* Poetically, some may refer to the residents as *los criollos*, but the social connotation of *los negros* remains. The population is predominantly Argentine from many generations back; there are, however, impoverished Russian-Germans, Italians, Spaniards, and Jews who have adopted a simple existence—that is, a style of life symbolized by *asado*, *mate*, a specific speech pattern, a *rancho*, and a slow pace.

Barrio San Agustín has its own plaza. Commercially the barrio depends primarily on the small retail stores called *almacenes*. The retailers frequently serve as knowledgeable middlemen willing to assist clients with their purchases in the city and to lend cash at high rates of interest. They can secure most items needed by the local residents who might not be certain how to make purchases on their own. Unskilled men work as peons for the municipality, the slaughterhouse, or the tile factory, while women and girls may work as housemaids. Those who have some skill may seek employment with the government. No professional men reside in this area. Barrios never host any city celebrations. The general public stereotypes these barrios; frequent knifings, great wine consumption, broken homes, and prostitution are prevalent here. In other words, for city people the barrio life is noted for its lack of *cultura*. Actually, modernization is under way; with a kind of frontier spirit, some people have begun building "modern" homes. The better-off residents orient themselves toward the city center, ignoring barrio life.

Juan Perón, Argentina's president from 1946 to 1955, won great support from barrio residents as he became the symbol of lower-class aspirations. And still today, Peronismo can count on a following from this area.[7] Usually pictures of Juan and Eva Perón decorate the walls inside the *ranchos*.

Some barrios in other areas of the city have been developed through government housing programs, and architectural innovations have been introduced. Many open lots give an appearance of semi-rural living. Areas such as Villa Sarmiento continue to expand as country and pueblo people migrating to the city aspire to enter into a generalized urban middle class. Such people build homes by stages, moving in before construction is completed.

Center-city people view the barrios as physically distant. Jokingly, a resident of the city put a barrio resident in his social place by remarking, "I thought I would have to put chains on my car to get to your house." Place of residence is intimately connected with social standing, and discomfort is evident when one does not live where he should according to his personal social image. It is not unusual to find barrio residents with social aspirations who are unable to move upward in the social scale but who are constantly planning to move toward the center of the city. All progressive barrio residents entertain such desires. Barrios are part of the city, but socially beyond it and alone.

The variables of profession, income, housing, level of aspirations, participation in public life, membership in clubs and other voluntary associations, and level of education stand in direct relationship to the city areas. At the city center, including the areas along the river and facing the city park, all these variables are expected to converge, supporting the ideal. The city center is conceived as something higher in status; it is a symbol of what the city truly is, a symbol of progress and social distinction.

The plaza and El Centro combine to form a powerful force influencing all other sections and directing change. The position has his-

---

[7] "The years of Perón's rule emphasized one inherent threat to the military position —the rise of the lower classes. The strength of labor unions, the effectiveness of demagogic appeals to the masses, the threat of a worker militia, the lower-class distrust of the military—all contributed to making the armed forces and the lower class distinct, and often rival, pillars of the Perón regime" (Scobie 1964:220).

torical support, and the balance is well-established. The configuration outlined although not the result of a planned design has become the way of living. Residents of the city are indeed conscious of their social standing and fitness. They find comfort in being like others, and discomfort when differing from the immediate social environment. To be where one belongs socially is an expected consequence where stratification is an active principle affecting the city's social ecology. The organization of the variables into a workable, publicly recognized model orders the social phenomena of the city.

The City: Paraná's Nomenclature

Names assigned to public places and streets provide another way of looking at the city, one which correlates with the residents' social orientation and reveals considerable historical depth. "Place naming, star naming, maps, myth and tale, the orientation of buildings, the spatial implications in dances and ceremonies, all facilitate the construction and maintenance of the spatial patterns of the world in which the individual must live and act."[8] There is variation by district, and a pattern similar to that expressed by the informant.

San Martín and Urquiza, the major thoroughfares of the city, are the boundaries for the four *cuarteles* and are named for the national hero of independence years and the opponent of the dictator, Rosas, respectively. At the intersection stands the main plaza, named Plaza Primero de Mayo to commemorate the adoption of the Constitution of 1856. A large statue of General José de San Martín on his horse dominates this setting where important historical figures and dates are obvious. At this oldest point the city began, and here one should begin to study it. All that is most valued converges at this point; one can make no better claim than residence near the intersection of San Martín and Urquiza.

Cuartel 1 is framed by streets named after three national heroes who participated in the country's struggle for independence or later helped to maintain its unity: San Martín, Urquiza, and Alsina. Streets in the northern section of the district bear the names of other national leaders of the 1800s and the names of places where the struggle for

[8] Hallowell 1955:186.

SOURCES OF STREET NAMES

▲▲▲▲▲▲▲ Names and Places of International Significance

▨▨▨▨▨▨ Argentine Provinces and Regions

⫿⫿⫿⫿⫿⫿⫿⫿ Towns and Cities in Entre Ríos

■■■■■■■ National Figures and Patriotic Symbols

∘∘∘∘∘∘∘∘∘∘ Local Figures

xxxxxxxxx Criollo-Gaucho Complex

Fig. 15

independence occurred. The *cuartel* has two open areas: Plaza Güemes, named after the leader of the gauchos in the province of Salta, and Plaza Berduc, named after a man who distinguished himself as a local, provincial, and national political figure and as a philanthropist. The street north of Urquiza, known as Andrés Pazos, bears the name of Paraná's first mayor, elected in 1813 when the settlement, which had been depending on Santa Fé administratively, became a separate village. "He was a man of the upper social stratum," stated a local historian. Most north-south streets are named after provinces of the republic, while several east-west streets carry the names of the most important towns and cities in the province of Entre Ríos. It is hardly surprising that the street next to San Martín should be named Corrientes, after the "sister" province of Entre Ríos. As one moves east from San Martín, one finds names of provinces increasingly distant from and less developed than Entre Ríos.

An important commercial avenue in Cuartel 2 is named Echagüe, after a governor of the province shortly after independence. The naming of the street was in recognition of his help and enthusiasm in improving educational facilities in the city. Many of the streets in this *cuartel* have been named after national political figures, including L. N. Alem, Irigoyen, Belgrano, General Ramírez Rocamora; also frequently used are the names of local political figures such as E. Carbó, Echagüe, Racedo, and Sola; local professionals include Soler, Palma, and Agote, and a local priest, Cura Alvarez. The remainder of the streets in this district commemorate national patriotic dates, such as 25 de Mayo and 9 de Julio, or carry names of sites of historical importance during independence: Gualeguaychú, Maipu, Chacabuco, and Monte Caseros. Three streets have been named after the smaller cities of the province: Villaguay, Feliciano, and Gualeguay. Residents of the area are thus surrounded by many historical symbols about which they learn from the school history books.

Street names in Cuartel 3 contrast with those in Cuarteles 1 and 2. Residents are reminded of nations and capitals: Spain, Peru, Italy, Paraguay, and Montevideo; provincial cities: Diamante and Concordia; the patriotic events of Ituzaingó (a battle site) and Libertad;

President Pellegrini and such local figures as Bavio (an educator) and S. Vásquez (a historian).

Streets perpendicular to San Martín in Cuartel 4 have received names of important national figures, such as Mitre, Rivadavia, Laprida, Garay; one street has been named after the great Spanish writer Cervantes. The streets parallel to San Martín were given names of provinces, with those nearest the plaza receiving the names of the most important, best developed provinces. Three of the streets farthest away from the main plaza were named after Central American countries, while one was named Los Vascos, in memory of the early group of enterprising Basques.

In an outlying section (Barrio San Agustín) streets are named after historical criollo symbols and after places and things found in folk literature. While street names in the city give an orientation toward modern Argentinismo, this outlying barrio surrounds people with evidence of an earlier period of history, *criollismo*. Street names in this area include El Pingo (a good horse), El Rodeo (the rodeo), El Estero (a flooded area of the pampas), Los Jacarandas (a tree linked to the gaucho life), El Jilguero (a singing bird), Los Arroyos (the creeks), La Cautiva (a famous poem), and other rural elements related to the gaucho tradition.

In non-criollo barrios, such as the one east of Alsina Boulevard, the streets have been given names of local personalities whose descendants continue to reside in the center of the city. Streets are named for professors, mayors, governors, and community leaders who have worked for the benefit of the city. Residents have very limited knowledge of these local men or their participation in local life. City officials, of course, do recognize these names, and it is a matter of pride for the family when their ancestors are honored in this public manner.

The Paraná pattern of street and plaza names, with correlating social implications, is repeated in other Argentine cities. The more important, the more highly regarded, and thus the more valuable symbols cluster near center city, as do elements of wider national and international significance, and more generally, items associated with *cultura. Criollismo* is relegated to one outer section, while another outlying barrio pays homage to locally prominent personalities. Streets named for national heroes and national symbols frame the city proper and separate the *cuarteles*. It is interesting to note that names which serve to integrate all Argentines into one nation, in this instance function to separate the four quarters of this Argentine city.

The People: Their Ethnic Background

In the setting described—with the architectural variation and the street-naming pattern—evolved the social groupings and relationships of Paraná. Thus we proceed to a discussion of the most important component of the city: the different kinds of people who arrived at various times from the founding of the village to the present and who live and identify with certain quarters of the city. The ethnic heterogeneity of the city emerges as an important factor in its historical development. Only a profile of the distribution and changes in the ethnic composition of the various sections will be here presented.

Argentina is a country composed of and developed by immigrants beginning with the Spanish Conquest and the early colonization. Following independence in 1816, immigrants from other European countries were added. The greatest number came from Italy. From 1860 to 1910, "1,880,000 of the immigrants to Argentina, or 55 percent, came from Italy. Spaniards added another 880,000, or 26 percent. The French accounted for 5 percent, while the rest were Russians (primarily Jewish), Austrians, Syrians, English, Germans, and Swiss in that order."[9]

Argentine society, both rural and urban, cannot be understood without considering the contribution of immigrants. They came to Argentina, particularly during the years of economic boom from 1882 to 1889 and from 1904 to 1912, to get rich quickly and then to return to their native country. The rural areas were believed to afford the greatest opportunity. Land could be easily acquired with the help of mortgages from government or private colonization programs. The immigrant could become a sharecropper (*medianero*), a

[9] Scobie 1964*b*:29.

tenant (*arrendatario*), or a transient rural laborer (*golondrina*).[10] Most immigrants, however, found the rural setting disheartening. They were forced to live in isolation, without urban institutions and services to which they had been accustomed in their native land.

By and large the more recent immigrants were politically and socially aloof and faced much hostility from the native population, descendants of the sixteenth-century *conquistadores*. On the other hand, the Argentine entrepreneurs, many of whom were of recent European origin, "welcomed the European peasant as a necessary tool to build Argentina's economic greatness. Yet they could develop little feeling or understanding for the dirty, ragged, illiterate and apparently stupid masses that poured off the ships."[11]

To the isolated *chacarero* (small farmer) and the European immigrant too long submerged in total isolation, the towns and cities began to look inviting. Most of the towns of the interior catered to the basic needs of the farmers, their businessmen serving as middlemen in handling the grain and other products for fast transport to the ports. Among these people of the towns, one finds many Europeans whose story of success is simply that they abandoned the *chacra* "after a few lucky harvests and invested their savings in a shop or piece of land in some town or city."[12] Those who remained in Argentina, perhaps economically stranded, began to see changes in the second generation. The latter were Argentinos. In the city, more so than in the countryside, the second generation rejected all that was European, even forgetting the exact geographical origin of their ancestors. This was more frequent among the Italians, Spanish, and Swiss, and less so among the Germans, English, and Jews, whose children were educated to appreciate and identify with their European culture.

On the variable of ethnicity, the gross pattern that emerges is that the four *cuarteles* have a lower percentage frequency of Argentine

---

[10] The term *golondrina*, which literally means swallow, has been applied by historians in discussing the transient rural laborers. These people, very frequently Italians, would travel between Europe and South America, arriving in each place in time for the harvest. Their annual movements suggested the use of this term.

[11] Scobie 1964b:125.

[12] Ibid., p. 70.

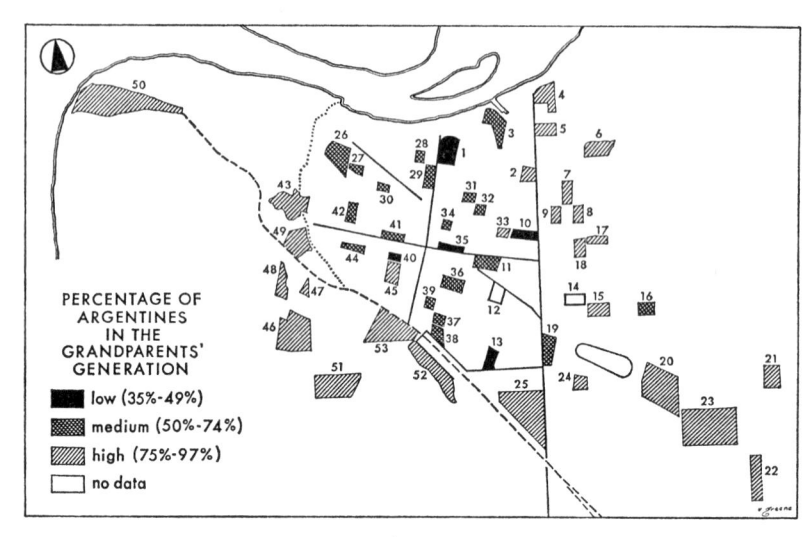

Fig. 16

ancestry than the barrios.[13] Argentines of several generations tend to reside in the barrios, which explains the *criollismo* stereotype applied to the people there.

Despite the high degree of homogeneity of the city districts suggested by a first glance at statistics, a detailed examination discloses a more complex ethnic configuration. During the field study twenty sample families were surveyed in each of fifty-three blocks (see fig. 16 for specific blocks). The blocks sampled show significant differences in percentage frequency distribution of Argentine versus European descent. Figure 16 gives the general distribution. Middle-aged individuals with a European father and mother tend to reside toward the center. Their parents migrated during the latter part of the nineteenth century or during the first decade of the twentieth century.

The situation portrayed by the data could be biased by the nature of the statistical sample. However, discussions of the pattern with

---

[13] Over 82 percent Argentine in barrios versus 63 percent Argentine in *cuarteles* (IPRUL sample of 50 blocks). The question asked on ethnicity is historical since it is the parents of the heads (husband and wife) of household (i.e., grandparents) whose ethnic background was recorded. Although more European parents can be found in the center, the larger percentage of interviewees were Argentine born.

The City and Its People 73

informants familiar with the history of the city population corroborated the statistical findings. Some interesting features can best be illustrated in Cuartel 1. Blocks 1, 10, and 35 show the largest percentage frequency of foreign-born grandparents and consequently have the lowest percentage frequency of Argentine born ancestors. The respondents in block 35 are Argentine born, in contrast to those in blocks 1 and 10 where the male respondents were born in Europe but were married to Argentine women. A similar situation holds in block 13, Cuartel 2, and in block 40, Cuartel 3.

Centrally located, block 35 brings together a number of variables already presented: large and comfortable, if not luxurious, homes; a concentration of professional families with secondary and university training; more and better material possessions; and memberships in city clubs.

Block 1, located at a distance from the plaza, conforms to the general pattern of the city; with increased distance from the center, there is a decrease in sophistication. The architecture is simpler, and the educational level of the population is considerably lower than in block 35.

Block 10 also presents a reduction in general economic, social, and educational levels relative to block 35. It is obvious that, while this area is closer to the ethnic composition of blocks 35 and 1, socially it is similar to the situation of blocks at the center of this *cuartel*.

Blocks 35 and 10 have immigrants of different periods; the former contains immigrants from the 1890s, while the latter has those from the years following 1930. In both cases the parents of second-generation informants show a similar trend in having married someone of their own ethnic group. In the first generation only 20 percent (in block 35) and 16 percent (in block 10) mixed ethnic backgrounds at marriage. In the second generation, although all were born in Argentina, there is a significant difference between the two groups; block 35 appears more conservative on this ethnic issue than block 10, as shown in table 6.

The figures in table 6 seem to indicate a more liberal attitude among the latest European immigrants (block 10). Supported by the active role played by ethnic associations in the years around 1900,

Table 6. Marriage by Ethnic Background (Percentages)

	Block 35 1st Generation	Block 35 2nd Generation	Block 10 1st Generation	Block 10 2nd Generation
Non-Mixed*	80.0	61.0	84.0	23.0
Mixed†	20.0	39.0	16.0	77.0
	100.0	100.0	100.0	100.0

* With Europeans, particularly those from the same country.
† With those of Argentine descent.

the parents of those in block 35 were able to preserve some degree of separation of their group and to resist ethnic merging. The associations were centers for compatriot meetings and for marriage arrangements in or outside Argentina; the group pressure to preserve Europeanism was very intense. As will be discussed later in this work, ethnic associations became less and less significant for the Argentine born, particularly following 1930, although the ethnic identification continues to be strong in the grandparents' generation. Now marriage partners are both Argentine born. Even though the data do not show it, great importance is attached to having European ancestors; the distinction between European-Argentine and Argentine-Argentine ancestry continues to be in some cases a source of social prestige, particularly at the time of marriage.[14]

In comparing these two blocks, one finds a significant drop in ingroup marriage among the second generation in block 10. Here, 84 percent of the parents married within the same ethnic group, but only 23 percent of the children did, while in block 35, 61 percent of the children did. As may be seen in table 6, in 77 percent of the total number of households the spouses show different ancestry; Italian on one side and Spanish on the other prevail. There are also Russian and Italian, Italian and Argentine, Spanish and Russian, and Spanish and Argentine marriages. Blocks 3, 31, 32, 33, and 34 show similar interaction, although this population descended from settlers

[14] It is necessary to indicate that stereotypes for each ethnic group influence interaction to some extent (see chapter 4). But parents of Spanish descent will not oppose marriage of their son to a woman of Italian descent, so long as she is a good person. "She is different from her group," is an important phrase in these cases.

The City and Its People

who arrived earlier than those of blocks 1, 10, and 35. The intergroup relationships present a situation similar to block 10.

Table 7 illustrates the distribution by ethnic identification in each *cuartel* of the city. The lead is taken by the Italian group.

An overall impression of the Argentine Paranaenses' place of birth is given in table 8. The largest number, close to half of the sample, were born in Paraná, about one-third were born in the province and migrated to Paraná (many of these reside in the barrios), and almost one-fifth were born in other provinces (a slightly higher percentage is found in the four city *cuarteles*).

Social Areas Sketched by a Paranaense

When my informant spoke about the subdivisions of the city and their functions, undoubtedly he presented a subjective evaluation, but

Table 7. Distribution of Paranaenses of Foreign Descent

Ethnic Identity	Cuartel 1 (total = 265)	Cuartel 2 (total = 150)	Cuartel 3 (total = 65)	Cuartel 4 (total = 174)
Italian	36.6	55.3	38.4	45.9
Spanish	22.2	9.4	29.2	17.5
English	—	—	—	2.1
French	2.6	0.6	3.0	3.8
Swiss	0.7	4.0	—	2.7
Russian	9.4	12.1	—	2.7
German	1.1	2.0	—	3.2
Lebanese	—	—	—	1.1
Turkish	0.3	60.6	—	1.1
Arabic	1.1	—	—	1.6
Syrian	3.3	3.3	—	1.1
Greek	—	—	—	—
Austrian	2.6	2.0	—	0.5
Polish	0.7	—	—	1.1
Yugoslav	1.1	—	—	—
Czechoslovak	—	—	1.5	—
Rumanian	—	1.3	—	—
Hungarian	—	—	—	0.5
Belgian	—	—	3.0	0.5
Latin American	12.0	8.1	13.8	9.3
Japanese	—	1.3	—	—

Table 8. Percentage Distribution of Argentine Paranaenses by Place of Birth

	Paraná	Entre Ríos Province	Argentine Provinces
Cuartel 1 (total = 407)	47.4	34.2	18.4
Cuartel 2 (total = 245)	48.6	37.9	13.5
Cuartel 3 (total = 118)	44.9	32.2	22.9
Cuartel 4 (total = 292)	44.5	29.8	25.6
West Section Barrios (total = 375)	50.9	40.3	8.8
South Section Barrios (total = 662)	41.5	40.2	18.3
East Section Barrios (total = 885)	44.8	44.9	10.3

NOTE: Each section had a small percentage of foreign-born individuals who were not included in the above calculations. There were 39 in the West Section, 17 in the South Section, and 178 in the East Section.

still this image of the city was his operational model. The physical, observable reality and the sentiments arising from the social conditions constitute the model—one widely shared by the residents. It is their way of viewing and organizing the city, and through time, as individuals meet and interact according to these attitudes, the social situation and organization are reinforced and the image is maintained.

The informant's description started with La Zona Central, an important axis of the social network of the city, located between Plaza Mayo and Plaza Alvear.[15] Well-to-do families like to own land and homes in residential areas along the banks of the Paraná River and in the area of Urquiza Park. There are families who have acquired economic status and are in the process of social ascent. They become conspicuous in the city by building houses or purchasing land in the most desirable section.

From the informant's point of view, some degree of traditionalism

[15] Although this material is not presented as a quotation, it is an informant's theorizing on the functional-social organization of space in his city.

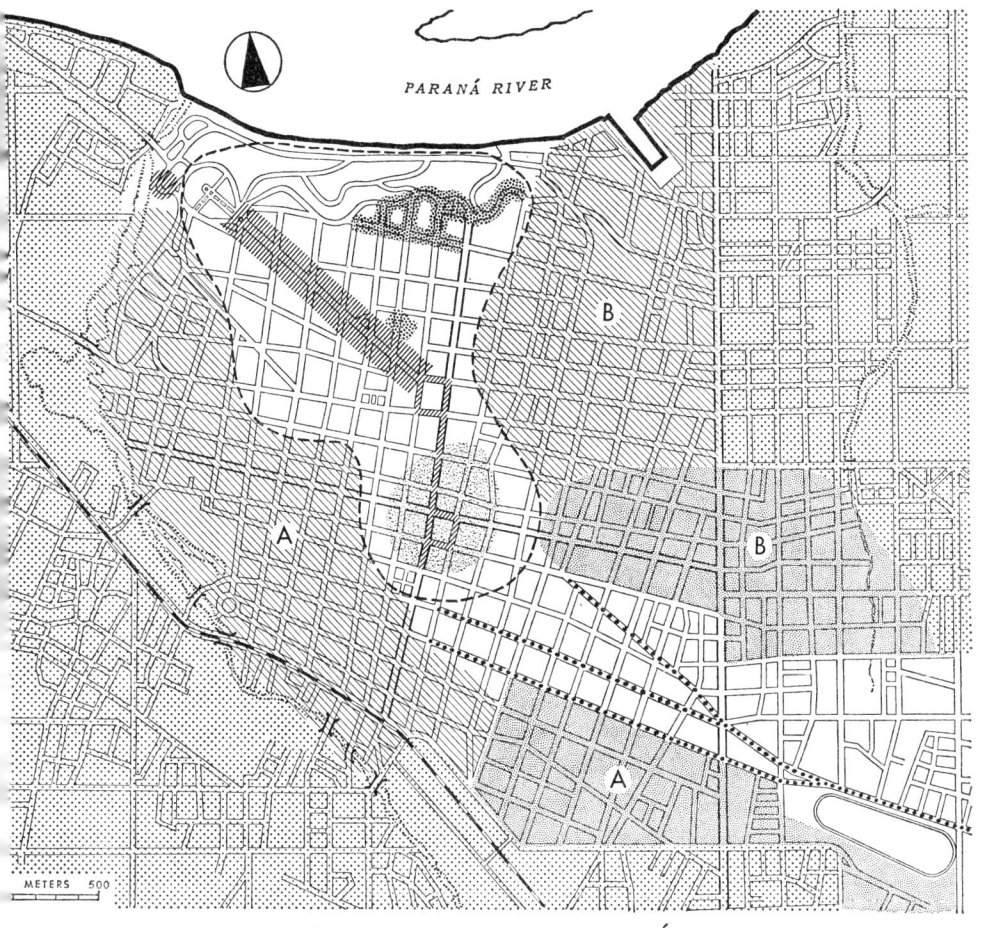

AN INFORMANT'S SOCIAL MAP OF PARANÁ

ZONA CENTRAL

ZONA SOCIAL NO. 1

ZONA CONOCIDA MAS ANTIGUA

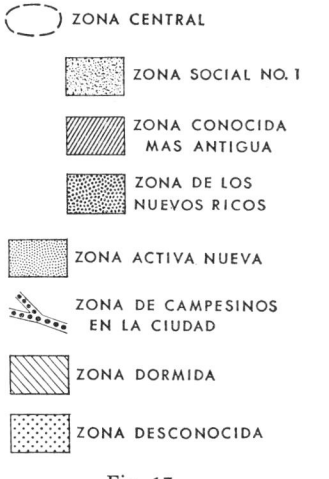

ZONA DE LOS NUEVOS RICOS

ZONA ACTIVA NUEVA

ZONA DE CAMPESINOS EN LA CIUDAD

ZONA DORMIDA

ZONA DESCONOCIDA

Fig. 17

is implied when there is a church of some importance in a neighborhood. Families residing most closely to the churches, such as the San Miguel Church in Plaza Alvear, are not all families of *linaje* or *abolengo* (of old tradition and name); proximity to the church enhances one's social standing. Many of these families now have married children who have moved to other sections of the city because the old neighborhood is too small to accommodate the expanding households.

In one part of the *zona central* that extends through Rivadavia Avenue reside the *familias conocidas*, the well-known families, known not only for their distinction historically but also for their general social and business activities. This area can be characterized as the *zona conocida más antigua*, the influential zone. The residents' mental image derives from the fact that most significant elements in the zone are old (*antiguo*), thus giving the area historical standing. Around this core there are many intermediate areas with families who feel socially well qualified. Land values are high, and professionals and businessmen of importance aspire to live here. Some people who once preferred to live around the main plaza, *zona social no. 1*, now choose the river's edge because of the beautiful view there (*zona de los nuevos ricos*). The main plaza and its surroundings, however, still remain the heart of the economic activities of the city. For a Latin American city, it is not strange or coincidental that the economic and social powers coexist in the same zone.

Economic competition with the *zona de campesinos*, thus referred to because it connects the country with the city, has increased in the last decades. Some businessmen feel that Gualeguaychú Street is an important thoroughfare for business and income. This is the area of many Syrian and Jewish businesses and residences; here country people begin to spend their money. The area thus functions as a filter for the city. Here small businesses (*tiendas*) are distinctive and conspicuous in each block. This is a zone with much movement and activity with diverse economic transactions.

Comparatively speaking, the rest of the city is residential, and the image is that of lower economic and social status. Informants tended to refer to the remainder of the city as the "sleepy zone," the *zona dormi-*

da. Subsection "A" constitutes a very old section of the city (see pictures). Some of the houses reflect the age. It is a "sleepy zone in the mental sense," declared the informant. Although there are families in good financial condition, it is simply an old section of the city, lacking the social prominence of the *zona central.*

Zona activa nueva A is viewed similarly but is considered more active. The houses are newer because it is an area of more recent expansion of the city. Although houses here are smaller, they have an appearance of architectural modernity that contrasts with the other areas. Here "people aspire to material well being." Military, skilled laborers, and technicians tend to reside in this subzone. Some may open businesses other than the traditional *almacén,* such as repair shops for automobiles, radios, or televisions.

The image held is that the *zona dormida* has no significant ethnic composition, and one never hears people referring to an area as that of the Italians or the Spaniards. As the informant stated it, "How can people speak nowadays in terms of ethnic descent when everyone has the same background?" If the Spanish element dominated at first, the Italian came as a second layer and overtook the Spanish in the twentieth century; and if the first generation did not mix, the second and third did. The Basques, who used to reside in the Bajada Oscinalde, have dispersed and many now live in the *zona central.*

As one enters the *zona dormida,* it seems that the *ambiente* begins to shift and acquires more of the barrio life style. "Here is the paradox: although the inhabitants are in the city physically, they continue to maintain a rural disposition—that is to say 'dull,'" observed the informant. People become oriented toward their own blocks and their own local, small merchants.

The informant pointed out that a striking distinction at present is the use of air conditioners. In the *zona de influencia,* residences have air conditioning, while in the *zona dormida* they are totally absent and considered out of place. Air conditioning is as much a distinction today as the refrigerator was twenty years ago. It follows the line of social and economic importance and begins in the central area of the city.

Beyond Alsina Boulevard one finds secondary economic centers. Here are shops such as the dressmaker's, the barber's, boutiques, and repair shops for cars, bicycles, and watches. This section is considered to be "tacked on" to the city. The attitude toward the *zona activa nueva B* reflects a sense of separation and intrusion and is reminiscent of the attitude held toward the past European immigrants. It is something yet to be accepted. The closer the shops are to Alsina Boulevard, the access route to the city, the greater is their volume of business. All these elements make this section of the city a zone of *empuje* (push) and earn it its name.

On the western side of the city, across the railroad tracks and Antoñico Creek, the very poor (*humildes*) reside; recently, however, there has been construction of modest homes, housing projects, and small businesses. The people of the city center consider this an unknown area and a social void—*zona desconocida* or *anulada socialmente*. The typical inhabitant, particularly the early residents of *ranchos* or humble homes, "cannot be trusted." Local tradition continues to point out, although with some distortion, that people of ill repute —prostitutes and thieves—congregate in this area. Nevertheless, the zone has been undergoing continuous modification. Here unskilled laborers, peons working in municipal services, construction workers, and domestic servants reside. Separation from the city, accentuated by the natural topography, resulted in the city's neglect of many of the area's basic public needs. It is, in addition, a zone of sporadic political activity with a tendency toward social unrest; when Peronismo flourished it became deeply rooted in this area.

The social monopoly of the city is centered within the *zona central* where reside a large majority of the people who feel proprietary rights over all things of social and historical importance. They would consider giving up their central residence as social death. It is interesting to note, as the informant pointed out, that most of these people tend to hold images of themselves—images based on generally accepted premises—that they, like the zone, are of *primera categoría social*.

In conclusion, everything classified as of *primera categoría* is found in the central zone of the city, directly connected with the central plaza. "These are the people in the candleholders" (implying social prominence), was the expression used. Though the central zone produces the political leaders, the bulk of the constituents are in the zones of *activa nueva, dormida,* and *desconocida.* It is in center city that high-level politics occur, that political maneuvering is discussed over coffee, and that the tribune of the pueblo holds forth. Because of this concentration of strength at the center, the constituents from other zones are either apathetic toward politics or produce leaders of extreme tendencies.

The sketches provided in this chapter, particularly of the people's background, lead us to the important question of how early European colonists, as well as those thousands who arrived after independence, have organized themselves in the social context of the city. Thus, our concern is with the nature of their Argentine society and culture. The setting of this city is not exceptional, but is, rather, typically Argentine, depicting the characteristics that have been most important in the country's development.

The heterogeneity of the city is an important factor when discussing the concept of culture in this situation. How the ethnic groups reached understanding, what cultural features they now share, and what distinctive character has evolved in the context of the city are among the most basic and indeed the most difficult questions to be answered. Straightforward answers may not be found in one single chapter, but the scheme of this work provides guides and sufficient data to allow author and readers to understand the nature of Argentine culture and the structure of the society.

Paraná is a city, and therefore a symbol of a complex community and society. The ethnic plurality is evident; one cannot help but raise the question of how the way of life (culture) and the people (society) are integrated by the Paranaenses. Are the elements brought in by Italians, Spaniards, Germans, Jews, Swiss, Syrians, and others preserved, overlooked, or combined in some intricate way? What, we may well ask, are the social principles responsible for the organization of the city? This is our first level of inquiry. Many of the Argentine towns and cities have a multiethnic background. Paraná is no exception. This is not altogether a unique phenomenon; it is common to North America and the Caribbean area, among others. The question raised by our Paraná case, as a segment of the total Argentine experience, is: what dynamics characterize these people, their society and culture? How should one begin to conceptualize life in an Argentine city only indirectly affected by industrialization? To find the answers we must plunge into the setting where man forms his social relations and begins his search for the road leading to his personal and social goals.

II. The Setting for Social Relations

... whether young or old, criollo or mestizo, general or laborer or lawyer, seems to me to be a person who shuts himself away to protect himself; his face is a mask and so is his smile. In his harsh solitude, which is both barbed and courteous, everything serves him as a defense: silence and words, politeness and disdain, irony and resignation. (Octavio Paz, *The Labyrinth of Solitude*, p. 29)

3. THE SPACE FOR SOCIAL RELATIONS: THE *VECINDAD*

Vecino (neighbor), *vecindad* (neighborhood), and *barrio* are terms constantly used by Paranaenses. They appear to be crucial concepts in Paraná's social structure. In this chapter I shall attempt to convey an image of life by describing events in one middle-class neighborhood. Familiarity with the neighborhood is necessary for understanding elements that intimately affect the individual and his orientation. Selected aspects of neighborhood life, as experienced by *vecinos*, should form the profile of what *vecindad* means in this urban setting. The neighborhood on which we focus is located nine blocks from the central plaza, and by adding or subtracting degrees of *cultura*, wealth, education, and ancestry we can conceptualize the social profile in the center city or in the barrios.

Vecinos and Vecindad

In a modern city social diversity is inevitable, and for Paranaenses this characteristic is essential to the definition of a city. As one moves away from the central plaza, a professional's neighbor may be a retired, unskilled laborer; a person of British descent may live next to a first-generation Italian, or an Argentine of early Spanish stock may be next door to a Turco, a German Jew, or a Russian-German; a wealthy person, educated and gentle, known in the neighborhood as a *campechano* (a frank and hearty rural man), may live next door to an Italian family without *cultura* that operates a shoe-repair shop. The cobbler's peasant background, passed on from his immigrant parents who came to Argentina in the 1890s, is retained in his Italian style of life. The professional uses the services of his cobbler *vecino*, and on the way to work both exchange friendly greetings. Privately, however, the professional judges the cobbler as *medio guarango* or *medio ordinariote*, that is, socially rustic, but a good man. After living side by side for twenty years, each comes to consider the other a reliable and hardworking *vecino*; they accept each other, but understand that cultural and social differences prevent further intimacy.

In the setting of these ethnic, social, and economic variations, social life among *vecinos* has little common ground. Each household maintains a strong sense of familial intimacy—there is an undisclosed life within one's own walls. In contrast to the constant public gatherings in the *zona central*, in the *vecindad* the rule of etiquette is that "each one should be in his own home." Toleration and calculated avoidance protect each family style. Neighbors seldom discuss differences openly, but guess at them. Differences are glossed over as long as one keeps "to oneself." This style gives the city its social character.

Every morning at 5:30 newspaper boys and men run from door to door in the neighborhood crying *"Diario."* Each adopts a characteristic chant, and clients recognize their own delivery boy by his melody. As the streets become noisier, the neighborhood awakens; car engines start up, and the night's rest comes to an end for all *vecinos*. Housewives or their maids come out on the sidewalks with brooms and buckets of water to begin their household chores. *Vecinos* clean the sidewalks in front of their houses, and some even clean a portion of the street, ridding it of accumulated dirt, paper, fruit peelings, and horse droppings.

In the summer, the windows of the homes are open in the early morning and remain open through the morning cleaning period. Thereafter, curtains and the outside iron or wooden blinds are tightly closed. The house is now considered clean and is kept dark and cool for the rest of the day.

Children, wearing the white uniforms of the public schools or the uniforms of private schools, depart for classes before 8:00 A.M.; their fathers leave for their places of employment. Most people in the city depend on public transportation; city buses are crowded at this early hour, causing much complaint over inadequate service. Other means of transportation include bicycles, motorcycles or scooters, and walking.

Stores in the neighborhood open around this time also; housewives or maids begin their daily rounds, purchasing food for the day. Children who attend the afternoon session at their school may also be running some errands. Shopping for the day's needs requires stops at the butcher's shop (*carnicería*), the green grocery (*verdulería*), the bakery (*panadería*), and the grocery (*almacén*) for staple items. These activities can be time-consuming for the housewife; she also must clean the house and prepare the big noon meal. The entire family returns home for two to three hours for this meal and a siesta.

During the busy morning hours, the women of the various households pass each other on the street or in stores, greeting each other formally. Sometimes they stop for lengthy conversations, though even when in a hurry brief mention is likely to be made of the weather or of an event announced on the radio or seen in the newspaper or on television. On these shopping expeditions, a housedress is worn, perhaps covered by an apron. A woman with servants is unlikely to appear daily in the street, and the apron is left to the maid. The daily routine brings everyone in contact in the neighborhood; through the years each one follows the other's state of health, degree of happiness, and general well-being, which may provide topics for speculative conversation with the local storekeeper.

The daily visit of the door-to-door vegetable man is a common sight in the neighborhoods. He arrives at the same time every day. A *verdulero* is familiar with the likes and dislikes of each customer and offers specific items for particular meals. In many cases he may trigger ideas for the housewife undecided on the day's menu. He stops only at his established customers' doors; only in cases of urgent need does a non-customer approach another neighbor's *verdulero*, and this with a certain amount of discomfort. It is etiquette not to interrupt transactions with customers, and for this reason noncustomers must appear hesitant in their approach. Neighbors gossip about city events or about other neighbors with the *verdulero*.

Several vegetable men serve the same neighborhood. Some bring their produce in horse-drawn carts; others may push a hand cart. Those arriving on foot carry baskets over their arms; in contrast to the traditional *verduleros*, they go from door to door or approach someone standing at a doorway, who may sample a product even when she has no intention of buying it. A housewife may dismiss the salesman with a curt "too expensive," perhaps concealing her limited budget. Sampling from several ambulant salesmen enables the housewife to become familiar with prices, and to assess her standing with the family's *verdulero*, especially concerning just how much she needs to bargain with him. A neighborhood housewife enjoys the opportunity to sample the daily prices from her own front door.

The milkman in a horse-drawn cart, the bread man in cart or small panel truck, the delivery boys, the postman, the garbage collectors, and the very poor who rifle the trash for saleable items such as paper, bone, and metal, or for food, are all part of the expected array of morning transients in a residential area.

An hour before noon the neighborhood streets quiet down again. Only the need for a forgotten item will cause a housewife to appear in the street at this hour. At the store, she will explain that the item had not been placed on the morning's list, or that a relative who had not been expected would be dining with them today. At noon, when children return from school, they are sent to the store for soft drinks, or wine for the table.

The sounds of cars stopping and doors opening and closing can be heard through the whole length of the street. These noises indicate to other *vecinos* the arrival time of a particular neighbor; such sounds are assimilated into one's own time and orientation. Prediction becomes part of one's own insular existence while separated by patio walls.

The sounds of the children going to and from school signal a significant break in the activities and rhythm of the day. Those who attend the morning session (*turno de la mañana*) return at noon; before siesta time, another group of children, mostly girls, leave for the afternoon session (*turno de la tarde*). People's activities shift the composition of the household; each day the family comes together for every meal. During the noon dinner hour, sound trucks appear in the streets advertising movies, a circus, or political activities. At this hour the announcers expect to reach both parents and children. Usually the members of the family discuss city events together.

Early summer afternoon hours find life at a virtual standstill. The cool, darkened home is a welcome relief from the subtropical heat, and the siesta is "desirable for the digestion" after a heavy noon meal. In winter an hour in a warm bed is also a relief from the cold of the unheated home.

The shift in the neighborhood population in the afternoon is readily noticeable. People who work in public offices remain at home unless they have other afternoon employment. Older children, especially boys, are more likely to be at home in the afternoon. Those whose business activities require that they return in the afternoon generally leave before 3:00 P.M. Again sounds mark their departure time: a motor starts or a man walks by with characteristic step that neighbors recognize. Thus adults, at home most of the time, keep up with outside activities. This orientation is part of fulfilling social existence. Few vendors roam the streets, though there may be an occasional person offering bargains on some item or a middleman selling fish caught during the morning. In winter, on a pleasant day, people sit in front of their homes sewing, knitting, drinking *mate*, or chatting with their neighbors while warming in the sun.

Another characteristic sound throughout the city is the tolling of church bells. They ring in the early morning for Mass; family members, especially the women, attend services on Sundays and holidays. Saturday afternoons (British Saturday) and Sundays are very quiet in contrast to the other days; there are no vendors in the streets and businesses are all closed. Catholic churches are scattered throughout the city, and *vecinos* attend according to their social rank. Neighborhood-oriented people attend services in the closest church.

Weekday afternoons, particularly after 4:00 P.M., the streets are filled with the noise and laughter of children playing. Groups of boys band together to form what adults call *la barrita de chicos* or the *barra de la vecindad* (the gang). Since children are not expected to enter the home of a neighbor without an explicit invitation from a parent (a rare occurrence), children meet and play on the sidewalks and in the streets. They may play soccer, pedal around the block on their bicycles (if their parents can afford one), engage in mischievous behavior such as knocking on a door at dusk and running away, or gather in front of a shop to watch television. Mothers may dispatch younger siblings in search of older brothers or may ignore them until they return for late dinner. Girls do not congregate in gangs; it is unladylike. They may be seen with one true friend sitting at the entrance of their own home or strolling along the sidewalks. It is customary for a few neighborhood children to gather in front of a home under a window in order to get the attention of the children of the household, fully expecting that their presence will entice the other children to come out. Schoolboys find it difficult to concentrate on studies and often parents need to order the group away rudely. Especially at siesta time, parents have no hesitation in informing the group that they are not welcome. On this basis, neighbors find grounds for criticism concerning children. Because they assume that children are mirror images of their parents, the blame is placed on the parents.

In the afternoon, between four and five o'clock, adults appear at the door to assess quickly the social situation of the street. Young teenage girls gather at a doorway for conversation, ceremoniously greet neighbors who pass by, or flirt with teenage boys whenever possible. A wife carries *mate* to her husband who sits on the front steps. Life appears casual. Women wear afternoon frocks instead of the housedresses worn during the morning. Everyone tries to be at his best at this hour on a weekday, according to his own "social image." As evening approaches, neighbors bring chairs to the sidewalk and sit there for hours enjoying the cool breeze. There may be some contact with other neighbors, but usually each stays with his own immediate family group. Children avoid the adults and try to stay out of sight of those known to be difficult (*delicados*). Not all neighbors, however, will be

The Space for Social Relations   91

seen sitting outside. The more sophisticated and socially aspiring individuals, the city-oriented ones, are less likely to be standing on the sidewalk or sitting at the front door. Persons of the neighborhood social setting with time on their hands truly enjoy this phase of life. The pattern is more intense in middle-class sections of the city, that is, several blocks from the central plaza.

Couples *en noviazgo* (in courtship) with non-neighbors may be seen at doors or repeatedly walking back and forth along the sidewalks if their families have approved their romance. After the first greeting of the evening, the couple may ignore adults, but self-consciousness is evident. If parents approve their daughter's companion, even though the couple is not yet officially engaged, the boy may bring the girl back to her front door after the parents have returned inside. The couple is allowed to visit at the front door, but no chairs are provided for them. This pattern is most widespread in the middle-class neighborhoods. At either end of the social continuum young people are less likely to spend leisure evening hours in this fashion. House visits are common for the poor, while encounters at clubs, cafes, and in the plaza are more common among people active in city social clubs. Servants of the upper-class families follow middle-class courting patterns, perhaps while caring for their employer's children.

In each neighborhood there are retired men who, while watching grandchildren, simultaneously "police" the neighborhood socially and converse at length with the storekeeper and neighbors passing by. Often they question maids about the habits and mode of life of their employers. And the employer tests the loyalty of his employee in this situation as well. Reserved persons dislike being observed, and avoid conversations with the "curious *vecinos*." One can ignore the "policeman" of the neighborhood, but in so doing, is likely to earn the label of *orgulloso*—haughty or snobbish.

In a *vecindad*, anything unusual attracts attention. People constantly ponder outside events. A firecracker fired at a time other than New Year's is certain to bring at least one member of each household to the street. Much speculation follows about the reasons for the strange noise. Was it a children's prank? Did they have their parents' permission? Did they realize the dangers? Was the owner of the house at home when the firecracker went off? All of these are questions to bring up. The incident remains a topic of conversation for many days.

This profile of neighborhood life constitutes a model; innumerable variations may be found, mostly according to the social category of the neighborhood. It is logical to expect some patterns to be more widespread than others. For instance, in the center city one does not sit outside on the sidewalk, but may stand at the main entrance to the house or on a balcony. The greengrocer and the grocer do not play the same role in all neighborhoods of the city. There is more individuality and a greater sense of personal freedom within the three or four blocks around the central plaza than beyond. But one's public social sensitivity, curiosity, and dependence on neighbors remain constant whether in a *vecindad* or in a barrio. Perhaps in different settings the general urban ecology does not allow one to observe the same rhythm of life. But the pattern here described is recognized by all.

Interpersonal Relations: A Case

The close study of a neighborhood in Cuartel 1, seven blocks from the central plaza, permits us to penetrate into basic aspects of the social and psychological dynamics of neighborhood life. The following profile is the interpretation of an informant judged by his neighbors to be an average, socially sensitive person with an excellent knowledge of the social setting. The informant's mother and sister were also highly sensitive to social differences, well-informed, and able to analyze the past and present situations of their neighborhood. The informant spoke of his neighbors as follows:

> The *K*s are a family in a high economic class. The father is known in the *vecindad* by the nickname of "the skinny one" [*el flaco*]. Actually, they are not in a high social class, but they feel that they are, and therefore, they like to appear as members of that class, that is, to pretend [*aparentar*]. They isolate themselves in an attempt to demonstrate publicly that they are above others in the *vecindad*. They separate themselves socially from the rest and behave like well-to-do people. This, together with the fact that they are nowadays well-off with a modern home, causes them to be considered upper class in the *vecindad*, but not in the city. They have maids, but they have less

The Space for Social Relations

money than their next-door neighbor, the storekeeper of the barrio. The *K* family and that of the storekeeper are both members of an important club of the city and hold canasta parties in their homes with people of their social group. Some members of the *K* family are well-known in the city and occasionally can mix with high society.

Below these two families is a group of four families. We consider them high middle-class even though they certainly have more money than the previous two families. They have a modern car, good television sets, and everyone dresses very well, but they are not in the *alta sociedad* of the best city club. The men, instead, are members of the club of the *vecindad*, though they go infrequently. These people interact more with *vecinos* than the first two families [*se dan mas con los vecinos*]. If there is a clique, it is formed by these four families. Their sons and daughters are all trying to become professionals in colleges and universities.

Below the four families mentioned above are thirteen families which are middle class; but economically, life has been a continuous struggle for them. They are employees who try, through education on a part-time basis, to climb and maintain their appearance on a par with the previous four families. This has been difficult. Inflation has affected them, particularly since the support of each family depends on one person alone. The saying in Spanish is "*es un esfuerzo muy grande para mantenerse y subir.*" [It's a great effort to maintain a position and climb socially.]

There is a Jewish family which owns a store; but they have no friends and never show interest in their *vecinos* except for business. They would not consider visiting anyone, and no one would consider visiting them. They are in total isolation, even though they have a good business. The opposite is true of the Russian-German owner of a store on the other side of the *vecindad*. He and his family are *muy conocidos*; that is, everyone knows a great deal about them. They are more open. One seems to have more confidence in them, and they are, therefore, more popular in the *vecindad*.

The preferences and the social proximity illustrated in the description above show social maneuvering as a game. The relationship among *vecinos* falls into three active categories: friend, neutral, and enemy. For some *vecinos* it is most difficult to comprehend human nature and to predict human sentiments. This confusion gives no clear guide for lasting interpersonal relations; among unrelated individuals closeness and intimacy constantly fluctuate. "*Vecinos* are like volcanoes, always ready to erupt," reflected a Paranaense.

Vecindad in the Past: Continuity[1]

In the past, *vecinos* residing near the plaza recall, the social setting was exciting. "Life was very gay and interesting," remarked one informant. In the afternoon women of the neighborhood sat on their balconies observing the street and each other. They even conversed from balcony to balcony. The families of important ancestry (*abolengo*) acquired valuable property around the plaza. The others "were people of little social weight (*no pesaban*); they were people from the *loma* (hill above), and those of us from the center did not know them. People of humble origin lived in barrios around the cemetery."

Families of elite ancestry seldom left their homes yet they remained well informed about the general moods of the city and intimately informed about their equals. "People even knew what time their neighbors went to bed by the noises of the front door closing." There were stories of the private lives of other families. For instance, one of the ladies of the elite felt that she should never show hunger in front of her husband, and so she spent much of her time resting and being served food in her luxurious bedroom. Informants remember one household of several elderly spinsters who spent many hours of the day keeping careful watch over their neighbors' movements and much time on their balcony during the afternoon observing the passing scene. From the balcony, ladies of the house were able to show their latest acquisitions in clothing and jewelry.

Because parents restricted the movement of daughters, much of the courting (*afilando*) was done from balcony to balcony or from street to balcony. Daughters could go out only when accompanied by a servant, some other member of the household, or a school companion; it was improper for a couple of high social standing to be alone. Some of the young "companions" were characterized by their ability to arrange encounters with persons of another social level, avoid parents, and properly bypass some of the rigid rules of those days. They were known as *las tiradoras de la vecindad* (the matchmakers of the neighborhood).

[1] A brief look at the period before 1900 should help to place present patterns in proper perspective. It should also bring other structural aspects into focus. The material in this section is based upon statements made by older residents of the city.

The Space for Social Relations 95

Grandmothers watched everyone's movements. They were perpetually involved in defining the social rules of their class as these were observed by their ancestors. Granddaughters went for outings in the afternoon in the company of their grandmother in a semienclosed buggy drawn by a horse and driven by the family coachman. All effort was exerted to appear most proper and different from the majority of the population, in order to prevent lowering oneself (*rebajarse*).

During specified hours of the evening it was socially proper for marriageable daughters to stroll in the plaza if accompanied by friends. Boys would stroll around the plaza in the direction opposite the one taken by the girls. After plaza hours gentlemen and ladies of this class would gather in one of the households for conversation (*tertulias*). Families whose economic reputation had decreased (*venidas a menos*) withdrew with proper excuses and dignity from these social appearances.

Rivadavia Avenue, now a distinguished residential area, was a setting for promenades (*paseos*). On Sundays and holidays many people combined walks in the plaza with strolling down the attractive Rivadavia Avenue. Several individuals with *cultura*, wealth, social position, and important name (*apellido*) built elaborate mansions along this avenue, thus opening a new prestigious residential area away from the plaza. Provincial officials residing on this avenue set the social tone. Later, the *nouveaux riches* built more practical and less luxurious homes than those of the nineteenth century. This is an interesting example of a city area, surrounded by humble people, that in a few decades became a distinguished residential area. Adjacent to it was a *barriada* known as *las latas* (the tin cans), a place to avoid. The move to the new area required considerable courage, and the first residents must have been truly pioneers.

Near Echagüe Avenue, five blocks from the main plaza, a Swiss family lived at the boundary between the downtown area and the barrio area. A first-generation Swiss informant described the style of life as that of "a great family with many social differences." There was cooperation; in those days servants would come to borrow tools and other household necessities. While the humble European residents of the barrio interacted with each other daily, families of ancestry nearest to the plaza remained apart. Invitations were extended for exceptional family celebrations, but polite excuses were returned. Those nearest the plaza were descendants of Argentine families of distinction. Within the neighborhood, the spiritual links between families of ancestry and the first-generation immigrants were limited. The elite women did not establish intimate relationships with the immigrant women. "Privately, they referred to us as the 'European gringos.' "

Political views in those early days tended to follow ethnic lines. Neighborhoods of immigrants were noted for their strong liberalism and desire for change, while *vecinos* near the plaza had a reputation for conservative political views. "The fathers," remarked an informant, "tended toward some liberal philosophy, while the women, being passive, followed a conservative and tranquil style of life. The difference may stem from the fact that daughters attended Catholic schools run by nuns, while the sons were more likely to attend public schools."

Immigrants, particularly men, clustered in ethnic organizations. The average immigrant could not hope to be accepted in the city's main social club, whose members were exclusively elite and of traditional families. In Italian and Spanish associations, intelligent immigrants came together, and in their daily gatherings members had an opportunity to air their views opposing the oligarchy of the city. The ethnic associations and the Club Social fostered the division between the foreigners (gringos) and the Argentines. In the course of time, this trend started to reverse itself. "While several elite families lost fortunes that their children were professionally ill equipped to recover and thus perpetuate the elite tradition, some immigrant children acquired education and *cultura* and rapidly gained social distinction. A very high *clase media* emerged and started to develop its own social organizations." A few of the immigrants who had been educated in Europe were able to speak several languages, and they came to Argentina with the specific objective of acquiring large tracts of land. In this they did not succeed, but instead acquired city property and participated in educational programs. It would seem that particularly the educated immigrant woman presented a serious threat to the aristocratic Argentine woman whose formal education was limited and who had few interests of her own. By ignoring immigrants and exercising mannerisms of their class, the aristocracy maintained—even widened —the social distance between the two groups. The upper class, trying to assert that they were the "owners of the city" and, by definition, should have control of the city's destiny, made the immigrant *vecinos* feel like social intruders.

Reports of other situations in the city indicate more egalitarian sociability; greetings had to be extended to anyone passing, whether well known or not. There is much agreement concerning the basic principle for the social ordering of the neighborhood; it was a place in which to reside, but not necessarily a corporate entity where one found his closest friends. Daily domestic chores, purchases from the greengrocer, and visits to the *almacén* brought people in view of each other and promoted further acquaintance. In some city areas, however, neighbors of thirty years continued to live almost like strangers. Casual daily greetings and exchange of a few phrases were the extent of the association. There had always been, according to informants, a clear-cut differentiation between "carrying on the life of a *vecino* and carrying on the life of friendship."

In conclusion, the older residents of Paraná, by their attitude and social acts, forced the eager European immigrant to find families of similar background with whom to interact. For many years, the situation was difficult for the sensitive and uprooted European who had to cope with Argentine Paranaenses who felt superior as "owners of the city." By the time immigrants started arriving, a strong social network of the city elite already had been established by marriage, political action, and membership in the Club Social. To the immigrants, traditional families displayed a united front in the spirit of a "family" defending a way of life and a superior social status. In a newly formed democratic nation, people were not hesitant to speak of social and ethnic differences. The egalitarian principles were for and of the political sphere; the social differences based on lower and higher, inferior and superior, were an expected quality of daily life.

The Ethnic Classification of Vecinos: Ethnic Background

Contrary to what happened in other parts of the Americas, ethnic stereotypes in Paraná did not arise from immigrants clustering in particular city quarters, barrios, or neighborhoods. Although one may find a high concentration of Jews or Italians in some areas of the city, this seems to have been dependent on recent business opportunities and available properties. Ethnic stereotypes in a neighborhood nowadays are used to explain unusual behavior and customs; each stereotype is general and accepted regardless of class position. They are the stereotypes of "the street."[2]

An Italian is generally portrayed as having blond hair, white skin, and blue eyes. There are southern Italians with darker skin and black hair—a physical difference significant socially within the Italian group. The dark Italian can be, and has been, confused with the dark "native" criollo—though the Italian can claim lighter skin (*la piel más blanca*). All Italians are rated above criollos and are known for their skill as shoemakers, mechanics, and construction workers; they may own a business or be employees. Criollos stereotype the average peasant Italian as one who can be easily tricked and frightened by supernatural events or fear of the afterlife, and as one who is rough, rude, and insensitive to the suffering of others. Many of the city's social problems such as vandalism, banditry, thievery, and begging are attributed to the arrival of this ethnic group. Immigrant Italian barrio dwellers (*conventilleros*) tend to maintain a low standard of morality. It is thought that the men are lazy, living at the expense of their wives, who are believed to be more industrious than their husbands. It is also believed that they will not argue face-to-face, but would rather talk behind people's backs. In the stereotype, families are said to accumulate old things; they are stingy (*pijoteros*) and impose discomforts on themselves to save money. Educated or not, all receive the nickname of gringo. But if a blond or lighter-skinned Italian possesses *cultura* and has an understanding of the European refinements of life, that person is placed outside the model of the poor peasant immigrant.

Physically, Germans are stereotyped as tall, blond, with blue eyes and very white skin. True Germans have enjoyed a high intellectual reputation. They are characterized as highly moral, extremely hardworking, responsible people and excellent entrepreneurs. They are

[2] The following models are derived from observation, general conversation, and directed interview.

seen as austere and creative, leading a systematic life and maintaining their homes in perfect order with many comforts. Because of all these traits, the criollo feels that the true German is worthy of respect and should be considered an example. For the upper-class Paranaenses, *cultura* distinguishes the Germans from the others. A German, however, is noted for being proud (*orgulloso*) of his "race" and tends to feel superior and socially insulated.

The physical description of the true German also fits the German peasants born in Russia. The Russian-Germans are in a marginal position, neither German nor Russian; they are classed in a lower social category. Popularly known as Rusos, they are considered coarse peasants (*campesinos brutos*) with little intellect or imagination. The stereotype is based on the assumption that the Rusos are naive and believe everything they are told; they are easy to fool, superstitious, and cowardly. The Ruso cannot assert himself as he faces aggressive people. He is believed to be typically peasant—humble, fearful, and resigned to the fate of life. He is perhaps the least gifted individual in regard to intelligence and perspicacity (*viveza*). He is of the rural village, with a strong group orientation and a social personality characterized by closeness and intimacy. His Spanish is not only limited, but characterized by a strong foreign accent; Low German is his language. The Ruso, though not successful as a businessman, is a hard-working countryman. Educated Rusos with *cultura* prefer to pass for true Germans.

The Jewish group is distinctively stereotyped. Physically they may be dark or light-skinned, usually with a prominent nose. Jews are eager to invest in higher education for their children, and the difference in *cultura* between fathers and sons is striking. The stereotype of the small-business Jew portrays an individual whose eagerness to make a good profit interferes with his *vecindad* client relations. The stereotype holds that taking advantage of others in business is an innate Jewish characteristic, but this is done only to save and invest. Seldom are profits used for more than standard comforts, they usually present a front of economic hardship. They are so concerned with profit-making that they find little time to display merchandise with elegance. Because family members are involved in the business, there is little domestic life. Jews are less sentimental toward national or historical symbols. The younger university students, however, are becoming less involved with their religious tradition and are participating more in the national political sphere. To call a non-Jew a *judío* is to offend; to make a *judeada* is to cheat or betray someone. In terms of aspirations, informants tended to rate Paraná Jews above rural criollos, Rusos, Italians, and Turcos.

Anyone from the Near East belongs in the Turco group. Jews from non-European countries, Syrians, true Turks, Arabs, and Egyptians are all labeled Turcos. In the physical stereotype, the Turco male is of average height, dark-skinned, with bushy eyebrows, heavy beard, and a prominent nose. Because of their social personality, Turcos are placed below the criollos, yet rated above the Italians, because of their eagerness to work in small business enterprises. In general, Turcos are known for their habit of taking advantage of uninformed clients, and shoppers know that with a Turco they must bargain with determination. The Turcos and the Jews share many characteristics of the stereotypes, but the Turcos are considered less shrewd (*vivos*). Turco, like *judío*, can be used as a form of personal insult. A Turco's place of business is not neat, and frequently he is involved in buying and selling used merchandise. Any disarranged store is said to be like that of a Turco. They are considered to be given to gossip and superstition, and are suspicious and quickly roused to anger.

Spaniards known for rowdiness and the inclination to exaggerate receive the nickname of *gallegos*. Physically, Spaniards are small, with black hair and a modest appearance. They save their money at the expense of the enjoyment of life. They give the appearance of poverty and need. An uneducated Spaniard may be rich but look poor; he will exploit and dominate his children. He believes that hard work makes a man and that education produces a soft, weak personality. Because of the Spanish heritage in Argentina, early Spaniards rated highly, and the ones arriving now easily fit into the national life. Argentine culture (unrealistically, I believe) is considered an extension of Spain, and thus Spaniards enjoy a privilege denied to other foreigners. A Basque shares many of the generalized Spanish characteristics, but in the stereotype he is associated with dairying and is well known for his economic and social success.

The stereotypes appear strongest among third-generation Argentines of predominantly Spanish and Italian descent in the middle social category. The informants derive their information from observing the first-generation immigrants in Argentina. In each group undoubtedly there are those who do not fit the ethnic stereotype, and many Paranaenses dismiss all stereotypes and do not use them under normal conditions. Nevertheless, the ethnic stereotypes are frequently used in conversations among *vecinos*, particularly when interpersonal relations are not smooth.

Argentines are usually unable to distinguish Russian-Germans, German Jews, and poor Germans by appearance; they class them together in a single category. This grouping leads to an intensive use of behavioral stereotypes as a way to differentiate individuals. A *vecino* may look like a German and behave with much *cultura*. His general image may remind people of the German social stereotype, and in the neighborhood he may be nicknamed *alemancito*. If, however, he only looks like a German, but does not behave according to the stereotype, people may say that he is like a *rusito* and remark, "What a pity, since he could pass for a German." The ethnic stereotypes, when used, are meshed with social and behavioral traits and are not simply based on a person's descent.

In public, people are expected to ignore features of the stereotypes; cordiality and tolerance guide interpersonal relations. Everyone tends to think that he stands outside the stereotypes. A person of economic means who through the years has acquired *cultura* (refinement) is known first as a *persona bien* and secondarily as a German, Jew, Italian, Turco, or *gallego*. As he joins clubs of the city and participates in public life, he rapidly leaves behind the ethnic stereotype of his immigrant ancestors. Comments made by people of higher social status about a successful person may run something like this: "In spite of his upbringing, there you have him, a *persona bien* and *respetable*." Such cases give reason to question the accuracy of the ethnic stereotypes.

In the neighborhood, ethnic stereotypes may or may not be taken into account. Unusual behavior is attributed to them, but proper social manipulation tends to erase the ethnic mark. The interplay between stereotype and individual recognition is first tested in the *vecindad*.

Social Class Stereotypes

Vecinos are not only ethnically typed, but also socially classified. When informants spoke of their *vecinos* of humble origin, they were not classifying people merely on an economic basis; behavioral elements enter just as prominently into the stereotypes. According to the stereotype, men of the *clase baja* work as peons and unskilled laborers. They are vicious, frequenting bars known as *boliches*. The family does not appear as a unit in public. Men go out to be with male friends, and women rarely leave the house for recreation. Rough speech (*guasos*) is characteristic among these people. They visit and help people of the same class, but do not greet people of a higher class.

This stereotype also depicts the *clase baja* who form a large proportion of the population in barrios and *barriadas*. In the neighborhoods, families of noncriollo backgrounds who exhibit these characteristics are known as *gente acriollada*. In addition to the social traits, physical typing is an important factor in the minds of those who classify people as *clase baja*.

The generalized *clase media* is a most heterogeneous group. According to the stereotype, the first subcategory—the *clase media baja*—is made up of laborers. Sons usually follow the same trade as their fathers. They own plain, modestly furnished homes. Generally they are neat, and live in a family group. Men spend their leisure time in clubs of the barrio and *boliches*. The men's social groups are divided by age, thus fathers do not go out together with their sons. Women stay at home. People of the *clase media baja* relate easily only to their equals or those below them.

People in the higher subgroups of the *clase media* are likely to be small entrepreneurs. Sons seek an occupation different from their parents; many hope to become professionals and are willing to work in order to earn money for school. People in this group know how to plan and save money for important purchases such as a new house. Women dress very fashionably. Drinking is not associated with this type of individual. The men of the household may leave the house with other members of the family. Husband and wife appear together on the sidewalk. Men, however, like the central plaza, frequent the center-city coffee shops, and seek male companionship in clubs of the city. Personal friendship becomes important: one needs companions to be seen with in the plaza, bars, clubs, or shows. These people tend to look European and to exhibit good manners in public. Their language is adaptable, and although it may have an accent of the *clase baja*, the vocabulary is more refined. A moral life is considered proper, though more so for the women than for men. The middle *clase media* is well-informed in local affairs. They attempt to establish relationships with persons of better social and economic status (*de mejor alcance*); they are social climbers.

The upper classes, in reality, are not so homogeneous as locally portrayed. They are professionals and employees of distinction in banks, the government, or large companies. Children follow the profession of the father, but prefer to work with a high degree of independence. Their houses are comfortable and modern; television, travel abroad, and servants are considered essential. The family may own a *casa quinta* (a house in the country for weekends). They may be seen in public as a family, though usually this is limited to the husband and wife when they go to the center of town or to organized dances or theatrical and musical performances. Men do not attend the clubs of the neighborhood. Children attend places of entertainment different from those of their parents. The upper classes have the deferential regard of the lower and middle groups; they always show good manners and interact smoothly with others. They may be several generations removed from European immigrant ancestors.

Because progress and modernization are important values, it follows that those socially lower undertake to incorporate step by step whatever seems feasible from those above. The process of acquiring social sophistication goes beyond the efforts of one single individual or one single generation. To work out one's personal relationships in an active neighborhood constitutes a sensitive social game, perhaps simple to imagine, but difficult to describe without losing the "spirit" of it. On the basis of the combined ethnic and social stereotypes, strong personality types emerge; a *vecino* becomes enmeshed within the network, and escaping from it becomes a major personal concern. Through the years, only ingenious, calculating, and highly motivated individuals succeed.

Experiences in a Vecindad: A Case

Classification of people in terms of life style or ethnic background begins and finds its best expression in the neighborhoods and barrios. (For the people of the city who are active in the city clubs and the plaza area, the ethnic stereotype yields to the social.) The case of one family living in a neighborhood not far from the central plaza illustrates the dynamics of the situation.[3]

The head of this Jewish household said that as a child he had lived in a neighborhood noted for the predominance of *familias tradicionales*. The block was a "museum of residences and people." Although the Jewish family was industrious, with a second generation of university educated individuals, social contact in the neighborhood was difficult. The informant gave three reasons: their ethnic background, their relatively recent acquisition of wealth, and their lack of connections with any city family of ancestry.

The social exclusiveness was evident among children; the constant presence of their *niñeras* (servants exclusively in charge of children) strengthened the distance. As a youngster, the informant was impressed by the homes of the traditional families, some of whose forebears were important political leaders in the province. He had always been curious to know how things were inside those houses and just how such people lived. As the opportunity to visit inside a home never materialized, his interest intensified. Children were well dressed each time they appeared at the door, whereas members of the Jewish family dressed up only to go out on the sidewalk or to a secondary plaza toward which their social activities were oriented. He recalled an incident when he asked a child of his own age to visit the latter's home, and the child answered, "No, you're a Jew." The refusal was sharp

---

[3] The case is not presented as a typical model in all *vecindades*—major variations occur—but it does provide useful insights.

and dual in nature. It was social by right of birth (the Jew was not of the aristocratic level), and it was ethnic.

The Jewish family later moved to a middle-class section of the city. The informant recalled that in a relatively short period of time he was playing with neighboring children on the sidewalks and, strangely enough, he had gained access to the interior of two neighbors' households. He was at first classified as Turco. Perhaps because of the mixture of backgrounds in this neighborhood, even though ethnic nicknames—*alemán*, Turco, or *turquito*—were used, the general mood stood in sharp contrast to the former place of residence. *Vecinos* realized soon that in the new family there was economic power; the Jewish family's children were receiving a good education. They became known as *la familia judía bien*. In the beginning, there was a good deal of curiosity as to how the father made a living and where certain household items had been acquired. There were many opportunities for adults to speak to each other in the streets and for children to deliver messages over household walls. Adults, however, never invited each other into their homes.

Feelings in the neighborhood to which this Jewish family moved changed radically during the Perón regime. Suddenly the ethnic stereotypes were applied forcefully, affecting *vecinos*' attitudes toward each other. Now the neighborhood had a *jefe de manzana* (chief of the block), a member of Perón's *vecindad* organization. The person selected had "inferior *cultura*" and had always been characterized as an "unhappy" *vecino*. An Italian baker with fascist ideology, he supplied bread to the neighborhood; but soon it became evident that he was also searching for information through his customers' children. *Vecinos* suspected that he passed neighborhood information to the authorities. Parents now hesitated to send their children for bread and instructed them not to answer any questions. There was fear, and the children learned it quickly.

Stories about Juan and Eva Perón circulated, and in the neighborhood an atmosphere of fear and mutual distrust arose and prevailed for several years. One day, for instance, a *vecino* builder told one of his workers that Eva had died (she was actually sick at the time). This was reported to the police, who questioned the builder for hours. For the Jewish family, social discrimination by class and ethnicity experienced in one neighborhood was followed by a political situation that precipitated a general state of confusion and personal distrust. As a result of the two experiences, they decided to withdraw from public view; trust was, even more, a rare quality in neighborhood relationships. "Now we are in a *vecindad*; we have *vecinos*; but socially we are not in the *vecindad*. This is our choice."

Vecindad implies social unity, but interpersonal relations are not harmonious, and it is far from being a corporate social group. *Vecindad*, remarked an informant, is a "crowd socially linked by curiosity and envy." Refined etiquette, tolerance, and acknowledgment of each other in daily encounters conceal the tension and the absence of loyalties. Historical events in the last three decades in Argentina and Paraná have affected subtle levels of people's ideas and ideals. If social distance had been the expedient social formula, after Perón it became a more definite established way of neighborhood life. Because of the psychological tensions of the past, however, people have begun to question whether this is the right way to exist, and some fundamental changes may follow.[4]

Behavioral Clichés

Behavioral clichés provide another level for classifying people and can outrank the ethnic and social class stereotypes in importance. *Vecinos* first place a newcomer into an ethnic or class mold, then observe his conduct in public in order to form an opinion about his character. The clichés are presumably part of a system of abstract ideas about man. Through them a *vecino* may be singled out and removed from the group stereotypes. The ideas formed about a *vecino* and his family conform to one of several models. A person and his family can be classed as *gente mala*, bad people; *gente bochinchera*, noisy people (socially loud); *gente peleadora*, quarrelsome people who cannot get along socially; *gente humilde*, plain people (also *gente modesta*); *gente abandonada*, careless people; *gente cargosa*, annoying, abusive people; *gente guaranga*, socially ordinary people prone to abusive speech; and *gente aislada*, distant people.

[4] See the definition of culture, p. xviii.

These characteristics typically belong to people from *barriadas*; neighborhoods in transition also find families exhibiting some or most of the above traits. Then the phrase "such people belong in a barrio, with the people without *cultura*," is used.

On the other hand, there are the opposite categories (note the use of *muy*, "very") expected from educated and city-oriented individuals: *gente muy democrática*, unprejudiced people; *gente muy dada*, people socially open; *gente muy correcta*, proper people; *gente muy campechana*, people with the friendliness of country people; *gente muy orgullosa*, haughty people; *gente muy distinguida*, distinguished people; *gente muy conocidas*, well-known people; *gente de mucho copete*, lofty people; and *gente muy bien*, wealthy or very socially proper people.

In *vecindades* some persons, by the nature of their birth, may be classified (note the implications beyond the literal translation of the Spanish phrase) as *gente media*, people of limited economic means; *gente baja*, people with no refinement and low morals; *gente criolla*, usually, lazy people of the country; *gente venida a menos*, people whose social standing has decreased; *gente extranjera*, recently arrived Europeans who are neat and progressive; *gente de pueblo*, unsophisticated small-town people; and *gente negra*, the poor, who are socially undesirable.

Vecinos use these clichés in conversations. Once a family has been placed in a category, and their position has been accepted by the public, only an event beyond expectation can effect a change. To remove a stereotype, moreover, is most difficult within one's own place of residence. The neighborhood gives one an identity. The remark "*quien diría de una persona tan correcta*" (who could expect something like this from a person so proper!) is typical. When changes do become evident, the characterization must be adjusted. In most cases changes occur at the economic level, while personality characteristics remain constant. A family may become wealthy and pass from poor to well-off, but remain *ordinariote*. A wealthy family, well-known, *correcta*, and with *cultura*, may become *venidas a menos* in the event of financial loss or shame caused by misbehavior. *Cultura*, however, remains constant, even though the family is facing embarrassment. Public withdrawal is then in order; they become *gente aislada* (distant). In this way the family hides the economic decline and protects its social heritage.

In every neighborhood some *vecinos* form an informal power structure. They promote interest in the lives of others, involve themselves in applying labels and spreading views. The oldest residents feel and act like *patrones* of the neighborhood, and after observing and evaluating the behavior of others, discreetly spread their views in casual conversations at stores or clubs. Such people, who are in touch with the doings of the *vecinos*, control the "social thermometer" of the neighborhood. There, members of a family must cope with the public image the *vecinos* have formed. A progressive young person may dislike the stereotype and find it inaccurate, but he still recognizes its existence. Discomfort derives from the assumption that *de tal palo tal astilla* (a splinter from the same trunk), which explains the behavior and personality of related persons.

Each person represents all other members of his family. The genetic assumption perpetuates a family's stereotype. Everyone is aware that all *vecinos* are weaving the texture of each other's social fabric. The father's profession or ethnic background serves as a point from which to start speculating. Later on, as a biography is constructed, the personality level is reached. To choose the right friends and associates, to avoid those who do not fit the social ideal of the family, to maintain a distance from those who possess certain traits but not others, and to be socially neutral are subtle or explicit family demands. The real difficulty arises because seldom does the individual from the middle group come from a situation where social traits adhere completely to the model. Allowances must be made when one speculates about new associates and how they might enhance or deter social avenues.

Social consciousness is not an all-consuming pastime. The concern emerges during exceptional social occasions, such as weddings, birthdays, public activities, informal social gatherings, or in the school. Feelings of social distinction then become apparent through conversations and conspicuous consumption. People's social concern may be manifested either by avoidance or by the search for new relations. It is common for neighbors to speak to each other on the sidewalk, yet there may exist a tacit understanding that, because of their social station, they should avoid each other elsewhere in public, or assume a formal stance like *desconocidos* (strangers). Each social situation is well calculated and determines the emotions transmitted in social interplay: either a definite *acercamiento* (nearness) or a social *distanciamiento* (distance). The attitude *vecinos* assume corresponds to a combination of the ethnic social model together with an evaluation of the person as an individual; the further the distance, the more formal will be the attitude adopted by the one in the higher position, who feels that he commands more social "power."

By general belief, *vecindad* implies a life of social togetherness. In the donor culture (in Spain, and particularly under the Moors), *vecindad* was a corporate unit. In Paraná, *vecindad* is a collective term for areas away from the very center of the city. It has become a personalized entity in that each *vecino* perceives the boundaries differently. Where distance from one's house to another prevents continuous exposure, that point becomes the limit of one's *vecindad*. Residents in the "intensive exposure zone" are the true *vecinos* and form the *vecindad*; those to whom one is exposed less are the *medios vecinos*, and beyond there are simply people "in that part of the city."

To true *vecinos*, one owes special deference, regardless of whether relationships are good or bad. Variations in greetings communicate feelings and one's judgment of the other. To the *medios vecinos* one can show partial or total aloofness. A short, barely intelligible greeting, or only a nod, may suffice to acknowledge familiarity and show respect. To the *desconocidos* or strangers goes silence. It is from among the strangers, however, that one will select a spouse. Seldom do children of true *vecinos* intermarry. The principle was stated well by an old resident, who said, "It is a habit created among *vecinos* not to entangle oneself with other *vecinos* (*no meterse con nadie*), but there is the basic need to be in tune (*estar enterado*) with the *vecinos* and potentially in contact with each other; yet one must keep one's distance." This statement bespeaks the intricate relationship between the individual and the *vecindad*.

The forces of the immediate social surroundings influence the formation of the cognitive system. With the ethnic, class, and personality stereotypes in the background, Paranaenses have chosen to remain reserved and distant in the *vecindad*. They become more and more preoccupied with their personal image in the city. For the people who are "of the city," the *vecindad* remains imbued with stereotypes and behavioral clichés. As might be expected from the mixture of these elements, Paranaenses emerge with an acute social sensitivity and consciousness.

4. THE *VECINDAD* STYLE OF LIFE: AN URBAN PARADOX

The concept of *vecindad* is not unique to Argentina. In Paraná, however, although *vecindad* is not a corporate unit, it still has sufficient meaning to be acknowledged by all. Very early in life, a child becomes "of his *vecindad*," and his social formation develops within the framework of his experiences with *vecinos*. *Vecindad* is the stage for daily encounters.

Within the *vecindad*, several points of reference act as nodes essential to the understanding of the style of *vecindad* life. One such nodal point is the corner grocery store (*almacén*). Daily shopping for household necessities brings *vecinos* into public view of each other, and the *almacén* functions as a clearing house for *vecindad* and city information. Every two or three blocks there is a cluster of stores that draw *vecinos* from the area.

The *clubes de vecindad*, organizations sponsoring athletic and social activities, provide another focal point. In the daily and weekly activities *vecinos* (primarily men) interact; annual events, in conjunction with a general festivity, often attract participants from other *vecindades*. The New Year's Eve street-corner celebration—and to some extent Carnaval—are other *vecindad* events that may bring visitors from the outside. (The number and standing of the visitors depend on the *vecindad*'s reputation in the city.)

The home (*el hogar*) and the family (*la familia*) do not enter as units into the social action of the *vecindad*. The home constitutes a personal and guarded sanctuary. The mother, the figure of *santidad*, and the father, the provider and administrator, together guide the home's intimacy and sentimentality. The church and the school, although in the *vecindad* or barrio, also can provide non-*vecindad* fields of action. Encounters in school and in church can be very distant and impersonal; people can behave as strangers (*desconocidos*). Schools and churches belong to the city, rather than to the *vecindad*, and are not integral to the *vecindad* social fabric.

The Almacén and the Social Network

The Argentine knows that the *almacén* (some of the stores with a stock of more selective food products are called *despensas*) in his *vecindad* is needed by the *vecinos* for the smooth running of their households. Servants, children, and housewives make one or several trips to the *almacén* every day. *Almacenes* generally open at eight o'clock in the morning, close during the siesta hours after noon, and reopen in mid-afternoon for another four hours of business.

Most frequently an *almacén* is one room of the owner's residence and is usually located on a street corner. An average store serves approximately four blocks, providing goods for residents living in all four directions. A large *almacén*, equipped with telephone and delivery boy, may have clients from other areas of the city, but the greater part of its trade is still from the *vecinos*.

In the center of the *almacén* there is a long counter where customers stand waiting to be served by the *almacenero* or a member of his family, usually his wife. Products generally are behind the counter within the storekeeper's reach only. Some *almacenes* far from the center city have an area of the store furnished with tables and chairs set aside for wine drinking and card playing. In the lowest-class section of Paraná (the barrios) where there are no clubs, the *almacenes* become *boliches*, the informal meeting places for men.

The social and economic level of the *vecindad* determines the quality and selection of products. In socially mixed neighborhoods, the *alma-*

cenero stocks his shelves with items of the quality demanded by the majority of his clients. His attempts to cut across this plural social setting result in a good deal of leveling of the merchandise.

Self-service is not practiced; it is in fact discouraged. The client requests the amount and quality of the item desired. Customers become well informed of each other's buying habits; patterns of domestic life and the economic trend of a household become publicly known. Clients with an open account have a small book, known as a *libreta*, in which the *almacenero* notes the date of purchase, the description of the item, and the cost. The *almacenero* has to make an identical note in his daily charge book for his own control. The transaction with each customer tends to be long, and when many items are purchased, the storekeeper may be occupied for half an hour with one customer alone, while others wait standing along the counter, listening to the conversation between *almacenero* and customer. There is always some time to mix brief social conversation while orders are prepared, even though waiting customers may become impatient, particularly when the conversation is of little general interest. At such a time, a child or an anxious adult is entitled to interrupt with, "*Despácheme, que estoy apurado*" (Would you take care of me; I'm in a hurry).

The *almacenes* of a barrio or neighborhood are small businesses with a relatively small margin of profit. Their economic situation has been further complicated by the instability of the national economy. One *almacenero* estimated his profit at about 20 percent, adding that if there were fewer *almacenes*, the merchants could move a larger volume of goods at a lower price. But since each *almacenero*'s volume of business is small, all must sell at a higher price. Under highly inflationary conditions, an adept *almacenero* may purchase large quantities of some product. If the product becomes scarcer and retail prices rise, the *almacenero* profits. But the *vecinos* keep close watch; consequently an *almacenero* seldom exhibits his business success. Clients are always ready to speculate when an *almacenero* suddenly buys a new car, new furniture, new clothing, or more property. *Vecinos* feel that they are helping *almaceneros* to become rich. Speculation on his entrepreneurial activities and profit-making can place the storekeeper in an awkward position in the neighborhood. Is he a good *vecino*, or is he only an *almacenero*? If he stays within a just profit, then he is a good *almacenero* and, therefore, a good man.

In the past, the credit system with its *libreta* (credit book) was a means to attract *vecinos* as clients. With this credit system, *vecinos* were allowed to pay for their purchases at the end of each month. In the years 1964–1965 the *almacenero* faced the continuous devaluation of the peso, and it became hard for him to extend credit. Some were forced into bankruptcy after overextending their credit. The situation became so tight that *almaceneros* now avoid offering credit. This, however, has led the *vecino* to view the *almacenero* as a hard person, interested only in himself, over-apologetic about not offering credit, and not serving the neighborhood as an *"almacén de barrio* should." *Vecinos* feel that an *almacenero* should understand that *vecinos* may get behind in their financial obligations, that they intend to pay, and that he has an obligation to wait. While this was possible at other times, presently it is not good business. Entrepreneur and customer carry on a quiet struggle.

Inflation has strained the relationship between the storekeeper and his clients, who are accustomed to a personal credit system. When a payment is overdue, adults appear less frequently at the *almacén*, sending their children so as to avoid an encounter with the *almacenero*. In time, the storekeeper may send a polite message to the family through the child. A typical reply may explain that the husband's salary has been delayed. Tension increases and the customer must be careful not to display any sign of new luxury; he is watched by the *almacenero*. In such cases proper etiquette requires that the *almacenero* appear patient, conceal his own feeling, and not embarrass his client, who is also his *vecino*. An offended client may intentionally delay payment, and for the *almacenero* this may result in a significant loss.

It is not unusual for an *almacenero* to lend cash. A client and *vecino* may unexpectedly send a child with a note requesting cash in order to pay a gas or electric bill. The note explains that the husband did not collect his salary, or that he is not at home and did not leave any cash. In such cases, the *almacenero* must act with much tact in order not to hurt feelings or to acquire the reputation of being uncooperative and

The *Vecindad* Style of Life

interested only in exploiting *vecinos* for his own personal benefit. "*Vecinos*-clients expect a great deal from an *almacenero*, but we truly cannot afford to meet their demands. Those who have tried have faced bankruptcy. Credit in inflationary times is convenient for the *vecinos*, but it is detrimental to the operation of the *almacén*," remarked an informant *almacenero*.

The role and position of the *almacenero* in the neighborhood were affected by the Perón regime. The key position of the *almacenes* in the neighborhoods' social network was convenient to the regime. Some *almaceneros* had an intimate personal knowledge of their clients, useful to Peronista leaders. Peronista clients, on the other hand, used the political situation against the storekeeper if he perhaps pressed a debt.

Under normal conditions, storekeepers find time in the afternoon for conversation with *vecinos*. When dealing with clients, "one must be the same to everyone, regardless of the social or ethnic stereotype," confessed one storekeeper. Because of the sensitivity in the neighborhood, *almaceneros* joke loudly with children and youngsters in front of adult customers to keep conversation at a trivial level. Joking is in the form of *cachadas* (verbal tricks). A child may be told that he is something he is not, or it is suggested that he has done something shameful. In the presence of other *vecinos*, the child feels defenseless and embarrassed. An *almacenero* may be taken seriously, since he is believed to be a well-informed person. A *cachada*, therefore, may interest *vecinos*, since it may be half-true, but it frustrates the child. A well-mannered (*bien educado*) child must remain silent or only smile at the adult's remarks. Answering back to an adult is poor manners. If a child were to reply, the storekeeper would at some point let the child's parents or other adults know that the child had been disrespectful to adults in his store. Parents usually dismiss any such incident as insignificant, but if the dignity of the family has been violated, there is retaliation. One might delay paying a debt or withdraw patronage from the *almacén*. This does not enhance the reputation of the storekeeper; his social position may be awkward if many of his customers take similar action.

Currently, there is a great deal of tolerance, but because of past experience and future uncertainty, mutual caution underlies interaction between storekeeper and customer. Some clients attempt to ingratiate themselves with the storekeepers, expecting to receive better service, better prices, and special trust. "The assumption is," said one informant, "that one never knows when one's family may suddenly need help and the *almacenero*'s friendship." A wise storekeeper stated:

> On account of our business in the *vecindad*, we hear and we learn a great deal about families in our *vecindad*, but it comes in one ear and goes out the other. In this way we can keep ourselves neutral. But you cannot easily imagine how careful we must be; we are constantly watching ourselves and training our children not to supply information about anyone: customers, *vecinos*, or ourselves. This is difficult inasmuch as everyone knows that the *almacenero* is a bank of knowledge and could gossip. On the other hand, our reservation may be resented by friendly clients who interpret this as an indication that we do not have trust in them.

Interpersonal relations are delicate for both customers and storekeepers. One *almacenero* said: "The best thing for me and my family is to listen, avoid serious conversations, tend to agree with everyone, and remain at home when the store is closed. At times it is a lonely existence. Our true friends are in another part of the city. It is safer this way."

The storekeeper and his family develop a social personality that enables them to face complex neighborhood interpersonal relationships with neutrality. Economic success is closely linked to success in handling daily neighborhood interaction. Storekeepers who assess well their clients' moods and problems succeed in business; those unable to understand just what it takes to be a storekeeper in the neighborhood soon meet with failure, particularly if a close competitor is handling the encounter situations ably. Neutrality is the complement of success, but one must also be sympathetic, friendly, and trustworthy. When husband and wife work together in the *almacén*, there is compensation; one of them can maintain a harder line than the other.

Having a reputation for being honest is most difficult; the answer lies in not making a mistake that might be judged as cheating. A neighborhood storekeeper remarked: "Our beginning in this *vecindad* was very difficult. We have always given the proper change and made

The *Vecindad* Style of Life

sure that the paper money was not too old. The transactions with children sent on errands by parents are particularly difficult. Parents are most ready to accuse us for their wrongdoings, for instance, their overspending without consent. They say, 'He takes advantage of the children, so we must always be on guard.' " In part the *almacenero*'s role in the neighborhood is shared by the butcher and the vegetable man. With them, however, *vecinos* can talk about the quality of the products, which tends to vary from day to day.

Street vegetable vendors (*verduleros*) may serve several neighborhoods; housewives like to think of them as neutral figures, a position very difficult to maintain. Vendors sense the social differences from one neighborhood to another and from one *vecino* to another. Some pride themselves on serving only the *gente bien*. Business is simpler when one deals with only one type of clientele; each vendor adjusts his social orientation accordingly. He maintains a business relationship during daily calls to individual households and does not divulge personal information. Nevertheless, much is learned from vendors about city and national events as they quote and misquote comments and evaluations of news made by their clients.

Information reaches *vecinos* through various routes. The storekeeper is as localized in the neighborhood as the *vecinos*; vendors are involved with a more diverse clientele, and their topics of conversation are broader. At mealtime the family discusses the various—occasionally contradictory—reports and a coherent version of any event is put together.

Clubes de Vecindad

There are approximately thirty clubs within the city limits of Paraná. Most clubs had a modest beginning and remain small, serving people of the immediate vicinity. Some, however, expanded and achieved a city-wide reputation. These became known as "clubs of the city" in contrast to clubs of the barrios or of the *vecindades*. The antiquity, the social sophistication, and the economic power vary from club to club and are criteria used for classification.

Each club may distinguish itself by organizing one or several athletic activities—bicycling, *bochas* (Italian *bocce*, a type of bowling), soccer, basketball, swimming, or tennis. Clubs with paved courts may sponsor activities with more social prestige like roller skating, hockey games, and dances. Clubs with soccer fields may also have a merry-go-round or other amusement-park facilities; or their field may be used by a nearby school for gymnastics. Because of the national interest in soccer, a club with a soccer field attracts a wider membership and brings esteem to the *vecindad*, particularly when the local team leads the city or provincial league.

Daily club activities are exclusively for men. Clubs are open all day long, but the largest number of members come in the evening. Some clubs have indoor *bochas* courts, and many have a canteen serving wine, beer, and soft drinks. There are card tables, casino, and billiards. Some card games were brought from Europe, others are indigenous to Argentina (*truco, escoba, chinchón, loba, monte,* and *siete y medio*).

Card tables are placed in the halls, and the men separate into groups. Age seems to determine the division; men of middle age share one table, leaving other tables for older, retired men or younger ones. Around each table some men stand watching and waiting for their turn to play a game. Skill in the game, friendship, or long acquaintance attracts partners. Although club members do not necessarily play for money, an atmosphere of casino competition underlies all activities. Most commonly they play for the wine that they drink during the game. A player, skillful in his game and *simpatico*, is chosen for interclub contests.

Players carefully watch each other to make sure that all play fairly. Those known for their tendency to cheat acquire the reputation of *tramposos*, and are especially watched or avoided. When a conflict is discovered, an ethnic stereotype may be used to explain the player's behavior. Then the usual atmosphere of gentlemanliness and mutual acceptance becomes strained. If the traits of the ethnic and social stereotypes describe the person well, the reputation of being *tramposo* gets firmly established. Repeated cheating may lead to personal and neighborhood splits. The club president and the council may request the members at fault to withdraw because of their inability to get along with other members.

Conversations in clubs center around political issues, labor problems, and the city. In this setting there is always a person who can turn a serious conversation into something light, bringing forth laughter and *cachadas* (teasing). "This is, after all, an institution for relaxation from daily burdens," remarked an informant. The club is filled with boisterous voices, *cachadas*, and loud laughter accompanied by friendly pushes and embraces; club language is noted for its *grosería* (coarseness). Gatherings in the club generally last until midnight. Some members come only on specific nights; others attend daily to meet with acquaintances.

Club anniversaries are celebrated with social dances, which are frequently open to the public for the benefit of the club. The press gives a short review of the club's history in which the importance of the club's association with the neighborhood is emphasized. For example, the thirtieth anniversary of Club Urquiza was reported as follows: "The club was born in the populous barrio of La Campanilla. It was founded on June 3, 1935, by a group of enthusiastic soccer sympathizers who were taking hours from their daily activities to cement the prestige of this organization, modest but meritorious from all points of view."[1]

Another club, Peñarol, was founded November 18, 1926, in the barrio Los Pinos with the objective of organizing a *vecindad* soccer team to compete with other clubs. The members of this club present themselves as La Familia Peñarolense. On the thirty-eighth anniversary of the club, the press described some of its achievements through the years and praised the cooperation of the active members with the residents of the barrio.[2] A third club, the Libanés Sport Club, celebrated its thirty-fifth anniversary with a dinner and speeches.[3]

Keeping a good public image is crucial not only for the sake of the club, but also for the sake of the *vecino*, the *vecindad*, and the city. Neighborhood clubs, when possible, install as president some professional of an upper social category. Each neighborhood, owing to its diversified social demography, is likely to be able to find someone with a city reputation to serve in an executive position.

[1] *El Diario*, June 1965.
[2] Ibid., November 1964.
[3] Ibid., February 1965.

Newspapers often publish articles in which one club airs its resentment toward another or accuses someone of mistreatment. Later, the other party has a chance to redeem its image through the press. One club presented a note to the Paraná Soccer League accusing a referee of unfairness. The players had shown their resentment, and the referee had threatened to end the game. Moreover, the referee had behaved disrespectfully toward the captain of the team. Each point of complaint was listed and evaluated in the local press. Whenever clubs are accused of dishonesty, they defend their position and deny the charges, claiming that the organization can prove the honor of its members and leaders. The public statement usually reads that they never have and never will lend themselves to dishonor in their sport. To defend the honor of the club is to defend the honor of the *vecindad*.

Neighborhood clubs have limited financial resources and therefore are unable to modernize their facilities. Membership dues are low, and inflation has intensified the problem. In a few cases, clubs acquire additional funds by sponsoring public dances that families of a lower social standing frequently attend. In one instance, a club held weekend dances with a well-liked orchestra. For some time, mothers were happy to accompany their daughters to the dances. But as the fame of these neighborhood dances spread, the number of men of "questionable social and ethnic reputation from lower barrios" increased. One informant remarked that "the inferior status of the outsiders brought about a radical change in the general atmosphere of the club. Behavior became *grosero* (coarse), and the moral reputation of the club fell rapidly. Consequently, good people stopped attending the dances and sought other places for weekend recreation. The club's past reputation is only history now." Poor administration, together with a decline in the social tone, it was felt, brought general disrepute and rapid decay to the club. On weekends, the club now serves a clientele that the neighborhood itself rejects.

Once the bad reputation of a club has been established, the public image is difficult to change. In one such instance, a club changed its board of directors in an attempt to bring back an atmosphere suitable for families. Their efforts did not succeed. Although the neighborhood's physical appearance improved and its economic and social

The *Vecindad* Style of Life   121

standing changed, the club continued to be patronized by people of a less-reputable neighborhood. Financial considerations forced the club to continue sponsoring public dances for a group of people whose standards and aspirations did not measure up to those of the *vecinos*. The situation caused friction on various levels: within families, between families, and from one neighborhood to another. Discriminatory social tactics were used when people met in the streets of the neighborhood. Outsiders, particularly women, heard derogatory comments and subtle disapproving gestures censoring their intrusion into neighborhood "territory." The neighborhood was at "war" with the club and its clientele. The club could not afford the standards of the aspiring middle-class *vecinos*; the public dances were necessary for the club's survival.

Over a span of two decades a neighborhood may change and progress to a higher social level while the neighborhood club lingers as a vestigial reminder of a different past. In such situations, *vecinos* support the club less and less, as they seek membership in city clubs. When a neighborhood club does not reflect the social aspirations of the *vecinos* and when the imbalance is publicly noted, everyone feels social discomfort.

From the women's point of view, the men's neighborhood club is a *centro de perdición*. Mothers with social and educational aspirations for their sons attempt to hinder their active participation in the club. As a result, there arises a significant difference of opinion between middle-class husbands and wives with regard to the husbands' and sons' membership in the men's clubs. Among the middle class of semiskilled workers, the father is commonly more realistic than the mother in the assessment of the family's potential status. In general, a man in this category is satisfied with presenting himself in public realistically, while the wife, constituting a force behind the children, aspires to better social conditions through further education, better clothing, and avoidance of clubs that may deter social mobility. Two opposing sets of goals, one supported by the father, the other by the mother, thrive within the family, causing embarrassment and a split in the social activities of a family. The mother may afford some upward social mobility and may accompany or vicariously encourage her children in this trend; the father, because of ethnic background or his personal desire to continue his activities in the neighborhood club, stifles social ambitions.

In contrast, semiprofessional and professional husbands and wives feel that a local club should not receive their support. For them, it is socially appropriate to be members of a city club known for its distinguished history and social sophistication. Mothers feel that such clubs are less likely to "ruin" the character and morals of young persons. In addition, the city clubs accept women; their presence, people believe, neutralizes the social setting and encourages proper behavior.

Middle-aged and older men in skilled or semiskilled occupations constitute the majority of the active members of a modest *vecindad* club. The youth of a progressive neighborhood or of a progressive family prefer to spend time in the central plaza, in the center-city coffee shops, or at the movies, and when economically and socially possible, as active members of a city club.

In summary, clubs reflect the social standing of their members, not of the neighborhood. The club may be either sponsored or avoided by *vecinos*; their participation depends on the social standing of the club and their aspirations. It is difficult for members to handle the economic burden necessary to move the club from the category of a "modest club of the *vecindad*" to a "club of the city." Even though a neighborhood or barrio club may boast of its athletic accomplishments and its dances, the public behavior and appearance of its participants indicate its social standing. In a socially mixed neighborhood, families with ethnic and social distinction would attend an activity of a neighborhood club only if it equaled or excelled their own standing. Lower-class clubs may become places for the adventures of young men of upper social categories; with friends, they sometimes attend a neighborhood club dance and enjoy an evening of diversion. Such adventure is concealed from one's family; it is hardly the type of event to share with mothers, aunts, or sisters. The discovery of this clandestine activity may bring personal discomfort and social embarrassment for the family. Grandmothers view it as an indication of failure to inculcate the proper social values of their privileged ancestry in younger generations.

The *Vecindad* Style of Life 123

Essentially, clubs are meshed with the social standing and dynamics of the neighborhood. Strong sensitivity of club members about the social category of their club is evident. *Vecinos* may feel that through the club they can stabilize their social standing. By the same token, the stratification of clubs may assist a *vecino* in rising socially. When an aspiring member finds that the club hinders his social development, he withdraws and, without sentimentality, severs his personal relations with the club members. He remains physically in the neighborhood or barrio, but socially belongs elsewhere in the city.

Vecindad and Carnaval

As mentioned in an earlier chapter, Carnaval is a popular fiesta for the *gente del pueblo*, the masses. "For them Carnaval is a release from the monotony of their social class," stated an educated Paranaense. It is then that humble people may come to the city proper for the official *corso* (evening parade). "During *corso*, the poor people have a right to the city," remarked one informant. "It is a *fiesta del pueblo*, a fiesta of the people."

Members of active barrio and neighborhood clubs prepare floats; dances are planned for the nights of Carnaval celebration. Each individual masquerader and each float (twenty-three in 1965) are registered in the name of the barrio, the neighborhood club, or the city organization. Cash prizes offered by businesses and by the city encourage competition. Newspapers advertise registration in advance and attempt to spark enthusiasm. The queen of Carnaval is chosen from the princesses selected beforehand by neighborhood and city clubs. She receives a cash prize along with clothing and jewelry. The queen then parades with the official floats and is "crowned" at a dance in one of the clubs. It is interesting to note that in 1965 the crowning ceremony was held in a club in transition from neighborhood to city status, a club typical of the middle class.

A city committee plans the celebration and arranges a series of eight *tabladas* (pre-Carnaval appearances) several days before Carnaval. The largest neighborhood clubs open their doors to barrio people. On an improvised stage, *comparsas* (persons masked and costumed) and other groups perform. A middle-class informant pointed to the style of clothing, dancing, hair-do, and make-up as indices of performers' and audience's lower social level. The elegant manners observed by the audience enhance the modest setting of the club. "Behavior lacks spontaneity and is highly stylized," remarked the same informant. He felt that their sophistication is fashioned after people from the upper class. The refined manners appear somewhat awkward since there is little *cultura* to support such public social behavior. "It is analogous to acting on the stage," the informant suggested. The manners of the upper social group may be "appropriate for their class, but they seem awkward for those below, who copy patterns and use them outside their social context."

On the three days of Carnaval, the parades stretch along Echagüe Avenue and include single marchers, small groups, and large coordinated groups representing barrio or neighborhood associations. Officially, all are required to pass by the judges' stand twice. Masqueraders may choose clothing of the opposite sex, may play on the stereotypes of an ethnic group, or may depict some mythical or historical character. Viewers crowd the sidewalks and applaud the floats they like. Floats exhibit the names of barrios or clubs, giving them a public sense of corporateness that is far from the structural reality. Carnaval reinforces the public images of the neighborhoods and their characteristic traits. People expect different degrees of sophistication and artistry from each neighborhood according to the existing social or ethnic stereotype. Through the years each neighborhood develops a reputation for its presentations.

A popular activity of Carnaval days, particularly for the young, is throwing water in the streets. Anyone walking in the streets during specified hours may become the target for a bucket of water thrown from a doorway, a window, a balcony, or a terrace, as *vecinos* act out their friendly or antagonistic relationships. A *vecino* may appear suddenly with a bucket of water and surprise another who has only been curiously observing the activities of the youngsters in the street. Water throwing within a neighborhood is not so much of a threat as is the appearance of a car or truck from another neighborhood. On such occasions, the youngsters may shout, "Inside! Boys from the barrios are coming!" The girls may unite as a group to attack the visiting boys while neighborhood boys look on. Or they may decide to help the neighborhood girls. This is, then, no longer a "battle" of the sexes but of neighborhoods and barrios. Mothers inside their homes watch carefully and are ready to intervene if the play goes beyond decency or if the dignity of a young girl is offended.

During Carnaval much of the rigidity of social interaction and taboos suddenly breaks down for a few hours. Aggressions and personal dislikes may be shown in a spirit of gaiety and fun. But any public display must be carefully calculated; it is a propitious moment to measure and corroborate stereotypes. Carnaval may strengthen cliques in the neighborhood or widen gaps between *vecinos*. Adults remember Carnaval experiences in their neighborhoods with delight; later in the year a story of an encounter with "bad" *vecinos* brings laughter and amusement.

The activities of Carnaval, both the *corso* and the water games, are primarily enjoyed by the masses. The upper classes may take vicarious pleasure in viewing neighborhood activities, but they never participate in the water-throwing games in the street. If they wish to enjoy this activity, private arrangements are made to play on the beaches of the Club Social or at a *casa quinta* (country house).

Molding Relations in the Vecindad

Classifying people according to available stereotypes is basic to the *vecindad* way of life, and information passes from *vecino* to *vecino*. The process is neither short nor simple; furthermore, it is accomplished subtly. Each *vecino* adds his interpretation and his own dramatic touch, converting statements into personal opinions: a *vecino* is "transformed" into many things that he neither is nor intends to be.

While a new *vecino* speculates on the general character of the neighborhood, established *vecinos* study him and begin their speculating. The new *vecino* realizes that everyone is forming a personal opinion about him and eventually will find a category for him; but he cannot predict where he will be placed in the collective neighborhood "mind." The combination of factors for classification works differently in each neighborhood, depending on its ethnic and social composition.

Source of income stimulates much curiosity. First there is an attempt to learn how a job was acquired, and if there was any political involvement (*acomodo*). Then there will be speculation about what would be expected from the recipient in return. *Acomodo* may enhance a family's reputation by showing that the family has pull—*cuña*—through friends in other social brackets.

A *vecino*'s description illustrates some basic aspects of neighborhood life.

Vecinos are interested in the movements of other *vecinos*. Traveling fascinates people and is of social significance. It is a way to judge one's economic position. If a person or his family take frequent trips to Buenos Aires, or some other expensive vacation, *vecinos* immediately begin to wonder about their sources of capital. There is an effort to determine through friends or relatives just how the traveler manages the cost of long trips. If the *vecinos* speculating on the matter happen to be of another political persuasion they may link the traveling with pilfering of government funds. On the other hand, if the traveler is a professional man, people are likely to accuse him of charging too much for his services. If a person travels, but is of modest means, it is said that capital for the trip came from needed savings or the sale of some small property. Extravagant spending that brings poverty is ridiculed.

Traveling plays an important role in the social reputation of *vecinos*. Those who always find it possible to travel arouse envy in those who are eager but not able to do the same. Inability to travel is a sign of inferiority; one feels economically deprived and socially less able to achieve prestige. Conversations about incidents on a trip increase resentment in some *vecinos*.

Family social events—weddings, birthdays, engagements—evoke much concern and speculation from the *vecinos*. They comment about the family's resources, the degree of ostentation, and the style of the festivity. Much attention is paid to the dress of guests. Women stand at their doors to watch guests as they arrive; remarks and gestures manifest approval or disapproval. If the fiesta takes place in a modest home of a laborer, one is likely to hear comments such as "they have little but they certainly enjoy spending it on fiestas," or "they have been able to surpass the rest in the *vecindad*," or "the father must certainly love his daughter."

On the other hand, if the family has a good social position outside the neighborhood, the neighbors observe the festivity to see whether it parallels the family's economic level. If the fiesta does not reach the level expected, *vecinos* wonder if the family is in economic difficulty or just stingy. Dress determines which of the guests represent the elite group of the city. These are occasions for *vecinos* to test each other's true social standing, particularly if the social activities exceed the social boundaries of the neighborhood. If the situation does not match the family's social image as seen daily, then the family should brace itself for subtle ridicule. This may not be openly expressed, but everyone involved knows the neighborhood opinion.

Casual conversation in the neighborhood *almacenes* and on the sidewalks touches on conduct and morals, particularly of single girls and bachelors of neighborhood families. Does the boy or girl go out every night? Does he have friends of questionable background or reputation? Are there changes in a couple's relationship? Is the boy serious about the girl? *Vecinos* construct an opinion according to the facts gathered along the grapevine. The prevailing tendency is to discuss and judge a *vecino* for his imperfections; speculation about the causes follows. Once more the ethnic or social stereotype may be used to explain the facts. When the individual's behavior corroborates a stereotype, a family may find no choice but to learn to live with the assigned characterization.

Courting at the doorstep usually lasts many months. *Vecinos* then have the opportunity to gather facts to determine the "true personality" of the girl and of her parents. If the couple's behavior is "decent," they do not seek dark places to show their affection; furthermore, a "good" couple does not mind the company of older people or siblings. If the neighborhood openly disapproves of a couple's behavior, the couple, in an antagonistic response to the neighborhood, may choose to act dramatically. *Vecinos* then have even more reason to manifest their feelings on the basis that public morals of the neighborhood are being violated. Frequently, single girls become socially aloof and ignore the public judgment. *Vecinos* and the family then reach an impasse.

Social honor is an important concept in the life and world view of each *vecino*. Loss of personal honor or *vergüenza* (shame) results from "immoral" behavior, breaking sexual taboos, ignoring household needs, being a person of the street (*persona de la calle*), drinking in excess, stealing, intentional disharmony with *vecinos* resulting in open feuds, political misbehavior, and dubious *acomodos*. Children begin to feel shame when they reach the age of social consciousness. Being blamed for or suspected of some wrongdoing causes shame. The actions of any one member bring shame to the whole family. A "shamed" family may adopt any of the following patterns: (*a*) not appearing at the front door where *vecinos*' gestures might be perceived as an indication of censure; (*b*) living in physical isolation; (*c*) avoiding interaction at all costs, even to shopping in other areas of the city or at the local store at odd times of the day; (*d*) ignoring *vecinos* by assuming an air of "I don't care"; or (*e*) becoming very serious and restrained. Someone in shame maintains distance by his attitude and gesture; the absence of amiability is immediately noticed. Such behavioral patterns in time can make the *vecino* a social enigma to others; being an enigma may enhance honor and dignity. To appear offended is to blame the *vecinos* for calumny. "Avoidance may not be complete in the physical sense, but it approaches completeness in the spiritual sense," remarked a Paranaense. The immediate reaction is social withdrawal of the guilty party and those related to him.

The assumption that in life no one is totally "perfect" relates to the nature of shame (*vergüenza*). Eventually it may fade away, particularly if the "shamed" recognizes the fault. "People forget," is a common phrase, although everyone knows that things of the past may be revived if socially needed. But tolerance is part of being human. Through the years, therefore, it is possible to reestablish one's social position, even in the extreme case of a suspected illegitimate child. The person must be willing, however, to renew her acquaintances and attempt to regain some of her reputation. "But the person can never be the same, because there is, after all, *that* in her life which cannot be totally erased," commented an informant. The nature of a fault determines the time involved to set things straight: the graver the misdemeanor, the longer the term. *Vecinos* expect a time of repentance. They feel that the shameful incident was "a lesson in life not to be forgotten"; it can make a socially arrogant individual a more humble person. Following the crisis, the passage of time and some changes of *vecinos* may facilitate the resumption of public appearances. If separation from one's own family and neighborhood is necessary, this is in itself a punishment. However, this eases the tension between the family and the *vecinos*; the incident is avoided in daily conversations.

According to a popular truism: "A person who assumes a neutral social position in his *vecindad* and neither offends nor is offended leads a more tranquil social life." For a majority of "well-bred" *vecinos*, one's success in the neighborhood depends on how well one can exist in social neutrality. One informant's generalization proved rather revealing. "In their own minds people separate 'life of the *vecindad*' and 'life of friendship.' These are two separate aspects of life." The two may occasionally overlap, but it is more likely that with the psychological pressures of a neighborhood, "life with friends" will be found elsewhere.

The heterogeneity frequently found in neighborhoods yields "a complex web of interpersonal relations." Life in a neighborhood is a "life in proximity, but it is not necessarily a life of friendship." One informant remarked:

It is better for a family to remain inconspicuous. There is distrust and a general lack of *cultura* because we have not arrived at that point of *cultura* when people no longer look at each other's pettiness. One is alone for fear of criticism. Furthermore, if a *vecino* becomes overly friendly when he has not been given any encouragement, then we conclude that such an individual will soon approach someone for a favor. Only relatives or close friends of the family visit freely. The latter we call *apegado de la casa* [close to the household]. Such people are seldom of one's own *vecindad*; and whereas they may come to visit every day, a next-door neighbor may hardly be greeted. In a town this size, and in the economic context in which we live, somehow or other we feel that everyone knows everyone else, and everything is potential public knowledge.

The general advice was not to become too deeply involved with *vecinos*, nor to remove oneself completely from them. A person who knows how much importance to give to the *líos de vecinos* (difficulties among neighbors), and is able to continue the routines of life with a dignified attitude places himself on a superior level. As he surrounds himself with an aura of respect, he increases his personal prestige. Usually it takes many years to achieve this status. The death announcement of such a person might read that he "knew how to earn the respect and sympathy of all his neighbors." Such a person knew how to be *conforme con la vida*, and knew how to display this.

On the other hand, there is always someone in the neighborhood who tries to "get back at" *vecinos*, someone who feels persecuted and constantly looks for social favor. Such a person gossips, promotes scandals, and seeks social disharmony. He will be avoided, although tolerated.

To be *conforme con la vida*, one must guard his own image and that of his family and pay heed to *lo que dirán la gente*—what people will say. Public amiability is the general neighborhood etiquette; one does not always express his own opinion unless the feud is completely in the open and the social break is such that greetings are totally denied. "What people may say" is a first lesson for young people in neighborhood life; it is a tool used by parents to cause children to conform to established rules and to avoid *vergüenza*. One's actions in the face of what people might say determine to a large extent the social attitude and career in the neighborhood as well as in the city.

Vecindad in Celebration

Vecinos hardly ever come together as a group, only an accident brings them all out into the street. Although the New Year is widely celebrated by clubs, a handful of neighborhoods are known for their New Year's street-corner dances. *Vecinos* gather at one street corner next to the *almacén*. Although many are not involved in the organization, each one closely watches the preparations and speculates whether the family should join the celebration.

Late in the afternoon, *vecinos* appear at their doorsteps as usual, but this time their attention is turned to the street corner. Children run back and forth and report to their parents any changes from the previous year that they have observed. Adults check the children's information and then share it with others. Soon people feel obliged to participate, at least as spectators. This may mean that some neighborhood tensions have to be overlooked. At dusk, songs dedicated to *vecinos* are announced over the loudspeaker. In these announcements, deference is paid to professionals, to teachers, and to persons of importance by the form of address, such as "to señor X and his friendly family." To small business people and others of lesser social category, the dedication is made by using the person's nickname: "to Shorty and family," "to the Italian and his family," "to Luisito," "to the shoemaker on the corner."

Excited children move between their houses and the corner, but adults hesitate to venture into the center of activity. Teenage girls stroll up and down the sidewalk speculating on the success of the event. At about 10:00 P.M. many families leave for the traditional *fin de año* (end of the year) dinner, an intimate family celebration. Before midnight, people begin to reappear at their doorsteps, and with the fireworks, sirens, and church bells, the excitement increases. The moment for greeting the New Year has arrived. Sons and daughters pay respect to their parents; *vecinos* having enough *simpatía* toward each other may cross the street to extend best wishes for a happy New Year. Those of higher social standing do not make the first move; discreetly they acknowledge the greetings of others from across the street. The situation truly reflects social standing, social personality, and the social history of each family. *Vecinos* are still aware of the various stereotypes, but there is a spirit of relaxation. The announcer plays the host and through the amplifier invites families by name. "People like to be begged" [*se hacen rogar*], remarked the informant, "It is part of our way." Finally adults, carrying their chairs with them, move slowly toward the scene of the festivity. Youngsters gather in groups and block *barras* (gangs), making themselves conspicuous by outbursts of laughter. Such gaiety is in sharp contrast to the reserved attitude of the adults.

The music grows louder. Finally, a married couple steps into the middle of the street for the first dance, and youngsters applaud them. Soon boys of the neighborhood *barras* will each invite a girl for a dance. Everyone is very much aware of being watched, and aware of *vecino*'s comments about their dancing. *Vecinos* carefully note who is dancing with whom, who greets and who is greeted, and who is ignoring tensions of the past. All this new information is fed into the neighborhood grapevine, and a new image of a *vecino* or of a family may emerge. The celebration is in full swing until 2:00 A.M. Young people are the first to leave to participate in the more formal dances of the city and neighborhood clubs.

During the New Year's celebration the social distinctions and frictions are relaxed. A student from the neighborhood may dance a few times with a girl from a modest household. There is general sociability for the moment. Thereafter the impersonal style of life returns, and the quality of relationships remains substantially unchanged Frequently, the analysis of the situation brings the *vecino*'s stereotypes into clearer focus. Much of the behavior observed during the gathering reinforces firmly held beliefs. Afterwards, neighborhood life returns to normal, and the maintenance of social distance resumes its importance to each *vecino*.

Maintaining Social Distance

The definition of the ideal neighborhood way of life implies social unity that needs to be manifested by acknowledging others through daily greetings, brief comments, proper gestures, and periodic street conversations. Personal distance, however, is considered a social safeguard. A man who has lived in the same neighborhood for twenty-five years said: "I cannot claim to know much about my *vecinos*. I would only go to their house if they needed me; I see them on the sidewalk and in the *almacén*. For many years some *vecinos* have passed by my sidewalk, but we never started to greet each other. Now it would be embarrassing to begin, and therefore, we act as strangers. I know, however, what goes on in the neighborhood, but we do not mix with anyone as friends. We stay with our families. Each one remains in his own home."

This informant indicated that he had been puzzled lately because a retired teacher suddenly had a new car, and there were rumors that he was planning to build an addition to his house. Cautiously and with a certain degree of naïveté, yet not without elegance, he observed that "one cannot do such a thing on a teacher's salary, much less with retirement income. Who knows where the money comes from." He then

The *Vecindad* Style of Life

dropped the subject; this was simply his way of eliciting information from the other *vecinos*.

This man, the oldest resident on the block, has witnessed a great deal of change in his neighborhood during the past twenty-five years. Whereas the *quinta* style of life was common until only a few years ago, now he is totally surrounded by modern homes of teachers, public employees, and army officers. He is a retired city employee, and among the *vecinos* he rates at the lowest point; they consider him a social lag with the lowest level of *cultura*. *Vecinos* noticeably avoided him. During the summer he spent much time on the sidewalk in front of his house, greeted by some *vecinos* who pass by several times a day but ignored by most.

Another informant, of Russian-German descent, moved to a *vecindad* thirty-five years ago. He remarked that there is no intimacy among *vecinos*, although there is a spirit of *vecindad*. There is outward respect in greeting one another, but no visiting. People know each other well publicly, helping each other during crises. Only rarely does a neighbor give another the key to his patio to water the plants and care for the family's pets while the owner is away. *Vecinos* feel that this is *mucho compromiso* (too much responsibility) and prefer to avoid situations like that. A woman of Italian descent said, "Although we do not see our neighbors for days, we like to hear them in their patio." Invitations to close neighbors may be extended for family celebrations, "but one hesitates to attend because maybe the other neighbors were not invited," commented another *vecino*.

A professional man living a few blocks from the main plaza mentioned that in his block people approach each other only for exceptional reasons; if one needs to request a favor, it is done very hesitantly. "They apologize because they feel that they may be interfering with my private life. If a neighbor knocks at my door, I immediately assume that he has an important reason for coming and that it is not a visit. He is a *vecino* and must not be confused with a friend."

A sixth grade girl from a modest family entertaining social aspirations said: "In my *vecindad* there are good *vecinos*, but there are also ignorant ones. One can see that they are ignorant because they do not have good manners, they do not know their place socially, and their language is not good. . . . We, in our home, totally ignore this category of *vecinos*. We do not want to learn their names or other personal things about them, and to me, each time I encounter these people, it's as though they were newcomers to the neighborhood. We know that these people are very jealous and we feel that they cannot be trusted."

Just a few blocks away, in another neighborhood, lived people of a very similar economic level. One informant felt that the people of this neighborhood could not be trusted, and, therefore, "we allow only one boy, a good friend of our son, to enter our house."

The *vecindad* is the social field for a housewife. She can speak to other women, but she is not expected to establish too many intimate friendships. This would be a source of criticism from others. If a man passes her door and greets her, only a reserved "good morning" or "good afternoon" is proper. While a woman belongs in her home, a man may find a tight-knit group in his club (if he is club-oriented). This is particularly true in the middle social category.

The social distinction between those who are outgoing and those who are withdrawn is also important. There are potential problems with both kinds. The outgoing may become friendly quickly, but they might involve one in nasty situations of neighborhood gossip. The withdrawn may be maintaining social sophistication or using isolation to guard their category.

Although outwardly sociable, *vecinos* must maintain distance. The distance a man keeps in relations with his neighbors indicates his social standing, his economic capability, and his potential power in the neighborhood. The degree of exposure to public view is believed to correlate with the amount of *cultura* a man possesses. A teacher in secondary school, for example, does not habitually spend his time on the sidewalk; it is only on extremely hot evenings that he and his wife may be seen outdoors. Low-voiced conversations are the rule on the sidewalk, and patterns of behavior indicate the social standing of *vecinos*. Afternoon appearances on the sidewalk may show that *vecinos*' relationships are smooth. A newcomer, while on the sidewalk, may be invited to visit there with the less-reserved *vecinos*. They may indirectly inquire into the means of his livelihood, and at the same time may subtly, but clearly, inform him about the other *vecinos*. During the conversation, some negative comments are made about nearly everyone. This course of action allows a *vecino* to feel that he is placing himself morally high in contrast to his low economic position. *Vecinos* who sit on the sidewalk daily become very much aware of the subtle changes in the routine of neighborhood life. The "sidewalk sitters" are the critics of the neighborhood. A *vecino* wishing to learn some fact approaches such persons for information.

Although distant, *vecinos* are interested in other *vecinos* and "very observant," remarked one informant. "When inside, we are preoccupied with the outside, and in this way we mentally live with each other." The sounds of doors opening and closing in neighbors' houses give constant clues about activities and moods. By the pattern of sounds, *vecinos* can tell even which member of the family is coming or going. By the sound of a car's engine and the closing of car doors, one knows whether a neighbor or a stranger is arriving or leaving. Unfamiliar sounds receive most attention.

Social distance minimizes the chance of involving oneself in social discomforts. Younger members of the family usually follow adult patterns. It is not unusual for mothers to instruct their children to discriminate if this is appropriate to the circumstances. To ignore is to prevent proximity, intrusion, false friendship, and to keep young people from falling in love within the neighborhood.

The illustrations supplied by informants, as well as my observations and experiences in the field, point to many common elements among the elite and the middle class. The higher the social category, the more likely that their ways fit the Paranaense stereotype of an urban existence. In a typical neighborhood of the city, *vecinos* cannot expect to develop close relationships simply because they reside in the same neighborhood. *Vecinos* become used to each other, expect to see each other, but as city people they avoid establishing friendships. Cordiality, however, is accepted and expected. Everyone likes to think that neighborliness (implying cordiality) or *vida de vecindad* should be possible. In this Argentine urban setting, however, the ideal does not become a reality. All behave as if their family's social importance were higher than that of others. In contrast to the ideal, one finds avoidance and separation according to ethnic background and economic level; the result is interpersonal atomization. Such a degree of individualism in the structural setting of the neighborhood is indeed paradoxical.

To attempt to speak of neighborhood loyalty among adults is to force a concept that in the *vecindad* is obscure, if not absent. There is no group feeling; hence there are no loyalties except to one's family and relatives, and this allows independent and individual thinking. The lack of loyalties and confidence in others makes the discussion of personal viewpoints undesirable. Neutral themes in conversation, avoidance of social conflict, and general agreeableness and cordiality constitute the rules of neighborhood etiquette. Men in the club may speak of serious things, particularly political events; outside the club there may be occasional opportunities for conversations, but concern about what people will say (*lo que dirán las gentes*) limits the expression of one's viewpoints and opinions.

Social neutrality is basic to public role playing and results in an amalgamation with no lasting cohesiveness. Neighborhood cliques do develop, but most relationships tend to be short-lived. An outgoing *vecino*, it is said, may be at the apex of the neighborhood social network and may direct unification. Yet few such persons are known; they seem to exist as mythical neighborhood figures of the past.

In conclusion, personal distance in an atmosphere of group togetherness (*Gemeinschaft*) characterizes the neighborhood. Some exist not as *vecinos* of a neighborhood, but as *vecinos* of the city. City life for these is equated with independence and personal freedom, with their attendant loneliness. *Vecindad*, by definition, should provide group support, but people are still alone in the *vecindad*. The reality is a paradox difficult for strangers to understand.

While some Paranaenses would like to practice the ideal philosophy of *vecindad*, others actively avoid it. They orient their social relations to other parts of the city by sending their children to private schools, attending services in city churches, and participating in city clubs. Two major forces are evidently at work; perhaps the struggle between the ideals of an intimate neighborhood and total individual freedom sig-

The *Vecindad* Style of Life

nifies the expansion of a truly urban and modern way of life best represented in center city. The stylistic differences from one neighborhood to another may be no more than the spread of the truly urban elements from the center toward the periphery of the city, from the plaza to the barrios.

5. *VECINDAD* AND BEYOND: VOLUNTARY ASSOCIATIONS

City, *vecindad*, and barrio clubs, together with various other voluntary organizations, constitute a basic structural network in the city's social organization. They form a social grammar for each individual's existence and serve as avenues for movement from the *vecindad* to the city social environment or from one social class category to another. The structural organization, however, may leave a person stranded in his immediate neighborhood if he does not see the social opportunities or does not manipulate the structural potentials for his social development. But in every case, the institutional network provides channels for a clear social definition.

In the last two chapters we have established the general character of the *vecindad*. Now we will consider voluntary associations, not only as structural social entities, but also as frameworks within which individuals relate, and we will consider how, through the associations and organizations, *vecinos* may step out of their neighborhoods into the city. The main objective—to understand the individual in the context of a highly stratified society—remains primary, and thus the presentation will be limited by this aim.

City Clubs

Theoretically, each neighborhood club could evolve into a city

Vecindad and Beyond

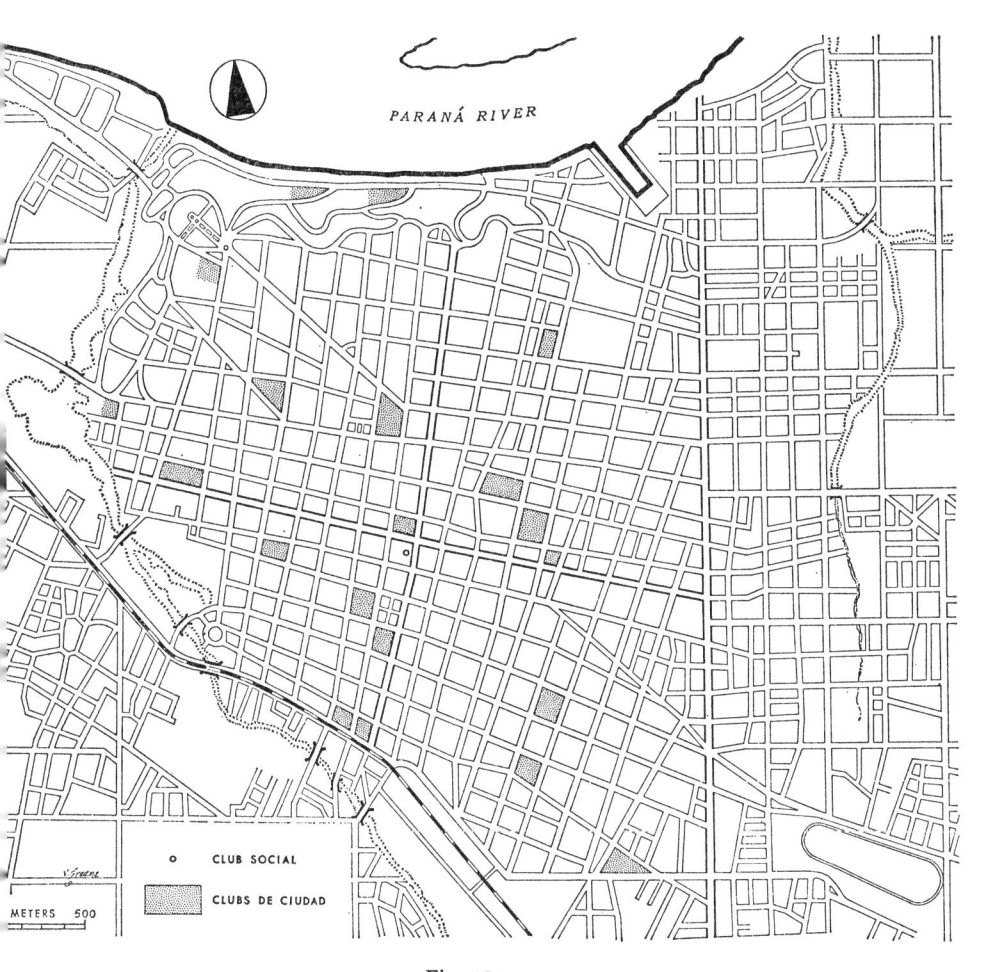

Fig. 18

club. In the history of the city, however, only a handful have achieved city status. The city clubs, in contrast to the small neighborhood or barrio clubs, draw members from all sections of the city, usually persons highly conscious of social status and constantly aspiring to higher levels. When a neighborhood club becomes of the city, members are expected to incorporate into their behavior the proper level of class sophistication. The location of the club building, the prestige and reputation acquired through the years, and the types of facilities offered to members determine the category of the club. Unlike the neighborhood clubs, city club facilities are open to both men and women (see fig. 18).

There are about fifty neighborhood clubs in the city exclusively for men with occasional activities for families of club members. Approximately ten clubs of the city have a wider membership, and their swimming pools, beaches, basketball courts, and soccer fields are open to families. Once a club acquires a swimming pool, it tends to open its facilities to a large, city-wide membership, but only three or four clubs can afford a pool or the combination of a pool and beach area along the river front.

Even though a city club is theoretically open to any person recommended by a club member, waiting lists are long, and admission into clubs with summer swimming facilities is not easy to obtain. Acceptance for membership usually depends on the social standing and reputation of the person sponsoring the new applicant. In some cases, preferential treatment is extended to guests in the city.

At the pinnacle of the city's social scale is the major club of the city known as the Club Social; to be considered in the upper social register, one must be accepted as a member of this club. Patronized by the elite families, the wealthy professionals, the educated entrepreneurs, the powerful landholders, the military, and the executives of the various branches of government, the club offers facilities for dining, with dancing on special occasions; it also sponsors a debutante party on New Year's Eve. A beach area along the Paraná River is reserved exclusively for members. As in other clubs of the city, facilities in the Club Social are set aside for gambling on assigned days of the month. Some members may join a group of gamblers from other social categories who are permitted to enter the premises of the club through the service entrance. The large halls, elaborate chandeliers, monumental paintings, heavy velvet curtains, mirrors, numerous attendants—even the sofa arrangements—provide a traditional European setting, which reflects the social aspirations of the minority responsible for setting a style for others within the city.

Club Social membership nowadays is less exclusive than in the past, as pointed out by one young member who remarked: "We now let many *nouveaux riches* become members because we need their financial support; but they can be socially ignored . . . and of course they suffer. They need the membership of the club, but with this treatment they become less and less active. We can then continue to dominate." According to a member of the middle category, "The club attracts professionals from middle social levels who are known to aspire to a higher social status, and who, once accepted into the club, try to imitate the behavior of the elite. But for those who cannot consistently act according to the expected mores of the group, the situation may be socially frustrating."

Wealth is necessary for membership in the Club Social, but of more importance is the intention to identify with the style of life of the traditional and elite Argentine families of the city. Even though the Club Social is a club of the city for *vecinos* of the city, its membership is limited to a small group of the city population; the Club Social is a society club, and society means the elite.

Currently the Club Social includes three categories of individuals: members by right of birth, whose ancestors took life membership for all their descendants; those who have "bought" membership through wealth and education; and those who have recently become members. The differences based on birth and parentage bring about distinctions within the club and stimulate the formation of competitive cliques. The old traditional families (elite of the upper class) ideally would like to keep the club exclusively for those who are known to have good ancestry. This proved too impractical, however, since many of the traditional families are no longer wealthy. Realizing that they are needed, the newly accepted families with wealth, but without the prestigious ancestry, have formed their own cliques. At the election of officers the divisions are most noticeable. The newcomers have been campaigning to extend the functions of the club to an upper group of the middle social level that has acquired high social standing through political leadership of national importance and through education.

Only a handful of clubs offer a style that is attractive to the middle social category of professionals. Among the upper-middle-class clubs are the Club de Estudiantes, the Rowing Club, the Lawn Tennis Club, and the Jockey Club. They limit their membership by sponsorships and high entrance fees. Swimming pools, exclusive beach areas, tennis courts, basketball courts, rugby fields, racing boats, bars, and, in some cases, restaurants are the main attractive features of these clubs. The choice of government employees, teachers, and professionals, these clubs also attract members of the Club Social, especially the teenagers.

The clubs of the next social plateau, with members drawn from a large section of the city and from *vecindades,* include people who prefer a less competitive social situation. Among these clubs, with a social orientation not so broad as that of the city clubs, are the Club Belgrano, Club Echagüe, and Club Paraná. These clubs have sports facilities such as large stadiums for soccer, basketball courts, paved courts for skating, and courts for hand and paddle ball; one club has a swimming pool. Weekend dances with good orchestras attract members and city people from neighborhood clubs.

Clubs of the city emphasize outdoor summer activities such as boating, sailing, tennis, and swimming (either in the club's outdoor pool or at their river beach). In contrast to the busy summer season, the winter months are quiet; some clubs have indoor facilities for card games, dances, or dinners. (Weather conditions allow the tennis club to remain open throughout the year.)

An educated man of the upper middle class summarized the relationship between social category and clubs in the city by saying:

> The Rowing Club and the Club Estudiantes are the largest ones; here you will find the elite of the city, and even the aristocracy as in the Club Social. The clubs' premises are of interest to youngsters from families of the *gente conocida* [well-known people]; there they can feel above everyone else. In clubs of lower social standing, the membership is of a lower middle category and then there is confusion with the neighborhood or barrio clubs, which are composed of people from the lower middle class and the humble people [*gente más humilde*]. The difference in the club's style is very notable; at dances many adults sit around the dancing area; they are the parents or the persons accompanying young girls. Close chaperoning is still an ideal but is disappearing in clubs of the city.

The process of joining a city club separates individuals who grew up together but whose educational paths diverge. People with a good degree of *cultura* are readily accepted into the city clubs. A working man from a *vecindad* and with a secondary education would feel inferior (*se siente inferior*) there. Conversely, an aspiring professional drifts away from the neighborhood club in order to mix with people of higher social standing. In a city club, however, he cannot easily enter into the power structure of the club, since one of the requirements is a time depth in the social life of the city. It takes more than one generation to become fully established in a city club. By contrast, in a neighborhood club he would find immediate *camaradería*, and a feeling of one big family.

Ethnic Associations

Activities sponsored by ethnic associations cut across neighborhoods and social classes. Currently only a few ethnic associations are strong in the city, supported by people who feel that these associations have been transformed into a form of social club free to some degree from the social class consciousness of other clubs. The associations of ethnic groups were important organizations aiding immigrants at the end of the last century. They provided a place where people could meet and interact solely on the basis of shared ethnic or nationality background.

The arrival of immigrants in this part of Argentina constituted a phenomenon which, similar to that in the United States, generated new social institutions and processes. With enthusiasm, the first immigrants built their ethnic associations. They served as a means for ethnic unity in a strange nation, and most of all as an extension of their own country. This was a place where things of the Old World could be discussed and the new surroundings considered, a place where one could observe the others who were also deciding whether to give themselves to the life of the New World or to remain unaffected by it.

Société Française de Secours Mutuel was founded in 1861; in 1864 the Italian Society was founded. By 1894 there were several organizations sponsored by Italians, including Unione a Beneficenza, Soccores Mutuos, Operai Italiani, and Italiani Meridionale. Later they all banded together in the Italiani Uniti. Another modification occurred in 1910 when the Patriotica XX Settembre and the Italiani Uniti joined together and became the XX Settembre de Mutuos Soccorso. The Sociedad Española de Socorros Mutuos became an active organization in 1918. Two other societies, strongly identifying with specific regions of Spain, formed centers. They are the Centro Vasco and the Centro Asturiano, which were formed to assist the poor Spanish residents in Paraná and those passing to other areas of Argentina. Each society built a large *panteón* in the cemetery for the use of its members. The members and contributors supported the associations.

Immigrants arrived in economic need, but brought skills and a strong desire to improve their personal economic standing. In the early periods when Paraná was a village, immigrants felt alone and insecure. In this atmosphere the idea of an association to assist immigrants in adjusting to the Argentine social situation was most appealing. The attempt was to reproduce some of the basic social features of their home country. The earlier immigrants were comparatively adjusted to the surroundings of the area by the time new groups of immigrants arrived. Within the ethnic associations, the earlier immigrants formed a group of experts in the new setting.

Immigrants generally stayed in the places where they first settled; they did not consider moving to a new frontier. In contrast to the situation in the United States, there was no gold rush and no following of the fur trade. Immigrants found themselves in cities, located in the midst of rich soil. Small and large landowners, the rural dweller with a small business, the aspiring youth who wanted education, as well as the European immigrant, all aimed to reside in cities. "The talents and abilities of the nation were concentrated in the urban areas, and especially in Buenos Aires. Rather than a frontier, Argentina had a city."[1] The high aspirations of the immigrants in the city added important new elements to the culture of Paraná and brought about an exciting confrontation with that which had been in existence since colonial days.

It is interesting to view the ethnic organizations in terms of the

[1] Scobie 1964*b*:163.

Vecindad and Beyond

sociopsychological accommodations made by their members. The activities of the Italians in their centers, for example, had an effect against Argentinization. Many immigrants continued to be *muy Italianos*, loyal to their country. A large number of them never learned to speak Spanish correctly. It was characteristic of first generations in the new setting to continue their ethnic patterns; as the second generation moved forward, the cultural distance between the two became very evident. Young people were more likely to support neighborhood or city clubs, while parents spent their time at the ethnic centers exchanging views about Italy. The first generation could not cope with the surrounding social forces affecting their children. The *familia*, however, kept the home as a sanctuary to preserve many basic ethnic traits.

Events in Europe affected relations among Europeans in Paraná, between groups and within groups between the first and second generations. During the 1930s, among the Italians there were the pro-fascists and the anti-fascists. The *Italia libre* movement opposed totalitarianism and racial and religious hatred, and supported full equality among men and the separation of church and state. Some of the Italians in Argentina were associated with a large movement "to fight the influence of Mussolini's fascism on the fifteen million Italians in the New World."[2] The years of war were a time of much internal friction and hostility resulting in factionalism; many left their ethnic centers.

The Spanish association was very active in the city until the Spanish Revolution. The split during the Spanish Civil War weakened the association, and many members withdrew their support. Serious disagreements over issues relevant in Spain arose among members. As the society weakened, no more *romerías* fiestas were celebrated. During the First World War members of the French Society went to France to defend their country; others organized "Kermesses" to raise funds and collect food and clothing for the people of France. Active members of the society still speak very favorably of the "mutualist spirit" of their members at that time.

[2] Cochran and Reina 1962:146.

None of the ethnic societies now has many members born in the Old World. Second- or third-generation Argentines maintain some social activities to perpetuate the memory of ancestors. There is no longer any need for the original functions. In some cases the associations have become cultural centers and sponsor lectures on history and travel, exhibit works of art, represent their group on national holidays, exalt their cultural past in Argentina, and provide the proper setting for the perpetuation of a religious tradition. General interest in languages, typical of Argentina, provides the opportunity for the associations to offer classes in Italian, French, Arabic, English, and Hebrew. The following centers are noted for their cultural programs: Unión Suiza, Sociedad Italiana, Sociedad Friulana, Société Française de Secours Mutuel, Asociación Croata, Sociedad Unión Arabe, Unión Residente Paraguayos, Asociación Sirio-Libanesa, Asociación Argentina Israelita Sefardi Religiosa y Cultural, Asociación Israelita, a chapter of the Asociación Argentina de Cultura Inglesa, and Alianza Francesa. Germans and Russian-Germans have not formed ethnic societies; the Protestant Russian-Germans meet together in the programs of the Lutheran Church.

The activities of ethnic associations have little relation to neighborhood life. Members come from all sections of the city; the active ones are usually of the upper middle class. Among other functions these organizations have attempted to counteract the ethnic stereotypes and the social discrimination that results from their use. In the competition for recognition, the exhibitions of high *cultura* from Italy, France, Switzerland, or Spain have generated many intellectual activities within the association.

The French Society, formed in 1860, continues to have some active descendants interested in maintaining the memory of those who pioneered the development of the city. They attract public attention by placing plaques and flowers along the walls of the French mausoleum and publishing newspaper biographies on each anniversary of the death of important members. Only a handful of these people know the French language, although their French names remain prestigious. The Spanish Association sponsors a fiesta on Columbus Day, October 12. At a lunch for this occasion, a learned criollo usually gives a speech. The society has now passed to the category of a men's club. It still offers its members medical attention, pharmaceutical services, and burial places in the society's *panteón*.

With the exception of the Jewish Center and synagogue, the ethnic organizations are largely symbols of another historical period. They are preserved for sentimental reasons and for some economic benefits derived through their cooperative services. It is generally felt that the societies have been transformed basically and that they cannot keep alive the Old World traditions. Today, Paranaenses are no longer interested in the early issues, and will be even less interested as Argentinization increases. If the ethnic clubs are to survive, they must function like city clubs or centers to promote the fine aspects of the Old World *cultura*. Their facilities testify to a flourishing period, but the membership points to a definite state of decline.

Service Organizations

There are many other organizations that fall outside the categories of neighborhood and city clubs or ethnic associations. The service organizations fulfill other functions. Their sponsorship comes from those who are inclined to humanitarian, artistic, or economic interests. Specialization and social distinction play an important part in the activities of these organizations. Service organizations, depending upon the nature of their activities, may concentrate in a *vecindad*, or they may concern themselves with issues relevant to special groups in the city. The local newspaper daily announces activities of organizations under the subheading *Vecinales*.

The *vecinales* associations are the truly voluntary organizations of Paraná. Their beginnings are never complex. Usually a group of people single out a problem or issue and organize to handle it. Once the work has been completed, the organization is disbanded or is transformed into a permanent social organization. A few of them have become important in the city structure, partly because the problem with which they deal continues to exist, such as poverty.

Through an association, *vecinos* may come together in a movement of neighbors (*movimiento de vecinos*), frequently in defense of their own rights. In 1965 there was an effective movement against the municipal officers for having raised city taxes. An organization known as Defensa Vecinal had its informal headquarters in neighborhoods and barrios. Its only objective was "the legitimate defense of the people's interest." *Vecinos* joined together and pressured the local administration to revise its position and to bring "just and reasonable solutions." The Defensa Vecinal advised the people not to pay their taxes until the movement could publish a communiqué recommending the best course of action. A Comisión Intervecinal coordinated the activities of the Defensa Vecinal for ten neighborhoods. Each neighborhood organization sent delegates who elected officers to negotiate with municipal authorities.[3]

Such temporary movements rapidly organize *vecinos* for collective action. Directives for the *vecinos* interested in their activties are communicated through the local newspaper or disseminated by loudspeakers mounted on moving trucks. These trucks move from corner to corner and from neighborhood to neighborhood reaching everyone, whether interested or not, with their blare of music and announcements.

In the barrios, active *comisiones de vecinos* deal with the limited public facilities. The lack of paved sidewalks, running water in the homes, sewers, and electricity has become a political issue in the barrios. Active *comisiones* at times have gained support from candidates for political office.

Independent from the *comisiones* are the *uniones vecinales*, also informal associations. The *unión vecinal*, as the name indicates, brings together *vecinos* and their leaders to put into action some program in their immediate surroundings or to participate as a group in public activities of the city. They may offer flowers at the cemetery in memory of an outstanding *vecino*, erect a statue of a national or local hero in the neighborhood plaza, or assist in some way with the work of the local school.

Experience has shown that a number of public issues can unite people who are physically dispersed and unfamiliar with each other. Under normal conditions, a *unión vecinal* is kept active just long enough

[3] From records, this issue appears to have been one of the most important movements in challenging the power of the municipal political authority.

to satisfy the *vecinos'* immediate wishes. The most active organizations are found in rapidly changing barrios, away from the city center. The *comisiones vecinales* hold meetings in local school buildings or in barrio clubs. Usually they conclude the meeting by deciding to send a petition to city authorities in which they request land for a plaza or a playground for neighborhood children, first-aid supplies for a barrio dispensary, programs to fight inflation such as one entitled Pro Abaratamiento de la Vida (for lowering the cost of living), or the beautification of streets by planting trees. These *comisiones*, acknowledged by the city authorities, could be used to influence voters during political campaigns. But doubts prevail about the pledges of candidates. As *vecinos* will confess, "From the promise to the doing there is a long stretch."

Amigos de Calle San Martín (the city's main street) is composed of representatives from each block of the street. This organization selects delegates to speak with the mayor of the city about the problems of drainage in the downtown streets, the state of garbage collection, the problem of street cleaning, the appearance of houses along the main street, and the damage done by organizations' painting propaganda slogans on their walls. The great increase of traffic in the street also causes concern.

Voluntary associations or the local government may appoint special *comités* and *comisiones* to handle specific tasks. For instance, there is a *comité* that comprises delegates from each of the Protestant churches, the Catholic diocese, the Rotary Club, the Israeli Association, the Lions Club, the military, the federal and provincial police, and the city government. This *comité* is responsible for the moral order in the city. Among other things, they evaluate the movies to be shown in the city. *Comités* and *comisiones* are formed to honor the flag, to honor motherhood in the Monument to Mothers, and to honor the schools and teachers. When the job has been completed, recognition is extended to the participants, and the group is dissolved.

Federated *cooperadoras* (twenty in Paraná) give aid to schools and hospitals. Members' monthly dues support programs aiding the schools. In some cases *cooperadoras* work for park conservation, as the Cooperadora Enrique Berduc. This organization attempted to bring to the attention of the provincial, municipal, and military authorities the need for conservation and redevelopment of the neighborhood in the area of Parque Berduc.

Several voluntary associations, usually women's groups, do mainly charity work. The Sociedad Hermanas de los Pobres (Sisters of the Poor) sponsors benefit dances and collections for the support of an orphans' home. The Sociedad Damas Vicentinas raises funds for the poor, the sick, and the hospitals. Other similar groups include the Sociedad Mutuos Unión Suiza, Sociedad de Socorros Mutuos, Sociedad Dante Alighiere. Madrinas del Amparo Maternal have as their purpose the protection of children below six years of age. Each of the above associations is recognized in the city in terms of the social class the members represent. Many of the active women are socially aspiring individuals.

There are also Friends of the Needy People, Friends of the Blind, and Friends of Children. These organizations advertise subscriptions in the local newspapers and request contributions to be placed in containers located in businesses in the downtown area. (Public announcements advertise the need for help, and the quota for the pledges, but no public announcement is made of the success achieved.) On the containers, announcements are printed that the proceeds will go for a daily glass of milk for each needy child in a barrio school. The Centro Amigos del Ciego de Entre Ríos sponsors a Week for the Blind. A committee of the organization collects donations on the streets and prepares a program featuring lectures by doctors. Members visit the blind in hospitals and finally may have a luncheon for the members and their spouses. Many of these organizations are extensions of social clubs and clubs of the city.

There are professional centers for teachers of primary schools; in such centers former pupils and teachers meet together. There are also centers for commerce and industry, centers for retired people, and centers for traveling salesmen (*viajantes*). The members of the Centro Commercial e Industrial met in March 1965 to voice their feelings and to find means of impressing upon authorities the need for improving the "deficient services of the ferry," which were causing great loss to businessmen and affecting businesses throughout the city.

Vecindad and Beyond

On other occasions, this center delegated a number of its members to speak with the mayor about tax reduction. Sometimes these associations serve as middlemen between the parties concerned and the authorities.

Another type of organization is the *círculo*: Círculo de Suboficiales, Círculo de Oficiales, Círculo de Maestros, and Círculo Médio Obreros. Each of these prepares programs and lectures or acts as a group for the improvement of a profession. Almost every week the plaza of the city is adorned with luminous signs announcing the week of some *círculo*. Programs are planned, and social gatherings of professionals take place. Seldom does a week pass without some activity, and the city people enjoy the changes as benefits of city life.

In addition to the Asociación Docentes Nacionales, the Amigos de la Facultad de Ingeniería de Paraná was founded to promote higher education in the city. The Syndicate of Newspapermen requires its members to participate actively in the Amigos de la Casa del Periodista (Friends of the House of Newspapermen). There is also the Sociedad Vendedores de Diarios (Society of Newspaper Vendors). Others that might be noted are the Liga de Jubilados (League of Pensioners), and the Liga de Inquilinos (League of Tenants). The Liga de Madres (League of Mothers) is active in one of the churches; it was organized to sponsor and maintain a library. A great many of these organizations rent space from clubs or public buildings. Administrative work is usually conducted in the house of an officer of the organization.

In addition there are organizations involved exclusively in cultural programs. Their activities concern people of the city. They may not come together as a single group at any time, but they are recognized as interested in doing something as "friends" of the city. Some of these organizations have become well known, for example the Amigos de la Música, an association responsible for organizing classical music programs. They bring artists of distinction to the city. There is also the Amigos del Museo Histórico (Friends of the Historical Museum), which is active in collecting documents on the history of the province.

Many organizations appear to have a special interest in preserving the memory of historical events and defending constitutional principles. These include Asociación Croata "Rey Tomislav," Asociación Verdiana, Asociación Juvenil John F. Kennedy, Asociación Cívica Mayo-Caseros, Asociación Pro-Patria. The memberships are small, and each is known for one annual activity. An interesting case is the Liga Social Pro-Comportamiento Humano, which was formed to exalt the values of "good living" as the "mainspring of a civilized society."

Another more recent organizational development is the formulation of groups known as Peña. The purpose of these groups is the preservation of folk music and criollo speech. At meetings local artists perform, and afterwards criollo food is served. Each Peña has a criollo name, such as El Lazo, El Aromito, Cielo Azul. These link themselves to barrio organizations by performing for the benefit of *cooperadoras*, schools, or charitable institutions.

Last but not least are associations formed for political activities. Political parties are active in municipal, provincial, and national elections. During election year, political parties rent space in each neighborhood and barrio for their campaign headquarters. The political propaganda is disseminated by the use of public-address systems mounted in trucks that pass through the streets, each reiterating the same propaganda. Membership in a political party is considered a very personal and private thing. In this sense it parallels church membership.

An Informant Views the Voluntary Associations

Anthropologists owe a great deal to informants who, perhaps responding to their own intellectual interest, have willingly spent many hours describing the situation and interpreting a cultural phenomenon they know intimately. The following account represents the views of such a man of the city, an entrepreneur, third-generation Argentine, a descendant of Iberian grandparents, high in the social stratification of the city. Although he is related by marriage to an old elite family, he is not too active in this category.[4]

[4] The material presented here was studied independently in 1965, and in 1967 it was discussed with the informant. During the interview the informant was guided

"In general, we all tend to think of the 'club' with the stereotype that the club is a place in which to waste time, but socially necessary. This belief is widespread, particularly among women of the struggling middle class. But the idea of indolence related to social and sport clubs has many variations. The intensity from family to family varies and is difficult to assess. But the fact remains that the city is full of clubs and associations, closely linked to the three social levels represented in the city.

"Theoretically, anyone can become a member of a city club as long as he can afford the dues. Once one is in, the social discomfort experienced when trying to participate indeed discourages many people. The clubs have their reputation and people know how to play the social game; by the time they decide to join, they know whether they can take it and how they can use the situation for their own social objectives.

"Although the Club Social is of the city, it is a representation of the elite. One cannot very well separate the Club Social from the city, but paradoxically it is not a club of the city even though it is in the city and for the city. It is socially exclusive, and while the members of the Club Social can be in other clubs, those in other clubs cannot be in it unless they qualify by rigorous social standards. I remain in the Club Social because of family tradition, and although I was a member of other city clubs, I have recently withdrawn from the Estudiante, Golf, and Business clubs. Another member of my family, however, belongs to the Rowing and Estudiante clubs as well as the Club Social. It is all a matter of personal convenience; the clubs offer the possibility of more social variation.

"Some of the city clubs enjoy excellent social prestige, and those families or individuals who can afford join them. One in this category is the Golf Club. In some ways this club competes socially with the Club Social. Those who have not been able to become members

---

into the subject of voluntary organizations and was encouraged to give his personal views and interpretations. This additional information constitutes not only a check on the author's views and interpretations, but will also allow the reader to enter the world view of one Paranaense. His views are presented not because they are typical or representative, but because he is a Paranaense, curious and critical of social processes.

of the Club Social or feel that it is not to their liking have found a way to figure socially through the Golf Club. They are socially noticeable because they can afford an expensive sport. Professional activities and intellectual interest—elements that count high among this group —produce a social style different from the traditional one associated with the Club Social.

"Rowing, Estudiantes, Jockey, and Progreso are definitely city clubs; they are open to all, although one knows that there is a natural selection. Those who feel qualified will try to become members. The Progreso and the Jockey clubs cooperate, and the traveling businessmen, a profession of prestige, tend to congregate here to eat and to play billiards, cards, and chess. Entrepreneurs of importance prefer the Club Progreso, while some are also active in the Jockey Club. In the Jockey Club there are a substantial number of public employees who form a group popularly known as the *burreros* [a term used for those who gamble on horse races]. Essentially, these two clubs are exclusively for men, although on special occasions members may invite their wives. Some of the organizations, such as the Rotary Club, carry prestige because of their attempt to sponsor intellectual activities, and the Lions Club because of its interest in relieving community problems. But the Lions and Rotary Clubs are not in the very center of the social structure.

"Barrio clubs are not located in the main section of the city. They are clubs *in* the city, but not *for* and *of* the city. Personally, I must belong to clubs of the city because of family tradition, and although my profession may take me to areas of the city where the barrio clubs predominate, I have never visited them. Sometimes they may have good public dances and one may attend, but in my case and for the people of my type, we are mentally dominated by the idea that anything central begins with the Club Social. What is outside is of another social setting and we tend to be uninterested. However, one must admit that the Club Social seems to be undergoing changes, and many traditional people feel that it is in decay. However, for the *nouveaux riches*, the club is not declining, and they would like to keep its reputation as a club of *sociedad*.

"In general one can safely say that the people of the very low

Vecindad and Beyond

social strata do not bother to think about clubs or anything that acts like a club. But as soon as one begins to move up even in the lower class, one sees that persons who have a constant source of income will use an *almacén de barrio*, generally known as a *boliche*, as a place to congregate, drink, and play cards or *bochas*. It is an informal way for men to congregate daily. From some of these *almacenes* grew the barrio club. However, the intense activity of the true or typical barrio club emerges in the middle-class sections of the city where the residents have no great aspirations to figure socially at the city level. The lower middle class—people with practical skills and public employees such as chauffeurs and janitors—will patronize a barrio club. When one gets into the high and aspiring middle class, one finds people who are barrio club members and who also belong to city clubs and guild organizations. Among the higher middle-class group, one finds minimal association with the barrio club; and if people are members at this level, it is done from charity, as a contribution, and there is no intention to use the club's premises. The *clase alta*'s main interest lies in the Club Social, followed by interest in the Golf Club and other city clubs.

"In the *vecindad*, women feel that the club for their men is a place of *perdición*, a strong theme that has been the source of family friction and even separation of spouses. When a person in public office finishes his work, spending the rest of the afternoon and the evening in the club with friends gambling and talking about sex and women, then there is tension, particularly for a socially aspiring wife and her children. It may cause them social embarrassment and mothers usually want to discourage their sons from following in the footsteps of their fathers.[5] There are other *vecinos* who are truly oriented to the neighborhood club and whose wives do not seem to object. This may correlate with low social aspirations, which separate them from neighbors who are searching for avenues to climb the social scale. The social distance among these *vecinos* can be enormous. This is very dramatic in barrios in transition. Complaints are frequently made public through the local newspaper, where *vecinos respetables* complain

---

[5] "Las buenas madres no quieren que los hijos aprenden las manias del padre."

about the noise made in the barrio club because of fights, drunkenness, and the attraction to their dances of undesirable women. For families with social aspirations who want to *aparentar* [figure] socially, publicly expressed disapproval makes them feel socially vindicated.

"It is interesting to note that while men, in the general sense, dominate the barrio clubs, women tend to dominate the social situation in clubs of higher social standing. Currently the clubs exclusively for men are disintegrating: this is the situation of the last few decades when the public role of women has definitely changed.

"Another element should be considered in the discussion of the clubs and voluntary organizations, and it may, in some cases, account for their longevity and success. The barrio clubs may have links with political parties, particularly during election years. There are, of course, two sides to the story. When clubs intertwine themselves with political activities, they expect assistance if that party comes to power. Clubs always feel that they do not receive enough and, therefore, have been deceived.

"With the exception of the Israeli Association, the ethnic associations are no longer strong, and one has the feeling that they are on the decline. Some of them have annual dances, and most of them have their own buildings. Many first generation immigrants can maintain a general identification with their place of birth through an ethnic organization. Some of the active members are individuals who did well economically, but who still have no clear identity; their thoughts are not clear. We call these people *gringos atravesados* [mixed-up foreigners]. They are socially isolated persons. Ethnic associations provide a place for people of the same origin to get together to promote Europeanism as a model and as a symbol of *cultura* and to teach their language. In some cases the successful son of an immigrant, perhaps as an act in memory of his parents, promotes the activities of the association, visits the old country, and returns to lecture on the values of his ethnic group. However, it is an attempt to revive the past. These organizations are becoming weaker each year and have not yet evolved other social functions. They have lost a battle, and one has the impression of empty premises.

"The Russian-Germans in the city have the Lutheran Church,

Vecindad and Beyond

which functions both as a church and a club; there, as in most Protestant churches, the rich and the poor come together as 'brothers.' The economic class distinction may be recognized, but it is not played up to any degree; on the contrary, equality is what counts. Traditional families would not consider joining the Protestant churches; it just does not go together with the image of this group. There are several congregations in the city that bring together people of specific economic categories, but in general they are from the middle sectors of society.

"The proliferation of organizations is a fact, and the local newspaper gives the impression that their activities have a direct relation to the needs of the city. Newspapers frequently portray an enthusiastic image of the club, but it is the special terminology of the newspaper, and one needs to understand this reality. To the outsider who does not know the situation, the editorials and announcements can give the impression that thousands of people are deeply involved, but we, the public, know what goes on. The newspaper also makes the ethnic associations appear very active, although they are not.

"From the point of view of the member, the club fosters the general and idealistic image that the organization is a great cause and that members act as a great family. But the fact is that many of the organizations are losing their souls because the founders or the elders find it impossible in these modern days to transplant their objectives to the present generation. Nowadays all clubs complain of the same disease: of a total membership of, let us say, four or five hundred, only twenty or thirty are active and truly dedicated members; in a sense they support a club for themselves. Many people pay their dues, hesitantly and from a sense of obligation, but they seldom take advantage of membership.

"The internal life of the clubs of the upper classes suffers from social trauma, struggles of a competitive class society, and the fact that people are highly conscious of trying to create an appropriate image of themselves. Many of the organizations that have activities related to the general economy of the city—the *centros gremiales* [guilds]—may be considered very positive. My pessimism leads me to believe that any of those centers directly related to one's economic well-being—in vulgar terms, the stomach—march well. The centers of wholesalers and retailers, the salesmen's guild, and other similar labor organizations are all strong and can exercise political pressure, particularly during election periods. The guilds for entrepreneurs are active and have a large membership, but the element of social distinction is of less concern than that of leadership and power.

"This situation contrasts with organizations for charity. In my pessimistic view, I feel that their activities are social role-playing by ladies in the high social strata. Again, I repeat, that in many cases this is all a means to social distinction or *figuración social*. What goes to charity does not compare favorably with what is gained socially. It is also known that all the social activities held in the name of charitable groups, including dances, bring a great many very enjoyable social hours, but this does not match the amount left over for the charity. It is not profitable. We are not generous people in deeds, though we like to think we are. In general we keep everyone busy in the name of social problems that persist without proper solution. It is like patching an old wall. One knows that within the charitable organizations there is much social envy displayed when those who like to shine socially attempt to become members of the governing body, particularly to become president. I have the feeling that there is a strong desire to do a great many things and to do them well, but because of a complicated social web, self-interest, and that strong social desire to shine—that eternal desire to climb socially—nothing is done properly and the effect of all is diluted. The charitable institutions have been operating for many years, but I feel that they do not go to the real source of the social problems in our city. Perhaps there is a fear of eradicating the problem because then the social activities would stop! But really we all are so used to seeing poor adults and children in the streets that we become blind and feel that the problem is not so serious.

"Because there is so much social stimulation and social politicking in a stratified society such as ours, the spirit of true community is greatly diluted. Of course, the public intentions are always excellent, but unfortunately they are not properly carried out. It is a society that functions by random pulls—*a tirones*. One must recognize that in our

Vecindad and Beyond

social milieu there is a great distance between the manner and the public image on the one hand, and the sentiment and reality on the other. One transmits this spirit to his children, and it is, I think, a very generalized sentiment that we do not want to discuss or acknowledge."

Participation and Support

The obvious question is why a highly stratified city population supports so many clubs and associations. The first answer suggests that this is the way a contemporary city society must be organized.[6] It seems to be traditionally Argentine to seek membership in one or several social and sport clubs. To belong to *el club* implies social fulfillment, although in many cases active participation in the club may be limited to only a few occasions. It is the thing to do—*un compromiso*. Those who cannot afford to belong may claim membership, but dismiss it with disaffection, implying that the club is not good enough for them. To be a member of city organizations is the way to demonstrate publicly that one is part of the city social machine and shares the viewpoint of some majority, whether this be of one's social class, city, barrio, or neighborhood.[7]

City club members, in particular, do not develop a sense of corporateness, although each member derives social guidelines and orientation from the club. With a few exceptions, city club members are prone to complain that in the club they have found no group spirit or true loyalties. Instead, as elsewhere in their society, they feel intense social distance and personal dissatisfaction. Many are members because one cannot afford not to be—it looks bad—but at the same time such members are reluctant to attend functions where they may

[6] In a sample of over 500 individuals of the professional and semiprofessional groups, 50 percent were members of a sport club; 10 percent were members of a social club only; the remainder were distributed among the mutual and cooperative organizations, church, school, and ethnic organizations. In a similar sampling among laborers, there were 37.7 percent in mutuals and cooperative organizations, and the remainder in school and church organizations.

[7] Minority groups, such as the Protestants, take a stand against clubs as worldly activities. They cut off their members, especially their youth, from the social circuit. By curtailing the freedom to become part of a whole, part of the network of clubs, they restrict the individual to a limited social participation.

feel social discrimination. As in neighborhood life, the basic spirit of individualization, of depersonalization, and the surrounding aura of keen curiosity about people's material well-being and social background all find expression in the club life. Appropriateness of behavior stands as a guiding principle for interaction. Although appropriateness is not always clearly defined, it is perhaps the most crucial criterion for determining the quality of interaction.

In city club activities members tend to congregate with relatives and adopted members of the family to appear as one group. Through the club, the household extends its activities and its image into the public domain. If such combined appearances occur often, other members begin to talk of "the group of X," or of those who sit at "the table of X." These cliques may last for many years without significant changes. One adopts this technique because he desires to be an active club member, socially conspicuous, but wants to avoid facing the world alone. Others are necessary. As a consequence, many individuals suspect others as *interesados*, using each other's social, economic, and political prestige for personal advancement; this interferes with the development of true and deep friendship. Friendship is relegated to the sphere of poetic possibility.

An important club is informally divided into cliques, frequently linked to the power structure of the club and the power structure of the province or the city (this depends on the social category of the club). The splitting is in terms of social correspondence, *simpatía*, common interests, long-time friendships, or marriage, and not in terms of internal issues of the club or outside political views. The small cliques constitute a strength of the club; clubs without such small groups often cannot promote interest and good attendance. In cases where emphasis is on the "great family," particularly in neighborhood clubs, the splitting into groups is not a dominant feature.

Club activities are controlled and directed by the younger and middle-aged men. An informant remarked: "There are years in one's life when one is full of enthusiasm and needs to be in the public eye socially; the clubs provide the opportunity. At an older age, even though one continues to be interested in the club's sports activities, life tends to be more subdued, and only rarely does one attend the

Vecindad and Beyond

club. One becomes satisfied with old friends, especially if they have been important political figures in the provincial or national government. But life has altogether another meaning for us older people now."

Ideally, it is felt that the club should follow democratic principles in handling its internal affairs. Within the club, egalitarianism is highly encouraged. By a process of natural selection, however, most clubs maintain social and economic homogeneity, but "equality is a myth; most people like to promote social differences," confessed an informant. To enjoy oneself (*divertirse*) is a theme of the club, but the strong social consciousness in the background frequently stifles enjoyment. Under the veil of a general sense of esprit de corps, people seek to bring out individual social distinctions.

During the Perón regime, the clubs, particularly those with social distinction, came under much attack. There was fear in those days that the exclusive gathering of the elite might be cause for closing the club. The government sent inspectors to see that pictures of Perón, and particularly his wife, decorated club walls. Although clubs complied with the dictator's wishes, basic social principles were being violated. The traditional families in the Club Social became highly sensitive to the government intrusion. Members became politically suspicious of each other; the traditional and frequent political discussions were avoided.

For purposes of comparison, we will turn to a club of lesser social importance, a neighborhood club over half a century old. It is a club noted for its emphasis on soccer. Some of the oldest members of the club, who joined in their youth, recall the early events of the club's history. This club, like most neighborhood clubs, had a modest beginning. At first it rented land for *bochas* courts behind the property of an Italian family. Finally with the assistance of the municipal government, the club bought its own land. The older members remember when children of both members and nonmembers came to the club's grounds to play.

The club is known for its intense bonds of *compañerismo* among the older members who have grown up together. To outsiders, they convey the impression of a group of active people dedicated to maintaining the association. There is also a large group with minimal interest in club activities. The active members constantly lament that currently *vecinos* do not support the ideals of the organization, do not want to work, and do not want to cooperate. One of the old members remarked, "Time has changed." The founders still supervise and accuse officers of a lack of dedication to the club. This general mood, together with a difficult economic situation within the club, suffices to bring out a feeling of decline.

In this case, and in contrast to the city clubs, the administrators of the club are older men. Though the membership list includes over 1,000, it is estimated that only 10 percent are active. Each time a club election is held, finding candidates for officers becomes a serious problem. "In contrast to thirty or forty years ago, the young people do not want to work for the club. Now there are other ways to spend leisure time outside the club, and the club suffers from the modernization of the present." An informant stated that a major difficulty in running a neighborhood club is the attitude of members who always seem to be against anyone in power, even though they themselves have elected him. Most members expect the club to provide services without their effort. The failure of a club to articulate with the neighborhood social status may be another significant factor that accounts for the absence of motivation.

A survey of neighborhood clubs of the middle social category shows the following similarities:

1. Only 10 percent of the members are active, manifesting a sincere interest in the destiny of the organization.
2. Club membership is exclusively for men. Women are invited through their husbands on certain occasions to open club events. There has been some discussion of admitting women, but so far no satisfactory solution to this problem has been found.
3. Only a small proportion of those who use club facilities have any interest in its administration. Members believe that they are buying a service, and when they come to the club, they expect to be served.
4. Older members, with older ideas about the neighborhood club, are in administrative positions.

Vecindad and Beyond

5. Persons join a club because of enthusiasm for sports, or because the club is close by and provides a place where one can find acquaintances, be among peers, and to some extent remain neutral in the neighborhood. Club members generally manifest little concern for the social problems of the neighborhood, except in a token manner.
6. Life among people of the middle social bracket is a constant economic struggle, and they do not wish to undertake an additional economic responsibility for a club.
7. Many clubs have disappeared; those that have managed to remain active show very little growth. Occasionally a club may receive some fame by sponsoring dances or winning first place in a sports league. Through political "friends of the club" some benefits may be derived.
8. The large group of socially aspiring individuals now see neighborhood clubs as weak social organizations. Although clubs may show physical improvement, people say that "spiritually they are weak." Some of the clubs, whose beginnings were not only modest but were also known to have included persons whom people from center city classified as "bad people," have attempted to change their social and public image. To improve the facilities of the club is to move with the general trend of society. Accepting women into the club would probably elevate the *cultura*. Some clubs hope to include children by adding libraries and television. Though plans like these have been discussed, no club has adopted such programs.

Vecinos, Vecindad, and Clubs

The *vecindad* clubs, the city clubs, and other voluntary associations open a series of social opportunities for individuals in the city. Organizations counteract the attitudes that emanate from the world view and tend to atomize interpersonal relations and leave the individual standing alone with the family.

A middle-class person may start his club life in a neighborhood club, but as his career progresses, he may join different organizations until he reaches a satisfactory social standing in relation to his economic potential. He obviously has moved from a neighborhood social being to a city social being. He does not necessarily drop all old memberships for new ones. Often one belongs to more organizations than he is able to participate in actively. The clubs are looked upon as social resources to be used according to moods, shifting interest, and friends. An individual of the city occasionally spends leisure time in his neighborhood club, but if his social position has advanced sufficiently, he may feel part of a wider circle linked by a city club. He has no time left for neighborhood activities, although he continues to support the club merely as *un compromiso de vecino*.

It is clear that the social network outside the individual's immediate circle of relatives is formed by contacts made in organizations. Between a person and the "others" stands a series of formal organizations either of a barrio, a neighborhood, or the city. If the organizations were to disappear, the contacts would dissolve. Thus, in the game of life, players who become less active or abandon the club soon fade away. Since an individual's action could offend the dignity of others, the interaction through the club protects the individual. In other words, a person conceals his prejudices as he proceeds to abandon both his club and friendships in order to continue his upward social movement. Some persons through an organization perform humane deeds such as helping the needy, alleviating social problems, and supporting the arts. By the same token, if the organization fails to carry out this obligation and fails the individual, the blame is not his. He does not experience a sense of personal failure; rather it is the failure of the organization.[8]

Individuals, by the same token, can become conspicuous in the public eye by means of an organization. When the organization makes its public appearances, the members derive self-satisfaction without great personal effort. During national celebrations, organizations present sumptuous arrangements of flowers at the foot of a statue of a national hero. At such a time pride is shown in *mi club* as it figures in the social network of the city. It seems to indicate that membership

---

[8] This is contrary to the situation of *vecindad*. There is no organization to represent or to speak for individuals. Each individual is himself responsible for his actions.

Vecindad and Beyond

in organizations constitutes safe conduct of some importance, depending upon the individual's social category.

Membership in a city organization is part of the "civilizing process," the process of citification.[9] To exist without a club means living in a social vacuum. An individual standing alone, without organizational ties, appears incomplete to others. The lack of institutional loyalties makes his position rather tenuous and not the least admirable to others and to himself. Those who do not participate in voluntary organizations or in church activities, but live exclusively within the family circle, are considered to be people *muy de su casa*—of their homes. Companions are found through activities in organizations rather than through associations in one's place of work. The *compañeros de club* carry a different emotional pitch than the *compañeros de trabajo*, and both differ from simply a *compañero*.

The importance of clubs is evident to a stranger or to a new resident. Clubs separate those who are of the city and those who are outsiders; a sure way to be socially counted in the city is through membership in a city club. Restaurants and bars give the opportunity to feel the pulse of public life; but one's social position cannot go beyond that of a transient visitor as long as participation in city organizations does not become a reality. If socially convenient, an acquaintance invites the newcomer first to visit the club of which he is a member. For those planning to remain in the city for some time, the acquaintance may secure a guest membership. The position of the club in the life of the socially active people is indeed central. A person without club membership faces a social handicap when he has to offer hospitality to strangers or outsiders. One's house is not open to strangers; the plaza and public places are neutral locations and only for casual interaction during business hours—at other times one enjoys recreational facilities of the club. The club and its events are the topics of conversation and a point of strong social reference. The city club is the most likely vehicle to introduce strangers to the city's social activities. The neighborhood club, on the other hand, is more removed for a city guest; only very close acquaintances may be invited to *mi club*.

[9] Seldom does one find an average Argentine pueblo of less than 5,000 people containing voluntary associations and clubs.

The clubs and ethnic societies constitute a potential avenue for establishing contacts; it is here that one can cross paths and learn enough about others to decide whether a person is *simpático* and a *persona interesante*. Avoiding interaction within the club itself is the established institutional way to transmit the opposite feeling. Without a doubt, the social and ethnic stereotypes are active; they are dropped only if the person proves to be exceptional from the point of view of social manners and local standards. In exclusive social clubs, competition is apparent, and it is not strange to find a person left in a social vacuum surrounded by the club's cliques (*grupitos*). On the other hand, if the person has political power, economic position, or other available resources, the isolation is less noticeable; but it becomes evident that there is a "relationship of interest" (*interesados*) that is played around the new person.

The attitude of members clearly manifests a lack of corporate sentiments. Members expect organizations to maintain the proper social status and to provide them with avenues to high social standing and social brilliancy. Generally people do not come to a club to make something out of it or to give of their personal prestige or status; rather they expect to receive from the club services and social standing. People with corresponding social images expect each other to behave within the club according to their social class.

The aims and activities of the club do not promote group integration. With the exception of the Club Social, organizations seem unable to foster sufficient loyalty and group cohesiveness. A general survey of organizations shows many different degrees, particularly when the consciousness of oneness is a criterion for the formalization of groups; associations, clubs, and *ligas* are only quasi-groups in this sense. Social, ideological, and intellectual interests bring people together, and potentially each group may become socially corporate. Participants seem to be more apt to make formal associations and to behave in the style of members of a crowd. Organizations have fluctuated. Only a handful of associations, particularly at the upper level of society, have enclosed themselves within social and psychological boundaries. There exists the predominant feeling that club members, as well as *vecinos*, form an aggregate of people formally organized.

Vecindad and Beyond 167

For the socially ambitious individuals, associations are viewed as a means to an end. They are part of the general social scale and tightly interlocked with the principle of social classes. This *campo de acción* reinforces the fundamental principles of stratification. The social entanglement is complex, resulting in social sensitivity characteristic in this city at this juncture of its history. The superabundance of organizations in which people may come together in various degrees of permanency makes all this possible.[10]

In conclusion, it is evident that *vecindad* is an elusive concept in this Argentine city. In the minds of the inhabitants, life within the city's boundaries is marked by a lack of corporateness and obligations among neighbors. Social formality promotes avoidance; it is difficult for newcomers to begin interaction. Much must be learned before *confianza* is established. Then the knowledge may prevent sociability. Yet readiness to perform favors is expected at critical moments in the life of a neighboring family.

The construction of houses and the walled patios foster family seclusion and secrecy. The family social activity is internal, personal, and hidden from the neighbor's view. Furthermore, seldom do neighbors borrow or lend freely. If such behavior does take place, it implies strong ties like those between relatives. Otherwise it can be taken as

---

[10] Some of the voluntary associations and clubs may at times have participated in politics. Presently, political activity is a personal matter. Political propaganda is centered in the headquarters of each political party, and no formal connection is evident between voluntary associations and political headquarters. The social, recreational, and mutual roles of the association take precedence. Argentina's political life has been in constant flux since the Perón regime and that which is apparent at one period of time is not so at another. A systematic social history of the voluntary associations in Argentine cities is therefore needed. The inadvisability at the time of the study of becoming involved in political activities (in political headquarters or labor unions) was very evident. Anthropological research subsidized from outside the country placed upon the author restrictions he chose to observe. Thus many questions concerning political life cannot be answered, although the reader will find sufficient information to see the overall pattern within a city, a pattern that finds its roots in the past.

Labor unions cannot be expected to be very active in an administrative type city. Paranaenses are not concerned with labor union activities, whereas in industrialized cities of Argentina unions represent a powerful political bloc. At the time of the field work, no one broached the subject of labor unions or their relation to the social setting of Paraná, although there were many opportunities for doing so during informal visiting and interviewing.

an intrusion on privacy, and annoyance can be subtly expressed by hesitancy and tardiness in responding to the request, or by making excuses.

Without a doubt, the variety of ethnic, economic, educational, and social class backgrounds obstructs the development of close and corporate neighborhoods. When interaction occurs on a casual or informal basis, the code of good manners takes precedence, and at all levels the ideal is to maintain a good conversation about local or national political events, business trends, or social problems. By contrast, in the clubs conversation can be light. Jokes, women's talk about clothing, shopping, family events, and social and political gossip are common topics for conversation. The type of club (whether it is a neighborhood or a city club) of course determines the nature and the dynamics of the conversation.

No doubt the importance of having companions in public places motivates people to join clubs, associations, and centers. But these do not seem to be conducive to meeting new people or to making new contacts. A newcomer finds it difficult to break the social shell in his neighborhood; the task is no simpler within the clubs.

The neighborhood constitutes an important social matrix for children and adults, and clubs and associations link individuals from different walks of life. Neither setting seems to develop a sense of community or a collective representation. On the contrary, there seems to exist a very strong social atomism, perhaps supported by the world view. Personal reserve paralyzes further development of social intimacy and reliance upon each other as *vecinos*. It may be that this case in some ways supports the metaphor of sociologists like Brooks Adams, who said that "society was becoming a dust heap of individuals without links to one another."[11]

[11] Homans 1950:457.

Entre Ríos: From the Country to the City

Entre Ríos Countryside

Approaching Paraná

Entering the City

A Tobacco Farmer beside His Home

A Russian-German Farmer

Farmyard of a Russian-German Family

The Country and the City

The City Seen from across the River

The City: From the Plaza to the Barrios

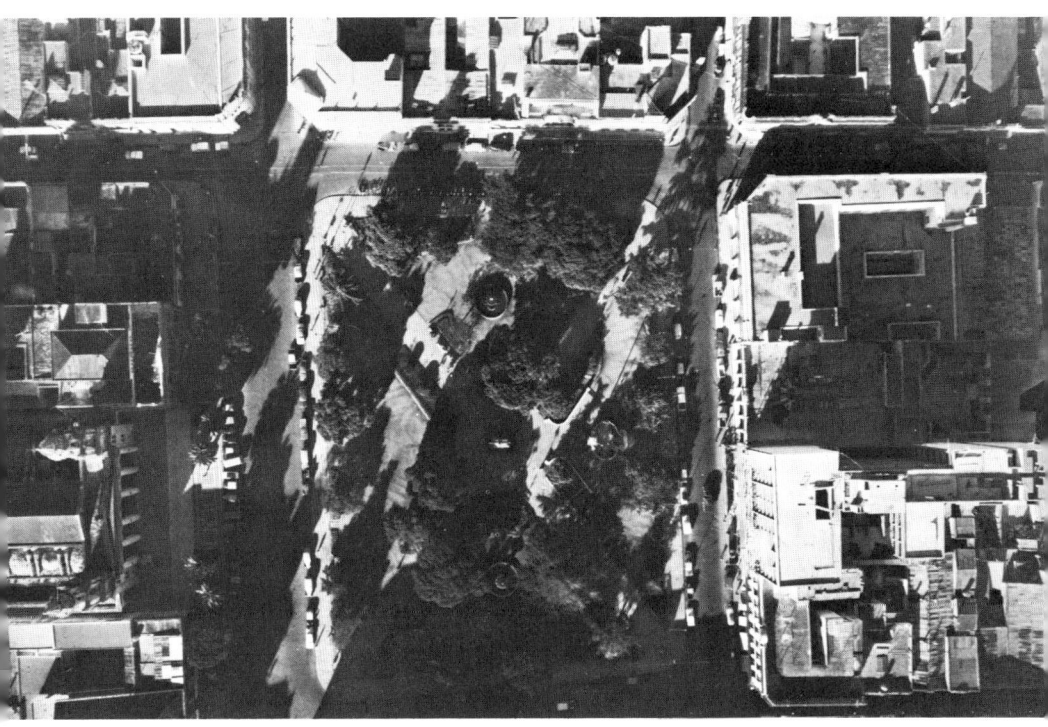

La Plaza Central: The Heart of the City

The Cathedral after Eleven O'Clock Sunday Mass

City Hall (*right*) and the Normal School

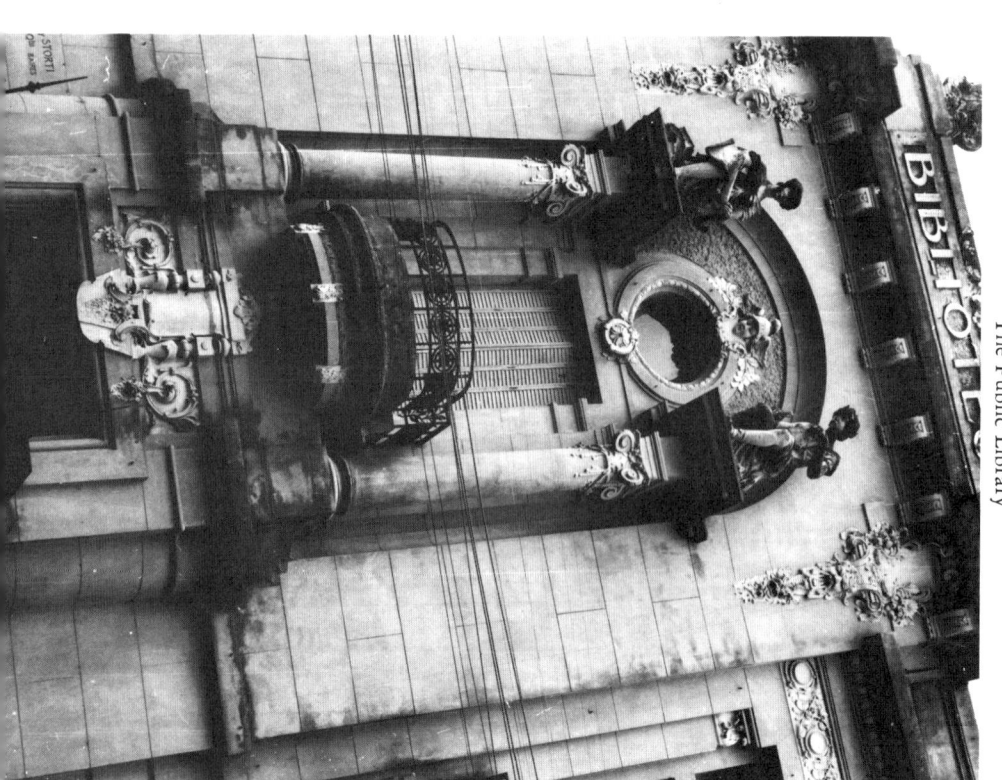

The Public Library

Second-Floor Residence of a Socially Prominent Family

Club Social

Traditional Residences in the Central Part of the City

Traditional Residences

"Modern Style" Residences Overlooking the Paraná River

Asociación Español, Showing Spanish-Moorish Influence

Residences of Early Basque Immigrants

Residences Farther Away from the Plaza

25. Modest Middle-Class Homes with "Modern" Architectural Details

Rancho Homes of the *Clase Baja* on the Edge of the City

Barriada of *Rancho* Homes

Fisherman's Home along the River

Vecindad Life

A Middle-Class *Vecindad*

Retailing Soda Water House-to-House

Green-Vegetable Seller

Milk Delivery

Carnival Water-Throwing Game among *Vecino* Children

Public Celebrations

ival Pageantry

Funeral Procession Leaving the Cathedral

...oration of the Mass at the Statue of Justo
... de Urquiza

Participants and Spectators in Observance of a National Holiday

III. Principles of Social Organization

> People . . . are very prone to differentiate themselves and others, and even those of us who most piously affirm man's basic equality cling tenaciously to privilege and rank. (John J. Honigmann, *Personality in Culture*, p. 133)

6. SOCIAL CLASS: THE BASIC MODEL FOR SOCIAL ORGANIZATION

Clases alta, media, and *baja* have been in the past and continue to be a powerful principle for separating people and things; it is an overall model of operational importance. The situation, however, is not so simple as portrayed by the model; it is, after all, an abbreviation of a very complex historical phenomenon, but it is a manageable model for everyone's daily existence, and a way to order and lump together large numbers of city residents who in turn acknowledge their social standing in life. Each level sets a normative orientation that individuals must adopt.

This chapter contains only profiles of the behavioral environment for each of the three classes. The reader will notice that the data presented to describe each of the social levels are not comparable. Instead, for each level the style of its own image is stressed. Since the material is organized in terms of the image from within, I have allowed the theme for each social category to emerge as much as possible in its own natural way. The lack of parallel material, particularly in such traditional areas as religion or political interest, illustrates the differences in each level's orientation and world view.

Clase Baja

The area of the city inhabited by the poor people is reminiscent of a rural setting; it is a pleasant environment of barrios and *barriadas*, not comparable to the *favelas* of Rio de Janeiro or the *villas miserias* of Buenos Aires. The appearance in Paraná is modest but relatively neat. Some houses are built of brick with a fence and a courtyard; others are the traditional *rancho entrerriano*, with or without fences. The general appearance of these barrios resembles a small rural settlement of earlier historical periods.

The reliable laborer, the poor rural immigrant, the person who gives up the search for steady work, the lazy, the lonesome and discontented, the foreigner without resources or friends, and the exploiters—all reside in such neighborhoods. Outsiders refer to all persons of the *clase baja* as criollos or *los negros*, implying a behavioral distinction for this "race." Although black hair and dark skin prevail among these people, they are far from being truly black, and the term *negro* has a social rather than a racial meaning.

In these areas, life moves at a relaxed pace. Some children attend school, while others may work as newspaper boys, shoeshine boys, or simply help with the household chores. The father may be a construction worker, garbage collector, sweeper, janitor, watchman for the *municipalidad*, or a laborer in the nearby tile factory. Those who are not permanently employed but work sporadically are known as *changadores*. Women take care of the household and sometimes, on a part-time basis, wash and iron for middle-class families.

Most frequently the homes consist of only one room and a kitchen but occasionally they may have two rooms. Most houses stand on municipal land. Facilities like running water, sewers, and electricity are not always provided; children and women fetch water from an outdoor spigot. Carrying water and going to the store are part of the traditional *mandado* pattern, which keeps the children occupied. There are no clubhouses in this area, although a small *boliche* (bar) may attract men to gather for drinking and card playing. Only a few men venture to a nearby barrio club; besides wine-drinking and card-playing facilities, the clubs may also have *bochas* courts and sponsor weekend dances.

The city people of the higher classes usually come into contact with the people of the *clase baja* as domestic servants or laborers. In a few cases upper-class people may have a fairly accurate view of these people's way of life, but more likely they perceive the *clase baja* as a conglomeration of people of *mal vivir* (low standards). Center-city residents feel that a lack of *cultura* and low morals make the lower class persons undesirable and even dangerous.[1] Undoubtedly, there are considerable variations within the *clase baja*, but the general model of the criollo way of life, that of a poor rural existence, is widely held. In reality, the life of these people is not well known outside their class. Accessibility to such information would demand close association, something that others consider undesirable. The simplicity of life and the old technology used for building houses in the low-class barrios indicate to the city residents poverty and social problems. The range of variation in conduct and sophistication passes unnoticed by the other classes; they perceive a homogeneous situation tinted by a low economic standing. But much diversity exists among the *clase baja*. Variations exist without proper recognition, but the stereotype overshadows the social and cultural reality to a casual observer.

A Fisherman of the *Clase Baja*

On the bank of the Paraná River, on land that belongs to the municipality, in one-room *ranchitos* live the fishermen of the lower class. As long as the weather is good, much of the daily activity occurs outdoors in the courtyard. People are received and entertained under the trees or in other shady places. While sitting and conversing with friends, one observes activities on the river and in the neighborhood. Adults dominate the scene; the father and mother carry on the conversation with other adults, while children watch passively and quietly. Usually, to entertain an outsider, the father will order some-

[1] I was, for example, advised by a city elite person not to trust the people of the barrios on account of their unpredictable behavior.

one to bring the family pictures, particularly those of the children's first communion and family weddings.

One fisherman lived in a one-room *ranchito* with a small outdoor kitchen and a latrine. His wife, from the Chaco province, was of Indian descent, and they were legally married during one of his trips to the north. A sixteen-year-old daughter helped the mother with the smaller children; a younger daughter lived in a *vecindad* of the city with an aunt (the father's sister), who had married well. Because of the *vecindad* style of life, she was now of the *clase media* and, from the father's point of view, well-to-do.

The fisherman spoke very proudly of the daughter in his sister's house who was receiving a good education for a better way of life. He said, "My sister is helping me to raise my large family. My daughter comes to us on holidays and on her birthday to celebrate with us, and she shares a well-made cake with her brothers and sisters." The older daughter had just finished the sixth grade, and the father again indicated his happiness: "I do not want her to work as a maid now. I'd rather she stayed at home helping her mother until she gets married. She's now the fiancée of a boy who helps me with fishing. He is still a minor, and his mother is separated from her husband. In order to marry, permission from the father is necessary, but no one knows where he is, so the boy will have to wait until he becomes twenty-one." The couple would like to live in another city, but only temporarily; the return seems necessary because, as the daughter remarked, "When one is sick, one needs to be near one's family." At the time of Carnaval, the family goes to the center city and enjoys the parade of masqueraders and floats. The older daughter attends a neighborhood club dance with her fiancé.

When the fishing was good, this independent river fisherman paddled his canoe upstream several hours each day, setting his lines across the wide river and alternating supervision of them with throwing his nets in clean areas used collectively by several fishermen, called *playas de pesca* (beaches for fishing). He joined the other fishermen there, where each took his turn at combing the beach.

There were times of the year when fish were not abundant in the river. He then helped in the maintenance of nearby weekend homes or worked in the construction of modest houses. On one occasion when no work was available, the informant was chatting in his home and shouted to a fisherman passing in a canoe, "*¿y de ahá?*" implying "what happened?" Since this was a poor season for fishing, the answer was "nothing." The informant then explained that knowing this would be the outcome of the day, he, therefore, had stayed home. There was too much wind in the early morning, and the water was too cold for fishing. "However," he said, "I feel ashamed to be at home all day doing little, but if there are no fish, why should one spend one's energy and be cold in these winter months?"

When the famous *surubí* and *el dorado* come down from the northern tropical regions of Paraguay, fishermen together might spend several nights on the river islands. Each day one man would take a trip to the beaches of the city with the fresh fish and, after selling them to the middlemen (daily waiting at the beaches in the late afternoon), proceed to buy supplies, report to the families of the other fishermen the good news and well-being of the men, and then return to join the rest.

Some of these fishermen took their sons with them. A twelve-year-old boy was already capable of remaining on the island in the company of other fishermen, and parents felt proud of this. If he happened to lose an expensive net at the bottom of the river because he misjudged the beach, the incident was taken as part of the process of learning and he was, therefore, not punished.

At home, men do not help in the kitchen; but while fishing on the islands, they prepare their own food, usually meat and vegetables boiled in a common pot by all the fishermen. *Mate* is passed around all day, but no wine or liquor is drunk. The men usually talk about incidents of the past, difficulties with large fish, and speculate on the conditions of the river and the weather. The fishermen spend several nights at work, and if there is little success in relation to their efforts, then "one becomes upset. When we have no good results, everyone is nervous although each tries not to show his feelings. One tries to take an hour's sleep until the turn comes, but it is difficult to rest because of the tension. Some may doze for a few minutes, but one is constantly afraid to miss his turn by sleeping. So, the nervous system is tired under normal conditions, but it is even worse when fishing is poor."

A fisherman, in order to be well-equipped for his activities during the entire year, has to invest approximately 150,000 pesos, that is about 1,000 U.S. dollars, to have nets of different types, hooks, camping equipment, and canoe. Financially, the fisherman can never be ahead, but he can cover expenses if he lives modestly. However, the informant fisherman knows what good standards of living are and would like to improve his own. He blames the inflationary trend and political instability for his general lack of progress. "I cannot get ahead and, therefore, we have to continue to live a very humble life."

His social manners have a touch of sophistication. He is, however, reserved with strangers and rather distrustful of any person who acts with *orgullo* (haughtiness). Once a relationship is established, there is warm and friendly interaction, usually with the sharing of food and *mate*. Eventually the constantly used phrase "Excuse us, because we are poor" begins to disappear. In a sincere friendship, social inequalities can be overlooked.

These fishermen are very alert and can verbalize their thinking quite well. They are relatively well-informed, but they find no time to visit the downtown area of the city. Their information comes through various middlemen. One fisherman was surprised to learn of a new, impressive hotel being built near the main plaza.

This description is presented as only one example of the *clase humilde*, sometimes referred to by middle and upper groups as *negros*.[2] It is more representative of the fisherman style of life and less representative of people who have not acquired a skill. The fishermen have a steady occupation in comparison with others of the same class who work sporadically. The informant thinks of himself as a man of the *clase humilde*, but he is proud of his achievements as a fisherman. Because of the nature of his work, he is in touch only with certain aspects of the market system and of life in the city, as he perceives them from a distance. Only for Carnaval does he go with his wife

---

[2] It should be pointed out that people of this class refer to themselves as *clase humilde*; the higher classes call them *baja* or *negro*.

and family to the city proper and then only to that section of the city (Echagüe Avenue) prepared to receive the *gente del pueblo*.

"*Clase Baja*" in the City

Further interaction with the people of the *clase baja* brought other insights into their way of life and thinking. Newspaper boys and girls from the barrio criollo families spend most of the day and evening in the streets of the city; shoeshine boys and men also spend most of their working hours around the central plaza. Errand boys may help in small businesses and commute daily from their barrio to the downtown area or live with the families of their employers for an entire week. Some beggars and garbage combers appear in the downtown section of the city in their daily rounds.

The independent young shoeshine or newspaper boys usually plan to get steady employment; in their daily routines they come in contact with customers who could give them the opportunity to advance. Stories of such good fortune abound, and though the reality may be different at least the contact in the streets is possible. Thus, hopes motivate these young people to wait for a long time. While young, they maintain a good degree of optimism, hoping that someone will trust them and offer them the chance of their lives. So, the theme of "losing many great opportunities" to make good money and to live with comforts is recurrent in their conversations with clients. Frequently, they learn about openings in hotels or other service establishments around the plaza, and they make a formal or informal contact. Then they are told to wait until called. They will wait patiently, sometimes for several years, hoping that one opening or another will materialize; through "friends" or the local political leader they may eventually find a permanent job. As the years go by, though, personal resentment increases and, if all attempts have failed and "society" thus disappoints them, they become apathetic. They feel rejected and find support in associating with others who have had similar experiences. Some entertain the idea of migrating to a bigger city, such as Buenos Aires, but as a shoeshine boy remarked, "If with acquaintances here, I cannot find decent employment, what will I do alone in an unknown place?"

The people of this group make a simple social distinction between themselves and the rest of the people of Paraná. The people in the city proper are all lumped together into a single category, probably as a consequence of the social insularity of this poorest class. For them, there is a duality: *los ricos* and *los pobres*. Anyone who lives *arriba* (in the city) is considered better off economically, and regardless of the amount of wealth he might have, he is placed among *los ricos*. The economic subcategories that exist in the middle class and the very basic distinction between the middle category and the traditional families are irrelevant in their thinking. This conception of the dual class system is an oversimplification of the political and economic situation, but may be practical from their own point of view.

When these people come in touch with the intricacy of an urban society, often they feel unjustly treated. There was much resentment in one case when children were sent home from school by the teacher (high in the middle class) to change their white uniforms because they looked dirty. The father felt much shame (*vergüenza*) and explained that he was an honest person, which could be proven by the fact that he had not been in court yet. But in the winter, it was difficult to wash and iron the one white garment every day. Such circumstances arouse bitterness and class antagonism. The *clase baja* people distrust the entire political organization and the political leaders. "There is," one informant said, "a lack of patriotism among us; one knows that through politics people can become wealthy."

The failure to organize themselves for "community" programs is well known. Fourteen *vecinos* were selected by the city government to cooperate in the plans for improvement of their barrio. The committee successfully collected money and sponsored dances to raise funds for improvements—primarily to provide running water and electricity in the houses. The committee accumulated eighteen thousand pesos, but the city officials did not act as agreed. Fearing the money would be lost, the group decided to spend it on a fiesta for children at which toys and sweets were distributed. That was the end of the committee.

The city government has also attempted to organize associations and chapters of political parties to provide centers for meetings and

Social Class: The Basic Model

recreation. None of the programs succeeded totally. After hours of work in the city or in the barrios, the life of these people is at home or visiting friends and relatives.

In matters of politics, the *clase baja* men tend to lean toward the holders of power. Peronismo, as might be expected, had much support in this area, but it did not bring about basic changes in the style of life and thinking. Many items given in assistance by the Eva Perón Foundation (sewing machines, beds, mattresses) were soon sold and the proceeds spent on food and wine. Peronismo, however, continues to symbolize for them the true spirit of patriotism.

One senses a level of simplicity as people of the *clase baja* interpret the city's social stratification. Even individuals who have associated with important families and have observed the style of life in other homes view the situation practically and simply. There is, for instance, the case of a mature criolla woman who for many years has been in the domestic service of the upper-class families of the city. Thirty-five years ago she moved from a farm to Paraná. Having lost her Indian mother at an early age, she spent the rest of her growing years with an older sister. With a child out of wedlock, she came to work for a second-class city hotel. After a few years she found the work too hard and left this first job to start working as a servant for some families in the city, particularly those residing in the downtown area. With her earnings she bought a small piece of land outside the city and built herself a modest house in the traditional style. Her daughter was brought up in one of the city's Catholic schools and is now married and lives near Buenos Aires. In conversation she expressed herself in the following way:

> After I left the hotel, I began to work for a family of *sociedad* [meaning high class], and the *patrón* was a person of high level in a company. I think that they were old families [patricians] in the city. This person was not the same as the first *patrón* I had in the hotel, who was not of *sociedad*. I worked later on for other city families and they all were, more or less, like the second *patrón*. I think that they are all of first *categoría* in society. These people, in general, are different because they have education and they have important ancestors. Recently, I have been working for the relative of an important leader in Argentina and I am happy. The people in the city are

divided into first, second, and third *categoría*. Of course, there are very low people, but those people are the beggars and they do other bad things. They are altogether another type of people, people who go for wine and laziness. My barrio is made up of people from the country and they are very criollo; we are all modest, because we are people from the country, and some have Italian or German blood. The people in the second and the last group became Peronistas in Perón's time, while the people of the first categories, my *patrones*, were for the freedom of the people. The governors are usually from the first *categoría*; servants are from the third *categoría*, and some of them have caused a great deal of disgust to their *patrones*.

Her general attitude toward people and life is very peaceful, and she usually agrees with persons speaking to her, particularly if their status is high. She calls herself mestiza because her mother was Indian and her father of Spanish descent. She places herself in the group of the *gente criolla*, and in the social group of the *humildes*. Her *patrón* remarked that she is of the *clase baja*, and added that, as a person, she is exceptional and can be trusted; she is alert, and in general her personal qualities bring her high esteem.

This woman's view of the social stratification of the city is manageable and follows the usual pattern of the three levels. Being at the bottom, she speaks of *categoría*, rather than social class, and of *humildes* rather than *clase baja*. She recognizes variations among people in the *clase baja*, but explains it in terms of personality.

For people of the *clase humilde* only a few personal acquaintances form the basis of their social orientation. Their understanding of the social structure is limited, inaccurate, and frequently difficult to explain. In the background of much political turmoil and general economic uncertainties in 1965, these people remained generally peaceful, as if they were watching another "political show." After Perón, they were left out once more, and their feeling was that whatever politicians said did not go beyond the word itself. To remain relatively poorly informed has its advantages; it permits one to continue his day-to-day existence, hoping for economic gains through more labor benefits. One need not plan to improve his material well-being; one can lead a life revolving around the immediate family and the barrio. The *clase baja* is physically in the city, but psychologically they are outsiders. They watch the gross political movements and understand only portions of the national and local events. They see the government as the organization totally responsible for solving their economic problems. And the quiet feeling of exploitation prevails.

In the matter of religion, the *clase baja* people are not institutionally oriented. By tradition, they belong to the Catholic Church and have been baptized. Religion is something very personal, and the basic doctrines of the Church are only partially understood. Interest in religion is very low, and only the general aspects of religion and the rites of passage (baptism, first communion, marriage, death) are matters for concern. The attitude toward death is one of resignation, and many of them feel that it is not even worth attending a funeral. "Once one is dead, one is dead!" replied one man when invited to attend a funeral in the house of a neighbor.

The *creencias* (superstitions) are many among the people of the *clase baja*. There are many incidents and signs in nature indicating future events in a person's life. One should know some of these things in order to do what is proper at the appropriate time. This is one way to avoid crises. The crying of an owl at night is a bad omen; to counteract it one must go outside and insult the bird or say the phrase "*la yeta*" (the bad omen is for you). Then one must make the sign of the cross. Salt spilled on the table means that there will be a disagreement with relatives. The amount of salt spilled predicts the seriousness of the problem. There are hundreds of combinations of elements used to predict life events. Interesting is the fact that most of them are known and used by people of other social categories.[3]

The death of children can be the result of the evil eye (*mal de ojo*) by which means a person in possession of strong power bewitches people. If someone causes a death, he does not necessarily do it intentionally, although it might be related to envy. The accounts of beautiful children who were looked at by envious people and became ill afterward suffice to prove the point. The combination of envy and evil eye can also cause the death of a *vecino*'s animal.

To be *engüalichado* means that something has been done magically

---

[3] Many of the superstitions can be traced to Europe.

by a *curandero*, on behalf of another person, to make a loved one reciprocate affection. The curers are naturally gifted individuals and obliged to use their gifts for the benefits of their fellow men. "Doctors cannot cure certain things," remarked an informant, "they do not know how to do it; only the *curanderos* or *curanderas* can perform the curing." So when the death of a child is believed to be because of the evil eye, *vecinos* blame the mother for carelessness and for not using the services of a curer in time. The curer can also treat *empachos*, which is anything from minor indigestion and loss of appetite, to more serious difficulties. The cure is simple: the curer assesses the *empacho* and usually pulls the skin in the back of the child. The illness is cured if there is faith, claimed an informant of this class who believes in the power of individuals to cure: "I have faith, *veia señor pa' que decirlo*. She was a very beautiful young lady; she cured me of *empacho* and urinary difficulties from one day to the next, but she married, and then she stopped curing because she loves her husband more than her power." The *curanderos* also have prayers and formulae to help the curing: herbs, salt, and sugar used in special ways help to keep peace within a family.

Many other aspects of the general world view could be studied through the specialist who supports and encourages individuals of this social class to think and behave according to these folk traditions. A *curandera* residing in a barrio served her people as well as those from the middle class who accepted many of the basic principles with which she works. Excerpts of an interview with her as she read a team member's future illustrate aspects of the world view that she shares with her own clients.

I am going to look into your future, and there is a little bit of difficulty in your personal life. You are preoccupied, you are anxious and fighting within yourself; this can be the triumph in your life. But you are preoccupied with something. You must think carefully about what I am saying. You had a trip, worries of documents, for some business. . . .

What is embracing you with your five senses?[4] Is your wife pregnant? I think that she is, that she is sick in her reproductive organs and that is the

[4] She repeats this phrase each time she is ready to change the subject.

reason she is not well. She's very weak. Many difficulties, . . . many difficulties because you used to live a very happy life with another woman and now she's married. You cannot get her out of your mind. You think of her and you are preoccupied with that person.

This is the pattern she follows as she throws cards and comes out with more answers. She usually speaks about problems in personal life, trips, anxiety, lack of sleep, sexual problems, house building, illnesses, suggestions to get a wife pregnant, ways to beget a male child, friendships, enemies, future business, etc. In the end, everything seems to come out well if the client follows her advice. Prayers and herbal preparations of her own can be used for help. She is usually very quick with words and boasts of successfully predicting illnesses, cures, or political events. Our informant indicated that she sees the formulas written on the walls and this, she says, is something strange "since I don't know how to read or write. But I know the nature of those formulas." When she receives the formula, then she knows what to tell the client on subsequent visits. The person may come for the first time and later can just send someone with a written message. The *curandera* searches the future in it and sends a verbal message back to the client. The informant was careful to indicate that she does not work on abortions, but she can help anyone to *engüalichar* (enchant) the person who is responsible for a pregnancy and does not want to be married.[5]

In the normative orientation of the people of *clase baja*, nature plays a vital role; some of their basic ideals, values, and standards spring from the fact that man is in nature and nature is in man. In conversation, analogies to well-known processes and facts of nature are frequently made. Often, for the sake of discussion, human beings are animalized and animals are humanized. The speech form varies when animals and objects are conceptualized as possessing something

---

[5] One of the local historians said that the *curandero* is "the true minister of the popular medicine, the man whom the pueblo trusts without fear or shame . . . knows all illnesses and all remedies . . . is like the doctors in spending hours on books. Sells life, foretells death to the hour and the minute . . . convinces and cures few, but confuses all and is always right" (Reula 1963:178).

that is human. In relation to philosophical generalizations about man, such analogies can be forceful and final. One cannot easily argue against these assumptions. The forces of nature and the mysteries of the universe are basic to their explanation of human existence.

Interpersonal Relationships

Generally, people of the *clase baja* are pessimistic about the nature of human relations. The theme that it is better for each *vecino* to be in his own home indicates a general atomization of human relations. There are many persons who are considered crafty (*pícaro*), envious (*envidioso*), and ingrateful (*desagradecido*). Certain of these personal traits were accentuated in Perón's period. Nevertheless, one should be able to trust and assist relatives (*parientes*). Acquaintances beyond the nuclear family are viewed with reservation. Although it is impolite to show one's true attitude, the reservation precludes complete trust or *confianza*.

Adjectives used for the evaluation of human behavior emphasize the "good" or "bad" nature of a person. Older people speak of rambunctious youngsters as *mal educado* (badly brought up), *muy peleadores* (fighters), *medio loco* (half crazy), *malo como un perro* (bad as a dog), *incorrigible* (unmanageable), *charlatán* (gossiper), and *haragan* (lazy). These insulting clichés may be applied to children, adults, or to groups of *vecinos*.

In the barrio, people may speak with contempt about *vecinos*. A barrio has all types of individuals, remarked an informant: there are *gente humilde mala*, people who do not leave others alone, people who live like *indios* (a stereotype for those living a near-animal existence); then there are *gente humilde buena* who mind their own business (*no se meten con nadie*); and finally, in between, *gente humilde regular*. Yet, a *vecino* may become a confidant and then be classed as a "brother," that is, an intimate friend, but everyone agrees that nowadays "brothers" are very scarce.

In this modest setting, the dignity of man, here associated with the criollo style of life, stands out as a valued characteristic. Economic shortcomings may be overlooked, and a person may say, "I am a criollo and live like one," or "I live like a criollo in the city." It is not historically accurate, but this image of themselves helps to give them a sense of spiritual well-being.

People of the lower class see themselves as a different race, and this keeps them apart from the rest. As such, they conceive of themselves as correct and intelligent, yet inferior and physically different because of their dark or weathered skin. They believe that these traits are biologically inherited and exist in their own blood at birth. Therefore, they accept their fate in life; one knows from birth what he is and that his social place is determined. Material surroundings may be changed, a house may be improved, but the social image remains constant. Behaving with dignity constitutes a significant part of the traditional criollo value system within the basic concern of *hacer la vida*, making a living.

The individuals of the *clase baja* play on the concept of dignity. This concept in itself brings about a very different self-image from that of slum dwellers. This is most obvious when they interact with outsiders. Dignity means seriousness. Cleanliness, proper clothing, proper speech are other important elements in their value system; one lives in poverty, but with dignity. If these duties are not met properly because of neglect, lack of economic means, ignorance, or laziness, the internal differentiation becomes significant. Extreme families, who receive the name of *tirados*, exist below all human dignity and often are compared to animals by a well-off and respectable criollo family. The better people, in contrast, have steady employment and a modest one-room brick house; children attend primary school; contacts with *patrones* are maintained to keep avenues open for children.

The family, the friend, and the *patrón* are three institutionalized spheres of interaction that demand constant attention. The criollo feels it necessary to manipulate relationships to his own advantage, and thus to derive economic, social, and psychological rewards. These manipulations, usually verbal, counteract the criollo's feeling of being continuously exploited and always having to guard his dignity. The strength of the theme of guarding oneself and those things with which one truly identifies is such that group relations are difficult to establish, let alone to maintain. To be left alone is ideal, but on the other hand one cannot live alone. Association with others is predicated on the assumption that one relates to others in order to reach specific material or nonmaterial goals. It follows then, that when a relationship no longer serves, it is discarded as useless.

From these basic premises one can determine his psychological state and social position and predict a series of disappointments for himself and his family. The values in his own world view do not bring him personal security; instead, he is faced with the fear that he can be left alone in the world.[6]

Clase Media

As one moves from the outskirts (the barrios) toward the plaza, the styles of houses change and the way of life seems less rural. A larger proportion of people in this section of the city are of recent European ancestry, some only one generation in Argentina. During the massive immigration of Italians, Germans, Swiss, and Spaniards in the late nineteenth and early twentieth centuries, the *clase media* became a definite group in the city and was later augmented by rural migrants. Ideally, the *clase baja* is residentially associated with barrio, while the *clase media* is associated primarily with *vecindad* and *vecindario*.

In contrast to people above and below them, the *clase media* presents a greater variety of ethnic, economic, occupational, and educational backgrounds. Informants noted, however, that "in general the *clase media* are all the same"; an examination indicated the reverse. Furthermore, these people are mostly guided by stereotypes that are linked to differences in income, education, ethnicity, and place of residence in the city. Social judgment is colored by social discrimination, differentiation, evaluation, and competition that underlie the rather superficial layer of unity.

As in the case of the *clase baja*, the *clase media* can be subdivided into several economic levels. There are *personas bien* of the *clase media* (entrepreneurs and professionals) who model themselves after the upper class. Their aspirations and standards are so high that few

[6] Henry Schwarz III, while a graduate student at the University of Pennsylvania, was a research assistant in the study of Paraná. He gathered data on the *clase baja* by direct participation and observation during the year of field work. Some of the findings from his 1966 manuscript report have been incorporated into this section.

Social Class: The Basic Model

families can meet them in full. Education, particularly secondary education, is important in their lives. Then there are the *empleados* and small entrepreneurs of the *clase media*; they model themselves on the life style adopted and adapted by the first group in the middle class. Finally, the poorest and least-educated people, laborers, are not far removed from the *clase baja*, and their life style is frequently indistinguishable from that of the people of the barrios. Nevertheless, Paranaenses still perceive a fairly uniform general image of an individual of the *clase media*.

The basic cultural assumptions supporting class distinction and the constant pressure to evaluate and classify families socially have developed strong social sensitivity in the middle classes. Very prevalent is the unceasing concern with problems that arise from the social stratification system of the city. The bases for evaluating individuals and locating them on the economic and social continuum weigh heavily upon their minds.

Persons of the *clase media* with an intellectual interest enjoy getting involved in discussions about class distinction, status differences, participation in voluntary groups, degree and definition of *cultura*, and etiquette. Their arguments express the feeling that differences among human beings need to exist. Distinguishing and separating those below poses no problem, but seeing the differences between themselves and those above is a difficult intellectual exercise. Consequently, members of the *clase media* do not readily agree about social classification. It seems as if distinctions should be very real, but at the same time, in the mind, the lines are not clearly demarcated. The criteria are indeed many, and the number of possible combinations hinders quick and easy perception.

One informant defined those in the *clase media* as people struggling economically who "in poverty have saved, have acquired property, and have been able to achieve some degree of comfort. By the same token, they are individuals who have lived an exemplary life, have taken pains to educate their children, and so have brought *cultura* into their homes. They have consecrated themselves to hard work for the achievement of the younger generation. They are indeed the *buenos vecinos de la ciudad*."

The degree of social sophistication is an important variable among the people of the aspiring *clase media*. One aspect of this is the distinction between those who do not work with their hands and those who do. The professionals and semiprofessionals—teachers and office workers in government or business—constitute the upper level of the middle class; the others—carpenters, mechanics, chauffeurs, janitors, small entrepreneurs—are at the other end of the social spectrum.

A new person coming into the city to establish residence raises the curiosity of his *vecinos*; his economic position is guessed, and if it is on a par with the neighborhood, everything goes smoothly. Source and amount of income are important determining elements; particularly it is important to learn what a neighbor does with his money. This always provides a good index from which *vecinos* can speculate on the quality of another human being. The economic variable is an important one, even more so than intellectual ability. If the person can afford a great deal more than those around him, this will arouse envy and social separation, and the simple formula that one with money associates with others with money and that one without it associates with another on an equal level is substantiated. When a stranger moves into the neighborhood, there may be awkward moments as some *vecinos* seek social opportunity through him.

When in the public eye, there is self-consciousness; the individual attends to himself, to his elegance, to his proper behavior and speech. Proper choices of friends and proper public behavior are seen as expressions of the individual's responsibility and good citizenship. By the same token, improper behavior and appearance can be taken to indicate social irresponsibility, deception, lack of patriotism—an uncomfortable and burdensome social background with which no family would wish to live. It has become usual to apply the criteria of *cultura*, half *cultura*, or no *cultura* as sure indicators of distinction within the middle economic group. The common assumption is that the economic level and *cultura* should correspond. When specific cases are considered, however, the correlation does not always hold. There are well-off people without *cultura*, and there are poor people with *cultura*.

An individual searching for recognition of his achievement of *cultura* tends not to be humble and frequently distinguishes himself for his dogmatic assertions. The amount of *cultura* seems to correlate with the ability to communicate verbally an image of one's level of literacy. Discussion is not so much a matter of logic as one of passionate involvement and personal belief. Economic level, degree of education, and occupation of ancestors are additional variables that act upon the individual's social standing.

In the *clase media* each family unit is identical in structure, although the intellectual resources, the economic level, and the degree of formal training bring about fundamental differences in the family's life style. The absence of a strong religious or political attachment, which might engender uniform principles of action, leaves the individual to his own cultural development. The family is the only place where one can freely entertain a private point of view; ideally, adult members of a family must tolerate each other, even when they hold widely divergent opinions. Each person knows that some views are proper within the household and others are for the street and public places. Social success is related to the use of each in its proper situation.

Voluntarismo (will) does not seem to be a normative concept in this sector of society. Relationship implies personal benefits and, by definition, one must be on guard since, sooner or later, one may find that any particular relationship was no more than a means to an end. Seeking intimacy soon after introduction or immediately on moving to a new neighborhood leaves the newcomer open to suspicion. It is therefore preferable to ignore others publicly by being more formal. When overdone, this brings forth the criticism that "he believes himself to be important" (*se las dá de importante*).

Education constitutes a means for economic, social, and cultural advancement. There are many cases that could be cited of parents who make a marked effort to prepare their children for higher social levels. One informant, who entertains high educational aspirations for her children, summarized the prevailing viewpoint of many who have been able to secure secondary education and like to display social manners and economic progress:

It is very important to place an individual. When I speak to a person, I can quickly capture his social status and his personal worth. The person speaks in a manner that I can recognize, and I can see something of his education [level of *cultura*], and quickly I know what he is. On this basis a person becomes *simpática* or *antipática*. Women are perhaps more sensitive to apparent social differences than men who need to be in daily contact with people. But the social levels must be distinguished. I have and keep my *ambiente*, my *círculo* [clique], and I will not go with another person to another *ambiente* where I cannot feel comfortable and congenial, although I am capable of behaving in just any *ambiente*.

The inability to acquire formal education precipitates a feeling of social inadequacy, and this can be accentuated if the person is not too far from a humble background of immigrant parents. Many parents in this class want their children to become professionals, so they do what they can, hoping that "with luck" they can provide their children with formal education—a degree is socially significant. In this way some parents who work hard and probably have secured the help of older siblings to put at least one child through university training can feel part of the son's success. Education is looked upon as an excellent investment, inasmuch as it should bring about a better life for all the members of the family through the one who acquires professional standing.

An individual feels strongly embarrassed by the other family members when they are unable to maintain what he considers the necessary social refinements. In some middle-class households, however, where many of the social and personal elements coincide, social peace exists: the parents and children are equally elegant, interested in theater and concerts, intelligent, well read, sophisticated, and generally aware of European *cultura*. Their formal education may not be the same, but each has acquired the correct social appearance, and there is pride in each other's social accomplishments. They may belong to city clubs and further accent the situation by their superior attitude toward *vecinos*.

There was the case of a widow who appeared in public with her daughters and son. They were all proud of each other; they have kept high standards by combining their economic resources, thus pulling together for the benefit of the household. No one became less than any other and there was a general predisposition to be more *cultos* (from *cultura*). They studied languages, participated in choir, and engaged in artistic activities. The family shared each other's friends, and the mother in particular provided entertainment for friends who were "adopted" into the household. The friends became extensions of the family, like her own children. The son and his friends frequently took the mother to public events and performances, while the daughters attended other activities with their friends. The sharing of friends by all members of the household is an important consideration in understanding this case, which stood in contrast to many others with an uneven household situation. "Where there is *cultura* and a desire by all members to achieve *cultura*, interpersonal relations are harmonious and social progress is attractive," declared an informant.

Cases like the above are not frequent. As a person ascends the social scale, he separates not only from his family, but also from his friends in the neighborhood. The following is a quotation from a conversation with a person of the ascending *clase media*:

Those boys in the neighborhood who have decided to study soon will separate from those boys who do manual labor. I, as a student in the Escuela Normal, no longer continue the companionship with those boys with whom I used to play and go to primary school. I have kept only one as a close friend. We used to be each other's shadow, but I face a problem now because he does not feel in *ambiente* with my student companions. It has become difficult and takes a great deal of work each time we appear together in public. He feels socially very inferior because he does not have sufficient education. He feels also that he should not continue going out with me, and a separation has come about lately; the separation is not caused by serious conflict.

The same process occurs between parents and children. When children surpass the level of the parents' education, there is then a feeling of not being of the same quality. Once children of an uneven family background start secondary school, parents may face problems. A son, for instance, may demand good clothes and freshly ironed white shirts, requiring excessive attention from his mother. He may go out and find *compañeros* in the plaza, be with them, but hide from them his family background, living conditions, and neighborhood. Parents worry over their son's whereabouts, types of friends, and loyalties. In one case, the mother cut many corners in the household economy to provide her son with secondary education. As the years passed, he became socially removed from the household. The mother felt that her son was "escaping" from her, and that she could not derive enjoyment from his development. The discomfort was obvious. From the mother's point of view, the son, now educated, had adopted a trend in his social life that could not be stopped. The son's behavior meant an emotional loss for the mother, as well as a loss of investment.

Children are frequently reminded that education represents sacrifice for the family; it is an investment, and a return is expected in the long run. In this sense, the acquisition of a degree constitutes a "medal" of achievement for the parents and for those who assisted in the support of the household. To have a child studying is a source of much pride for the parents, who build a monument to themselves in this way. On the other hand, the difference from one generation to another results in family tensions. Children often recognize the efforts of their parents, but they face some embarrassment in being professionally, economically, and—most important—socially distant from their parents' level. Only the high respect accorded parents by everyone in the society prevents a total breakdown.

One middle-class informant described the situation for middle-class families as unbalanced—*una situación muy desventajosa*. The generation gap nowadays is wide; at play there are feelings of inferior and superior intellectual capacity. First, there are many illiterate and almost illiterate parents in the middle economic classes; and when the children finish the sixth grade, some realize that their parents are judged by society as "inferior." It follows, then, that among children there is a definite consciousness of the ignorance of their parents. Emotionally the situation is most difficult when, on account of education, youths want to bring changes dividing a household.

One informant described a *vecino* who was born in Spain and had little formal education. As an adult in America, he became literate. He is a successful small entrepreneur and can afford a university education for his son. The son is studying in the university, and the father is reported to have said: "I should confess to you that there are many things I see wrong and cannot correct in my son; I cannot impose my reasoning on him anymore, because he tells me that he knows more than I do. He has more *cultura* now on account of his studies. In a sense I feel very incomplete, uncomfortable, and inhibited in this situation." The same situation occurs many hundreds of times.

In light of family dissatisfaction caused by generational differences, parents may hesitate to continue their support, particularly if it has been financially strenuous for them. In instances where studies are not finished and the son takes a job to help the family, he does not have the feeling that he should be able to live an independent existence. While he remains in the city, he must continue to reside with his parents. The discomfort caused by conflicts between his desire for independence and the ties to the parental household usually results in attempts to move to another city. If the son were to take separate residence in the same city while unmarried, this would be considered a shameful rejection of the family and an act of dishonor.

People expect an unmarried son or daughter to remain in the parents' household, even if conditions are crowded and socially unfit. Only a person who was previously married and has been left by his spouse may remain in separate quarters; these cases are very rare. Social mobility is achieved individually, yet separation from one's family is looked upon as very improper. It may be seen by others as an act of *vergüenza.*

To declare that the father is a laborer or even a skilled worker can cause *vergüenza* for someone who is in Normal School. Society imposes a bond between father and son that is hard to break. In higher social circles (among members of a city club, for example) there is always that boy or girl who has been able to qualify as professionally outstanding, but someone may always remark, "But the father is another thing." And this is a way "to put someone in his proper place." The normative orientation demands high respect for parents' experience; education and social inequality, however, create conditions that bring psychological stress. The social and the psychological expectations add to this. "The tragi-comedy of *My Son the Doctor*, by Florenzio Sanchez, is not altogether fiction in our present situation," observed a Paranaense.

There is no doubt that the aspirations and the standards of the middle group are high for their means, and, as a local sociologist phrased it, "irrealizable." Paraná is experiencing problems caused by a growing middle-class population with secondary education and ready for a semiprofessional standing in the city. A nonindustrialized city like Paraná can offer only a few career opportunities. Consequently, there are many restless, apathetic young individuals searching—with the aid of their families—for an economic niche in the city before considering other places in the country. Many face an acute problem: they finished secondary school, passed the years of military service, and now randomly look for opportunity. Under these conditions one's future becomes a matter of luck; manipulation of acquaintances and people in political power can help to shape one's future.

For young people there is always the possibility of establishing a romance (*noviazgo*) with someone of a higher social level. The first reaction of the girl's parents is to find out as much as possible about the background of the boy's parents and his family, but less about him. If the parents are found socially incompatible, the obvious disequilibrium brings adversities to the young couple. A long *noviazgo* demonstrating "true love" may be the solution. To marry in another town or city also avoids some social entanglements.

Conversations about religion with the members of the *clase media* reflected a variety of styles. Their interpretations are frequently not shared by the Catholic Church. People associate religion with baptism —Catholic by birth—but barely concern themselves with other aspects of religion and its relation to salvation. Some are interested in religion philosophically, and others manifest religiosity by attendance and support of the position of the Church and the clergy. A substantial number of people are against the clergy, but not against a Christian way of life. And a final group is composed of persons who are against the Church, the clergy, and all aspects of the Church considered magical. They do not consider themselves Catholic, but may be of other persuasions—humanists or atheists. It is still the *clase media*, however, that fills the churches and participates in the public processions. Outside the Catholic tradition there are groups of Protestants (Lutherans, Methodists, Baptists, and Seventh-Day Adventists), and

Social Class: The Basic Model   195

the Jewish people. The variability adds to the dynamics of the plural images that one should have of the *clase media*.

For each type, there are degrees of convictions, degrees of identification, and differences in the approach to faith by scientific, humanistic, or pseudoscientific methods. Individuals hold personal convictions and explanations for natural phenomena and are ready to seek the *curandero* for solutions to personal problems. Such problems and the illnesses associated with them are considered mysterious and not always empirically demonstrable, but indeed possible to resolve outside the teachings of a religious tradition. The same individual who seeks the help of a *curandero* may rely on scientific findings for other kinds of curing through a doctor or even a psychiatrist. The assumption that medical doctors can be of much help for illnesses of the body may be strong, but still may need to be qualified. To believe another power can cure is not unreasonable, particularly at times when medicine cannot provide further help. As has been indicated, it is assumed that nature has inexplicable aspects, and there are things in one's daily existence that must be accepted as such.

The *creencias*, general beliefs that certain happenings are signs of good or bad luck and that the horoscope published in the local newspaper should be consulted daily, seem to be important for some and not for others. But generally people in this class talk a great deal about it. Housewives are more sensitive to this predictive method, and often a wife will remind her husband or son that an event, personal or general, has been predicted, and therefore precautions must be taken. Other formulas may be used to escape possibly undesirable consequences. The difference from the *clase baja* is that, as one ascends, there is more public rejection of such beliefs. Doubt prevails and some members of a family feel ambivalence about the causal relationships in these matters.

"*Clase Media*" in the City

The *clase media* with its great diversity is intellectually conceived as a functioning group, but in reality this does not appear to be so. The lack of esprit de corps invalidates the reality of the concept, and in itself constitutes a contradiction. The prevalent theme seems to be "each one in his own home to avoid people's talk—*lo que dirán las gentes.*" Behavior and thinking are not necessarily dictated by the group, but are in the realm of private initiative; self-expression and individualism constitute in theory an integral part of each person's image. To speak of the *clase media* as a group is only a figure of speech, since group unity is not an intrinsic part of the people's orientation. They do not live or act as a group guided by structural principles. They are, in theory, people grouped and sandwiched in by others from above and from below. The struggle is not to become like those below, but to become or at least to compete with those above. Quite evident is the effort to separate themselves from the very low categories in the *clase humilde*, poor people whom they do not even wish to understand, whose social problems are blamed on their inability to progress—on laziness, the criollo style of life, wine, and unemployment. On the other hand, the *clase media* also makes an effort to maintain separation from the *clase alta*, which, for all practical purposes, is most difficult to reach socially.

It may be interesting at this point to note an upper-class informant's comments about the middle class.

There the *clase media* was in all its splendor. Lower executives of companies and some employees with guests were in the dinner party, and one could not help but notice how wives and daughters glittered. To my way of thinking, these people had an opportunistic orientation as a common denominator. Their behavior seemed to have been dominated by the constant gratification provided by their superiors. The night was boring and empty, at least for me. Conversations were trivial and full of negative gossip about other individuals; but the world seems to be moving in this direction.[7]

The writer Sabrelli speaks about the *clase media* of Buenos Aires as follows:

Middle-class people value reputation, personal appearance, and fear what the rest may think of them. One depends greatly on fellow men, and one lives dominated by the fear of what people may say and of the rumors and the scandals. Their concern with morality takes them to the

[7] Personal communication from an informant, May 7, 1967.

cult of childhood, to a nostalgic attitude toward the lost years of their own irrecoverable infancy. . . . Hypocrisy is, therefore, the fortune of the middle class.

The enormous disproportion between what the middle class imagines or wants to be and what it actually is forces them to live in simulation and concealment, closing all open and frank communication, preserving always a cold distance with fellow men.[8]

This description by an Argentine writer coincides with our characterization of middle-class Paranaenses. When a family wants to figure in society, the social game becomes very intense. "Here we have the valuable individual," remarked an informant of the *clase media tradicional*, "but those who are not valuable want to be so at any cost; those who are outstanding and esteemed individuals live a peaceful existence, but those who want to be recognized live anxiously, gathering money to do something with themselves and for their appearance. If money does not do it, then there is always the possibility of establishing an association with someone of an upper category in order to activate one's own social mobility."

Another informant stated:

The present situation in the city can be noted for the abundance of cases where the social dislocation of individuals is apparent; this is the result of our modality of life and conceptualization of life and people. Most of us feel that the social sensitivity exists to the extent that one must continue to be very careful in public or it can sometimes work against the individual. Public punishment in a small city like this, so much oriented toward class differences, constitutes a constant potential threat. But one learns to live in this way, and it does not seem very difficult. It becomes, after all, just another way of life. I feel that someone in a large city like Buenos Aires perhaps can easily hide his identity and personal characteristics, but certainly not among us.

Some informants indicated that a "personal state of confusion within the bulk of the population, that is, the middle classes, correlates with the general national political discomfort." It was then implied that the differences in *cultura* have penetrated to higher levels of the

[8] Sabrelli 1965:76, 77–78, 88. After the data had been collected and the general interpretation had been reached, the work of Sabrelli was consulted.

culture and the tradition of the nation. If the local-national correlation does hold, it certainly demands further research. But, interesting is the fact that this type of interpretation and the logic of cause and effect are deeply imbedded in the present-day programs, plans, and particularly in the critical attitude of Argentines toward their own social context. Consequently, these people are concerned with the control of the political situation. They struggle to improve the economic situation for the country and for their own standing. The theme *"hacer la patria"*—in the sense of remaking the country—is thus translated into social action.

Clase Alta

The *clase alta* in Paraná is clustered in homes next to Plaza Mayo, Rivadavia Avenue, and Parque Urquiza. Residential proximity, however, is not the basic factor promoting group cohesiveness. More important are their consciousness of social distinction and their identification with ancestors who appear on the pages of history books. Although at first the *clase alta* may seem homogeneous, a careful examination reveals internal subdivisions and significant distinctions. Interaction and relationships among individuals of the *clase alta* are based upon their social differences.

A man of the city, whose intellectual and professional capacity and *cultura* permit him to be convivial with both those in the upper level of the middle class and those in the elite group, discussed with me at great length the subdivisions in the *clase alta*.[9]

The families with antiquity, patrician, well-known or *conocidas*, aristocrats, must all be carefully distinguished. Each represents a distinctive type, and each can be distinguished according to very specific criteria. They are all, however, the elite of the city, internally a very complex group. Time constitutes one of the main criteria for distinguishing the subcategories of the elite group. There are, today, a few truly patrician family names with a sense of antiquity, "as the aged wine." Only a handful of families can trace their ancestry to colonial

---

[9] The material will not be presented as a quotation. It must be kept in mind, however, that these are the views of an informant gathered in long interviews describing, analyzing, and discussing the city's social situation.

days and direct descent from someone who played a leading role in the history of independence. Among them a few have chosen to live a "faded away" life. An aura of distinction still surrounds their names. Their ancestors, leading figures in government and in professions of humanities and law, have been followed by generations of individuals who have tried to live up to the standards implanted by a past reality, but loss of land and economic means have set them back. These families, however, cling tenaciously to their names, since, under current economic improvements and modernization and through the general benefits available in a developing society, social return is always possible. The few families that can trace their past to colonial times and have remained socially active are the patrician families.

This group is followed by the *familias tradicionales*. They are relatively old families, having perhaps three or four generations of continuous laudable social performance in the city. Several generations have been political leaders, and the families feel that they are playing a role parallel to that of the patrician families in the early historical periods. Some have married into the patrician group. The patricians and the traditionals, although distinct from the elite point of view, are for those in the middle class a single group.

The *familias conocidas*, or well-known families, do not have deep historical roots in the city; rather in a comparatively short period of time they have become well known for their high level of *cultura* and social and political participation in the city. Through friendships and marriages with people of well-established families, they have been able to enter into the elite and are recognized as "arriving." Socially, the *conocidas* lack the aging process, that is to say, lack *la decantación*. These families are closer to a European immigrant background. Among them one finds immigrants from Italy and Spain who have succeeded in business and maintain good social and political connections in the city. The new landed families, professionals, and military officers can now shine socially with the help of their association with patrician and traditional elements. At this point the Club Social plays a most crucial part. The four groups, popularly known as *las gentes conocidas*, should be conceptualized within concentric circles, rather than in the more common sociological fashion from top to bottom. Historically, there would be no problem in indicating the position of the patrician families at the very top. But currently, the nature of their differences permits a circle diagram (see fig. 19).

It is not too difficult to separate individuals in the elite by their social backgrounds. Local history, street names, plaza names—all speak publicly about them. Although from the outside the group may appear uniform, internally even greetings exchanged on social occasions subtly express the distinctions. On the street the choice is simple: the man above makes the overture.[10]

The process of entering into society may or may not be simple. It all depends on the individual's level of *cultura* and the public uses that he makes of it. The whens and hows are topics for social speculation by those who feel that they are in control of approving or disapproving the entrance. There is no doubt that his public manner is one of the

INFORMANT'S SOCIAL CLASS MODEL

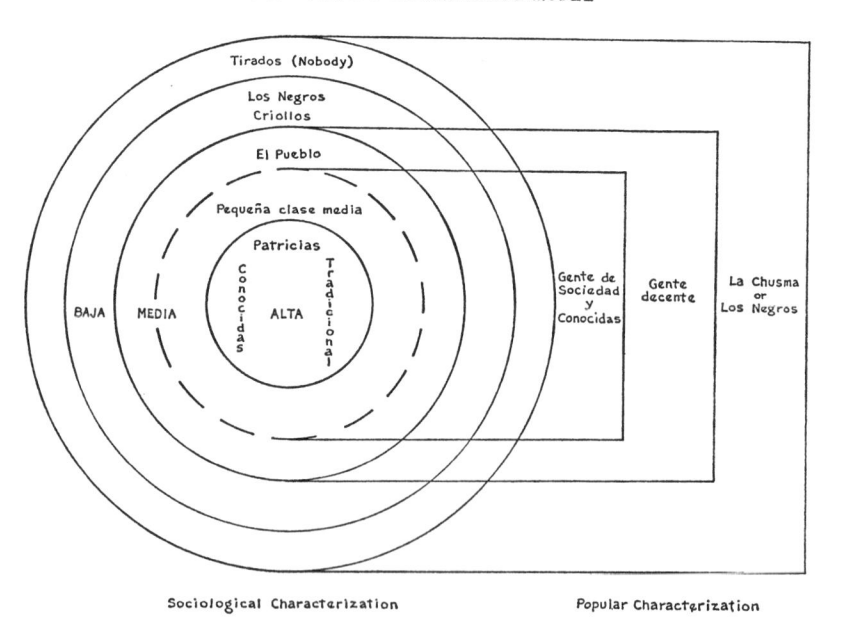

[Diagram: concentric circles labeled from outside in: Tirados (Nobody), Los Negros Criollos, El Pueblo, Pequeña clase media, Patricias; with BAJA, MEDIA, ALTA divisions and Conocidas / Tradicional labels. Rectangular overlay labeled: Gente de Sociedad y Conocidas, Gente decente, La Chusma or Los Negros.]

Sociological Characterization   Popular Characterization

Fig. 19

[10] This concludes the analysis of the situation as described by the informant.

most important elements; it must develop with his economic advance, particularly in the case of the *nouveaux riches*. The admittance is preceded by a long period of observation and rites of incorporation. Families of European descent with strong social aspirations have prepared the social ground for their descendants to climb. These families, striving to enter the elite circle, are going through the social transformation or social evolution allowed in this class system. The effort to combine and properly balance all elements—social background, economic solvency, and individual physical and social attractiveness—has not been a random phenomenon. Instead, it has been the conscious effort of several generations.

Since 1876 the Club Social has been the central institution for the *clase alta*. It was established to provide for the elite of Paraná a place of social insularity where "diversion, social harmony, and social relations may be cultivated."[11] The club sets the social tone for society, and all Paranaenses consider it the truly superior organization in the city. The superiority of the club and of the member families gives form to this general category of *clase alta* or *gente aristocrática*. The exclusiveness of the club separates its members socially from the other categories.

Individuals of the *clase alta* are very sensitive to the strong social push produced by the upper middle class. These people are active in city clubs that compete with the Club Social. There is the constant threatening possibility that more social interaction with the middle class has to come about as those with means seek membership in the Club Social. To *autocolocarse* (place oneself) at the level of the higher social categories, one must act with utmost propriety, a most rigorous demand. A European orientation, together with a personal knowledge of the Old World, serves as a springboard for persons who desire upward mobility. Being a professional *bachiller* (having a B.A. degree) and properly married, attending Mass at the proper hour each Sunday, being active in charitable organizations or in other institutions of *cultura*, and dressing in proper style (modern, but conservative) are excellent indicators of one's worthiness of participation in the Club Social. The degree of social acceptance depends on how a per-

[11] *Reglamentos del Club Social.*

son combines these factors. All public behavior must be well calculated to add that distinction to one's personal record. Possessing *cultura*, proper behavior, wealth, and a sense of style brings the further touches of social distinction; persons with distinction possess the means to wedge into the upper category of society. Proper ancestry, however, remains an important factor; several generations are required for a family to achieve social recognition.

The unbalanced sex ratio is another important problem to consider in the admission of new persons into the Club Social. Young men leave the city for study and thus pose a problem to mothers of marriageable daughters. Their absence promotes the incorporation into the club of unmarried military officers, high bank employees, university graduates, traveling company representatives, and successful entrepreneurs. The daughter of a conservative family of much distinction, for instance, recently married a doctor from a *clase media* family. It was considered a good match for the girl and the distinguished family. The boy is a professional, "intelligent and good-looking." It was stated that she would be able to continue her social career in the city. This is an interesting case, remarked an informant, inasmuch as in the past it would have been an unhappy match, and the girl would have lost social status and could not have "shone" in society in the same way. The present scarcity of young men, however, has changed the marriage strategy in this group. An accommodation of values and aspirations has been necessary in the last few decades. Young professional men, particularly outsiders, have become the newest addition to the social circles, and the management of the social situation is left to the wife and her acquaintances.

Some outstanding professionals of humble immigrant families have achieved social standing in a relatively short time. But this has been possible only when their social actions fall into the elite pattern. There are families of the middle class that are known among the upper class for having produced distinguished children. These persons have been desirable for interclass matches. Such a person, "by appearance, fine manner, speech, and appropriateness, reveals elegance and distinction," remarked an upper-class person. All the same, social ostracism is readily practiced, particularly toward those less concerned with preserving the status quo.

Different from the previous case is one in which one of the few available young men from a traditional family married a "humble girl, but pretty" from the *clase media*. In this case, traditional families resented the fact that he stepped outside his own class of people; there were many available women in his own social circle. It was considered offensive, and regardless of the sophistication and elaboration of the wedding, hardly any persons of his own class attended the church service or the reception. It was said that the new wife will face very unpleasant moments in the club. She should not try to shine and should be very careful in displaying her husband's wealth, because any ostentation, even if managed with the elegance of this class, will bring severe criticism and direct ostracism.

Nowadays, one finds old families that are very honorable but outside the elite groups of the city. There are also old, well-established families who by right of birth could figure socially but have chosen not to do so. Some active members of the Club Social feel that the traditional families are rapidly disappearing. "Only some families remain," said a person of Basque descent.

Most of them keep their name, but have no wealth. One by one, they have been left in a curious economic condition—with signs of wealth, but no money. It is not difficult to understand their social dilemma. They have lost a good means of income when they lost a large amount of land. The lack of concern with the future, so characteristic of them, has caused them to *malgastar*, overspend their fortunes. Consequently, some of the younger generation from this class have been forced to take jobs in the middle-class bracket in order to survive. However, they do keep in their souls the style that they inherit from their class.[12]

Everyone is informed about everyone else by daily face-to-face contact within each family. The oldest woman, usually the mother or spinster aunt, centralizes the family information and divulges it to other relatives. It is expected that this promotes strong loyalties among

[12] This represents the view of a professional person, third-generation European descent, who married into a traditional family of Paraná.

the members. The social news of the city is also discussed daily; one person brings to the attention of all the others news of political events and social happenings of the city.

When a public event does not carry the social tone that fits the standing of a person, the rule is not to attend. A concert of classical music made too popular will not have the elite in the audience, particularly if the proper invitation has not been made and places for them have not been reserved. The same pattern exists for weddings. The elegance can be outstanding, but "if the group decides" not to attend because of a wish to show disapproval publicly, then the elite will be conspicuous by its absence.

The nuclear family and immediate relatives play a very important role in the daily existence; visits and telephone calls are constantly exchanged. Family life was described by a lady informant of a traditional family in the following proud manner: "After my marriage, I did not let one day pass without visiting my mother. I visited her every day after lunch and my husband came for me after his work. We spent each thirty-first of December in my mother's home, and my brothers and sisters with their families came together. On the twenty-fourth I went to my husband's household. It was traditional to go to the in-laws' household on the twenty-fourth and to my parents on the thirty-first." And there are cases of middle-aged sons who married, but who twice a day stop by the central household to pay respects to their parents. This is conveniently done at the closing of business at noon and in the evening. It is now fashionable to watch television, and members of the family get together for special programs. It is known that not all individuals observe such family practices; it is agreed though that those who do are faithful to a tradition of this class.[13] Not only are they well-brought-up children, but they serve as models to their own children and represent a social fulfillment for the older generation.

The appearance in public of a united family is highly valued. Eco-

---

[13] This pattern is prevalent among "middle-class people with *cultura*," stated an informant.

Social Class: The Basic Model

nomic assistance from parents or grandparents allows youngsters to live up to the social level of the family. There are parents who contribute monthly to the maintenance of a married daughter's household so that maids and other comforts of their class may be afforded. This is not to be looked upon as an act of assistance; it is just what a family should do to maintain the social appearance of its members. Otherwise, it reflects on the parents.

La familia, composed of several nuclear families, usually makes plans together. The middle-aged members attempt to harmonize all social appearances. Much time is spent speculating about the formality of an occasion and the best way to fit into it. In unison the family can present a strong front that they feel to be appropriate. If one of the family wishes to attend a formal dance at the club, this is discussed, and other members may join. At the dance there will be a table reserved for the family and the close friends. As they arrive, the group becomes socially conspicuous in their circle. It will then be known that a certain family was at the dance, and such occasions permit the public to see the result of their coordinated planning of dress and jewelry, showing the family's tastes and values. If the whole group meets the occasion in superior fashion, this adds to their distinction and social success. There is also concern that "friends of the family" be in tune with the values expressed. Close friends are known for their high degree of conformity on the social appearances.

Another aspect of the general way of life with friends was well illustrated by the following discourse:

> I have four close friends and one belongs to a different social class. One of them is a very high-class person and his family used to have a great deal of land. They lost the land in the thirties and became *venidos a menos*, but now they are well-off again since one of them married into a family with wealth. Another friend is from a different province and has some ancestry in that province. He is a person with a great personality, but he lacks style. Yet, by his manner, one sees at once that he has background. The third friend is from a lower class of Paraná, while the fourth one is of *gente conocida*. Everyone knows each other well, although I have more intimacy with each one, an intimacy that does not exist between them. There is a

fifth person who has tried to become a friend of ours, particularly with me, but my two upper-class friends and I are keeping him under observation.

I find it difficult to maintain friendships with persons in the lower class, although I like my lower-class friend. But he cannot share with me the same public places such as the Club Social. He could go, but my acquaintances would make him feel very uncomfortable. My own family places people socially in *la loma* [the hills] and some in *medio pelo* [literally, half bad], or in *el monte* [the forest]. This categorization applies to my friend, so he will be between the category of *medio pelo* and *monte*; as a matter of fact, he does not know anything about his ancestry. I cannot hurt my friend or see others hurt him. Therefore, I do not talk about my grandfather's achievements. But at the same time, I must remain *parado en la loma* [standing on the hill] because, if I am not interested in my ancestors' achievements and myself, I will be going downhill very rapidly. I and my family are interested in maintaining our social standing and in honoring the social standing of our ancestors.

I have also been indoctrinated in the political tradition of the *partido conservador*, and I feel that the party adapts itself well to the Argentine reality. But this position, of course, will not appeal very well to my friend, and, therefore, we do not discuss certain aspects of politics.

I get upset when my people treat my lower-class friend, who has admirable personal qualities, disrespectfully—with *desprecio*. By the same token, you can imagine how I would feel if I were married to someone of that social category. Of course, some of my family would surely squash my plans. However, it is apparent that the *clase aristocrática* is coming to be a rather relative category for this day and age. Paraná is not like Buenos Aires or other cities. We in our own class are aware of our limitations, and our ancestry by comparison is probably not so important as that of individuals in Buenos Aires and in other countries. But locally we are a very distinctive group of people. In the streets, many people from my own college are aware of my origin, and I know that they try to use me as a springboard when they need to. I try to present myself as a friend of everyone, but I stand in "the hills" and can socially hurt others when necessary. There is the case of an acquaintance from school who is now "building castles in the air" because his fiancée happens to have more wealth than many of us. But his fiancée has no family or ancestry. I need to stop him one of these days, because he tries to look at his own friend with a degree of contempt. If he marries her, he will have his good name and her good wealth, but I must embarrass him one of these days and put him in his proper social place.

Frequently, traditional families express their own world view in the phrase "life is memory, and life is made of lived memories." The past and the present constitute two significant dimensions. To think of the future or to prepare for the future appears a grotesque thing. The future, by definition of their social standing, is a *fait accompli*. To be concerned is to lower one's own image. Here lies the greatest difference from the middle classes, who characteristically need to concern themselves with their future. By contrast, for the *clase alta* the future is in the present, and the past is also merged with the present. Their homes and decorations preserve their past; they are "museums." Inside each house there are portraits of severe-looking ancestors in conservative dress. An informant commented that these surroundings surely affect their mentality, and one has to be careful not to become a piece of the family museum himself.

In view of what these families represent historically, there is a strong affection for their past. The study of their present goes against their premises. The elderly individuals of this class frequently describe and remind the younger generations of the achievements of members of the families and of their contributions to history. Widows are particularly notorious for preserving the qualities and the achievements of their husbands in as vivid a way as possible. The husbands are portrayed as persons who lived up to the highest standards of the class, whose personalities and accomplishments epitomized the perfect gentleman and the truly humane man. The admirable quality of people of the past, according to present informants, is that they did not act inhumanely; they were loved by all the people and extended their professional services indiscriminately to both the rich and the poor.

From early childhood one learns to appreciate ancestry; through ancestry one finds his identity. Ancestors are not only presented as gifted individuals, but as models of perfection. One informant remarked:

"I resent all these things, but I cannot leave this style of thought and way of doing things. I would then be without the support of my group and I would be considered a deserter. I must even enter into the profession of law because it is in the family tradition and my ancestors were lawyers. We are in the history in this particular way. I could hardly think of one of us becoming a pilot of a commercial airline."[14]

Marriage is no different from selecting a profession. Uncles, aunts, parents, and grandparents are all involved and carefully consider who shall receive the family name. Marrying an outsider or someone of a different ethnic group or religion would be a mortal sin. "We are taught to struggle to the very end, but to stay in this class and to remain a closed group." The past must be transmitted to the new generations. The present generation must honor the past and live up to its standards; the past is then their future.

The situation of the past is also presented in contrast to the present as a very exciting period. Judging by those great men, intelligence, *cultura*, and friendship were intense and genuine. The elderly persons of the upper class now feel that the world around them is rapidly changing, and their present role of describing to the new generations their historical worth is extremely important. Furthermore, the image of persons of the past is supported by the names of streets, libraries, schools, museums, and other institutions. Their personal qualities—good public speaking, writing, knowledge of other European languages, gentlemanliness—and their contribution to history make of such individuals the ideals of perfection. In order to become a distinguished person today one must be on a par with those "great men." Their careers encompassed such broad activities that today it is practically impossible for anyone to achieve an equal level of professional success. This very fact places them on an even higher pedestal as models of tradition and *cultura*.

The younger generations are expected to identify with these high standards to the extent that eventually they should be able to speak about the family "heroes" as if it all had been a personal experience. The past must become something real in the present. In the process of growing up, the children are expected to learn sufficiently about the

[14] Note that no middle-class individual would speak in such terms.

achievements of their ancestors and to support them without questioning, living up to the standards that they represent. They must learn to cope elegantly with the present social situation and to honor those of the past. Grandmothers are very important in the transmission of these sentiments.

Upper-class traditional people realize that there are changes in the nation, but the life style, the aspirations, and the symbols inherited from the past must remain constant. It is because of the great regard and appreciation for things of the past and their continuity in the present, and the limited concern with the future, that *improvisación* can take place. It is not only a descriptive concept, but explanatory of many aspects of public life that concern the middle classes. Social and political programs are characterized by their short-range quality; their future consequences are not clearly anticipated or projected. It would appear that through improvisation many aspects of the traditional life can be preserved. For some public activities improvisation has become an accepted style and is considered as part of human nature.

Accommodation to a quality of life below the standards of one's own class is frequently discussed. Traditional families point to the difficulty of maintaining their style of life. For instance, the present situation of the country makes it impossible to consume imported European food and drinks proper to this class level. This is just one among the many material and political aspects of their lives in which they are compelled to compromise. The problem is to adapt to present conditions without giving up the upper-class ideals. In the past young ladies of patrician families who were courted by men of a lower social level preferred to remain single rather than to mix their social rank. Today their nieces and nephews are marrying professionals without social background. These upper-class individuals are ready, willing, and proud to be successful in their social manner; however, the competition with outsiders, particularly military officers, is keen, and the chances of marriage are limited.

Personal freedom and spontaneity may be absent by other standards; it becomes rather bothersome constantly to act in proper and formal manner in order to avoid criticism. The phrase, "what people will say," is not so relevant for this class as the phrase, "it does not fit you well" (*no te queda bien*). This is often used to correct a youngster. "One important rule in the process of socialization is to keep to oneself any displays of emotions when crises occur." In light of this self-image, Mrs. John F. Kennedy's decorum during her personal crisis in 1963 was greatly admired. She met their highest expectations, and they could not do less than to identify emotionally with the late president's widow. It is a rule for members of this class to go through life crises with distinction and dignity, without regard to their personal emotional state.

The European aristocratic traditions of France, Spain, and Italy have served as models in Argentina. Many of the Paraná homes include European patterns in their interior decoration and maintain a style of life that is locally conceived to be typical in Europe. Historical elements, archives, and family libraries have played an important part as symbols of distinction and *cultura*. People with wealth and land—*hacendados* or *estancieros*—adorn their homes with art pieces purchased in Europe or acquired through dealers in Buenos Aires. Families that identify with Argentine independence display colonial furniture. Urquiza's dining room, for instance, is presently the dining room of a *familia tradicional*. Although the house interiors are not publicly known, the taste of the upper class may be seen in public buildings and in the cathedral. Families responsible for the decorations of the cathedral thus direct the public taste by imposing their artistic values.

It becomes very clear that upper-class people are constantly concerned with a specific and unique style of life. Excitement is evident when at the end of the year new members present their daughters in society. There is much speculation and fear. Each family would like to capture the social brilliance of the occasion. This may even undermine the bases of some smooth social relationships. One informant said, "We live with models around us, and when we cannot meet the model in the true sense, then we practice *apariencias* (appearances). We live, more than anything else, under a veil of *apariencias*." *Apariencias* are ideals derived from the dynamics of the stratification model. Mentally, an individual tries to be a step above his economic means and social possibilities. He must learn to handle a second personality for public appearances. The elite think about this problem, live with it,

Social Class: The Basic Model

and constantly rehearse their public roles above their own social and economic standing. In this sense, the stratification model functions not in the background alone but with considerable strength in the foreground.

The participation of the *clase alta* women in the three churches of this city carries strong social overtones. Much attention is paid to the social fringes of all their activities. Some ladies are active in the charitable circles of Damas Católicas, others care for the altars and church decorations. There is also the Cofradía del Niño, and its members take the "Child" to visit the households of "brothers." Those with intellectual interests may be in discussion circles where theology and philosophical issues of the church are discussed with some outstanding member of the local clergy. The less traditionally oriented ones view the Church much as do people of the *clase media*; they are nominally in the Church, but participate only in socially important occasions.

In spite of their background, the *clase alta* may retain within their general world view a limited belief both in *creencias*, outside the formal framework of theology, and in the powers of the *curanderos*, whose services they may find useful as a last resort in some special situations. This is an interesting link of these people to the past; it may be a symbol of early days and a reliving of some of the early semirural situations. Much of the information on *curanderismo* is derived through maids, who can always testify to curing by words of the evil eye and *empachos* or to the fact that in the country the *curanderos* know the formulas to cure animals of ailments such as worms, broken bones, and digestive disorders. The case of an old lady suffering much pain in one leg was given as an example of the power of curing. The person did not want to give in to the power of the *curanderos* for a long time, but she was encouraged by a relative and the maid and finally visited a *curandero*. Arrangements were made through the servant. The *curandero* made the sign of the cross over her leg and applied some homemade remedies, and the lady's leg, long treated unsuccessfully by a medical specialist, became well. It was a two-day treatment with much success that clearly contrasted with the unsuccessful years of medical treatment.

Further conversations about *curanderos* revealed that some individuals in this class believe in their power. There are worms in animals (*empachos*) and other types of pains that can be treated by their methods, according to an informant. Most speakers, however, had not themselves witnessed curing, but knew of successful cases and felt that there must be some truth behind such stories. A case was mentioned of a *curandero* in a nearby city with the power to cure, only by words, a person bitten by a yarara snake. Many other cases were cited of individuals who had been advised by doctors to have an operation in a hospital but had their problems solved by able *curanderos*. One of the men in the group indicated that his own wife (of the upper category) was found to have the power to cure the *empachos* defined as "gastric pregnancies." However, in her own image of a lady of society, she would be offended if someone referred to her as a *curandera*.

During one discussion it was agreed that there are limits to belief in curers, and that excessive faith is superstition and ignorance. Those who have spent much time on *estancias* know about many formulas that country people believe and trust. A knife buried in the ground, for example, may cure a horse of certain illnesses when he steps on the soil above the knife. It was also agreed that a curer should be allowed to cure a body from the outside, but one should never eat or drink anything prepared by the curers.

On occasions the horoscope is consulted for personal matters and decisions. The desire to predict one's own personal luck is in the realm of the uncontrollable events such as happiness, illnesses, death. Therefore, it becomes an interesting game, but—an important aspect that contrasts with other classes—such things are never discussed with other persons, except close relatives and intimate friends. Such beliefs belong to the lower class, but, as one informant said, "There is a bit of truth in this mysterious life."

The most striking feature of the *clase alta tradicional* is the strong sense of corporateness, autonomy, conformity, and of belonging to a real historical past. Between the *clase media* and the *clase alta* there seems to be a qualitative difference, particularly in relation to corporateness. People of the *clase alta* identify with each other as persons, and the social network appears to be a very tightly knit system. There is indeed a tightly knit tradition maintained by the socially well-known families (the *gentes conocidas*). Their ancestors made history in pioneer days and these people feel that by the definition of their class they have inherited a clear sense of social destiny, priorities, and distinction.

The public identification of a *persona conocida* is frequent in the local press. The newspapers, at the time of death, for example, will make statements that the deceased is "a member of a *conocida* and *arraigada*" (well-known and rooted family) or "*conocida y tradicional familia* in our midst and deeply linked to the social circles of *la sociedad* of this city." This contrasts with the statements made for others, simply indicating that they were neighbors of the city or good persons who distinguished themselves by good performance in office. An active social sensitivity is imbedded in this recognition. In this context *conocida* means not only well-known, but also having historical roots, and it stands in contrast to other uses that refer to someone simply known in the neighborhood. In the latter case, the word *conocida* brings less social distinction than in the former.

In the *clase media* there is a group of politically active individuals who feel that they are making the country in the spiritual sense, *hacer la patria*. This position differs from that of the elite who know that the country has already been made by their ancestors (*hicimos la patria*) and that the administration of the country is now entrusted to them. Presently, a handful of families can claim pure patrician background; they are rapidly disappearing and the "*gente decente* of the *clase media* are taking over." There is, of course, Argentine authenticity among the patricians, but this cannot be confused with patriotism. In some cases patriotism may rate very low among the people who feel a personal obligation toward the historical past.

Aristocracy must be understood as a localized and relative concept in the context of the nation. This is, at best, a very high middle class. In Paraná, however, the term elite acquires tones of distinction that, although not acknowledged in the social stratification of the nation, parallels the case of aristocracies in other Argentine cities.

The local elite believe their life style cannot be grasped in the framework of the social sciences. "This approach," remarked an informant, "lacks the sensitivity to capture our emotions and what we really are. It is not of our class to convert the actions of human beings into items for cold analysis." The same informant asked, "How could a social scientist study upper-class behavior and capture with finesse the sensitivity that can be acquired only by growing up in the group?" The intellectually oriented individuals of this class feel that the group is a very complex historical phenomenon and not a simple matter to grasp and understand, especially through modern research procedures of the social sciences. "Our manner of being can only be understood by being born in our circles."[15]

A member of a traditional family summarized the present situation in a way worth incorporating as a conclusion to this chapter:

> Traditional families are the oldest, but despite the fact that they are old, they should have a high economic level. In this group there were those who were rich, but had lost much of their land and wealth; these people are known as *los venidos a menos*. For them, good economic standing is something only to be remembered. In the upper class, therefore, there are families relatively poor, but with social status derived from their ancestors.
>
> There is a relation between class and politics. The members of traditional families belong and have belonged to the governing class of people. Therefore, the prerequisites for the traditional families are antiquity, wealth, and political power in the city [as presidents of important institutions], in the province [as senators or governors], or in the nation.
>
> The Club Social is not open to everyone. A generation ago, the club was restricted to individuals with ancestry and wealth. Nowadays, those who can pay could theoretically apply for membership. But still, what the club looks for in a person is his degree of *cultura*. Members of the club look into the ethnic and racial background of a person applying, because there are some ethnic groups with little *cultura* that are not by nature s*impáticos*. The Club Social has the specific objective of preserving some degree of social purity in the city in the sense that the club is a place for the elite families, for the things that are historically old . . . for preserving the "race" of Entre Ríos. The families with deep roots feel like one, because of their common historical ancestry. Here, then, is the great difference with those who enter the club because they feel money means everything. Indeed, money may bring *simpatía* from someone, but this is only when, with

[15] There is an interesting methodological point made by the informant in this paragraph.

Social Class: The Basic Model

money, there is a touch of social distinction. Wealth without finesse brings *antipatía*, and such a person may be left in a social vacuum within the club.

The *gente conocida* or *tradicional* should be conceived as an integral element of the city and its history. They work and live in the city. This group centers its activities and thinking on the Club Social and values family reunions. There are many cliques, therefore, and some of them never meet unless there is a special activity at the club. However, they carry on their friendships with individuals who have been accepted by their families in cliques that were formed by them; they have been in familiar groups from early childhood. Therefore, other types of friendships, at work, become rather difficult. There is, indeed, a sense of superiority that people of this class do not want to lose. It is their patrimony, after all. Their feeling of affinity brings about a sense of pleasure in life. This identification brings a social unity that makes people feel happier. In contrast to other cities of Argentina, in Paraná there is not so much a sentiment of exclusivity as a sentiment of preference.

This, in essence, describes the most basic attitudes held by individuals of the *clase alta*. The *clase alta* consists of persons whose lives remain very formal; its dynamics center in close, corporate cliques, although all attempt to support the features of a class subculture. The need to accommodate to the changes of times becomes an imperative, but the meaning of life is found in their past. Variations from this pattern are many, but the ideal clearly emerges, although it may not be feasible for everyone to practice it totally.[16]

Paranaenses realize that the three-fold system constitutes an overall social scheme supported by the country's social history. Individuals have used and continue to use the models of each of the social classes as fixed points in the continuum of social stratification. From a practical point of view, the stratification model stands in the background for the evaluation of individuals' public behavior. While the model of any one class appears distant from another class model, in reality persons approximate the fixed points, and usually act according to the image of the level above their own.

The manipulation of this system by individual Paranaenses fre-

---

[16] For comparison, see the analysis of class and kinship among the criollo and elite groups in Buenos Aires province (Strickon 1962:500–515).

quently obscures the divisions of the overall model. Furthermore, the difficulty in placing families or individuals exactly can add to general confusion. The stratified model of society constitutes a system in constant motion, animated by individuals who are also in motion as they add, discard, or refine traits of the model. The motion of the system and the motion induced by individuals may at times be an obstacle to a clear perception of the city social system.

It is not unreasonable to conclude that public social life constitutes a dramatic social game; social contacts, contracts, and associations must be made for personal convenience. The desire to move upward or to remain in control of their social standing motivates individuals to practice complex social gymnastics. One can create confusion over one's social image by *apariencias*, a pattern that appears on all social levels; the greatest amount is found in the *clase media* and the lower levels of the *clase alta*. "*Apariencia* is the basic dynamic of our life style in Paraná," remarked a socially well-placed Paranaense of the *clase media*.

7. SOCIAL CLASSES: MANIFESTATIONS AND DYNAMICS

The Cemetery and Social Class

In Paraná, the correlation between preferred areas of residence and social class is direct. As a residential location, the center of the city has always been the proper place for families of the *clase alta*. The main plaza is the most desirable place for residential social distinction, particularly because everything that is most relevant in the life of the city occurs or is located in this vicinity. It is socially appropriate to declare one's intention to move closer to the city center; to dwell outside the imaginary inner circle of Paraná is to experience the feeling of social inadequacy.

As in the plaza, so in the cemetery a person's social position is put to a public test. The cemetery reflects important social values and constitutes a permanent public projection of the social and economic position of a family. Like the social ecology of the city, which it seems to copy, each section of the cemetery has a number of traits associated with specific social categories. Each tomb, with its decoration, is a public document and a reminder of the social standing of the deceased as well as of those related to him. At the tomb the social present and the social past come together. The cemetery is an accurate portrait of so-

Fig. 20

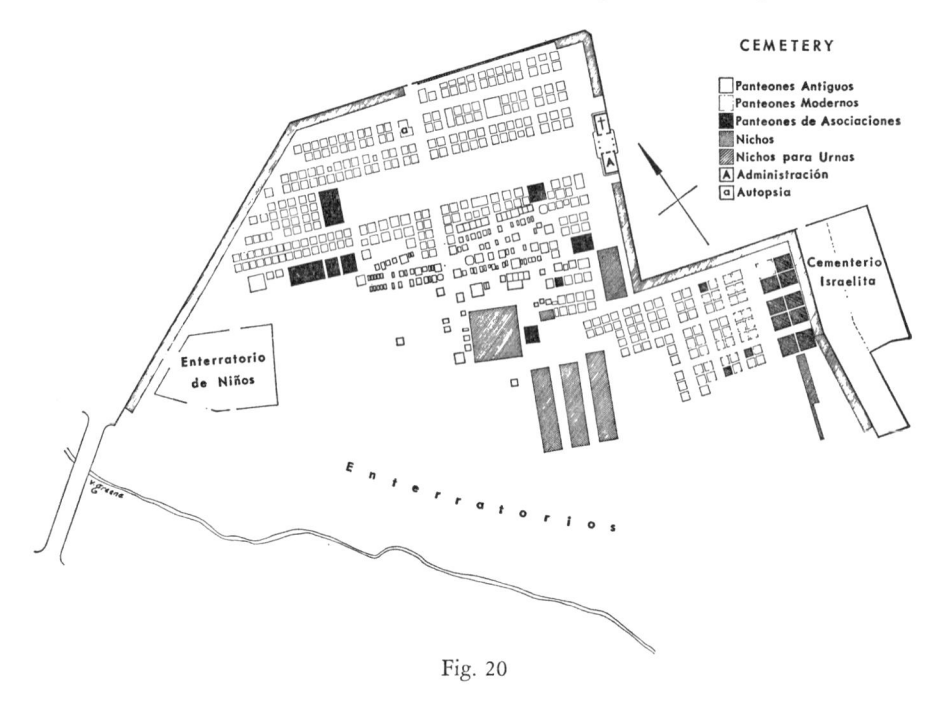

cial positions and a testimony to the families' past; it reminds the living of an upbringing with or without distinction, and it can become a disheartening reminder for aspiring individuals who live under the shadow of socially displaced ancestors.

Conversations with an informant about the cemetery indicated how the social implications of burial are evaluated, and a careful study of the tombs revealed that Paranaenses can easily determine the social standing of a family. For example, a person of an aspiring *clase media* background may today enjoy some social distinction through professional achievement. A pleasant personality and some "luck" make acceptance by the elite group possible. If a person like that dies suddenly, without having purchased a place of distinction for his final rest, the relatives face a social crisis. They might decide upon a temporary burial in a *panteón* (mausoleum) of friends or relatives until further arrangements can be made. If this is not possible, the family may bury him according to their means, perhaps in a nonmausoleum location.

Social Classes: Manifestations and Dynamics 219

But people immediately would talk: "After all their snobbishness and social activity, look where he ends—just thrown out in any old place." For a person who tried to be in a high social category to end up in a secondary place in the cemetery is considered awkward and socially shameful.

Historically, when the village of Paraná became a city, the cemetery was for the use of the *no disidentes*, the Roman Catholics; it was administered by the Church. The death of the wife of a North American principal of the Normal School precipitated the issue of non-Catholic burials. The municipal record shows that there was a petition in 1878 by a Protestant group (*disidentes*) applying for land to establish their own cemetery. This request was denied, but eventually Protestant burials in the main cemetery were allowed. Later one of the Jewish associations purchased a piece of land adjacent to the cemetery over which the Sephardic and the Ashkenazic Jews now share control. The Protestants now use the city cemetery, preferring burial in the ground rather than in niches.

In 1891 the public cemetery was reorganized: avenues and streets were constructed according to the gridiron pattern. Along the avenues the wealthy families purchased land and built family mausoleums. Names of the streets and avenues were socially significant, like the street names in the city. The title records show a division of the cemetery land into two types: the *primera categoría* for mausoleums, and the *segunda categoría* for popular burials in the ground (*enterratorios*). Thus each family could purchase a plot according to its social status within this dualistic system.

Today there are three types of burials corresponding roughly to the three classes: in the ground; in *nichos* (niches) the size of a casket, either in the walls of the cemetery or in the mausoleums of ethnic, religious, professional, or labor organizations; and finally, in the private family mausoleums. The tombs directly in the ground are located in the geographically lowest section of the cemetery along Arroyo Antoñico—the creek that has always been associated with the most humble class of people in the city. The ground tomb is rented for five years, and afterwards the remains of the deceased may be burned and the ashes placed in a container in the urn-niche wall of the cemetery. The ground tombs are simple, but in each case a relative tries to decorate the tomb in a manner appropriate to the economic means of the family—a wooden or wrought-iron cross or a crypt arrangement is quite popular.

Informants remember that two decades ago the ground tombs were outlined in cement and painted gray, which seems to be the color associated with the cemetery and the expression of sadness. Recently, with the change in building material, people began to utilize tiles of white, black, or vivid shades of blue. Though the patterns of arranging the tiles are fairly consistent, varied sophistication is still expressed. Natural or artificial plants in pots are often placed along the edges of the tomb; the ground may be raised in an elongated mound, or an outline of a wall may enclose the tomb itself. Some of the graves have a thin sheet of gray marble covering the ground. Somewhere the name of the deceased is inscribed together with the dates of his birth and death. Some graves have a cross with a big, inscribed, heart-shaped medal in the center; a photograph of the dead may also be attached. On All Saints' and All Souls' days (November 1 and 2), the families of the deceased clean the tombs, whitewash them, and adorn the graves with fresh or artificial flowers.

The next type of tomb in the social continuum of the cemetery is the niche, which an informant of the elite class readily assigned to the *gente media*, the middle class. The walls of the cemetery contain rows of niches; the height and location of each niche express degrees of social distinction. Recently the *municipalidad* built galleries two stories high with open balconies (see fig. 20).

The rectangular front of each niche varies. The family, according to its means, may place a marble front—light green, black, or white—with an inscription, a picture, a greeting from the family, and holders for candles or flowers; some caskets are exposed while others stand behind a glass door with a lock. The niches differ in quality, indicating degrees of prestige and artistic taste. Those who have *panteones*, however, feel uncomfortable about the idea of anyone being enclosed in walls in spaces the size of a casket. One of the elite men described the feeling: "I cannot think there are people without a *panteón*; I feel asphyxiated just to think about this type of burial."

Social Classes: Manifestations and Dynamics

Middle-class people without membership in an ethnic, labor, or professional association have no alternative but the niches. And each niche, as already suggested, becomes a personal expression of sentiment, its front decorated with a bronze inscription declaring love for the deceased and sorrow for the empty place in the family. The following are examples of messages on the niches (and only on this type of tomb):

Rosita: you will live forever in the memory of your parents and little brothers.

Patito, died at four, and you will live eternally in the memory of your parents, siblings, uncles, aunts, and grandparents.

Mother: we will not forget you in your eternal rest. Your life was an illusion, your death my unhappiness. Your husband.

Mother—you will live in the thoughts of your husband, children, and grandchildren forever.

Your death leaves an emptiness that no one could occupy. Your husband, children, and relatives.

Dear husband, you left this world and left me behind and forever I shall suffer with your children, who will not forget you for a moment.

To prove our love, our son, Francisco, after eight months of work, presented this tomb as a symbol of the high glory which will perpetuate your memory and your holy rest.

In Paraná, there is a feeling of great religiosity toward a deceased person, and expressions of sorrow and loss are accentuated as one ascends the social scale. The inscriptions, the photographs, and the candles seem to predominate among the niches and tombs of the middle class, while among the upper-class people, the individuals with *panteones*, expressions of sentiment are in terms of homage on each anniversary.

Some of the organizations of Paraná, particularly the ethnic organizations, affect the usual class model of burials. They possess large *panteones* for their members, who through mutual plans can secure a niche inside a majestic and ornate construction. The niches generally resemble those in the walls of the cemetery, but their location in a large mausoleum bestows a measure of prestige. These buildings are usually near the family *panteones*. From the public viewpoint, it is the association that is of importance socially, while members are significant only as they relate to it. Bronze plaques appear on the walls of the association *panteones*. In the *panteón* for teachers, for example, inscriptions on plaques honor the office of the teacher. Labor groups provide their members with mausoleums with niches for burial. Ethnic background as a criterion for separating the population is not so significant today as it was in the past. Still, the ethnic associations bring together the remains of Italians, Spanish, Swiss, French, and others. Because of organizations, then, people who would have been buried in wall niches or in the ground can sleep eternally with a large group centrally located in the cemetery.

The family achieves considerable satisfaction when it can provide the best possible arrangement for the burial of its member. For those in the lower class, placing someone in a niche brings prestige and social pleasure, the same feeling that an upper-middle-class family experiences when it can finally afford a *panteón*.

The family *panteón* is socially the most prestigious type of tomb. A sensitive informant reflected: "It would seem that the architecture of the *panteón* transmits feelings to the public about the social importance of the family and the social virtue of those in it. In this way, it effects respect and admiration from the public." The names of the families are displayed above the entrance to the *panteones*. Friends, co-workers, associations, or the government acknowledge the personal achievements of the deceased by donating plaques, which are unveiled at anniversaries. Friends and members of the family also send notes of sympathy on each anniversary.

The old *panteones* of the elite families of the end of the nineteenth century stand in one section of the cemetery (fig. 20). The *panteones* of this era, built of cement and plastered bricks, some with Ionic or Doric columns, are noted for their excessive height. Adjacent to these are the *panteones* of the early patricians' descendants and of the *nouveaux riches* who lived through a period of economic splendor in the early part of this century. At an exorbitant cost that would be prohibitive today, some families—many of whose names appear in books on local and national history—raised *panteones* of black marble imported from Europe. Such buildings, according to one informant, are "cold," but they are forceful projections of the social standing of the family and testify to stability and power. Next in line among the *panteones* are the less elaborate ones, with a white cement front and perhaps about four feet of marble at the base. The informant felt that this type of *panteón* was more *simpático* and human. As a consequence of architectural developments in the last decade, there are low, modern *panteones* resembling, in some cases, a "weekend house."

A *panteón* of any kind is an expensive proposition today—the cheapest costs several million pesos, and those in black marble "have no price." But *panteones* are still desired as portrayals of the family's sophistication. Some are decorated as chapels with elaborate entrances leading to a marble altar on which religious objects are displayed in glass cases. Coffins are exposed on the side of the altar, and covered with intricate, expensive, hand-made white lace. Each exposed casket is identified, but unlike the niches, there are no pictures or sentimental phrases. To make space for the new generations, sometimes the remains are cremated and the ashes are placed in urns near the altar. Some *panteones* have basements with shelves where a family places the remains of a faithful servant of the household.

Periodically, if not weekly, a traditional family sends a servant to place flowers in the *panteón*, to clean the building, and to polish its façade. There is an exceptional amount of activity to prepare each *panteón* for the first and second of November. The *panteón* doors remain open during these days, and servants or close relatives stay there to receive flowers and visit with others. Out-of-town relatives may come at this time and exchange information about the members of the family. On anniversaries, plaques, flowers, speeches, and Mass in the cathedral are part of the activities of a family. These are ways to remind people in the city of the importance, distinction, and achievements of someone who the family feels should be publicly honored.[1]

In general, when members of a family have lived in harmony, the father, his wife, their children and direct descendants, all share the

---

[1] It was surprising to find that in Seville, Spain, where social distinctions are marked and have been preserved through so many centuries, the cemetery does not display the social differences to a comparable extent. Also, the part of the funeral ceremony in which only men participate does not occur in Argentina.

panteón. These monuments are willed and are part of the wealth inherited by successive generations.[2] There seems to be no definite rule (such as patrilineality) about who qualifies for space, but it is assumed that the family will remain united even after death. Occasionally someone may be temporarily placed in the *panteón* of another relative if appropriate space is not available at the time of death. Some individuals may be deposited in urns, or the family may acquire a second *panteón*.

The people consider the cemetery as sacred land. During the day it is visited, but it is not desirable to do so at night. Many old, retired individuals speak about their experiences near the cemetery. There are many stories about strange cries and nonhuman footsteps in the night. Some of the ideas about the cemetery at night are related to the bad light, *la luz mala*, a light that is a mystery to everyone and is closely associated with gaucho experiences. It is believed that this light may follow people, and the fear of it keeps many away from the cemetery during the hours of darkness when valuable things could be stolen. Respect for the cemetery is partly based on fears that cross-cut all social categories. But this respect also stems from the fact that the cemetery is considered an extension of oneself because one's progenitors rest there. On the one hand, life ends in the cemetery, but on the other, the cemetery fixes one in a definite social category in the city forever.

Funerals likewise project the principle of class differentiation. At the time of a funeral those arranging it must think about the social status of the deceased as well as their own. The municipality of Paraná provides all funeral services, the arrangements varying in price. During the year of our residence in the city, there was a definite feeling that funerals were controlled and commercialized by the city government. Local newspapers commented about the situation, especially in reference to middle-class families. "Families of the *clase media* are affected, even at the time of death . . . because they must pay thousands of pesos . . . eighteen thousand pesos for the most humble services."

---

[2] The social impact of this clearly has an effect on the quality of interpersonal relations in one's social group. Much of the group sentiment discussed in this work is expressed in this particular context.

The government "requires that 50 percent be paid at the time when the service is requested." This may present great difficulty for the family, especially if the proper social image cannot be publicly displayed according to the norms of the social model.

Preparations for the funeral can cause much discomfort to the people involved. Though life is relatively peaceful when the family has accepted its real position, when it has lived beyond its means the moment of death becomes a moment of truth. The family must confront the set of social categories represented by the different kinds of funeral services offered by the *municipalidad.* This is an occasion when the social position of the family may be reaffirmed and its public image manipulated. The problem of public presentation becomes a conscious issue for all of the deceased person's relatives, and not just for the members of his household. The closest acquaintances wait and speculate upon the type of funeral arrangement to be made by the family. Family disharmony may also arise at this juncture. Some may disapprove of the arrangements made by the family, claiming that the very best was not provided for the deceased. This usually implies that those criticized lack a strong love or *cariño.*

Funerals are times to be publicly proud, particularly when one is able to meet the expected level of his social standing; but they are also times to suffer embarrassment if the ceremony is too modest and does not match the usual image presented to *vecinos.* The amount of energy spent and the concern and thought given to these occasions are directly related to their conceptualization of social class and their understanding of its importance in their society. Weddings are also excellent opportunities for people to judge the reality of class standing. But while a wedding can be carefully planned, there is hardly sufficient time for the proper planning of a funeral. Law requires the completion of the funeral within twenty-four hours after death.

Death is publicly announced in the local newspapers, either simply as a demographic item or with the elaboration of a social event. In the latter case, the newspaper will give recognition to the deceased on its front pages. But it is up to the relatives of the deceased to request more elaborate individual treatment. The article should comment on the individual's qualities, the extent of his acquaintances, his participation in clubs and other organizations, and whatever else is judged by the relatives to be important to the public.

For the elite group, the key to social distinction rests in the cliché phrase, "the deceased descended from a traditional family."[3] If the family is known to have been in the province for many generations and the ancestors had participated in the making of the society and the operation of government, then the deceased is distinguished by the standard phrase, "a member of a traditional Entre Ríos family." The announcement also states that the funeral and burial will be in the family *panteón*.

There are those who did not descend from traditional families, but their achievements in life have allowed them to enjoy a high degree of *cultura*. A person in this group will be noted by the phrase, "a person from a well-known family" (*familia muy conocida*). Interestingly enough, to be of a traditional family is also to be of a known family, but not necessarily vice-versa. The adjective *conocida* used before a noun also implies a degree of superiority, for instance, "X died, member of a *conocida* family in our social midst." For the middle class to announce publicly that the deceased received the last rites is very important. For the upper classes this is unnecessary, since the only way for them to die is within the Catholic Church.

In the case of the death of someone socially important but not belonging to a traditional or known family, the word *vinculada* (associated or linked) is used by the newspaper reporter. There are those who are "*vinculadas* by marriage and friendship to known families of our city." If the person is generally known for his commercial or professional activity, then "the person was largely (*ampliamente*) *vinculada* to well-known circles of our *sociedad*." (*Sociedad*, in this case, means the elite group.) If social prominence was not so outstanding, this is carefully indicated in the newspaper: the person was "*vinculado* to some *familias conocidas*." *Conocida* in this context refers to prominent families of the city, both patrician and well-known, of the elite group.

Further refinements are noted in newspaper editorials about funer-

---

[3] "Traditional" conveys the sense of being in direct lineage with patrician families. The adjective placed in front of the noun *family* gives further indication of antiquity.

als, weddings, or anniversaries of death. If an individual has achieved professional distinction and his parents are known to have founded a reliable entrepreneurship, then the family may be identified as a *"caracterizada familia"* of the city. The paper can go even further and indicate that the deceased person is a member of an old and *caracterizada familia* of the city or "an appreciated and *caracterizada familia* of our city." Other ways of expressing social standing include the following clichés: "a person from a noted family in our midst," "a person tightly linked to the general social *ambiente*," "a person rooted (*arraigada*) in the city."

Forms of announcements appropriate to personal and individual achievement underplay the family's social background. The word neighbor (*vecino*) appears frequently in the announcements and indicates some distinction in status. Announcements mention "a *vecino* in our midst" or "an appreciated, old, and respected *vecino* in our midst." The phrase "an old person" in the context of the middle economic group usually refers to an elderly European migrant from the nineties who can be distinguished for his "good life" and neighborliness. The status gradations as expressed in these phrases may appear as random choices; nevertheless they project important clues in the social network of the city.

The newspaper editorials about the barrios or the *quintas* of the city may refer to *residentes antiguos*, perhaps known for their political leadership. The newspaper uses the terms "respected" or "esteemed" and may carefully add the name of the barrio. It should be noted that the terms just mentioned are also used for upper-class men, but the naming of the barrio qualifies the situation and marks the social difference.

Some individuals have earned public recognition through activities in sport clubs and other voluntary associations. Biographical articles in these cases may overlook the family background, use the terms "good man" and "good citizen," characterizing the person as unselfish (*desinteresado*). Among the most frequent expressions are the following: "an individual active in different sports and also an active officer of a club," "excellent worker in a commercial house of importance," "a retired farmer," "a humble person" (*una persona sensilla*), "a dedicated official in the army." The death of an individual who remains very criollo—in the sense of a true son of Argentina—whose name is unmistakably from colonial days, is cast with an inescapable touch of ethnicity. It may be written that "he was a person with the values of those who have been born here and have worked our land and soil with honesty, religiosity, optimism, and clean spirit, helping to make this nation."

Ethnicity emerges as an important factor also in cases of individuals who, after many years, have remained "strangers" in the city. If the country of origin happens to be Great Britain, France, or Germany, the respective ethnic stereotype plays an important part. Although these individuals may have remained aloof to national tradition, they might have been models of *cultura*. By their activities in the ethnic centers, they may merit public recognition. When a Jew dies, his ethnicity is mentioned as also are his links to commercial activity and the Jewish group. The announcement will indicate that the ceremony will be held in the Jewish cemetery.

For the people in the city, the personal and social information in the newspaper appears very significant. They frequently comment that not enough has been said about what the person used to be, although this may stem from the shock that death always brings to the relatives and neighbors. Reports and biographical sketches in the newspapers rarely satisfy the socially aspiring families. They always feel that it was not totally correct, and thus become annoyed and resentful. (The same applies to reports of weddings.) The annoyance is less acute as one descends to the lower social categories. It is particularly noticeable in the middle class, where a strong cult of individualism requires the detailed enumeration of all the achievements of the individual. When the announcement is not proper, the newspaper offends those who pay tribute in this manner to an active person.

Like the social ecology of the city, the ecology of the cemetery and the entire complex associated with death and funerals exhibits social stratification and status differences. The actions of people within the city firmly fix the social symbolism at times of funerals or anniversaries of deaths.

Linguistic Differences and Social Classes

The Spanish spoken in Argentina has its unique characteristics. There is no major structural difference from the Spanish spoken in Spain, but the phonological, lexical, and idiomatic differences are obvious. Argentine speech is different from all the dialects of the Iberian Peninsula as well as from that of other Latin American countries.[4] We could therefore assume, even without historical evidence, that the Argentine speech community has been separate and independent from Spain for a long time and that it probably has never formed a single community with its neighbors.

To Spanish-speaking persons traveling through Latin America, variations in speech indicate country of origin, and any confusion in identification is surely linked to a change of residence after the age that dialect "sets." Each country of Latin America has its dialectal indicators, and since there are degrees of communality, smaller, more tightly knit social groups can be determined by the greater similarity in speech. So Argentines are able to classify other Argentines by their regions and provinces of origin. The first national division is that of people from Buenos Aires (Porteños), whose speech is considered urban. Anyone who does not speak in this manner is judged to be a person of the interior or of the rural areas and, consequently, a person of lesser prestige.

Each province differs from the others, although some provinces can be grouped by their speech similarities. To whatever degree these similarities are related to changes from the original Spanish, the provinces that share them can be believed to have formed a community. By speech alone one can determine much of the sociopolitical division of the country. Each province also shows differences between the speech of its urban center (the capital of the province) and its rural area. Since "city" speech usually carries greater prestige than that of the rural areas, immigrants to the city, particularly those entering the *clase media*, try to acquire the characteristics of the "city" speech. The in-

[4] Argentina was colonized by Spaniards from several dialect areas; therefore, different features have been combined.

tention here is not to describe the linguistic differences among the provinces; the purpose is to call attention to the fact that the social differences that exist are reflected in linguistic differences and that both were more pronounced in the past decades than at present.

The phenomenon of linguistic differences does not end on the regional, provincial, rural, or urban level; within a city, as a result of social variables, an individual's dialect depends partly on the group of people with whom he deals daily. The interrelationship of social class and linguistic dialect and style is obvious to all people and an important diagnostic feature for social judgments. Within a city, individuals with specific and constant characteristics in their speech are socially grouped together. Speech type is associated with cultural models that support the public stereotypes of social distinctions. So there is a circular process whereby a social grouping determines dialect, and that dialect determines apparent social class. Those social groups that are proud of their classification cultivate a speech style rather consciously. This is not surprising as a social phenomenon, and it is not presented here as unique for Paraná.

An analysis of speech points to a definite relationship between social levels and speech differences.[5] The range of speech variation corresponds to the social continuum with which the reader is already familiar. By analyzing speech, stopping at specific intervals of this continuum, one can sample the points where variations are most striking. Several linguistic indicators showed that the speech of individuals of a given social standing is more distinctive and more structured than was originally anticipated. The linguistic analysis is based on tapes of general interviews intended to gather information on behavior and oral history, not for dialect study. Nevertheless, many variables were immediately evident, although information on style was meager because of the interview situation and the presence of the interviewer.[6]

---

[5] I wish to thank Joel Sherzer for cooperating with me in the preliminary analysis, and especially Malcah Yeager for refining the first findings and assisting in the formulation of this section. Both were graduate students in linguistics at the University of Pennsylvania at the time of their association with this analysis.

[6] The analysis is presented in Pikean notation for greater accessibility. This is

Social Classes: Manifestations and Dynamics

The upper class in Paraná appears to use the [ř], "assibilated" long *r*. This is a common feature for old families of Spanish descent in many traditional dialect areas of South America. This upper-class indicator does not seem to change under style variation. The difference between this and the standard long *r* is very pronounced. Wherever other speakers use a trilled *r*, the Paraná upper class uses a sound much more like a "curly *z* or *s*." The [ř] may go unnoticed in Paraná; only the upper class and the poor criollos use it, and they use it to the exclusion of the standard long *r*. Thus:

Upper Class	Middle Class	
[řama]	[r̄ama]	for *rama* (bough)
[řElixiɔsU]	[relihioso]	for *religioso* (religious)

The second variable *ll/y* is realized by most of the upper class as [ž] (as in azure). Unlike its appearance in the rest of Argentina, the devoiced [š] (as in assure) is not a feminine marker in Paraná. That is, upper-class men and women both "whisper" [ž] in an appropriate phonological environment. The middle class currently pronounces the *ll* as [y]. There is:

Upper Class	Middle Class	
[žama]	[yama]	for *llama* (flame)
[baža]	[baya]	for *vaya* (go!)

However, the middle class is beginning to use [ž], especially those younger women who are very socially conscious. Thus:

---

slightly modified to allow for some uncommon phonetic variants: /ř/, for example, can be described as [žR] or as [ž] (as in azure), with *r* coloring. Because phonologically it holds the place of a trilled *r* in most Spanish dialects, it is most reasonably transcribed here as ř.

The terminology used here is taken from Labov 1964:102. An indicator is a phonetic realization of a group difference, but it does not usually change with style. A marker, however, shows social and stylistic variation and has consistent effects on judgment of group status. Information on other terminology of the field, as well as some background in the theoretical constructs of sociolinguistics, can be found in Hymes 1966 and Hymes 1967.

	Upper Class (men and older people)		Middle Class (upwardly mobile)	(socially minded women)	
[žama]	[yama]	[žama]	[šama]		for *llama* (flame)
[ɓaža]	[ɓaya]	[ɓaža]	[baša]		for *vaya* (go!)
[žo]	[yo]	[žo]	[šə]		for *yo* (I)

The fact that the middle class does not use [r̃] and that they realize [ž] vs. [š] differently from the upper class would indicate that their model group is not entirely the upper class, but a stereotyped impression of high-prestige usage.

The simplification of orthographic *cc* to [s] occurs in the more relaxed conversational styles of the upper class, although the school-oriented individuals tend to use [ks] in formal style. The middle class tends to use [ks] at all times. In Spain, many consonant clusters were not formerly pronounced as such, and have reappeared as clusters only because of the spelling pronunciation of middle-class South Americans. Subsequently, the spelling pronunciation has become the accepted formal South American pronunciation. The absence of the spelling pronunciation cannot be used as a simple upper-class indicator, because many of the upper class use it in their formal style. The breakdown for Paraná is:

	Upper Class	Upper Middle Class	Lower Middle Class	Lower Class
Conversation: *cc* →	[s]	[ks]	[ks] [s]	[s]
Formal:	[ks]	[ks]	[ks] [s]	[s]

The same applies to other spelling clusters. One could say that the middle class is marked by consistent spelling pronunciation. So, for example:

Upper Class	Middle Class	
[asion]	[aksion]	for *acción* (action)
[asionista]	[aksionista]	for *accionista* (activist)
[esakamente]	[eksaktamente]	for *exactamente* (exactly)
[aʔtualida]	[aktualida]	for *actualidad* (present)

Social Classes: Manifestations and Dynamics 233

One upper-class teacher makes a misspelling pronunciation in her speech. This may mean that although she feels a formal style should have clusters, she was not brought up with clusters in her dialect and now she overcorrects. In some cases this is more obvious because the cluster created may be a common cluster, although not the original one. This teacher says [asEkta] for *accepta* (usually [asEpta] or [asEta]). This is a common analogy—to make *kt* from a *t* that was originally *pt* because *kt* is more common. In many areas the *kt* cluster has become standard in such positions.

All of the upper class also use the strong Castilian /x/ at all times.[7] The middle class all use [ḥ] for /x/. This is one of the clearest class indicators. While the upper class uses the Iberian [x] consistently, the middle-class speakers just as consistently use the standard Latin American [ḥ]. So:

Upper Class	Middle Class	
[xImte]	[ḥEntE]	for *gente* (people)
[IxImplU]	[EḥEmplɔ]	for *ejemplo* (example)

At first glance the pattern of vowels appears erratic, but after analysis it seems there is a systematic difference between the allophonic distribution of the vowels in upper-class and middle-class pronunciation. In an unaccented syllable the distribution is:

	Upper	Lower	
Upper Class	Middle Class	Middle Class	Lower Class
Informal: closed vowels	open vowels	open vowels	closed vowels
Formal: standard vowels	(toward) standard	open vowels	closed vowels (?)

By comparison, the pronunciation of vowels in standard Spanish is as follows:

/é/: [E] in closed syllables [e] in open syllables
    [mEn·te] *mente* (mind) [me·te] *mete* (put)
    [mwEr·ta] *muerta* (dead) [mwe·la] *muela* (molar)
    [pEro] *perro* (dog) [pe·ro] *pero* (but)

[7] This is a strong velar slightly lateralized fricative. The closest sound to it is the German *ch*.

/ĕ/: The stress rules probably follow the syllable division rules. All the vowels are [E] vs. [e], and [ɔ] vs. [o], irrespective of environment. Those that precede stress are most open, followed by the post-tonic vowels.

From the above examples it is immediately obvious that the upper class handles the vowels in a very distinctive way. For the present study their informal speech is of primary concern. The middle-class dialect has vowels even more open than in the standard language. In the upper-class dialect atonic vowels are raised and centralized to a much greater degree than in the standard. In most environments the upper class realizes /ĕ/ as [I] or [i], with parallel realization for the other vowels.

Upper Class	Middle Class	
[mEntI]	[mEntE]	for *mente* (mind)
[pokU]	[pɔkɔ]	for *poco* (little)

Even in a stressed position a vowel after /x/ is also raised: [mEntI] but [xyIntI] vs. standard [hEntE] *gente* (people); [IxyImplU] vs. standard [EhEmplɔ] *ejemplo* (example).

Another possible social marker is /s/. It varies from [s] to [ḥ], [h], and [ø], and there are two distinctive environments: (1) the [s] at the end of words such as *dos pesos* (two pesos); *buenos* (good), *todos* (all), *estos* (these); and the preconsonantal [s]: *mismo* (same), *este* (this), *España* (Spain). (2) The [s] at the beginning of the words and in an intervocalic position: *son* (are), *peso* (weight), *oso* (bear). For the dialect here considered, position (1) is important. In Paraná speakers tend to "reduce" preconsonantal or final *s*:

Formal		Informal	
/eḥte/	/ehte/	/eʔte/	*este* (this)
/deḥpweḥ/	/dehpwe/	/depwe/	*después* (afterward)
/miḥmo/		/mīhmo/	*mismo* (same)

When *s* is pronounced, the upper class has an *s* that is very dental, giving it a much higher pitched frequency than a standard *s*. The *s* spoken by the middle class is very much like the American English *s*.

Social Classes: Manifestations and Dynamics

Besides the segmental indicators that have been listed, there is also a distinctive intonation factor or "melody." South American standard Spanish has the following characteristics in the formal style:
1. Loudness: rise for stress.
2. Syllable lengthens for stress: the greater the length, the more emphatic the statement.
3. Pitch rises for stress and lowers immediately after stress.

If the last stressed syllable falls at the end of a sentence, the rise and return are all on the same syllable: *caridad* (charity, while if it falls on the penultimate syllable—as is most common in Spanish—the rise is on one syllable and the posttonic syllable is again unmarked: *gente* or *gente*. If the stress is on an ultimate short syllable, the word (words) ends on a rise *yo*; if the last stress is an antipenultimate or before, the same modulation as for a penultimate stress is maintained: *contemporánea* (contemporary). In standard Spanish the end of an "unmarked" sentence, signal of your-turn-to-talk, is usually expressed by a drop; however, if stress is, as in Spanish, before the last syllable, the drop can be expressed as before.

In the rural criollo dialect of this area, stress is expressed by longer and more highly pitched syllables. It can be highly dramatized in conversations in which a person wants to appear more traditional or more regionally minded. Anyone who speaks in melodic fashion fits into the stereotype of a lower-class criollo, and may at times be referred to as *un negro* or *persona acriollada*, even though of German, Italian, or Spanish descent. Poor people residing outside the central area of the city manifest this characteristic in their speech. Young people who move into these areas tend to adopt this style in order to be socially accepted. In social groups that have such an intonation pattern, standard Spanish intonation is regarded as snobbish. Anyone whose reference group has the nonstandard pattern accepts that pattern as his own. Intonation is the least conscious dialect indicator but the one that apparently most freely varies with the social referent of the speaker. This would make it the most sensitive indication of present social reference (or, in the case of the younger people, of present social aspiration).

Some Paranaense intellectuals (because of their literary interests) and some professionals (such as lawyers) may choose to use the traditional intonation. People may refer to such a person as *muy criollo* or *muy argentino*, one who is or feels that he is a true, native Argentine with true regional allegiance. Women of the upper class use this style more consistently than men. The intonation (*canto*) has the following characteristics:

1. Change of pitch is used only for prominence or, secondarily, a duration change. Loudness never signals word or utterance prominence.
2. Pitch is lowered on most accented syllables (rather than raised), especially near the end of a sentence. On the last syllable of the utterance they often use the contour ⌢‿ rather than the ‿ contour. (This, of course, is subject to sentence contour meaning, which will not be dealt with here.)
3. A pitch curve from ‿ to ── is not discrete.

Contouring consists of retaining loudness constant, lengthening the stressed syllable, but changing pitch: instead of *gente conocida*, *gente conocida*; instead of *está malo*, *esta malo*. In addition, the older women do not use any modulation of loudness, and only rarely of duration. The younger women use pitch absolutely exclusively.

To summarize the differences in intonation, upper-class women use pitch changes on accented syllable and raise the pitch except at the end of an utterance, where pitch is lowered. Pitch prominence is "contoured" to return to the "base" pitch while still on the stressed syllable. In contrast, the middle class (*a*) shows a stressed syllable with pitch, length of syllable, and extra loudness; (*b*) raises pitch, lengthens the vowels, and makes the syllable louder in all positions in the sentence; and (*c*) makes a discrete pitch rise—pitch goes up on one syllable and returns to "base" on the next, unless the stress is on the last syllable of a sentence.

The middle class pattern is also the standard pattern. Some examples of the local intonation pattern follow:

ni la quiere conocer	nor does she want to know her
duros, todos iguales	hard, all alike
ay señora	oh, lady!
doña Paula	Paula
nunca	never!

This dialectal use of intonation patterns is quite different from that of the rural areas of Argentina. It is difficult to determine the pattern's origin, but at present it is a clear indicator of social influences.

In appropriate situations, people use the socially correct form or the grammatically correct form; these two styles do not necessarily correspond, and on some occasions the mixing of the two styles is socially ridiculed, particularly by upper-class speakers. Those who would like to appear of a social group other than their own must acquire the appropriate indicators for the group to which they wish to belong. As one informant put it with some wit, "As one becomes upper class, one must speak by elongating one's lips" (*estirando el pico*—elongating one's beak), particularly when names of certain important individuals are spoken. Some individuals maintain two speech styles and use them in appropriate circumstances. A middle-class secondary school teacher of Spanish descent views himself as an educated middle-class city person and as a real criollo. Correspondingly, he has two dialects: at times he uses a very middle-class set of features—standard vowels, [r̄] with the very citified multiple trill, a very standard Latin American modulatory intonation pattern. At other times, when he consciously or subconsciously wants to project an image of a *persona acriollada*, he uses raised centralized vowels, the criollo [ɾ̈], and the pitch contours described above. Because he feels that criollos use loud speech (a folk stereotype), he speaks louder when he switches into this dialect, a change evident to the most casual observer.

An elementary school teacher, also middle class, young, Buenos Aires oriented, and socially minded, likewise exhibits two dialects. At all times she maintains a strong [ʃ] for *ll/y*; she has even had enough contact with the upper class of Paraná to have a very dental [s]. She tries very hard to project an upper-class image. Nevertheless, it is still possible to tell her class by (*a*) her open vowels in unstressed position

—[muˑcɔ] (much), [pɔkɔ] (little); (b) her r is not assibilated, except right after the upper-class interviewer says something (understandably this is a very conscious indicator when it is used at all); (c) her consistent use of spelling pronunciations—even the use of ps—/ps/ in [psikɔlohíya] *psicología* (psychology); (d) her /x/, which is [h]; and (e) her modulatory prosodic patterns. In the very academic word *ejemplo* (example) she consistently, carefully enunciates the /xe/ according to the upper-class pattern. It is impossible to determine if this is merely a word she uses only in upper-class group situations or if the sense of the word and the presence of a high prestige auditor combine to "force" her into the upper-class pronunciation. However, when she uses other /x/+/e/ words, she uses her own middle-class system: [hEntE] *gente* (people), but [IxIEmplU] *ejemplo* (example). In the same way, words with r that she says immediately after the upper-class interviewer has spoken use [ř̌], while most r's are [ř].

As a rule, people make an effort to correct their speech pattern to accord with the situation. Once rapport is established, however, the effort to maintain correct middle-class pronunciation may be abandoned if the speaker no longer feels that his identification with that group need be (or can be) maintained.

It is interesting to note that the phonemic systems of the upper class and the poor criollos have many similarities. The historical relationships between the two groups may partially account for this. Both have been in the area longer than the middle class, and there was considerable contact between the two groups before the emergence of the large middle class. Also, both groups are of Spanish origin. Nevertheless, by topic content, style, and vocabulary one can easily distinguish the two groups, primarily because the level of education is so radically different.

Certain words are associated with the different social categories, for instance:

Upper Class	Middle Class	Lower Class	
presta	empresta	empriesta	to lend
fijese	aa...	a la fresca	(an expression of surprise)
poco	algo	chiquito	small portion

Upper-class individuals can afford to use words associated with lower-class speech without great consequences. In fact, this was particularly fashionable during the period of field work; but for individuals attempting to climb socially, the use of words and gestures of the lower class is not helpful.

Like burials in the cemetery, manner of speech also has its definite social position. This is not a strange phenomenon in contemporary modern society, but the degree of class consciousness in Paraná is such that it becomes part of the entire complex relating to the social distinctions daily acknowledged by all individuals. Speech form is, therefore, central to the understanding and operation of the most fundamental principle of social organization in Paraná, namely social class.

Cultural Orientations by Class

One way to view cultural variability is through the investigation of the members' awareness of self and, by extension, of "the world perceived as other than self."[8] Individuals in one culture share not only the physical environment, but also a behavioral one; they respond similarly to surrounding physical and symbolic objects. Hallowell lists several orientations provided by culture that structure man's response to his environment. Besides self-orientation, object, spatiotemporal, motivational, and normative orientations are all culturally defined. In Paraná, all these must be cast in the framework of the social class categories. In each class category, the behavioral environment is clearly defined, and an individual must transcend the boundaries of his social life in order to reach the behavioral environment of people in other social categories. This transcendence is conscious, and the consciousness itself manifests the reality of the cultural boundary. The psychological reality for the individual in the context of the aforementioned variables is part of his personal world view and that of people who share his behavioral environment. It brings a degree of actual or theoretical corporateness to each of the social categories.

A brief review of the basic orientations that Hallowell believes are provided by culture is most helpful in the analysis of each of the social categories in the city of Paraná. Self-orientation, object orientation,

[8] Hallowell 1955:75.

spatiotemporal orientation, motivational orientation, and normative orientation appear to be unique for each level. The culture provides each individual within it a perspective that is transmitted in the process of socialization and incorporated in the value system of each class.

Let us begin with an analysis of the general orientations of each class. First, we will consider the *clase baja*. For adults, the immediate circle of spouse and children constitutes the closest and most meaningful relationships. Outside this circle there are "one's people" with whom one may associate in public places but always with reservation. Some of these are the *gente buena* who can be friends, but this classification must be reassessed from day to day. Relations between adult friends are always brittle. Nevertheless, one does not avoid making friends simply because there is the ever-present possibility of an immediate end. The people of the *clase baja*, however, are most careful and maintain a reserved attitude toward others.

The fact that people can be crafty (*pícara*), untrustworthy, bad-intentioned, and ungrateful creates a feeling of suspicion expressed by aloofness. Occasionally two individuals feel that they can trust each other without reservations; then the attachment becomes intense. These two may constantly visit and assist each other. Everyone knows, however, that such relationships last only a short time. Relationships are also affected—augmented, predicted, or brought to an end—by specialists like the curers. Their negative attitude toward human relations, which justifies their role, perpetuates the assumption that close friends may become future enemies. The result, again, tends to stimulate individualism and social isolation and to abate organizational activity.

There is an imaginary social boundary separating the people of the *clase baja* from the "others"—people connected to one another through the Church, the government, clubs, business, etc. Generally, these are viewed as an assemblage of men striving to curtail the freedom of the people of the *clase baja* and pressuring them for their own ends. The people of the *clase baja* feel that the "others" prefer not to see and recognize the true needs of the *clase baja*. These needs are rarely assuaged by those in power, and this fosters the prevalent pessimism of the lower class. One might argue that the lower class should rely on their own efforts, but these are limited by their circumstances.

As a result, the elements of the culture intrinsic to the lower class come to be viewed very favorably in comparison with "objects" from the outside. Particularly, the close relationship to elements of nature is highly valued. The people of the *clase baja* live and act as if they were in a rural setting. Thus "the orientation of the self toward objects of his behavioral environment with reference to the satisfaction of its needs,"[9] as Hallowell defines the motivational orientation, is in terms of the folk model of rural life. The motivational orientation, which constitutes a substantial layer of the culture of this class, is akin to that which is considered traditional and pertaining to criollismo. The normative elements of criollismo—values, standards, ideals—play an important role in relation to the cultural orientation.

People's conceptualization of space and time Hallowell views as being very intimately linked. For the Paranaense *clase baja* there are ecological niches in the city in which individuals of this class—men, women, and children—can move about in the spirit of "owners" and creators. But these are definable, bounded sections, not the whole city, except during special occasions like Carnaval. Likewise, the present occupies most of the thinking of these people; the future on earth or the afterlife play a minor role in their daily concerns. The orientation toward the past is generalized and does not deal with ancestors. Rather, the stress is on the way of life that sprang from the country—the source of the "good life." Through the criollo complex, the temporal and the spatial orientations connect with the motivational and the normative orientations.

These generalizations that emerge from the data may be of only heuristic value, but they are representative of a model constantly in motion. Within the model, human beings are able to change—to expand, abandon, or preserve elements in order to meet their specific needs. There are, no doubt, significant variations within this group from individual to individual, but this general social configuration derives from the study of basic structural forms. There are transitional

[9] Ibid., p. 100.

social fields and marginal individuals that emphasize outside elements more strongly. When the basic orientations are lost, however, and the individual's social network shifts, then another social level is reached, and thus we pass to a consideration of the *clase media*.

In the *clase media* the nuclear family, the extended family, and a small number of individuals of trust (*de confianza*), considered as if they were of the family, constitute the most relevant circle for the individual. These are the people expected to come together during family celebrations, fiestas, and at times of need and crisis. The other circles surrounding the individual narrow as one moves further away from the nuclear family, where rights and privileges cannot be easily taken away or questioned. Beyond the family, there are people in proximity (neighbors, acquaintances, people of the city, people from the country, the rich, the poor). All are physically close, known to be inhabitants of the same city, but separated in thought.

The individual's self-image is guided by the concept of *clase media*, which is defined and used in a great number of ways. A further duality, however, in terms of *cultura* is most relevant in the context of the *clase media*. There are those who work with their hands, the *gente más humilde*, and those who do not work with their hands and are in or near the professional groups. The economic differences between members in these two categories may not be very significant, but the social distinction is sufficient to dominate decisions on association and identification. For the manual workers with limited resources, primary school and trade-school training are the educational goals; the children of white-collar workers—teachers, semiprofessionals, or professionals—are more likely to acquire secondary education (normal school for teachers, national colleges for a B.A., or business school). The social dichotomy is also reflected in the typology of clubs. The *clubes de ciudad* are patronized and frequented by those with a higher educational background, while the *clubes de barrios* are more apt to be supported by persons (particularly men) with less formal education, who are small entrepreneurs or skilled and semiskilled workers.

The concept of *cultura*, as already described, is vital to the orientation of men and women who desire social recognition. *Cultura*, the appropriate white-collar occupation, and wealth must be maintained

Social Classes: Manifestations and Dynamics   243

in the proper equilibrium to improve an individual's social position. This is very consciously pursued, especially *cultura*—the most attainable and valued quality. Ethnic and religious backgrounds are also variable among the *clase media* and serve as additional classificatory schemes. These attributes from the past cannot be erased, but one may overlook them or profess historical ignorance. Conceptually, the social environment is related to the "civilized ways of Europe." Within the setting of an ethnically pluralistic nation, distinctive for constitutional democracy, social equality should be operative.

In the normative orientation, deceit, incompatibility, animosity, cheating, opportunism, propriety, and patriotism are prevalent themes, strong enough to affect the orientation of the self. One can state fairly safely that an unfriendly atmosphere prevails at the present and prevents individual and mass progress. The behavioral environment is filled with personal anxiety. "Social distraction" offers a means to cope with the situation. Congeniality, indifference, social acting (*figuración*), and strong subjective involvement are linked to this notion and are utilized for the classification of individuals in this class. Interpersonal experiences based on these premises affect the people's disposition. The degree of personal sensitivity is further heightened by the thought of "what people will say."

Behind the normative orientation are the institutions of the larger society. The political and governmental institutions of the city, the province, and the nation are desirable sources of income. Economic success while in office is an implicitly expected possibility. Government is not only a source of income for many, but also is conceived at all levels as the entity responsible for the welfare of the citizens. Promises and planning for the benefit of the populace are rarely sufficient. Although numerous plans are made, they are rarely realized. The well-informed and perceptive middle-class citizen views development or potential development as a continuous process of improvisation that affects his own individual plans. Society is thought not to do enough for a person's future, and it is up to the individual and his immediate family and friends to plan and manipulate his existence.

The Church, on the other hand, is there to serve society. The clergy is perceived as a body of administrators of the Church. When it comes to the direction of individual habits of thought, however, and the question of the accuracy of the theological premises of the Church, the role of the clergy is underplayed. A large majority of the *clase media* is traditionally Catholic, but they like to believe that they are free-thinking. Religious diversity, however, is part of the definition of this class, and the amelioration of religious discrimination is very apparent in contrast to the past. Religious institutions alone are not responsible for the salvation of a man's soul; it is the function of the Church and the people to join in the common effort to manipulate the final destiny of souls.

The cemetery exists to perpetuate the memory of immediate relatives (a social rather than a religious function). In the cemetery the past meets the present; the past, as a social entity, stands still for those who have died, while those who are alive move into the social world of the future. This, indeed, places ancestors and contemporaries into distinctive social spheres. The social levels visible in the cemetery may not fit the present reality, and if social discomfort is experienced, then the past is underplayed to the advantage of one's social image. The public details of one's past are not part of the "behavioral environment and code." The combination of past and present is not so prominent in the spatiotemporal orientation of the middle class as is the combination of present and future. For the *clase media* the past was not a better time; rather, the present and the future should be better than the past. This conceptualization of time is powerful enough to attenuate the present, to overlook the past, and to convey a clear image of where a person intends to be in the future. The manner of perceiving time, obviously stronger in some cases than in others, is a basis for structuring goals, interpersonal relations, life standards, and values. The conceptual reality is probably guided by the way the temporal orientation is patterned.

Although scientific orientations are prevalent, particularly in medicine, illnesses unsuccessfully treated by doctors may be cured by the techniques of *curanderos*. There are mysteries of life that science has not yet comprehended. When an individual enters a situation in which the competition is uncertain, the *curandero*'s role becomes important. If there is some truth to the fact that human relations can be manipulated and that there is a way to bring about economic success and psychological contentment, one should try that formula; there is nothing wrong in trying.

The *humildes* and the people of the *clase media* may live side by side in some areas of the city; individuals of the *clase baja* may serve as domestic servants to those in the highest level of the *clase media*. Although there is physical proximity, the social distance is always obvious. The *gente humilde*, who live without the trimmings of *cultura*, are forced to remain in their own social and ecological niche. By the same token, where there is physical proximity with *clase alta* professionals, social distance is also kept. The social boundaries are well demarcated by membership in clubs and participation in public life.

The self, object, spatiotemporal, motivational, and normative orientations derived from the social context of the *clase media* result in a forceful cultural pluralism. The individual human being as a conceptual entity seems to overshadow the potential roles that might be played by institutions attempting to coordinate group efforts. Although the deviations from the model may be many, the essence constitutes a reality for most persons of the *clase media*.

If the emphasis on the present and future is relevant in the cultural orientation of the *clase media*, the temporal orientation for the *clase alta* presents us with a significantly different situation. The future is less relevant, leaving the present and especially the past in the most prominent positions. In the socialization process within the *clase alta*, individuals begin in the past and, it would seem, the present incorporates the future. There is a continuous flow from the past into the present and vice versa. In other words, one does not find the usual lines of separation into the three time levels. The past is very much a part of the present.

As has already been pointed out, the *clase alta* individual is very strongly oriented toward his own group. The individual alone is not prominent, as in the *clase media*. What one is, one owes to ancestors and to living relatives. "Family" in this class refers to a large group of individuals united by the symbol of those in the past. The forces of the past act upon each person to keep him within the group and thus to promote a degree of social unity. Individualism and personal achievement do not flow out naturally from the general orientation. By the nature of the historical unity, the whole family shares, lives, and recreates an ancestor's achievement. One might say that an individual is never alone and is always followed by his ancestors' shadows, just as he must follow the path of his ancestors' reputation. This is an important dimension of the spatiotemporal orientation granted by the culture of this group. The notion of a group having specified rights to a distinctive style of life and to public leadership stands out in the cognitive framework of individuals. The future has been prearranged by family and ancestors, and the stability of the system stems from the group's support.

School training is in the most exclusive manner possible. Private and Catholic schools are essential to this orientation; universities are the destiny of the *clase alta*. Men from the traditional families are conditioned to choose selected professions, law in particular.

The *clase alta* is not a totally closed group; ancestry and *abolengo* are important for the social separation of newcomers. In the *clase alta* there are people with some ancestry and others with none. But the latter possess desirable attributes such as wealth and *cultura* and have voluntarily sought membership in the Club Social. The Club Social constitutes the main and the most important filter for all the subcategories of the *clase alta*. Ancestry remains a crucial distinction that is usually manifested through the formation of cliques. Each family speaks of "our group," and these affiliations, sometimes reinforced by intermarriage, have been handed down through several generations. Individuals supported by their cliques may exercise exclusiveness and display the social differences within the social club. When it becomes necessary to protect the reputation of members of the club against other social classes, then overall unity emerges; there is a "we" standing in opposition to "them," the masses.

The masses are conceived by the traditional old members of the *clase alta* in a social continuum that goes from the *gente muy humilde* to individuals with good economic means. In some cases, the lack of personal contact with the classes below results in a uniform conceptualization of the masses. There are some individuals, however, with extensive contacts beyond the Club Social, and, in contrast, they show an awareness of the many and complex social differences existing in the *clase media*. Not only do they know that there are people beyond their immediate social circles, but they also know in detail the nature of their existence.

Among concepts guiding the dynamics of social relations among the *clase alta*, there is, first of all, a sense of having been born with a destiny. The nature of the links with distinguished ancestors fosters a sense of uniqueness, distinction, and separation from the masses. In the normative orientation, each person finds support for personal security and innate superiority. As one informant stated:

> One may talk about these matters with others who share the same perspective. To speak about one's own background to disinterested individuals results in pedantry. Nowadays, it is pedantic to identify oneself as the great-grandson of an early general. It is not a matter of feeling superior, but rather an immense satisfaction in having these roots. One learns to value that which is old in one's own blood. Changes in the economic system have allowed mobility, and some people have climbed to superior levels in the beginning of this century. In family conversations, one recalls the background of some individual who is the grandson of a butcher or another kind of small entrepreneur. Here is the difference from us: we can trace ancestors instead to governors, senators, presidents, or members of the legislative body.

The value placed on being gentlemanly and proper rules interpersonal relationships and displays of emotions. It is also a means to separate the *clase alta* from the others.

The social and political changes of the last decade have affected the strength of the upper class by curtailing the exercise of their socially derived privileges. Internal as well as external pressures exist and seem to indicate a trend toward decreasing emphasis on the socially privileged individuals. While the world around may appear chaotic to the *clase media*, the people of the *clase alta* are still in positions that "provide for an intelligible interpretation of events in the behavioral environment on the basis of traditional assumptions . . . regarding the 'causes' of events."[10] The *clase alta* perceives society in a very organ-

[10] Ibid., p. 91.

ized fashion. The rest of the people, the *pueblo*, are assumed to need an intellectual understanding of man and society. The views and interpretations of the people should, from the upper class's point of view, come from the elite.

The institutions of the Church and of government occupy prominent positions in the orientational configuration. Both are conceived and used as means to support a group's cultural ends, and in both cases the nature of the institutions provides opportunities for social distinction. The clergy and the Church are not separated, as was the case in the *clase media*. Religion can be derived only through membership in the Church and by observation of the sacraments. The rites of passage are carefully marked, either privately or in public, but always with the pomp of this class. The people expect this. Government, both provincial and national, is of much concern and is associated with their class image. This way of thinking is linked to the involvement of ancestors in the formation of the province and nation.

Participation in charitable organizations by women of the *clase alta* constitutes an attempt to assist in the alleviation of the social problems of the city. This publicly manifested desire to serve reflects a responsibility attributed to the upper class by literature. Within the group, the charitable organizations function as internal social outlets. Their dual function is evident. On the one hand, they extend assistance to the needy, and on the other, they fulfill the role of the upper class in the city.

Besides the gatherings in the Club Social, the gatherings of women in social circles bring together representatives of many cliques. In these situations public issues are discussed and judgment is passed. Our study of the city was discussed and evaluated many times. The members of the team who were studying the *clase baja* and *clase media* could be viewed only as subversive. The proper study of social history must be done only through the *clase conocida*. But the question was asked whether an outsider can do it properly when he has not grown up with the social sensitivity of the *clase alta*.

It would seem that, by definition of this class, the soul easily reaches its final place after death. There is an implicit public assumption that one's final destiny is part of the class definition. The family monuments in the cemetery, the celebrations of anniversaries, the offerings of bronze plaques and flowers in family *panteones*—all remind individuals to keep alive the memory of earlier members of the *gente conocida*. The cemetery and the clear view of each casket containing the remains of a relative are in the present, and through these there is a continuous association and identification from generation to generation.

If one compares the three class levels, there seems to be in the *clase baja* a good deal more room for expansion than in the others. By the same token, individual atomization in the lower class seems to be much higher. In the *clase media* the individual atomization continues, but superimposed on it are the institutional organizations and conceptualizations guiding human relationships. This is even more accentuated in the *clase alta*.

These descriptions are only profiles of the relationships of the most crucial and most vital elements to a class social existence. The Argentine cultural elements are present in all the class levels and in various degrees of sophistication; but, "the social orientation of the self" differs considerably in each case. Although the class system does not support much cultural continuity, mobility is feasible within the special conditions outlined.

Cementing Social Classes

The commonly uttered phrase *así es la manera de ser del pueblo* (this is the way to be of the *pueblo*) refers without a doubt to a cementing force created in the social history of Argentina. More precisely, the phrase relates to the individual's specific perception of and motivation toward social relations that are ordered by a system of categorizing and classifying individuals. This way of ordering diversities in Paraná—or for that matter in Argentina—is not something of the last few years but is imbued with the unique history of the population of the area.

The beginning of the system for social differentiation should be understood historically. The *clase alta* of the first centuries after the Conquest maintained that a few have inherent rights to handle the destiny of the people and to direct contact with European people. Thereafter, this provided sufficient ground to support a system of formal social differentiation. With much public pomp a minority became the dominant ruling elite; in this role they displayed behavior and speech style proper to a group in their position. Cohesiveness was derived from the distinctive feeling that history has reserved a place for the "chosen," a place to represent and to lead the *pueblo*. In the 1880s this feeling was manifested in the capital of the nation as well as in this provincial capital of Entre Ríos. Together with this feeling, the objective of Europeanizing Argentina became a significant concern of the ruling minority. McGann's insightful analysis states that the generation of the eighties held direct responsibility for "Europeanizing Argentina." He remarked: "If this decade were not a golden age, it seemed to the Argentine aristocrats to be its dawn. Provincial yet cosmopolitan; proud of their land and themselves yet quick to imitate the ways of other lands and other men; eager for internal peace yet on the verge of a bloody revolution; liberal in economic matters but conservative in politics; sensitive to the nuances of European culture yet adolescent in its domestic application; proud of their history but prouder of their future."[11] The phrase "quick to *imitate* the ways of other lands and other men" is significant; the model of the social system was not indigenous.

The classic work of Lucio V. López, *La Gran Aldea*, describes some aspects of life among the elite of Buenos Aires and illustrates the close affinities between that elite and Europe. López writes that it was not "chic to speak Spanish in the great social world; it was necessary to sprinkle the conversation with English words and French expressions, carefully pronounced, to credit the stock of a gentleman." The strong kinship with European tradition meant "good sense, experience, fortune, and in one single word, the decent people. Outside us are the rabble, the plebians. We are the head; the pueblo are our arms."[12] The elite conceived of social manners, public interaction, individual sophistication, and conspicuous consumption as part of a European tradition; land, wealth, and ancestry became the necessary conditions for the social standing of individual and family.

[11] McGann 1957: 65.
[12] López 1928:112, 41.

The important cultural process for small provincial capitals was adjusting the European elements, copied in Buenos Aires, to a new ecology and creating local historical symbols that would generate and support the new cultural style distinctive to the American experience. European *cultura* and *civilización* were forceful models to reproduce faithfully in Argentina. For the intellectuals, Europeanism had the elements of "reason, freedom, and welfare." An Argentine writer remarked that "to progress was to get out from under Americanization and enter into Europe."[13] Copying thus stood in the foreground of social development and was a process evident to Ortega y Gasset. After his visit to Argentina, concerned over what he had seen, Ortega y Gasset confessed that "a pueblo cannot choose among several styles of life; it either lives according to that which is its own or it dies."[14] But the economically able landed gentry (*los hacendados*) continue to support a style of life appropriate to their rank in society —a style that, like that of the upper class in other South American cities, has been in imitation of Europe.[15]

No doubt the European immigrants settling in this part of the New World must have experienced much disorientation as they discovered that Argentinismo—something supposed to have a character of its own—was an extension of the Europe that many had hoped to leave behind. It was paradoxical that the most European-oriented individuals represented the elite, but by virtue of their ancestry they represented also pure Argentinismo, sometimes referred to as *criollismo*.

While the Buenos Aires elite looked toward and identified themselves with the refinements of Europe, the interior cities of Argentina, among them Paraná, looked toward Buenos Aires and through it to Europe. The thriving metropolis of Buenos Aires was for the interior the symbol of Europe in America, and everyone was proud to have it in Argentina. In this way, a sense of Argentine Europeanism was channeled into the interior and modified according to the local economic possibilities and human resources. The interior cities, socially dominated by Buenos Aires, copied the strong sense of social differen-

[13] Mafud 1965:237.
[14] Ibid., p. 254.
[15] Wagley 1963:chapter 3.

tiation and also set in motion a highly stratified society. The Paraná elite maintained aspirations for national distinction and entertained the desire to belong to the national elite.

As one traces structural lines into the past, a picture of a particular kind of change emerges. It is somewhat intriguing that the change does not occur as change in the established principles that support the social structure, but rather it occurs as a substantive addition to the system itself. In the beginning we find a two-class system, with only an embryonic development of a third small group (see fig. 21). The *hacendados* constitute the traditional Paranaenses who, because of their family's antiquity, can claim more Argentinidad. Their names appear in the history books and in public places; their ancestry cannot be questioned. Those who cannot claim pure ancestry but can trace descent from very early colonists also enjoy a high degree of Argentinidad or *criollismo* and identify with the patrician heroes and Argentine folklore.

In the nineteenth century, Entre Ríos needed population for its rural areas. The *hacendado* class expected that European immigrants could contribute to the further Europeanization of their own society. Few of the leaders, however, estimated the social consequences that a massive migration would have on the country's social system and culture. With the influx of the nineteenth-century immigrants, the clear social boundaries of the past collapsed, and people were forced to compromise values, ideals, and standards. The exclusive style of life was questioned and relegated to a conservative and quiescent tradition; only a handful of families remained as models of the *clase alta*, or at least of what a *clase alta*—the *aristocráticos*—ideally should be. Ancestry, land, Argentinismo, and Europeanism, which had constituted the principal conditions in their orientation and prerequisites for classification as *gente de abolengo*, lost their primacy with the influx of the new population.

If the large number of European immigrants had not appeared on the scene, the social stratification would surely have continued to be based on the traditional dichotomy. The arrival of the masses of European immigrants during the nineteenth and early twentieth centuries

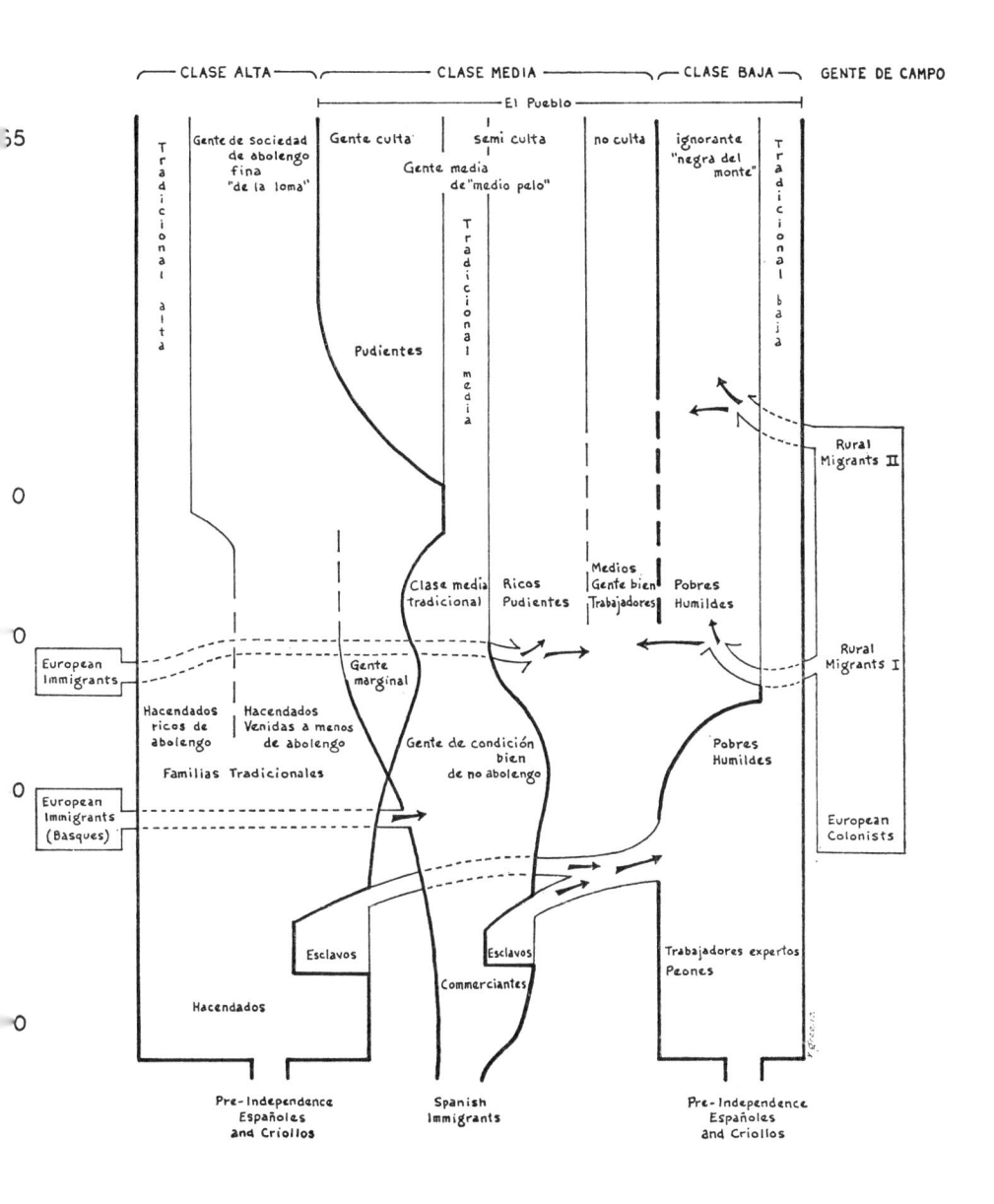

STRATIFICATION MODEL THROUGH TIME

Fig. 21

crowded the traditional groups—the elite and the pueblo or *los humildes*. The accommodation of these European foreigners (*extranjeros*) in Paraná proceeded rather rapidly. Newcomers found an initial social niche in the pueblo above the *clase baja* and proceeded in subsequent years to move upward and to achieve differentiation by their accomplishments in the New World. The *humilde* criollos, with and without *cultura*, were crowded by the new European population, and, by the same token, the *humilde* became even more distant from the elite.

After 1900 the European immigrants became the *clase media*. This rapidly formed social group soon advocated a new political outlook and sought social reformation. The heterogeneity of the *clase media* was emphasized by its members. People occupying the middle category became known as the *gentes decentes*, *gente de media categoría*, *gente de vecindad*, *vecinos de respeto*, and *gente con un poco de cultura*. For those residing outside the city proper, the names (with definite social implications) were *quintero* (horticulturalist), *chacarero* (farmer), and *colono* (colonist). To refer to all of them together as a social category the phrase *gente de campo* was frequently used.

At first the city people presented different social images as forcefully and as dramatically as possible. But with the passage of time, the emphasis on modernization, and the distance from the European-born grandparents, there remained less latitude for self-expression and social improvisation. The reason for the change seems to lie in the nature of the social system. It had become necessary to be on guard; economic competition, related to the social standing of the family, grew acute. Personal discomforts became obvious, and social jealousy was the inevitable consequence of the heterogeneous situation. At present there is still a mood of social instability, even within each level. Living together for less than a century has not been sufficient to bridge social and cultural differences or to prevent the internal misunderstandings attributable to the diversity of backgrounds.

Although traditional Argentine *cultura* remained with families of *abolengo* and those of non-*abolengo* who were entitled to claim social priority, the *extranjeros*, or second generation descendants of for-

Social Classes: Manifestations and Dynamics 255

eigners, soon also claimed the appellation of criollo.[16] The *extranjeros* made the first step toward Argentinidad as their descendants took a position within the established lines of the social classes and entered in competition with those who felt that they had more rights because of their long ancestry in Argentina.

The social arena became a truly dramatic setting for a number of years. The culture of the *clase media* was in formation and modernization began to play an important part. New generations reasserted themselves within the historical structure held constant by the old patrician families. Striking is the fact that the application of a great amount of time and energy to one's own appearance and to the external appearance of one's home became a recognized social phenomenon. A large number of individuals made this aspect of life essential to their social existence. Conspicuous consumption appeared as a strong element among the young generations of the forties and the fifties who initiated a total cultural break with Europe. The average individual continued to center his thoughts upon himself and seemed to lack any consideration of his social surroundings.

Elements of enculturation were clearly manifested as the *extranjeros* competed for higher positions in the social scale. The social game in the city was heightened dramatically as the desire for social mobility among the immigrants increased. There can be little doubt that the strong motivation to acquire rapid wealth, to refine their *cultura*, and to display the most appropriate symbols in public dramatized the social play. Paraná became a formal society—severe and conformist.

While the traditional Argentine Paranaenses displayed a sense of ownership and historical pride, the new arrivals or their first-generation descendants struggled to acquire an equivalent sentiment and to feel part of the destiny of the nation. Most immigrants' descendants preserved little knowledge of their ancestors' past and culture and looked toward their own future in Argentina. History, however, had placed Argentinidad feelings in the hands of the elite traditional

---

[16] By definition, criollos in the colonial period were all of those born in the Argentine of Spanish parentage, a claim which the second-generation Europeans of the twentieth century could similarly make.

group, their position supported by a well-established power structure. The Italians, Germans, Jews, Russian-Germans, Poles, and new Spaniards of the first generation were left with two alternatives: either to become part of the existing social structure or to center their social activities around their own ethnic organizations while passively watching their children struggle with the system. Those in the upper levels of the *clase media* tended toward a strong Argentinismo.

There can be little doubt that the point of reference for the population was in the past based upon the concept of the three social levels—upper, middle, and lower; this finds strong continuity into the present. As we take a central position in each level, the features become evident. In a social system such as this in Paraná, the application of the principle constitutes an unquestionable reality of the society. As uncomfortable as it appears to be for some individuals, it *is* a reality and, for a small town and city, an intense one. It is a phenomenon to be aware of, and, due to the openness of the system, one which allows an interesting social game during one's lifetime.

Furthermore, with the recognition of this social reality, defining the "self" and adopting a modus vivendi are clear; acknowledging it requires less individual effort. Public roles to be played, formalities to be observed during interaction, levels of propriety and social fitness, the uses of prestige symbols, language styles—all constitute the cultural content for the individual to learn and to use. The divisions of classes must thus be conceptualized as in constant movement. The people themselves continuously fluctuate only to reestablish the social equilibrium of a historical formal organization.[17]

The partial descriptions of each social level are only symptomatic of the strong differences with roots in a national past that, if neglected, would obscure the understanding of the present. The social hierarchy in Paraná is based upon historically conditioned social differences and privileges, and therefore an individual's place in it and what one is socially are not altogether his own social creation. From both a theoretical and practical viewpoint, social classes were in the past and continue to be the central organizing principle in the fabric of the city,

---

[17] For an interesting comparison with another Latin American city, see Whiteford 1960, particularly the material concerning Popayán, a Colombian city.

Social Classes: Manifestations and Dynamics

and only recently have people begun to question whether the principle can properly encompass the diversity of human gifts. Are modernization and the progress of a potentially industrial society compatible with a strongly class-conscious society?[18]

While social scientists have been concerned with this question and continue to deal with a variety of theoretical models, Paranaenses feel that the fundamental aspects of their social life cannot be easily modified. The renovation process has been stronger than the changes brought about by substitutions of the basic elements. An informant reflecting about life in Paraná said: "We understand ourselves and meet our obligations with the rules of our *cultura*. We as men elsewhere are the product of our own history. . . . To belong to a social category is to belong to a *tradición* and to be a Paranaense is to be in *la tradición Argentina*. Our conformity is based on our social history, a history which we must respect, believe, and continue to build upon with its fundamental assumptions. If we lose this perspective we will confuse ourselves."

---

[18] Many scholars concerned with the nature of social and cultural dynamics have addressed themselves to this point at considerable length. Classical contributions have been made by Émile Durkheim, Max Weber, Karl Marx, Alfred I. Kroeber, Pitirim Sorokin, and other social scientists. See Parsons, Shils, Naegele, and Pitts 1961, vol. 2; also for a useful bibliography of anthropological sources on culture change up to 1952 see Keesing 1953.

IV. Growing Up: To Live Is to Conquer

> The continuity of our cultural life depends upon the way in which children in any event receive the indelible imprint of their social tradition. (Margaret Mead, *Growing Up in New Guinea*, p. 155)

Introduction

The *vecindad*, the primary and secondary schools, and the army will be used in chapters 8–10 as reference points. They constitute the stages through which youth tests and finds the individual latitude allowed by his society.

Social boundaries exist by definition of the system. "To find oneself" (as in the case of North American society) does not constitute the most important concern in the life of a Paraná youngster. Rather to find a suitable life style and a career are the central concerns that begin early in life. This preoccupation is not his alone, but becomes his whole family's obsession as they become absorbed with the destiny of their children and themselves. Thus the family together may set up the *conquest* of life; conquering is a never-ending process. Through their children's future accomplishments adults may gain a social standing previously missed. The strong desire to "be" something develops a spirit of conquest (*conquista*) of human relations (*conquistar una muchacha, un amigo*, etc.) which begins in the *vecindad* and continues into other city institutions.

In this section we are interested neither in the traditional anthropological analysis of the socialization of children nor in the effects of that socialization on personality development. The emphasis is on how adolescents find ways to accommodate and to manipulate many of the cultural pressures that, in a realistic way, emanate from the city social system. By observing the process of adults interacting with young people and children, one can test the strength of basic orientations and social principles. By the time children reach the caretaking public institutions, their predisposition toward education as a means of attaining social success is indeed well established. In the tradition of the educational system, the child must conform to well-specified rules. His steps are clearly prescribed. Inasmuch as all Paranaenses have coped with the same institutional variables and organized them into a coherent system, the role of shared reference points becomes evident. Thus we shall return to familiar profiles—neighborhood, barrio, class—in an attempt to document institutionalized individual experiences that relate directly to the cognitive structure of the population.

In the chapter "Finding Social Boundaries" two assumptions underlie the discussion: that adults possess an inherent right to dominate children, and that as members of a household with a specific social standing, children are required to learn to manifest the adults' aspirations and social status. In the neighborhood, general interaction with adults takes place; companionships and friendships are formed, and children test and find the degree of personal freedom. The road is not as wide open as they might have been led to believe. The emphasis in the household on conformity demands a great deal from them; evaluating and discriminating in public become necessary. *Vecindad* is soon conceptualized as a paradox of physical togetherness and subtle social competition.

At the age of seven the child enters school, another context, which this time he faces alone. Prepared by the life in his home and the neighborhood, he finds in the school another situation for a *conquista*. The powerful orientation within the institution toward the acquisition of *cultura* gives rise to intense social consciousness. At this moment he becomes aware that the world around him presents strongly defined social boundaries. Life appears to the child as serious an enter-

Introduction

prise as his family has conditioned him to think. As life moves on, the pressures increase until induction into the army (for men), when by definition of that institution's charter everyone should be treated as social equals. It does not take long to understand that this is partially a myth.

As a youngster passes through these institutional landmarks it becomes clear that much is determined for him; he is constantly confronted with rigorous rules of what to learn, how to learn, how to accommodate, how to act, and how to think. It has been said that as a result of life experiences and the social context Argentines like to "be" something rather than to "do" something.[1] Paranaenses might share this national value orientation, but before committing ourselves to a point of view we must turn to some of the stages in life common to everyone.

Gillin, with his concern for the study of modern Latin American society and culture, became very much aware of the "social-position consciousness" of all Latin American people and furthermore of the Latins' recognition of *mobility*. He went on to explain:

> ... everyone is aware that he is born to a certain social position which is one of the facts of life, but at the same time he can perhaps improve this position. ... Thus, according to the Latin American pattern, one may rise in the social scale if he has the soul to do so; but at the same time one recognizes and accepts, at least for the time being, his position in society. He has no right to expect more. Strange as it may seem to a North American, the acceptance of the social order as given is not, for Latin Americans, inconsistent with the concept of individuality as they conceive it. At one and the same time, therefore, the average Latin American is motivated to maintain the established order and also to take advantage of it for his own personal ends with the help of his friends, including kinsmen of various types.[2]

In sum, Paranaenses share the Argentine national social-class orientation, which coincides also with that of other modern Latin American societies. Let us turn to a more detailed description of the ways culture, society, and the individual come together.

[1] Filliol 1961, chapter 2.
[2] Gillin 1955:496–497.

8. FINDING SOCIAL BOUNDARIES

Children and Adults

Adults feel that they have an inherent right to call upon a child and that, as members of the household, children should learn to represent adults and to assist in household chores. A "typical" neighborhood of the *clase media* was selected for intensive observation. In it there live office employees, small private entrepreneurs, retired government workers, teachers, semiprofessionals, and a few unskilled workers. It is also typical in that a variety of ethnic backgrounds are present: Jews, Italians, Germans, and Spaniards. The houses do not differ from each other in value; the lots are relatively small and have the traditional walled patios in the back. The neighborhood has touches of architectural modernity, currently an important middle-class value.

In the style of daily shopping, children are constantly sent for small domestic purchases. The oldest child usually gets more involved in the household errands than his younger brothers and sisters. When there are no children in a household to run errands, the housewife depends more on the services of door-to-door vendors. As children grow older (around high-school age), running errands is left to a younger child or to an older member of the household. Teenage girls continue the errands until they become *señoritas*. Certain errands are considered proper, while others can be detrimental to the social prestige of the household and its members. In the past, a child from a poor rural or city family would live with a wealthier family to run their errands and serve the traditional *mate* to adults in exchange for housing, food, clothes, and primary education. This arrangement released the children from their household responsibilities.

An adult from another household may ask a neighbor's child to run to the store for him. To do this, however, a tacit understanding with the parents is necessary; interference with the smooth running of a household would be resented.

When a child is sent on an errand to a small store or to deliver a message, he is expected not to stop or be stopped. He is performing an adult task and must behave accordingly. Any errand requires a precise period of time according to distance and hour of the day. When it is not accomplished as expected, the storekeeper may be blamed for not helping the household and for not listening to the message delivered by the child. If this happens repeatedly, *vecinos* may begin to resent the storekeeper. As the child runs in and out of the store, parents expect cooperation from other adults; the child is entitled to be acknowledged and respected—after all, he is representing the adults. He cannot be called a child of the street—*chico de la calle*, or *callejero*.[1]

When a child on an errand is invited by another to play, he should answer, "I am on an errand." Interference from another child is interfering with an adult activity, and therefore a "good" child must not divert another from his task. When two children on an errand get involved in a prolonged conversation on the street, discomfort on the part of both children becomes evident. Only "bad" boys defy adults and stop to play marbles for awhile.

A five- or six-year-old child learns to go to a corner store if there is no street crossing. Often he carries a written message for the storekeeper. While a six-year-old undertakes small ventures, older children are responsible for the important errands. The situation of errands clearly entitles the child to rights that are not proper to a child under other circumstances. He may say, "I am in a hurry" (*estoy apurado*) while tapping a coin on the counter. The storekeeper accepts this de-

---

[1] "To be of the street" is frequently used to indicate someone who is constantly wasting his time on the street or sidewalk and not helping the adults in his home.

mand because the child is voicing the expectation of the adults he represents. The child may be forceful, selecting merchandise, making negative comments, and rejecting if he finds the goods below the standards expected by adults. The child may talk back to an adult serving improperly; he may supervise the scales and check the weight, talk like an adult, demand attention, decide whether he should share information, and may even enter into some gossip. The child may demand better merchandise and openly criticize the business of the storekeeper.

When making purchases, the child may perceive himself as standing between two opposite poles; he needs to negotiate with both sides —his parents as well as the salesclerk. He must translate and transmit the standards of the adults he represents and get the best value for the money, bargaining when necessary. He must compromise between whatever the merchant convinces him to buy and what his parents expect. After each errand the child explains that nothing else was on display, or that everything was the same for the day, or that the best had already gone. The child may be sent back to return undesirable merchandise, but this is embarrassing and carried out reluctantly.

A child on an errand behaves according to a specific pattern that is allowed and defined by the situation. He would be violating the rules of etiquette if he were to use the same manner when buying candy for himself. He is then representing himself, and a child is expected to be submissive, obedient, and well-behaved toward adults. Otherwise, adults will classify him as *mal educado* (a poorly trained child), and this affects the dignity of the family, a highly sensitive domain. On the other hand, youngsters who are passive and well-behaved enjoy a good reputation among adults, and people speak of them as *todo un hombrecito* or *toda una señorita* (a perfect little gentleman or lady), coming from an excellent home. Each neighborhood has its own bad boy or girl among several very good, good, and regular children.

It was noted that public behavior of children concerns adults. They frequently advise and reprimand children, impressing on them that they are a mirror of the family when in public. The concern of adults toward the children in the streets constitutes a constant source of friction among parents, children, and neighbors. Good relationships in a neighborhood do not come easily; there are many covert feelings and much jealousy. In the *clase media*, particularly among the *humilde*, the better-off families can be the source of "attack" during Carnaval. There is public license to throw water at anyone who appears in the street. Unclean water thrown at a neighbor's child is a sure sign of personal disgust, disagreement, and is a clear communication of this message to the parents. Usually this is strategically performed toward the end of Carnaval days so that there is no time to respond to the message.

Parents are offended when an adult takes advantage of a child and treats him roughly, even if only verbally. Adults seem to assume that children have few feelings, and with this assumption they do not hesitate to act in ways that are conducive to developing fear. Conformity, particularly in the middle sections of the society, is enforced in many cases through verbal statements or physical actions that evoke fear. Rigid as such conformity may appear at first, as the child grows he learns the true facts. It is then that some begin to question and even disbelieve adults. They start to act without fear, perhaps slightly arrogantly, in order to cope with the hostile situation. Surely one should expect this to color the child's disposition and attitude toward adults.

Many techniques are used to elicit good and proper behavior from children at an early age. Parents may punish a child by forbidding him to go out in the street. As his peers make themselves known in the street by signaling, whistling, or calling his name, the child may begin to negotiate with his parents. If he does not come out soon, everyone will know that the parents have found out about some mischief through a *vecino* and as punishment have forbidden the child to go outside. Sometimes a child may quickly come out to say, "I'm not allowed to go out," or he may only shout this from behind closed heavy iron shutters. If the other children continue to insist, an adult may come out and tell them in no uncertain terms that the child is "occupied" and cannot play that afternoon. Usually the leaders will respond,"What a pity!" (*ché, que lástima*). The children may talk with the brother of the punished child and suggest that he negotiate with the mother to get the decision changed. The group applies a great deal of pressure by being sorry and advising the child to promise to behave

Finding Social Boundaries

well. Parents often give in to the group pressure in order to make it easier to send a child on an errand later.

School children reported that sometimes parents punished a child by sending him to spend several hours alone in a bedroom. A mother may also threaten the child with "I will let your father know about it" or with other strong verbal threats. For instance, a mother who dislikes spanking her child may threaten: "If you do not behave, I will take you to the doctor and he will give you a shot." Such threats are frequently used with a child less than five years old who dislikes taking siestas or going to sleep at night at the proper hour. A housewife who worked as a semiprofessional in a government office for the development of community programs indicated that she would "tell the children just about anything so they will go to bed and leave me in peace. If they hear friends outside playing, I tell them just anything even to hide the fact that they are their true friends."

In an *almacén* a mother used a similar technique when her child cried because he wanted candy. She asked, "Didn't you see what your father brought today? That big package contains more and better candy." According to *almaceneros* this is a common technique for diverting a child from his intentions to get candy in the store. One *almacenero* said, "Everyone does it, and one gets used to it. One even does it to his own children." There are lies—*mentiritas*—used in order to avoid an unnecessary purchase, particularly in cases of financial shortage. Very young children believe the adults, but as they begin to comprehend the situation, they may throw a temper tantrum in the store. Then the child will be physically punished until he learns not to demand things publicly. If the child persists and is hard to correct, he then acquires the reputation of being a difficult case and *mal educadito*.

Maids are noted for using the lying technique with the household children; consequently, servants often have serious difficulties in maintaining discipline and respect, particularly if they have abused the techniques. Informants agreed that lying to children is "an institutionalized thing." People use this method in varying degrees, and every child experiences it at some time. Although at home some parents avoid lying to their children, in interaction with other adults the child is bound to come across the technique. "It is effective," an informant added, "since it brings desired results and keeps the child in line with one's wishes." When the child is about five, the methods need to be changed; children begin to understand what is expected. To adults this means that the child learns to *conformarse* (accommodate).

In order to prevent a fatal accident, other adults may correct *vecinos'* children, especially if the interfamily relationship has been smooth. Very young children may be reprimanded when they take chances in the city streets. An adult passing by may say, "I saw your mother coming to get you," or "Your mother is coming to punish you," or "I will tell your parents that you are in the street and that you are getting my sidewalk dirty." The threats are frequent, and the whole situation may annoy older children. Occasionally a child may respond rudely to the ceaseless pressure from adults. "You may tell my parents if you wish; they will not do anything to me," may not be altogether an unusual answer to an adult from an aggressive child. The child will then be classified as a bad child. He will be verbally directed to correct his behavior, or he may be physically punished.

An effective verbal technique is to threaten the disobedient child (if he is less than five years old) with the "old man and his bag"—*el viejo de la bolsa*. A kind *vecino* repeatedly instructed two three-year-old boys playing with a bicycle to behave well and not to go too far in the block because *el viejo de la bolsa* is always around the corner looking for small boys to take away. When an old, poor man approaches, small children will run close to the parents or hide inside the houses until the "danger" passes away. A neighbor who supports parents by using this myth is showing concern and *cariño* for the child and the child's parents. In this way a *vecino* assists parents in the process of socialization without causing resentment. Sometimes an elderly woman, the mother figure for the *vecindad*, assumes a strong role in the training of the children in the street. Having been corrected by the "grandmother," the child may then hear from another adult, "I told you about it."

Small children should not be outdoors at night playing on the sidewalk. People view nights and an outdoor environment as hostile to defenseless children. Again *el viejo de la bolsa* may be presented to the small child as a folktale in an attempt to control an overactive child. As children grow older, they begin to realize the truth; they discover that *el viejo de la bolsa* is a myth. Nevertheless, at the sight of an old, poor man, perhaps a beggar, some adults cannot help but recall unpleasant childhood images. Youngsters in the neighborhood streets who no longer believe the myth, or perhaps want to test its validity, frequently bother such old men.

Daily observation of children in the neighborhood left no doubt that some of the *vecinos* were hostile to them. There was the case of a retired man who took siestas every day in both summer and winter. His wife remained alert working slowly and quietly in her front garden during the siesta time. When children came too close to her house, she chased them away. Noises disturbed her husband's rest, and with all etiquette she often complained to parents. But parents could always find someone else's child to blame for the noisemaking. Nevertheless, the message was clear.

The children of this neighborhood had to cope with another retired man, who spent much of the day on the sidewalk of his home. He watched children's behavior and passed on to others information about the public activities of all families. He was always ready to make recommendations to parents who in any way showed a willingness to listen. Although he felt rejected by many parents, he still continued in this role. Children knew that they would not be punished for anything reported by this man. On one occasion a child answered him, "You may go to my father, but he will not do anything to me." This triggered an argument between the man and the child, since in answering the child had stepped out of his submissive role and violated the rule of his relationship to an adult. He may also have offended the man's dignity, since a child's statement may be taken as a reflection of the family's opinion.

A woman who had been trying to remove a *barrita* (play group) of boys from her front steps found an opportunity. She discovered that her sidewalk was littered with orange peelings. Although actually a passing merchant had thrown them, she blamed the children who were standing on her portion of the sidewalk exchanging stamps. The woman, almost hysterical, started shouting at the children. The noise brought many curious adults to open windows to see what was happening. As the outburst subsided, the children slowly dispersed, parents closed the windows, and the woman was left alone in her window. The case was clearly and effortlessly dismissed. After the woman closed the heavy iron shutters of her house, the wife of a semiprofessional man remarked to a new *vecino*, "This is *vecindad* life; it is almost like a low-class *vecindad*, always the same thing. How can one keep children constantly inside the house? They need to go outside and run."

Although variations may be readily noticed from one neighborhood to another, neighborhood pressure on children prevails. Some methods for correcting children have changed when compared to older generations. A first generation Italian man reflected that a look from his father was sufficient to bring out his good behavior. Now children are left more to themselves; they cause problems that lead to friction among adults, observed an informant. "Children nowadays demand more; they require help to complete their homework, and we parents are soft. My child bores me with his homework every day." A child overheard his parent saying this and smiled with satisfaction.

Children and Vecinos

The children seek space outside their own homes for recreational activities. No one can take away their rights to the street and sidewalk area around their homes during their free time. Household activities are oriented toward the street, and people constantly move from the interior of the house toward the front door. Very small children may exercise their privilege to the street and sidewalk space when the mother is at the front door or when parents take chairs to the sidewalk during leisure periods of the evening. *Vecinos* put up with children playing outdoors during some periods of the day. They implicitly agree, however, that parents should take care that their children do not interrupt the siestas of *vecinos*.

Children may remain in the street as late as midnight on summer nights. It is not uncommon for a very young child to sleep on someone's lap while everyone sits talking outside. To reach the world outside the home for moments of nonrestrictive play and personal freedom is an escape from the seclusion imposed by the homes, walled and sealed from public view. When adults retire, children will follow.

Older children assume domestic responsibilities, but outside of that they use their time as they please. The smaller children depend upon constant adult supervision; they are a "problem" for adults. They must have direction, particularly since streets and sidewalks are not the safest areas for small children's play. As a child grows older (between twelve and fourteen), he is expected to settle down. He participates in sports through a club or spends his leisure at the door of his house reading a magazine, and perhaps casually visiting from door-to-door with other children of his neighborhood. Radio, movies, television (when available), walking (*paseando*), and visiting with relatives occupy the leisure hours of the day. Secondary school students spend much time studying, perhaps with a *compañero* from another neighborhood, to memorize the lessons.

Age is not a basic criterion that divides children into play groups; in any one group the ages may range between six and ten. Mothers do not make an effort to find a child of the same age as a playmate for their son or daughter. An informant remarked, "There is no need to separate children when there is no great difference between the age of six and ten. After all, they are all *niños*."

In the afternoons children begin to appear on the sidewalk to make a quick survey of the activities of their peers. A child can do this on his own initiative, as long as the time spent is short. When he intends to go out for a long period of time, he must request permission of his parents. The expression "I am going out to play" suffices both to inform and to ask.

In play groups, the older children are leaders and sometimes urge the younger ones into mischief. All neighborhood groups are well organized, and the younger children must comply with the wishes of the older. No doubt, in a segmented society such as this, the older children acquire a sense of importance if they happen to be leaders of a successful *barrita*.[2] If relations between *vecinos* are friendly, children find sidewalk playmates in the *vecindad*. Some play group games, others—like teenage girls—may walk back and forth, arm in arm, from one corner of the block to the other.

[2] Being a *patrón* and *muy hombrecito*—a man—is rehearsed in this early situation. Domination and submission are very strong themes.

Children encounter each other on the street or sidewalk; only on rare occasions, perhaps birthdays, may some of them be invited to the home of a friend. To bring a friend into the house requires special permission from the mother or another adult of the household; thus a child feels like a stranger in his own home. There is the unstated but real feeling that a neighbor's child invades the privacy of the home. If the relations between adults have not been amicable, the child, as an extension of his family, projects the image of the adults behind him.

A young man, age twenty, reflected on his childhood in the *vecindad*:

Before the age of seven I would play outside of the house with my brother and sister and their friends. They were all older than I, and they teased me a great deal. But I went with them anyway. Finally at seven, I remember having made my first friend in the *vecindad*. He was the grandson of the lady across the street, and he only came part of the year to stay with his grandmother. But we had things in common, and we called ourselves amigos. Since my mother was friendly with his grandmother, I became his friend. This friend was, however, two years younger than I; my mother allowed him to come into my house, and I went to his grandmother's home to play.

Of course, in the *vecindad*, there were many other children of my age, perhaps as many as ten or fifteen. My mother did not permit me to play with them in the street. She constantly told me that they were children of the street [*callejeros*], cheaters [*tramposos*], thieves [*ladrones*], and that they used dirty words [*malas palabras*]. Some of these children belonged to a family with whom my family had "fought" on account of my older brothers and sisters. My sister stopped playing with all of them. My parents constantly talked to us about the bad qualities of those in our *vecindad*, and prevented us from seeing and trusting each other. We avoided them constantly. I could not play with them; I could play only with that friend whom I have mentioned because my mother used to say he was *muy buenito*.

During the rest of the year, however, I felt the need to play with other children. There were many of them in the street and I was attracted. So little by little, I began to slip away from the house. The children were idle

Finding Social Boundaries

at that time of year; still my mother would not let me play with them, although they would include me in their play. This did not mean that I was readily accepted, so I did not waste the opportunity to find someone who befriended me. At first the children of my *vecindad* mocked me, and they said that I was spoiled, but on one occasion they showed me that I could defend myself. I did not care for that. In general I felt that the children wanted to play with me, and as I grew older I became good at many games. When I became older, my mother allowed me to be within my block, and we could meet and play soccer in another barrio. But I could not play ball in the open space behind our block. My parents believed that the children learned bad things from each other, and also some of the poor newspaper boys came there to take advantage of the younger children or to pick a fight with us. I escaped many times to that place, and nothing happened that I can remember. I was very attracted by the games in the street. As the years went by, I just went out into the streets to find the children from the neighborhood. We formed a *barrita*.

My real friend, when he was with his grandmother, continued to be my companion, and he was the only one allowed inside my house. This intimate friendship grew through the years because our likes and ways of thinking matched; we were encouraged to associate by adults. The friendship lasted until I was fourteen, then differences began to show because I went to secondary school and he began to work as a skilled laborer. I associated with boys from other areas of the city. From then on, I was no longer close to the fellows in my own *vecindad* or even my very good friend. Our ambitions and aspirations were different, and now I wanted to bring companions from my secondary school to play card games. My childhood friend felt uncomfortable and socially inferior with them.

This account can be accepted as representative of childhood and youth in the *clase media*.

Among children the competition for friendship seems acute. When there are many children in a neighborhood, divisions occur. The pressure of peers frequently forces each child to take sides. Since each child has his own reputation in the neighborhood that is supported by adult views, the associations follow these lines. Otherwise the child and those who associate with him acquire the same public reputation. Usually the division is between good and bad, meek and aggressive.

The characterizations often cause difficult interpersonal relations among adults. The reputation of being *un mal amigo* (a bad friend) is considered before parents and older siblings approve a friendship.

Children of the lower-middle social class are interested in each other's belongings, particularly bicycles, tricycles, and roller skates. While in the street, children learn to make small transactions; they use each other's bicycles, marbles, or roller skates. A good friend is entitled to borrow something valued; dyadic contract occurs early in life. In the frequent bargaining, children establish strong sentimental associations. Friction arises when one notices hesitation or distrust and considers himself hurt by unfaithfulness. "You are a bad friend" (*sos un mal amigo*) is a frequently heard phrase. There is also the threat, "I will not play with you any more unless you change your mind."

In tense situations, the bicycles may be roughly handled, particularly by those who feel outside a strong dyadic relationship. The following incident, after a collision of two bicycles borrowed by friends, reveals intimate aspects of the children's world. This single incident manifests nuances of relationships between children, manipulation of adults, and feelings of insecurity. In a collision the pedal of a bicycle was bent. The immediate reaction of the children was, "Do not tell your father. We shall get a hammer tomorrow and straighten it out. You take the bicycle inside and carefully cover the damaged part." The boy behaved as instructed, but his younger brother, who felt that he had been left out by the group, told the parents during the evening. The older child felt that his brother had betrayed his friends. The next day all the friends ganged up on the younger boy for not keeping the secret. Then the group decided that in order to maintain rights to the bicycle in the street, each was to chip in some money in case they could not fix it themselves and had to take the bicycle to a shop. But everything had to be done in complete secrecy so the adults would not become upset. Throughout the incident the power of the group was evident; the small child was afraid to go out into the street. For several days all children in the street avoided the parents of the child whose bicycle had been damaged. Since the incident seemed to bring no further consequences, soon the children were no longer afraid to pass by the house and face the adults. In the other household where the

Finding Social Boundaries

second bicycle was damaged, the parents ordered their son not to lend it to anyone because friends would not be careful with his things. According to the father, this damage was done out of meanness and invidiousness.

Another case illustrates the accommodations to the adult world and the relationship between children and adults. Two boys asked permission to go together to a downtown barbershop. They also wanted to go to an afternoon movie. Both mothers refused permission for the movie. After the haircuts, the older one convinced the younger to go to the movie anyway. They agreed not to say anything to the parents. The older child claimed that he could do it because "my mother tells me that she is not going someplace, but she goes anyway." The hours passed, the mothers telephoned the barber and found out that he had finished with the boys several hours ago. The barber added that perhaps the boys had delayed themselves in the plaza, playing without realizing that it was late. The two boys finally returned and blamed the barber for the delay. In the evening one of them told his parents the truth. He was obviously afraid of the embarrassment that would follow in his relations with his friend.

Another time two boys of the same neighborhood were separated after school festivities. They had been instructed to stay together until they were picked up. The older one, however, returned home alone. While the two *vecino* mothers were comparing notes outside their homes, worried about the return of the younger boy, he appeared with another child. Before he had a chance to explain, the mother of the older one said, "What happened to you, son, because John waited for you for a long time and looked for you everywhere and could not find you. Where were you?" At this point the guilty boy appeared at the front door and remarked, "Yes, I waited for you, and I waited and waited for a long time, but I could not find you." The younger boy and his mother felt defenseless, and it was evident that face-saving guided the reaction of the others. A series of incidents of this type provides sufficient grounds for the two families to become distant. The younger child was no longer trusted to the older one, and the mothers had to resolve the conflict if their relationship was to continue smoothly. Similar incidents occurred again and again, and finally the parents of the younger boy started restricting the time allowed for unsupervised play after school. The older boy, aware of the new development, avoided his friend's parents and became more demanding and aggressive toward his younger friend. The relationship between the two had its constant ups and downs from then on, while adults made an effort to overlook the situation.

For children, the *vecindad* situation can be both friendly and hostile. Neighborhood life by definition implies togetherness, cooperation, friendliness, and companionship; the reality, however, points to avoidance of intimate relationships in one's own neighborhood.[3]

The neighborhood provides the child with an orientation into his immediate surroundings; here he begins to put into practice the concepts that guide interpersonal relationships. The child very early distinguishes clearly between people who are related and people who are not related; between those with whom he may be congenial and those with whom he may not. He is taught that the world is divided: one can approach some with confidence and associate and play with them; others are not desirable. In between there is a neutral category of individuals who are unimportant in the child's thinking or in the network of his social relations.

The social spheres of children and adults are forcefully delineated; each group exercises different privileges based on role and the status of the age and sex. Through experiences in the neighborhood, the child may see the world as socially competitive and realize that he must begin to conquer it as he steps into life. Life is conceived of as a perpetual *conquista*, which begins in the neighborhood and continues through school into adulthood.

In the *vecindad* the child comes to a realization that there is a

---

[3] This is supported by the response of 1,097 individuals in the IPRUL sample to the question of the residence of their friends. 43.3 percent indicated that their friends were elsewhere in the city; 27.7 percent had friends nearby, but not in the same block; 10.3 percent nearby; 2.6 percent downtown; 5.8 percent outside the city; 7.6 percent had no friends; and 2.7 percent did not respond to the question. It is interesting to note that those who had nearby friends were living in areas of the city receptive to rural populations of lower economic level. The people were laborers. On the other extreme, the *clase alta* people also had nearby friends. In areas of the *clase media*, the data showed that the social network tends to be definitely outside the neighborhood.

Finding Social Boundaries

strong and powerful adult world that determines everything for him. The problem for him is what he can do for his reputation or what he can bypass because of his reputation. Society outside the household appears a highly competitive environment. This reality does not coincide with the implications of the definition that states the neighborhood should be a united group of *vecinos*. He finds that the social environment of the neighborhood is primarily for adults and that he needs to develop techniques to cope with the forces around him. The next important level the child must manipulate and conquer is the school.

9. ALONE IN SCHOOL

Children and School

Schools, as national, provincial, or private institutions, are divorced from the dynamics of neighborhood life. The national role of the schools is to impart *cultura* and to represent a high social level; the feedback from the neighborhood is limited. This chapter contains abundant material on the operation of a school located in a middle-class neighborhood, but it will be compared with a school in the *clase baja* of a barrio and a private school in the center of the city. Continuities and discrepancies between the social sphere of the neighborhood and the sphere of the school underlie the organization of the chapter. Examining the three social levels gives further insight into the children's formative development, as well as into the dynamics of school role playing, the city social class structure, and national orientation. The child enters a caretaking institution *alone* finding himself in the midst of a regimented style of life.

For the administration of education, the city is divided into sections composed of several neighborhoods. Each section is provided with one primary public school. Children may bypass the neighborhood boundaries in their choice of schools, but there is a tendency to attend the public school that is nearest. The city is served by seventeen provincial schools, four national schools at the outskirts of the city, and nine private institutions.

All school programs are the same, ruled by the Provincial Board of Education. The Provincial Ministry of Education, in coordination with the National Ministry of Education, prepares the school program. The nature of each subject and of the pedagogy is directed from above. There is, therefore, no latitude for innovation in the classroom; the *directora* and the *vicedirectora* closely supervise all teaching. The teachers follow the program, conduct classes in a uniform manner, and in all cases face the handicap of the limited budget assigned to the schools.

Children of different economic levels come together in the first grade. After the first grade there comes a division of those who can be promoted to the first superior grade and those who remain in the first grade because of personality or learning problems. The ones who stay behind in the first grade are separated from the newcomers. A special class of slow learners (with over thirty students in 1964) works under a regular teacher. From this group only about 10 percent reach the second grade after several years of struggling.

The progress through the grades follows a pattern: a large number of students repeat the first grade; after the next two years there are again the poor students (*mal alumnos*) left behind in the third grade. In the fifth grade many more drop out. Those who pass through the sixth grade with an average of about seven may qualify to enter into secondary school. The marks are scaled from zero to ten, three being failing. The dropouts—left behind, barely literate, materially poor, and with social and psychological handicaps—will become the potential labor force in the city for small businessmen, middlemen in the markets, ambulant salesmen, seasonal laborers in rural areas, or mechanics. Those who pass the third and the fifth grades are known by the school staff to have "better quality and to be of better families in the neighborhood." Teachers stated that some of the dropouts were sufficiently good students but that the household's limited economic resources constitute a serious handicap. In some cases the older brothers and parents cannot afford to put the younger ones through school. To finish the sixth grade is a considerable achievement for the children of poor families.

By the sixth grade there is a definite elite of those who have the means to continue secondary education. The social separation from the others now becomes evident and affects both children and parents in the neighborhood. Those who do not continue in secondary school may undertake a short course at an academy or night school. Some try for one year to remain at this transitional stage, and then the boys become apprentices in shops or businesses while the girls continue with housework or seek employment. A very small number of those in secondary education undertake university training.[1]

The description of the school and teaching methods will be centered on the primary school of San Martín *vecindad*.[2] This school is situated in an area where rural families and *pueblo* immigrants have built modest homes and displaced center-city residents have built more substantial ones. In this sense it is not representative for its antiquity in the city. San Martín incorporates and manifests all the elements and attitudes of a middle-class social level. The neighborhood is seven blocks from the central plaza, in one of the "active" zones of the city.[3]

The professions best represented in this area are technical workers (carpenters, mechanics, tailors, painters), small entrepreneurs (*almaceneros* and *tenderos*), military personnel (subofficers), and office workers. There are also four teachers, four agronomists, and five professionals with university degrees. A handful of people were born outside the province, some in Italy, others in Syria, but the majority were born in the province of Entre Ríos and have lived in Paraná most of their lives. All the children were born in Paraná. While most children attend the local provincial school, the professional families send their children to private schools or to the Normal School.

As in all schools in the city, San Martín has a morning and an afternoon session. The administration, the staff, and even the name of the school change with each session. The principal (*directora*) is the only permanent administrator for the morning and afternoon sessions. Each session is equipped to give instruction for the first seven years of the child's education, including two years of first grade. There is a

---

[1] Approximately 65 percent of the school-age children of the city are in primary school, 30 percent are attending secondary school, and 5 percent go to the university at eighteen.
[2] This is a fictitious name.
[3] See fig. 17.

general belief that the morning school is better, attended by children of the best families in the neighborhood, while children from families of the lower economic level attend the afternoon session.

For a period of three months the school was visited daily to observe classes and interact with students. The students were also observed in their neighborhood. But after a period of observing all the grades, it became evident that for our purpose one should concentrate on the sixth graders. During the seven years of school many children have been unable to continue because of economic or intellectual deficiency and have dropped out. The group studied thus represents a rather successful subgroup with ability and backing from their homes to progress through the primary grades.

This sixth grade with thirty-one students (seventeen girls and fourteen boys) had the following age distribution: five were eleven years old, sixteen were twelve years old, five were thirteen, four were fourteen, and one was fifteen years old. Seventeen attended the seven years of schooling in the same institution, never repeating a grade; of the rest, two repeated grades, four attended this institution only for six years, and eight attended this school for less than five years. The students' nuclear families were small; with the exception of three (criollos) who had six, eight, and nine siblings respectively, all came from families with four or fewer children. Ethnically, the composition is fairly representative of the population of the city.

As might be expected (see chapter 3) the largest group within the grade was of Italian descent; the few remaining were Spanish, Swiss, German, French, Yugoslav, Syrian, or Eastern European Jews. All of them were second-generation Argentines and not necessarily of a pure ethnic descent. Fathers with secondary education were employed in offices of the government and banks. Twenty-three mothers were reported to be housewives, two were schoolteachers, two were general employees, and two were part-time dressmakers or hairdressers. There was only one wash woman, who was of criollo descent.

These sixth graders fell into two distinct groups: those from families that were able to send their children to secondary school and those from families that would keep their youngsters at home, perhaps helping with some sort of family entrepreneurship until completion of military service or marriage. Only a handful would be able to undertake university training. At the end of the field work, twenty-seven students successfully completed the sixth grade, and four were asked to repeat it. Two years after the completion of the field work, four girls were attending the second year of Normal School; one boy had begun secondary education for a *bachiller* degree but had stopped after the first year; and eleven boys and three girls were in the second year of business schools. The rest had remained at home or were awaiting employment opportunity.

The School Program and Rules

For the morning session, the children arrive in school at 8:00 A.M. and remain in session until noon. The school day is divided into five periods, each separated by a few minutes of recess. The bell, like a church bell, marks the separations and announces the beginning and end of each period. Each student wears a white uniform, brings a notebook and loose paper for work, and buys a reading book and a dictionary. The same facilities are used for the morning, afternoon, and evening schools, thus nothing is left in school after each session. There is a class closet where illustrations, maps, and other class equipment can be stored.

The classroom in this school is typical, including the private school. The teacher was born in Entre Ríos, trained at the Normal School, and has been teaching for several years. She is married, of the *clase media*, and from a family with at least two generations in Argentina.

The classroom situation is highly formal; children are not allowed to speak to each other during class. While the teacher is in class, her permission is necessary for each individual act. Although the general rule is complete silence, a great deal of low-voiced talk may be tolerated at times, but the teacher may reprimand anyone at her discretion.

In the sixth grade, children take arithmetic, geometry, anatomy, geography, physics, language, grammar and writing, history, botany, chemistry, drawing, music, and physical education. A great deal of time is dedicated to arithmetic, geography, history, and grammar. A small library with some encyclopedias and manuals supplies the students with reading material. Some of the library books have been purchased with the cooperative funds of the school. The children themselves raise most of the money by selling chances throughout the school year for raffles; prizes are donated by city businessmen. Also each child pays a small annual library fee.

Most of the time in school is used for the dictation of each lesson, word by word, by the teacher; each student must take the entire dictation in his notebook. The teacher begins with the title and instructs students to underline it in red or blue; she carefully indicates each comma, period, and subtitle. Students constantly ask her to repeat phrases and words. A thirty-minute dictation usually will provide a five-minute recitation the following day. Some days teachers dictate lessons for four consecutive hours.

The lessons dictated by the teacher are usually short to allow all students to get every word. Lessons are usually composed of definitions, descriptions, and basic principles. Explanations may be offered as the teacher goes along, but the students are instructed not to copy them, just to remember. In some subjects the lessons are illustrated with exercises at the blackboard, where several students attempt to solve a problem. In addition the teacher usually dictates a few problems for homework. At home the children recopy each lesson and illustrate it with pictures from newspapers and magazines or by drawing maps. The following day each child presents his completed work. Each student also has to memorize the lessons dictated. In later sessions of the same subject, children are called to the front to recite. The teacher may ask the class to help the person reciting if he is not able to continue, and then other students raise their hands and say, "I'll tell you, señorita." When the teacher decides on the person, he stands up next to his seat and answers the question. He may be asked to continue the recitation, while the other student is sent back to his seat.

During the last few years work in teams (*trabajo de equipo*) has become popular in the curriculums of the schools. The class is divided and each team prepares a lesson in botany, or history, or anatomy. Usually the teacher attempts to mix the group by ability, so the better students act as leaders. The students consult books, prepare illustrations, and then teach the class. The five or six members of each team divide the assignment among themselves.

In one team presentation the students took over the class, while the teacher assumed a position of a listener in the back, grading each student's performance. The first did not have the text well memorized and waited for cues for each new paragraph. After the recitation he questioned the class on the subject. The other team members followed the same pattern.

The teacher does not specify in advance the amount of preparation required for the assignment and judges the efforts of the group after the presentation. The better students may get upset when the poorer team members detract from the total performance. At the end of the presentation the teacher may comment, "You all shine," or "You did not shine this time."

The team whose performance is always good becomes something of an elite group. The members may develop distinctive behavior and speech patterns. Girls in such a group in particular cultivate social distinctions. Work in a team may become difficult if individual differences, personal status, social class orientation, and aspiration strain interpersonal relations.

In the classroom the very serious students usually sit on one side and the less studious ones (*haraganes*) on the other. The class, however, has a reputation as a whole. After a periodic review of students' notebooks, the *vicedirectora* publicly evaluates the development of the class. Usually she is not satisfied. She advises:

You must work harder. I am not satisfied with your work. You write badly, you are not neat. In your special notebook first there is one type of writing and then another, and I don't like that. This class is not working well. Do you understand me? How could it be that only two girls will have a general grade of very good? You can work better, and we will see if the next review will show an improvement and better grades. I am not happy. Your work must be more consistent and more balanced. I am not saying perfection, because we are not perfect, but more evenness.

The teacher and the students listen to the admonition of the *vicedirectora*. With some embarrassment the teacher may add, "I have told you the same things, but you do not pay attention to me."

During an interview the teacher in the sixth grade did not hesitate to praise the good performance of students who were *muy cumplido-*

res (very reliable). These form an elite of the class; they meet all deadlines, are neat, studious, attentive, quiet, and are therefore, by the teacher's standards, intelligent. Students with the opposite traits are not intelligent and "show their social background," remarked the teacher. Most of these, however, dropped out before reaching the sixth grade.

Most students display some negative characteristics, and it is the teacher's role and duty to correct them. Trying to bring everyone up to the level of the very best students preoccupies the teachers. They must imprint on the child the desire to achieve the very best. Public shame stands as one important technique to bring about improvement. One student was having difficulty with arithmetic. He was in front of the class trying to solve an equation at the blackboard. The result was wrong, and the teacher remarked: "What you have there is wrong, and obviously you have not studied your lesson. You are getting behind, you don't pay attention in class. You may not pass the sixth grade."

Another time a poor student came to the front of the class to recite, hoping that some of those in the front row would help him remember the lesson. But the teacher was too close and his companions could not assist him. The teacher waited for awhile in complete silence. Then, using the formal verb form of address,[4] she said: "Don't you remember anything? Don't you know anything? Why don't you study? You are a lazy student!" A series of such remarks indicates that the teacher is ready to fail the student and might make him repeat the grade. In this case her voice and face were expressionless; the student sensed that some of the threats would not be carried out because his overall performance was not that bad. The reprimand was for the day, but the projection into the future was exaggerated.

In a history class a student who had been called to recite just stood silently in front of the class. Finally the teacher said, "You did not study, but you must defend yourself because you are old enough. Don't you think so, sir? And why didn't you study?" The student replied that

---

[4] The familiar form of *vos* is most frequent in school, but when the teacher reprimands a student she is likely to use the formal *usted*. In this way she becomes further removed and almost a stranger to the pupils.

he did not find the time, but he was obviously embarrassed. He felt even more embarrassed since the rest of the students in the class wanted the opportunity to be graded on a short and easy lesson. The teacher continued: "So you did not have time? And why?" This question the student could not answer. "You have studied badly this year, and half of the year is over," said the teacher as she recorded a failing grade and advised the student to pay attention.

Sometimes the teacher may call on a student who needs more help, but the call may be accompanied by, "I imagine that you do not know anything today, but come in front and see what you can do." If the student surprises the class and the teacher and knows the lesson, then the teacher may comment, "You see that when you study, you can do it. Go and sit down and continue studying if you want to complete the sixth grade."

If the student does not know the lesson, the phrase "sit down" means failure for the day. When this is accompanied by an adjective like *regular* (poor), or *bien*, or *muy bien*, the grade can be anywhere from barely passing to excellent, but the student never knows his grades until the end of the quarter. "Sit down," energetically pronounced, constitutes a threatening situation for the student and his *compañeros*. In general, students tend to suppress and disregard the criticisms made by the teacher in public. By not dwelling on the issue, the group forgets it, too, and after all, "It can happen to anyone," was the usual student comment.

During dictation students get behind, ask neighbors for help, and thus give the teacher a chance to reprimand the whole class. A teacher may interrupt a dictation to call on a student to recite part of the lesson. This poses a threat to everyone. The teacher pays special attention to the poorer students, and on account of their mistakes she can define norms of conduct and values for the others. There are many ways to get to one person through class pressure. For instance the teacher may say, "You all can hear that one of your *compañeros* does not work and likes to talk. I have asked you to work in complete silence."

While dictating, the teacher walks in the aisles stopping behind some of the students for spot checking. In a low voice she corrects spelling mistakes, pointing to the place of the error in the notebook.

If the work is bad and the student is not trying to improve, she may stop dictation to reprimand the student publicly. Dictation is frequently interrupted by requests for the repetition of a phrase; the teacher may decide whether she should repeat or let the student suffer the consequences on the assumption that he has not been paying sufficient attention.

When students do not follow orders, teachers are expected to become upset. For instance, when a teacher comes to class after recess and says, "Now remove all your books from your desks and sit with your hands over your desk," this clearly indicates that she is about to call on students to recite. A student may try to leave a book or notebook on his desk to study the lesson for the day. If the teacher discovers this, she again reprimands him severely and in public. Students, particularly the lively ones, are continuously threatened with punishment. The teacher may send them outside, and if the *vicedirectora* happens to see them there, she can punish them even more severely.

Slowly the hours in school come to an end. Students may begin to collect their books for departure. If the teacher has not yet given the order, this occasions another public scolding: "Who told you to prepare your books to go home?"

Students agree that taking notes is something very mechanical and does not require much thinking. One student said:

One writes and does not think; I try to study and memorize the notes later at home. I write whatever the teacher dictates, but frequently I'm thinking of something else and without realizing it, I'm writing whatever the teacher is dictating. One learns to do that. I'm thinking of a soccer game while I write, and sometimes the teacher knows that one is on the moon, and she may ask someone to repeat what she has just said. I'm not sure how I'm doing until the end of the year. One is afraid of not passing the grade. I think a great deal about grades, and I am anxious. I am afraid that sometimes because one does not behave properly, one may fail the subject.

Average and poor students tend to think that teachers are severe, distant, and indifferent toward them. The high status of the teacher must be acknowledged constantly. When a teacher or the principal enters the class, students stand up and greet her in unison. They do not stand up when a woman janitor walks in to deliver messages or material. In the street only the few exceptionally good students know precisely how to react to a teacher passing by. Others wonder: Should she be greeted? Does she recognize me? Is she going to answer? Should I greet her inasmuch as I'm not a very good student? If I don't greet her, will she fail me? Will she become angry and scold me in class the following day? Students face all these questions and uncertainties outside of class. Most of the time, unless the teacher is a friend of the family, the encounter is very formal or the child is not noticed.

Students usually remember one or two teachers who were unusually kind and good teachers. In most cases students differ in their evaluation of former teachers. One teacher may be considered very good by some students while others and parents consider her not so good. One fourteen-year-old student summarized the school situation in this way:

Teachers in general are *malas* [meaning rigorous and dictatorial] and only one in our school is considered a good teacher. We get tired with so much copying and writing of dictations. A teacher will place us against the wall for an entire hour as punishment, and if we fight she can send us to the school office. There we have to see the *vicedirectora*; she is *mala* and one must sign a book. After three times, we can be expelled from school. We get very tired and bored when teachers spend so much time talking, explaining, and dictating one lesson after another.

In the past when the teacher used to call my name in class to reprimand me and I stood up next to my seat, I used to blush a lot; the other pupils used to kid me about that. They called me "red." Now I do not blush because I am not so ashamed any more. Perhaps I am used to it. Sometimes I was reprimanded because I sat in the second row and when some of my friends did not know the lesson very well, I used to help them. When the teacher was not looking, I gave them the next line so they could continue to remember the lesson. To whisper the line means to be a good friend. Sometimes during a surprise quiz I can also help my friends and place my answers in such a way that they can copy the lesson. In this way I am assured that I will be helped when I don't know the lesson. But the teacher must not become aware of this, although she knows that one will do it when necessary. One must be careful, and of course everyone does it anyway. If one does not help a friend, one is called a *mal compañero* or a *carnero* [male

Alone in School

sheep]. We copy if the teacher does not see it, and it is not a bad thing to copy when one needs to improve his grade.

It is interesting to note that, in relation to school, children use an entire set of feminine terms: *la escuela, la maestra, la vicedirectora, la portera*. Although there are masculine counterparts, the majority of the city people have been taught by women or under the administration of women. (In the national schools, mostly established to conduct classes in rural areas and small towns, one finds more male teachers than in the other schools.) The teacher's role is equated to the mother's, and the expression "*la maestra* [the teacher] is like a mother" describes the role and elicits the proper response from the child. The inspector (*el inspector*), who is in the role of superior and who inspects and passes judgment on the school and the *directora*, is traditionally conceptualized as a male. However, the number of women inspectors (*inspectoras*) is increasing.

Language obviously affects one's conceptualization of the world. In view of this, the following pattern cannot be overlooked:

La casa . . . la escuela
La madre . . . la maestra . . . la señorita
El padre . . . el inspector . . . el maestro
Los niños . . . los alumnos
La familia . . . la patria

The sequence of terms in either the feminine or the masculine form dominates in the formation of the child's cognitive structure. The mother and the teacher are the two most prominent symbols, almost sacred by definition. To both of them people build monuments, offer flowers, and each has her day in the calendar. Not to pay the proper respect to them, not to honor them when the occasion calls for it, constitutes a grave social transgression, and only people without *cultura* could do so. The social punishment, both in the household and in school, is severe.

It is also interesting to note that the teachers are always referred to as señoritas, although the teacher may be the mother of several children. Within the classroom, however, the term señorita has connotations different from its usual use. Here the qualities of purity, youth, elegance, knowledge, *cultura*—all of which can be easily combined with motherhood—clearly emerge. The male teachers, who hardly exist in provincial institutions, are addressed as *señor maestro*, or in some cases simply as *maestro*. When children speak about their experiences in school, they refer to the male teacher as *el maestro* but to the female teacher as *la señorita* rather than *la maestra*.

The setting of the school calls for a sex orientation similar to that found in the home. The school and the family are parallel concepts and should evoke parallel images. Within the classroom, behavior of a sexual nature constitutes a serious offense, and any advances by word or in action are punishable by dismissal.

Formerly, in order to avoid difficulties at the age of puberty, the schools adopted the morning session for boys and the afternoon session for girls. Currently, the trend is to mix the sexes in the same class but to separate them through the seating arrangement. During recess boys gather together, while girls organize games in another section of the school's patios. Gymnastic hours are also separate for boys and girls.

The situation in school introduces the child to the notion that many aspects of social behavior must be perceived in terms of sex roles. This notion, already embryonic in the neighborhood, in school becomes a forceful reality for the first time in the child's development. It is as if a piece of society were made real for the child by imposing this principle of sex segregation. There are sex-defined social zones in school—beginning with the seating arrangement, continuing into the recreation, and affecting the dynamics of formal and informal groups. One must learn to act, to speak, and to think in terms of a world composed of two groups physically together but mentally and socially apart. This situation replicates the division between the spheres of children and adults. The world for the child is a duality: he belongs to one part and must accommodate to and conquer the other.

Social Interaction in the Classroom

We shall concentrate on studying how children apply the assumptions that they learned in the neighborhood to guide them in school situations. A sociometric questionnaire was prepared for the sixth-grade classroom. The children's response to specific social situations provided a means to abstract patterns of choices and to study interpersonal relationships. The teacher was instructed not to participate in the exercise, and the class was assured that the information would be confidential and had no relation to grades.

As part of the experiment the class received five hundred pesos to use as they pleased, so long as they discussed the alternative plans and reached agreement. They were thus faced with a real problem, in contrast to the hypothetical situations in the sociometric questionnaire. The results were important as a check on the general dynamics established through the first test. The teacher again was instructed not to participate in the decision making, not to give advice, and not to evaluate the decision afterward. Both teacher and students fully cooperated in the experiment.

As mentioned earlier, the group consisted of thirty-one students between eleven and sixteen from one *clase media* neighborhood, most of whom had attended the same school for at least four years. Most children classified themselves as of the *clase media*, above the *humilde* level. Three individuals were in an economic category above average, and a few were near the *humilde*. Although all were socially in the *clase media*, there were subtle economic differences. The members of this group were able to evaluate each other on an economic scale ranging from low (*regular*), through good (*bueno*), to very good (*muy bueno*). Table 9 provides more specific information on the students. It is interesting to note that, in their own classification for ethnic background, the use of criollo refers to a category of people with little *cultura* but with long historical roots in Argentina. Argentine refers to someone with more *cultura* whose parents were born in Argentina, very likely of European immigrant stock.

The questionnaire presented the student with hypothetical activity situations for which he was to select classmates. Questions were related to activities in school, at home, in the neighborhood, and in the city. Although the reasons for selection were not required, it was suggested that they be given. Additional information was derived through interviews with each person after the experiment.

Table 9. Paranaense Students

Identification	Sex	Age	Years in Same School	Father's Profession	Mother's Profession	Ethnic Background*	Economic Condition
1	M	11	7	employee	household	criollo/Argentine	low
2	F	12	7	business—wholesale	household	Arab/Argentine	very good
3	M	12	4	retail business	seamstress	criollo/criollo	low
4	M	12	7	business	household	criollo/Swiss	low
5	F	11	4	mechanic	employee (office)	Italian/Argentine	low
6	M	14	7	mason	household	Argentine/Italian	low
7	M	12	7	employee	household	Italian/Argentine	low
8	M	12	7	landholder	household	Polish Jew/Argentine Jew	very good
9	M	12	7	butcher	household	Argentine (European descent—doesn't know)	good
10	F	12	7	railroad employee	household	Italian/Italian	good
11	M	12	6	ceramic laborer	household	Argentine/criollo	low
12	M	11	7	landholder (agriculture)	teacher	Jew (Russian born)/Russian-German	very good
13	F	13	2	retail business	household	criollo/Italian	low
14	M	11	6	bank employee	household	Arab/Spanish	very good
15	F	11	7	retail business	teacher	Italian/Argentine	good
16	M	14	6	ceramic laborer	household	criollo/Italian	low
17	F	12	4	railroad employee	hairdresser	Argentine/Spanish	low
18	F	15	7	employee	household	criollo/criollo	low
19	F	12	3	mechanic	household	criollo/criollo	low
20	M	12	7	bank employee	household	Yugoslav/French	very good
21	F	13	1	employee	washerwoman	criollo/criollo	low
22	F	12	7	employee	household	Italian/Argentine	low
23	F	12	7	baker	household	criollo/criollo	low
24	F	12	4	policeman	household	criollo/German	low
25	M	14	9	mechanic	household	Italian/Argentine	low
26	M	12	7	traveling salesman	seamstress	Argentine/criollo	good
27	F	13	3	mason	employee	Italian (Brazil)/German	low
28	F	12	7	employee	household	Argentine/French	low
29	F	13	7	retail business	household	doesn't know	low
30	F	13	8	plumber	household	Argentine/criollo	low
31	F	16	3	marble business	household	Russian-German	good

* Criollo here is used in the sense of native: humble in social standing and economically of the lower class. The historical definition of criollo should not be applied here. The children's answer to questions of their ethnic identity was "criollo native" perhaps meaning truly "native of Argentina." In contrast, Argentine was used for those born in Argentina but from European ancestry, and they were in a higher economic category than criollos.

Alone in School

In selecting a team for class work, the students made a total of 140 choices, 54 of which were mutual. Most of the groups formed included both boys and girls. Expediency in fulfilling the assignment acted as the most important criterion for selection. Proximity of household, *voluntad* (will) to do the work, and studiousness were the most important reasons cited for selection. Students with *voluntad* took their work seriously and knew how to carry out assignments conscientiously to completion. This quality seemed more important than being the best student, although studiousness also counted a great deal and was held to include such qualities as good memory, industriousness, good behavior, good nature, leadership, and ability in public presentation.

Participation in the maintenance of the school garden was the next hypothetical situation. A total of seventy-five choices was made; very few were mutual choices: eight students received one return each, and one student had two mutual choices. Six of the thirty-one students chose across sex lines. Physical strength, know-how, and skill to do the work determined the preferences. Experience and enthusiasm counted in some of the choices.

Another question asked students to select teammates for sports—soccer for boys and softball for girls. The leading boy was a student who had distinguished himself in soccer in both the school and in his neighborhood. He ranked low in the class for other activities. The choices were not based on *compañerismo* or friendship but on skillfulness in the game.

Although the specific task in each of these cases determined the selection, still there seem to be some key individuals who were more likely to be selected. Students looked up to these classmates for their outstanding skills, but choices were not always mutual.

From hypothetical situations in the context of the school, we moved to considering choices of classmates for activities in the household and in the neighborhood. One question asked, "If you have a picnic in your house, whom would you invite from your class and why?" It was expected that the family would play an important role in the association of the child with others. The selections ranged from one choice for one student to thirteen choices for another. Eleven students mixed sexes in their selections. One person selected ten classmates who had also selected him. Three students had eight mutual choices, two had six, and the rest received between one and five. Some students wanted to invite only a group of boys for soccer playing but felt it would be difficult to leave anyone out because these boys would resent them. Only a few would invite the entire class, since they felt compelled not to discriminate. The most popular reasons for inviting certain students and not others were because they were "educated," friendly, *simpático*, good *compañeros*, and responsible.

It became evident that the group of boys felt very united in all of their activities, with boy number twenty in the center of several social groups. While the network for the boys indicated a successful picnic, the network projected by the girls appeared more limited. Interestingly enough, the appearance of two cliques in an open chain was also apparent in the classroom.

In selecting companions to go to the movies, the number of choices was greatly reduced from the picnic situation. (In the picnic there was a total of 212 choices; for the movies, 111.) One person selected eight classmates, another made seven choices, and one made six; five selected five students, four selected four, and ten made three choices; four students made two selections, and three wanted to go to the movies with only one classmate. In this question the division by sex is most evident. As one of the girls explained: "To go to a public place with a boy would be severely frowned upon by parents unless he is a relative, like a cousin, or someone like a brother." Another girl commented that to appear in public with a boy would cause people to think "in the wrong way about me and my family." The reported reasons for the choices were cast in behavioral and moral terms: being a good *compañero* and a good friend, being well-behaved and educated, not envious, responsible in public, behaving like a true señorita, and rating high socially.

The choices made for attending church bring the social and religious variables together. The results were significant and rather surprising. The total number of choices was reduced to fifty, with eight students choosing to go alone. Only ten students selected each other mutually and seven of them were girls. The pattern seemed to express the feeling that religion is something personal and demands the best conduct while in church. Only some of the students who go to church do not laugh or giggle or talk during the service. Knowing how to behave in such a way that does not bring *vergüenza* was a strong argument for the choices. Many children preferred to attend church with sisters, brothers, or cousins rather than with friends. It was not rare for the youngsters to argue that it was best to attend services alone.

The concept of *simpático* played an important part in the choices individuals made for associating with others. Although this is a relative concept, there seemed to be some consensus as to what constituted *simpático*. It seemed to be a personality trait, sometimes related to popularity and certain physical features that accompanied the appropriate personality traits. On the question, "Name the four most *simpático* persons in your class," only 107 choices out of the possible 124 were made. Boy number twenty and girl number two led in choices. They were the best students in the class and enjoyed the reputation of *muy simpáticos*. Both were members of families in good economic standing. Three persons were selected eight times, while all others received less than five. Seven persons were never chosen; they were in the category of *muy criollos* and economically toward the *humilde* side.

In conversations after the test, the children explained that *simpático* is something physical but has other important characteristics in the way a person is. He knows how to joke, how to smile frequently, how to behave well; a *simpático* person is good-natured, good-humored, and gentle; he enjoys life and has good answers for adults; he is sure of himself and tends to like everybody. Three students found it difficult to explain the concept; strangely enough, they were among the persons their classmates chose as most *simpáticos*.

On the question of intimate friends, student number twenty still received the highest number of preferences (nine); the rest were all below five. Friendship constitutes a complex social phenomenon, and the criteria are not simple to pin down. It goes beyond the concepts of *simpático* and *compañerismo*. To become friends, people need to know each other for many years. The relationship is almost like that of brothers. Friends must be able to trust each other, defend each other, and become preoccupied with each other's needs. Sometimes the mere fact that one has strong affection (*querer* or *cariño*) towards another is sufficient reason for wishing to be the friend of another person. All of the students' answers tended to be mature and serious, and to incorporate the feeling that this subject demands respect. The requirements for friendship are high and difficult, particularly since the feelings have to be reciprocal. Usually one is a *compañero* first, and when the feeling of *querer* takes hold, the two become friends. But being a *compañero* does not necessarily lead to friendship; these are on two separate levels. Many are *compañeros* and never become true friends (like brothers), but any two friends have gone through the *compañero* stage.

The data from the sociometric experiment allows the statistical testing of some hypotheses. In the *vecindad*, social and economic class and ethnic affiliation affect the classification of and interaction between individuals. There is a similar mixing of social class and ethnic background in the schools. Statistical tests were applied to the data to see how these variables influence relationships among school children.[5]

The first approach was to analyze the significance of the economic variable among the thirty-one sixth graders. An analysis of variance could show whether the popularity of students on one economic level differed significantly from that of students in another bracket. The group was divided into three economic categories: very good, good, and low. Although all of the students were in the *clase media*, the differences were still sufficient to perform the test. With an F-value of 5.45 necessary for significance at the .005 level, the hypothetical situations showed the following results:[6]

teamwork	17.60
garden	10.40
sports	
boys	1.19
girls	7.70
picnic	17.50

[5] I wish to thank Mr. Stanley Katz from the Statistics Department of the University of Pennsylvania for assisting me in the analysis of the data.

[6] Level necessary is not the same due to different sample size. In any case, this test proved insignificant. For the girls, however, the result is significant at the .01 level, where $F = 6.51$ is necessary.

movie	23.60
simpático	17.70
friends	1.42

Almost all tests proved highly significant; thus popularity seemed to be in direct proportion to the economic well-being of the person involved. It became possible to regress the economic level on popularity and derive a significant result. (Because of low sample size, sports was excluded from this test.) A simple ranking of 1, 2, 3 for the low, good, and very good proved inferior to a ranking of 1, 1.67, 3.5 respectively; figures are given in r values (strength of regression), where .55 is necessary for significance at the .01 level.

	Using 1, 2, 3	Using 1, 1.67, 3.5
teamwork	no correlation	.73
garden	no correlation	.657
picnic	.73	.745
movie	.777	.791
simpático	.68	.745
friends	.294	.336

If the linear relationship is accepted, it would seem that the difference between the economic conditions of the low and good groups is relatively small compared to the difference between the good and very good categories.[7]

The matter of choosing intimate friends proved to be one exception to the strong economic correlation. In this case the results were completely random. Boys' sports also yielded less than significant results. Apparently athletic ability is more highly regarded by boys than the economic variable. The girls still choose significantly on the basis of economic standing. The results differ enough to warrant the generalization that the girls at this age are more strongly oriented to economic status differences than the boys. Besides the economic orientation,

---

[7] Replacement of the simple ranking by the improved ranking brought improvements of 5 to 10 percent. This can have either of two explanations: either the variation is nonlinear and people of above-average means receive a disproportionate share of popularity, or the rankings are not equally spaced and there is less difference between low and good than between good and very good. Probably both explanations have some validity.

there is a strong tendency to choose members of one's own sex, even when the activity in question is a mixed one. This, however, is stronger for boys than for girls.

The same type of analysis of variance test was performed for the four ethnic groups: criollo, Italian, Jewish, and other foreign. The results were as follows (the level of significance of .05 requires F = 2.96):

teamwork	2.29
picnic	3.06
movie	3.30
simpático	2.64
friends	2.04

The cases of picnics and movies appear significant, but a close look at the data reveals a distinct problem; the reaction of significance is not consistent. If the Jewish cases are taken alone, they rate first in the picnic, movie, and teamwork; they rate second in *simpático* and last in friendship. It is therefore difficult to assign a general value for regression purposes. On a purely average basis, ranking seems to place foreign first, followed by Jewish, Italian, and criollo. Breaking down ethnic considerations into a general model was basically fruitless on account of the random fluctuation from situation to situation. Multiple regression tests showed that most of this variance was in fact a direct result of economic status. The inclusion of the ethnic variable into the regression equations did very little to improve the overall correlation.

Variable	Situation				
	Teamwork	Garden	Picnic	Movie	*Simpáticos*
economic	8.57	4.33	5.53	6.74	5.53
ethnic	2.62	1.24	1.80	2.15	1.28

The figures show that the economic variable is significant in every case (the necessary level of significance is 2.048 at the .05 level), while the ethnic variable is significant only in the teamwork and movie cases. For friendship, since neither analysis of variance test proved significant, multiple regression tests were not performed.

The tests indicate that the economic variable is significant in all cases, while the ethnic is significant only in the strongest regressions. With this in mind, one can examine the b values of the regression—that is, the direct effect attributable to each variable.

b value	Situation				
	Teamwork	Garden	Picnic	Movie	*Simpáticos*
economic b	2.90	2.28	3.57	2.88	3.02
ethnic b	.677	.474	.891	.72	.535

The strongest significance is shown by the teamwork variables, but the greatest average differentiations occur in the picnic situation. In the case of the picnic there is a greater difference between economic groups and more variability in the results; in the teamwork case the difference is less marked but more universal. Most of the sixty mutual choices that occurred in the picnic situation were between the very good and good; eighteen were between the ten children of the very good and good level, twenty-eight between one of those children and a low. Only fourteen mutual choices were between children of the low economic group.

The same tests were performed on a control group of girls in a private school. Most of the regressions performed were marginal, with r ranging from .22 to .52, where .47 is necessary for significance. The one factor that emerged constant from the control experiment was that the best regression coefficients resulted from the use of the 1, 1.5, and 3.5 spacing method. Again the privileged economic group enjoyed inordinate popularity in the sixth grade of the private school. The analysis of the ethnic factor proved inconclusive.

In summary, the statistical tests point to a markedly high dependence on economic status, while ethnic considerations play only a minor role in the selection of associations. The anthropological observations indicate that there is a conscious effort on the part of students in the middle and upper classes to choose in this particular manner.[8]

The dynamics of group relations in the class were further studied

---

[8] Mr. Stanley Katz remarked of this conclusion: "Surely, one might reasonably expect popularity to be based somewhat on economic status, but the extent of the correlation and the subsequent nonsignificance of other variables seems indeed odd."

by giving the students an opportunity for decision making. The class was given five hundred pesos to use as they pleased. It was predicted that (*a*) the group would encounter many difficulties; (*b*) the class would come to an impasse; (*c*) the students would lose their enthusiasm for the use of the cash; and (*d*) in apathy, anything would be accepted.

At first the class considered the assignment to be a simple problem; they talked about it during recess. The money was kept by girl number two, but no one was assigned to a position of responsibility. Each was given equal responsibility for the disposition of the money. The people who had received the largest number of choices in most situations remained in a position equal to all others. Their opinions were no more influential than others. As time passed, the discussions during recess turned to arguments accompanied by shouting. The good students became restless and apologetic for the failure to draw up a plan to use the money.

The first obvious division was in terms of sex. After awhile the girls wanted to buy a ball for their games, and the boys wanted one for soccer. Because there was not enough money to buy two balls, this idea was abandoned. The class seemed to be united in the opinion that the money should be used for the pleasure trip at the end of the school year. When they had to decide exactly for what it was to be spent, again there was chaos. Finally the teacher suggested that they remain in class for a half an hour after the session to make a final decision. (The investigator remained to observe the situation, but the teacher was not present for that special "meeting.") One of the boys assumed leadership and wanted to sample the opinions of his classmates. The noise and shouting became almost unbearable; students exchanged defiant statements and insults were shouted. (This was the first time insults were heard so liberally used among the school children.) There were also invitations to meet afterward in the street to settle the matter with a good fight. The matter remained unresolved.

Finally there remained four possible ways of using the five hundred pesos: (*a*) to buy a soccer ball for the school, but the girls opposed this; (*b*) to buy a ball for the sixth grade only, but many opposed this, arguing that the ball would be left after they graduated; (*c*) to give the money to the *cooperadora* association of the school; and (*d*) for a pleasure trip. These alternatives were written on the blackboard and a vote was taken. Two boys helped boy number twenty to record the votes. One student noticed that her vote was erased and misplaced; she stood up and angrily objected. Corrections were made, and from then on everyone watched the counters carefully. Often everyone talked at once, and the leader could not control the group. He wanted to give up, but his *compañeros* urged him not to. Finally he declared: "The decision is to use the money for the trip." Three students objected, but they could propose no alternatives. The students were tired and wanted to go home; they pleaded with the objectors to accept the vote. Thus the meeting came to an end. The solution was reached by exhaustion, and the students were not in agreement.

The next day many students complained about the decision. The teacher suggested that they could hold a raffle to increase the capital; other proposals followed. Someone suggested another after-school meeting and elicited vehement objections. The teacher took this opportunity to lecture the class on cooperation, but privately she said that the children should not be given the freedom to decide on matters of importance. She added, "Students are children, and what can one expect from them?" It is evident from this that the child, both in the neighborhood and in the school, receives the imprint of his cultural tradition; life for him is a continuing struggle.

Schools in the City

As in the case of clubs, schools also fall into two categories: schools of the city and schools of the *vecindad*. Families in good economic condition who have achieved a high degree of *cultura* and are constantly aspiring to still better economic positions send their children to the city schools. They prefer the Normal School for teachers which runs a primary school for practice teaching, private Catholic schools, or the number one provincial public school. Most of these institutions are located in the center of the city, while two, the Normal School and the private school for girls, are in the main plaza.

In the second category are schools farther away from the plaza and the center. The provincial government sponsors most of these institutions. The teachers are all women from the upper social levels who have been awarded degrees by the Normal School. Orders of the Catholic Church also run two private schools considered of the second category. Informants classified them along with neighborhood institutions, although these schools draw students from a wide area of the city.

Deciding on a school begins early in the life of a child, and he cannot predict if his parents will allow him to continue in the same school for several years to graduate with his own peer group. For the parents, the feelings of the child are a minor consideration. Some parents who identify with the neighborhood only partially tend to disassociate the children from the neighborhood by sending them to a school in another section of the city. In general, the parents' position is determined by their degree of class consciousness and intellectual and professional aspirations for the child.

The categorization does not apply only on the student level. Teachers feel social discomfort among themselves when they are members of a staff in which class differences are very evident. Identification and recognition of each other come as soon as a new appointment is made by the minister of education. Very quickly, teachers speculate about the social standing and the teaching ability of any newcomer to the staff. The interaction in schools among teachers, between teachers and principals, and between teachers and students is very formal. Class differentiation, sex, position, and age dictate etiquette for interaction. Properness, *cultura*, and distinction are demanded, leaving little margin for social errors.

One can observe class differences and social formality at student assemblies in the schools for the celebration of historical events. On these occasions students listen to very poetic presentations on the meaning of the event. A teacher will dramatically deliver a literary speech for twenty to forty minutes. Everyone must agree that the delivery was excellent, although few comprehend the speech. It is an adult presentation for an audience of children. When children become restless, the *directora* may stand and walk to the front of the auditorium. Without saying a word, she makes the children realize that the slightest movement on their part could result in their names being called, and then they would be severely reprimanded for disrespecting the sacred symbols of their country.

On these occasions school children are taken in formation to the central plaza. Each school appoints the best sixth grader to march with the flag. Instructions for the celebration come from the provincial government. High officials from the government, the church, and the military are represented. Ethnic associations also send representatives and offer flowers to be placed at the foot of some statues. At these times, the public appearance of teachers of high social standing with a school of a secondary category causes public discomfort. At these public gatherings in the plaza teachers learn about new appointments and gather material for later discussions among themselves. Those on the staff of reputable institutions can walk with pride and can shine (*lucirse*); those servicing modest schools prefer to remain inconspicuous in the public gathering.

Variation by Class

The program and organization of the schools are uniform throughout the city, but the implementation of the program varies by class. A lower-class school in a barrio of the city was observed. This school was founded to extend formal primary instruction to poor children and to provide manual training for them. During the morning hours they followed the regular school program, and after lunch they trained in practical skills. The teachers for the morning session received training in the Normal School; regular artisans conducted the manual shops. One member of the research team observed this school for the purpose of comparison with the previous case.[9] In his diary we find the following remarks:

Today I spent the day in school. I was well received by the *directora* and the various subdirectors, as well as by the teachers. While I was sitting in the office of the *directora* in charge of primary education, several mothers came with children they wanted to enroll. The mothers did not understand

---

[9] Henry Schwarz III, who was exposed to the Argentine system of education for the first time, offered some interesting points for comparison with the middle-class school. His orientation was based on a background of elementary education learning theory and the psychology of socialization.

the procedures very well, and the *directora* spoke to them as a sergeant might speak to a recruit. "You didn't know that you had to have your documents? Why not? Whom did you talk to before? What was her name? Why don't you know?" No effort was made to foster the mother's confidence or to bridge the differences of class status that separated the teachers and the mother. The curt treatment of the mother contrasted with the great show of interest and courtesy accorded to me.

The first class I visited was the sixth grade, composed of twenty-two students. The class ranged in age from little boys and girls of about eleven to big boys and girls of at least fourteen. It was an arithmetic class and consisted of a review of previously learned material. A problem was put on the blackboard, and each student tried to solve it in his notebook. Then the teacher would call on someone to do the problem on the board.

I was surprised by the attention paid to the class by the students. When the teacher asked for a volunteer, about half the class offered to answer. Other teachers often came in to ask questions, and the teacher had to leave the room several times.

The next class was a fourth grade, and the lesson was in grammar. The room was crowded; four boys had to stand up and a number of children shared a chair and a desk. One student wrote at the board in front as the teacher dictated. The students were called upon to tell which was a sentence and which was a phrase. In the sentence they were to point out the subject, the verb, and the predicate. The answers to the questions about grammar were all memorized. If the student did not know the answer, the teacher would help by supplying the first few words of the line as a cue. Formulas or rules were also learned and applied, as was the case for arithmetic in the previous class.

The teacher addressed the students as *señor* and *señorita* and used the formal "you." In both classes teachers made no conscious effort to establish a warm, personal relationship with students. Many of the teachers wore dark glasses in their classrooms, making eye contact impossible; those without dark glasses avoided eye contact. Teachers wandered up and down the rows and always spoke with a strong, snappy voice.

Whenever I went to a class or a shop, the teachers would listen to my explanation that I wanted to see the students working and did not care what they knew. They all apologized for the fact that the students did not yet know how to make this or that. One teacher came to me after I had been in her class and with obvious discouragement explained that the students came from families that had no interest in *cultura* and no interest in helping the

Alone in School

children to learn. She tried during the school year to teach the children good manners. She was very critical of the bad manners of her students. (At this point one student said, "I and John." She sharply corrected him: "John and I." But she said that she knew the children always reverted back to the bad habits they had learned at home.)

In the third period I visited the first inferior grade (first first grade, in contrast to the first superior). All the students had been through the grade before, some as many as four times. This class seemed restless—it was the third hour of the day—and the children did not pay much attention. The teacher told them to make three rows of certain letters in their notebooks. She then proceeded to make three rows of the same letters on the blackboard and said that the children did not understand instructions unless they saw the example in front of them. At this level children are more apt to report each other; for instance, one boy made four lines of each letter instead of three, and his companion reported him to the teacher.

This class was poorly dressed, and one of the students was Miguela, a girl who sold newspapers in the streets at night. The teacher knew her from the street and had appointed her to line up the class in ranks to march to and from the classroom. Miguela did the work like a sergeant. She acted with great force, pushing and pulling the others into position, and she enjoyed it.

In the afternoon I went to the barbershop, the carpentry shop, and glanced through the door at some of the other shops. The barbershop was very relaxed. The first few minutes the boys scouted around me and asked me such questions as whether Eliott Ness still lived and whether there were Indians and cowboys in North America. I was amused by one incident. I was wearing my dark flannel trousers and, as I had been walking in the dusty road, they had dust marks on them. The boys were very concerned and would not let me dismiss it as inconsequential. They insisted on getting a brush and brushing it off. This happened more than once.

The principal granted me permission to observe the shop. She advised me that I should be interested in the personnel teaching in the shops as well as in the students. They are people without *cultura*; they are just tradesmen who teach their trade and know nothing about psychology or teaching, therefore, what can one expect the children to learn? In the barber shop, the boys cut the hair of other boys, while the teacher walked about looking and criticizing, taking a snip here and there to demonstrate or to even up a mistake. On the whole, there was supervision, but the teacher left the boys very much on their own.

The overall impression from the visit was that the primary school program was poorly adapted to the needs of the students whom I knew well in their own *vecindad*. They had the same program as those from the center who were preparing for secondary education. The material learned was purely memorized, and imagination, understanding, and innovation were far from being encouraged.

Many more days were spent in the sixth grade of this school, and most of the patterns and generalizations were further corroborated. In addition, Henry Schwarz, who assisted me in the field work, also observed the students in the middle-class school. He reported:

The first and most obvious difference between the sixth grade of the San Martín School and the lower-class one was more active participation among the middle-class children. When questions were asked, and even before, the room was a sea of arms snapping in the air and students gasping, "I can tell you, señorita!" When someone was called on to answer, he jumped up and recited at attention. The impression was of a brighter group of children than the ones previously observed—more highly trained and more lively. They were also considerably more advanced in their lessons than the children in the same grade in the other school. In the lower-class school the recitation of the lesson was usually full of stumbling, and frequently the student would go back to the beginning, including the title. Academically, the group was a year ahead of the sixth grade in the lower-class school.

The teacher of the fifth grade appeared to be a very refined person with *cultura* in her upbringing. She seemed very conscious of herself and of her status; her diction and manners were very proper. She continuously reminded the class that a visitor was observing them.

In comparing the two groups of children, one could say that the middle-class children were more organized in their activities, more vivacious, better coordinated in motor movements, and bolder in their actions. The school patio was located in the middle of the school and was divided to separate the boys from the girls. I noticed that a group was playing ring-around-the-rosy, a thing that never happened in the first school. Another group of girls was skipping rope, and several boys were running around swinging under the railing of the patio.

The classes were conducted as in all schools: teachers dictating, students reciting memorized material. In the middle-class school, the students' free composition appeared very stylized. I was shown a composition with a very good grade from the teacher in which the student wrote about how nice it was to finish vacation and return to school. Another theme had to do with neatness:

"I care for my school things because they will accompany me all year round. I like to keep them neat so when the teacher asks for them they are pretty and give a good impression. I take care of covers so they will last longer, and I take care of the pages of the books so they will not become wrinkled and break. How nice it is to care for the books!"

These observations become meaningful in the background of the class structure of the city. The emphasis on physical appearance is very central and transcends the situation of the school itself.

In the private school, one immediately notices the obvious differences in the background of each student as compared to the other schools. Most of the students here come from higher economic levels, some from socially well-known families. Their families are active in the city, and they are people of the city and not of the *vecindad*. This distinction in itself is significant. The families of these students belong to city clubs and social clubs, and they know each other well from these few centers.[10]

When I arrived in school at 7:45 A.M., the students were already lined up in the patio for the flag salute. The girls all wore the same uniform: a blue skirt, white blouse, and a blue jacket. There was a minimum of artificiality in makeup and dress, and this was in contrast, indeed, to other situations where the same girls appear to advance their age by sophisticated dress. As the students were lined up, the *directora* reprimanded them for making so much noise when leaving the classrooms and for not being attentive during the salute to the flag.

The sixth grade began the morning classes with arithmetic. The teacher called one of the students to pass to the front of the class to write the first exercise on the blackboard. The entire class then was supposed to correct it. The student was slow and took a long time to reduce the numbers, so the teacher called on another student to continue. This person again was very slow and made many mistakes. Other students jumped to correct her. At this point the teacher spotted a student who was consulting something under

---

[10] The material on the private school was gathered by an assistant, Sandra Kerawalla, a graduate student at the University of Pennsylvania.

her desk. The teacher bluntly asked her to stand up and report what she was doing. The girl was sent to the front, but she could not solve the problem. Another student was playing with colored pencils and painting. The teacher, having noticed this, asked her a question about the subject. After much hesitation the girl repeated what another helpful companion had whispered. The teacher then had a chance to remark: "You can see that by repeating what others say, you can be wrong, because you were not paying attention to the class." The teacher then asked another person the same question and finally got the right answer.

During the grammar class the lesson was dictated, and then some aspects of basic grammar were reviewed. They talked about verbs, nouns, and other grammatical categories. One of the girls who doesn't pay much attention was frequently called to answer questions. The teacher usually would remark, "As you see, this *señorita* today was talking during class, and now she cannot answer. When will you abandon this habit and stop talking in class?"

The teacher finally dictated a lesson about the declaration of independence in Argentina. The classes were finished at noon, but before going home, all the students went to chapel.

It would appear that as one rises socially, one finds a more active and alert group of children noted for their sophistication and good manners. Social distinction and distance between teacher and students do not appear as striking in this school as in the other two. The social background is consistent with the amount of *cultura* expected from the institution. Both teacher and students seem conscious of themselves and their status; proper social manners are naturally practiced and considered essential to the style of life in school and at home. Children organize their activities rapidly and reach decisions with speed and efficiency.

There is no doubt that the private institutions are definitely related to people in the higher categories. It is expected that in those schools there will be more refinement and more exclusive selectivity of both teachers and students. The social and economic differences in these schools are thus less apparent. In the *clase media*, however, and particularly in the lowest sections, teachers must cope with different values that affect motivation and stimulation to learn. Learning the subject matter does not seem to have a strong emotional stimulus. Teachers feel that these individuals, products of a humble social condition, exhaust them physically from day to day. As teachers with high standards and refinements aspiring to teach in schools of first category or in private schools, they attempt to impose behavioral and work standards and ideals of interaction from another subculture. After four hours of classes, a teacher exclaimed, "My nerves are shot, and when I return home, I am in no condition to enjoy the rest of the day!" Disobedience and social disorientation seem to lie at the core of the problem. This situation brings discomfort and misunderstandings for both teachers and students.

School and Regimentation

Parents, like their children, view the school with a feeling of being threatened by it. One socially aspiring mother, a professional secretary, blamed the teacher for much of the misconduct and the weaknesses of her son.

There are many injustices in the school with the children. The teacher has been threatening my son constantly, and he fears that he will not pass the grade and thus won't be able to go to secondary school. The teacher keeps the children in fear [*sobresaltados*], and shouts and threatens always. I advise my son not to complain or answer to the teacher, because teachers will get back at you. There is no way but to bear them. It has always been like this, even when I myself was a child. If the teacher realizes that the child comes home and complains, and the mother or the father goes to the teacher or to the *directora*, then you will see what happens. It is better to abide with everything. My advice is not to go against the teacher. But one is always afraid that one's child may fall in disgrace, and then it becomes difficult for the child to get good grades.

Many parents reason like that, yet teachers feel that parents do not cooperate with them. Parents, on the other hand, view the teacher as a socially unreachable figure. Once more we can remind ourselves that life (and school) is a perpetual *conquista* for both the children and the parents.

There is a general feeling among parents and children that neat homework implies satisfactory progress, and when a child complies with the standard of neatness, he should obtain excellent grades. If the neat child is also well mannered, quiet, and recites well, there is no question about the grades he deserves. Thus the effort of the parents is to see that the child goes through all the formalities to earn good grades. Learning is necessary, but in light of all the other demands, analysis and understanding become secondary goals. For many people of the *clase media*, education is not so much for the sake of learning as for the sake of eventual economic success. For many parents, the content of knowledge does not appear so important as the diploma itself.

The school is an institution not only for educating the child, but also for "correcting" him. With respect to socialization, it shares many elements with the *vecindad*. The school has a duty to keep a child good (*buenito*) and to convert the *malos* into *buenos*. Adults expect that a child will develop into a good social being; society has given rights to the school to form the child's personality and to force him to comply with adult aspirations. The child must learn and internalize good behavior, *educación*, and *cultura*.

Teachers feel that they receive students from neighborhoods and barrios with low *cultura*. They are expected to perform the roles of teacher and social judge in implementing the growth of the child. Here lies the explanation for the constant concern of the teacher with correcting behavior, defining appropriateness, expecting correctness, and presenting adult standards to the child. As has been described, in each class the teacher constantly sprinkles the subject matter with advice and demands for proper behavior. Frequently there is more emphasis on appropriateness of behavior than on the subject matter itself.

In all of the schools, the teachers are constantly active, dictating, correcting, evaluating performance, and giving directions. Correcting manners and developing the child socially are considered important problems for the teacher, regardless of the school. This is more intense, however, in the low and middle classes. Students tend to be noisy, and teachers reprimand them publicly, threatening in the familiar pattern, "If you do not stop talking, I will keep you half an hour after school."

The class situation in any school and of any social category depicts eloquently the strong role that the society assigns to the teacher. The teacher gives her knowledge, and is expected to create; students merely repeat the memorized material and behave well for the reward of a good grade. There is no individual latitude within the system, and this affects the creativity of both teacher and students.

If freedom is an important aspect of the learning process as demonstrated by Sylvia Ashton-Warner in her book *Teacher*, the system of teaching and learning in the Argentine schools does not use freedom as a tool for learning. Ashton-Warner writes that "it is always not what is said, but the freedom to say"[11] which is part of an artistic moment of creation and personal experience. The school system under consideration here does not provide sufficient room for freedom of expression. The formality of the programs and the rigidity of interaction suppress both teacher and students. Criticism of performance is constant, and it can be intense when innovation is noted. From my own personal experience and observation, the basic and fundamental aspects of the national system of education have not changed over a period of thirty-five years.

Children do not have the freedom to write an essay expressing their personal thoughts. Thus the teacher never has the opportunity to explore what is in the child's mind. "The ability of the teacher to draw out and preserve that other line of thought"[12] and to remain a good listener hardly exists. Among the Maori, the students wrote their own books and each was different; among the Paraná children, each writes a "book" dictated by the teacher and patterned after the work of many generations who did the same thing. Each generation followed the instructions from the educational authorities in the proper department of the government. How close this "book" is to the single model conceived by the authorities determines the grade. Hence, the child's book is not a highly personal document to be analyzed for its content; and analysis of the child's intellectual and personality development cannot be based on the work he is doing in school.

In this system, teachers take upon themselves the task of conducting all the teaching by performing and modeling for the students. The listening is on the part of the student and rarely falls on the part of the teacher. When she listens to students, it is to evaluate them as they perform. In a sense she listens to herself as the child repeats the

[11] Ashton-Warner 1963:49.
[12] Ibid., p. 33.

material she has dictated. The closer the student's version is to the original, the higher the grade.

Thinking carefully through lessons given them is not encouraged; there is a lack of interest in what an individual may think, or how he reacts to the material presented in the classroom. Children frequently wonder about what the teacher says. One student dared to show her perplexity at one of the wonders of the world—the hanging gardens—and asked the teacher to explain. Her teacher answered, "Child, don't you know what hang means?" The subject was closed.

10. THE ARGENTINE PARANAENSE

Children's Social Images

Children throughout the city, no matter what their family backgrounds, are exposed in the educational system to the same administrative procedures and programs as those just described. The method of teaching and the material are nationally set and not adapted to fit the educational needs of the pupils. The program leaves little room for modification that would promote greater interest from the pupils. With the children's varied backgrounds and the common educational process, it is interesting to test the variations in conceptualization of the world by children of different classes.

To test the degree of variation, sixth graders in three schools of different social categories were asked to write a few paragraphs about life in their *vecindades* or *barrios*. The intention was to bring out a general profile of the social differences internalized by the children.

The first school was for the lower class, *la gente humilde*, and attended by children from the *clase baja*. Only the most capable children ready for a hard conquest manage to complete the sixth grade. In the barrio the "twenty-two" stand out among the large majority who have abandoned school or repeated the same grade several times. Half of the group are two and a half years older than the average group of children in the same grade elsewhere.

Analysis of the essays showed that the lower-class children entertain a poetic and romantic outlook toward their surroundings. Although much vacant space stands between the houses, the children viewed their neighborhood as an intimate, close unit. The first and most basic theme was the humbleness of their neighborhood; *humilde* was the concept used. This also served to classify the people in the barrio: *gente* or *clase humilde*. The lack of material comforts and urban sophistication contrasts with their strong emphasis upon nature. Nature seems to have an appealing influence on their perception of the surroundings. The essays refer to green pastures, empty spaces, trees and their shade, the colors of the different seasons of the year, and the singing of birds. The children describe these as happy experiences and present the material with much poetic sentiment.

When writing about people, the children mention honesty, good manners, and diligence and do not discuss the fact that "bad" people do exist in the barrios. Ignorance, enviousness, and gossiping make people bad. The children write about drunkenness, but it does not seem to affect the category of "good people," especially if the person exhibits the positive characteristics. They accept the widespread drinking pattern; drinking is a vice only if it severely affects the person's health and life. *Asados* (barbecues) and home festivities with relatives, close friends, and good neighbors are part of the complex of adult sociability.

Children are not left out; it would be difficult for the children of the *clase baja* to imagine the life of a barrio without the welcome noises of children at play in the empty spaces between the houses. The children run errands to the stores and fetch water; this adds to the surrounding outdoor sounds and is an integral aspect of social existence for both children and adults. Children are viewed as a source of joy (*alegría*) in their *vecindario* or barrio.

The essays also mention the lack of formalized activity in clubs. Clubs are considered necessary institutions when a barrio becomes more structured; they organize recreational activities for adults. Adults gather in open areas to play soccer or in *almacén*-bar combinations. Other sporadic recreations may break the monotony of life—a merry-go-round truck, a truck with amplifiers alternating music with commercial or political announcements, a door-to-door vendor with colorful trinkets, or the television set at a store charging viewers who sit in front. The bars are a kind of neutral place for the adults in this area, and they are a curiosity for children, for whom they are taboo. Noises, fights, and drunkenness are associated with bars. It is evident that the free movement of people always in view of each other—adults and children in search of an activity—is attached to the *alegría* of a neighborhood of low-class people.

For most of the sixth-grade students, darkness, the silence of the nights, the quiet of cold winter days, and the desolation of rainy days evoke sadness, loneliness, sorrow, and pity. Much of this feeling may be related to the reduced space that has to be shared under the bad climatic conditions. The houses are not only small, but also dark—a generally rejected quality. Poetically, one student wrote that in the night, "the barrio cries so it will not be left alone." On the other hand, spring, daybreak, and nights with a full moon symbolize happiness.

The frequent appearance of public entertainment brings the reputation of a happy neighborhood. Occasionally the circus may attract people from the surrounding areas, bringing and causing excitement. Sometimes gypsies camp in the barrios; the tents and colorful silk dresses excite children, although adults react with reserve toward the gypsies.

The outdoors—open courtyards, semienclosed areas for pedestrians, open spaces for soccer—is the stage for living. Activities in the open make people an integral part of the natural environment and also permit mutual evaluation. General moods can be assessed, and the degree of security can be predicted. Silence is dangerous; lack of movement implies boredom, sadness, and *miseria* (poverty).

In summary, those who are socially *humildes* do not conceptualize *vecindario* or barrio as a physical entity alone. The essays convey the impression that the *vecindario* is an extension of the people. Tranquility and the good life derive from the balance between the positive and negative conditions, and when balance exists, the situation in the barrio invites the development of appreciation, and social roots can be supported with dignity. The expressions and conceptualization of their neighborhood by these children constituted, in contrast with other groups, a very special portrait of their image.

The next group of children were from the San Martín School (see chapter 9) and of the *clase media*. For them, *vecindad* seems to represent a group of families sharing space in delimited city blocks. The children do not classify *vecindades* as humble, but simple; in turn, the better places are called comfortable, in contrast to simple. Nature plays no significant part in the life of these children. The only references made to plants, flowers, and trees are to those in gardens. The theme of the artificiality of the environment permeates all the essays in this group.

The concept of *gente*, or people, is very relevant but not just as people; the quality of people is emphasized. In general the group is evaluated as amiable, educated (not necessarily in the formal sense, but rather in the sense of possessing *cultura*), and united. The children portray the *clase media* as a perfect group. The physical limitations imposed on the people promote the group consciousness. There is a definite tendency not to speak about individuals as bad, as with the *clase baja*. That life is peaceful and people are amiable are the two most important themes in all of the essays.

Some children discuss indirectly the lack of smooth relationships in the neighborhood. Most children, however, are more likely to express these views in conversation than in writing. In interviews with each child after the essays were written, the same children who wrote about the peaceful existence in the neighborhood now spoke about the enviousness of neighbors, the gossips, and the lack of *cultura*. But all of this is excluded from the essays; the children write about the ideal of neighborhood life. Writing about the ideal in itself is an interesting aspect of the *clase media*.

The essays reveal the tensions in the relations between adults and children. (Only six persons, out of the thirty-two, consider children as a source of joy. These six reside in areas of the *clase baja*, and in the school they are known as *los negros*.) Children seem to feel that as long as space is provided for them, space that they can call their own, then life is gay and peaceful. When the physical conditions clearly delineate the spheres of adults and children and each can fulfill his needs without clashing with the other, then the essays strongly emphasize unity, friendship, and justice within the neighborhoods. Such conditions allow companionship and mutual understanding to develop between children and adults. The lack of available open spaces prompts statements that it is better for each person to be in his own home in order to avoid clashes with adult neighbors who dislike children.

The *clase baja* children conceive of joy in relation to the noises created by children at play and people moving about their day-to-day activities. Children of the *clase media* find joy in city noises created by traffic, public services, and at terminals. Such surroundings indicate development, progress, and *cultura*, and these symbolize the *clase media*. In the definition of *vecindad*, the formal recreation facilitated by clubs and open spaces and plazas or small parks plays an important part. Paved streets and sidewalks, solidly built houses crowded one next to another and surrounded by high walls create an urban setting and show modernization. Physical manifestations of *cultura* and progress make life gay. On the other hand, antique cobblestone streets, old houses, and lack of traffic or pavement symbolize sadness for the middle-class child.

For this class of people, *vecindad*, as a concept, remains an extension of themselves, although it is not realized as such. Limited space for public activities, economic differences, and social variations curtail individual self-expression. *Vecindad* is a physical entity somewhat removed from one's own existence. In contrast to the previous group discussed, the two variables (physical and human) are acting independently and frequently one against the other in the *vecindad*. The physical divisions (walls) between households add to the ethnic and economic plurality. Nevertheless, *vecindad* continues to imply togetherness, people's knowledge of one another, and lack of conflict. The ideal and the real seldom harmonize, and the discrepancy between the written essays and the conversations reveals the wide hiatus between them. The distance between what a *vecindad* should be and what it really is may leave an individual lonely and confused.

The next sixth-grade group attends a private school. Twenty-five of the girls are eleven years old, and one is fourteen. Ten are from elite, patrician, and known families; a few belong to an economically high group of the middle class, aspiring to be considered of the elite.

In the essays written by the sixth graders of the private institution, the definition of barrio or neighborhood does not coincide with the models presented by the previous two groups. The children do not attempt to describe the social aspects of barrio or neighborhood. The essays are brief, just a few lines; it appears that the orientation toward barrio or neighborhood as a social unit is greatly diminished. Instead, they are oriented toward the city and specifically toward the center of the city. The neighborhood is hardly something personalized and an extension of oneself as it is for the lower class and to some extent for the middle class. *Vecindad* does not bring an image of children playing outdoors, children on errands, or other activities in the open. As a concept it does exist for the children, but, as one student pointed out, "We live in society instead."

The essays of the *clase alta*, especially of the ten elite students, do not bring nature into the discussion of the surroundings and of the daily activities. Some mention wanting to live next to Paraná River because of the nice view rather than because of some personal relationship with elements of nature.

These children do not emphasize *gente*; they write about neighbors saying that "we are kind to each other"; everyone in the group is very *simpático* and cordial. Instead of the *clubes de vecindad*, the *clubes de ciudad* are important points of reference in the themes. Motor noises in the streets are presented as part of a progressive *ambiente* and part of life in the city. They are welcomed as indicating progress and civilization, thus making the residents part of it. The early morning activities—servants washing sidewalks, housewives purchasing merchandise from ambulant salesmen, delivery men making their rounds, people going to offices, children in uniforms going to school—all are cultural elements described in the essays as significant to the making of their surroundings and creating excitement in their existence.

The children associate sadness with the quietness of Saturday afternoons, when all businesses and offices close, and Sundays. Cold winter nights are also sad because no one is out walking and the streets are empty. Again, this group of children differs significantly from the first group in their conceptualization of sadness. For the children of the *clase baja*, noises that signify happiness and joy are of their own making; the *clase alta* children perceive noises as necessary elements, but with the feeling that noises are made for them and brought to them. Absence of noise means a lack of potential entertainment and personal recreation.

Obviously this group's view of *vecindad* does not coincide with the others. *Vecindad* is not a matter for consideration by families residing in the center of the city; *vecindad* and barrio are terms of folklore and cultural tradition. They carry little personal value because the upper class feels part of the social context and network of the city.

It is clear that the three groups of children conceptualize their immediate surroundings differently; without doubt, their views correlate with the adults' views in each social class. Within each group exceptions exist, but each diverging student was classified socially below or above the average background of the group. In the neighborhood or barrio, the child receives the first impact of the nature of interpersonal relations and derives assumptions that underlie his later public behavior. The lower-class people are very personally oriented toward the barrio. The barrio is in them, they are part of it; barrio life means living. Barrio can also be a central concept for the *clase media* of lower economic means; *vecindad*, however, is the reference point for the entire middle class. As one moves toward the center of the social continuum, particularly into the category of people with high social aspirations, the variations become greater. *Vecindad* no longer remains a real entity, and for the upper class it is not central to an analysis of their general orientation.

Children at the age of thirteen evidently have acquired a fairly clear concept of their social surroundings and its relation to themselves. Their identity, both public image and self-image, is rooted in their conceptualization of their environment. There is a definite gradient from the *humilde* group at one end, through the *clase media*, toward the upper class at the other extreme of the social continuum. In the middle class the relationship between neighborhood as a social unit and the children appears from their writing to be intimate.

Friendships, companionships, and avoidances begin within the neighborhood. What one is in public is derived from the characterization of one's neighborhood. While primary schools group children by neighborhood, the situation changes in secondary schools, which draw students from the whole city. Secondary schools are arenas for many awkward social situations. Students residing in a poor barrio, with parents who cannot compensate socially for their residential location, are socially handicapped, especially if they want to associate or study with someone from a higher class. They then must choose a style of friendship that will maintain social harmony and personal tranquillity. One solution is to cultivate the friendship in public places. In exceptional cases a student may become a friend of someone in a higher social category, and then he usually becomes a friend of the family. They consent to the friendship and may even encourage the association. There are also friendships limited to school (*amigos de escuela*). The sorting during the first year of secondary school is rapid. The real reasons for the mutual discrimination are rarely stated, but selection occurs, and the pattern perpetuates social distinctions and the intimate relation of *vecindad* to individual.

Planning for the Future

As described above, one's self-image is intimately linked to one's area of residence. In addition to describing their present environment, the children also responded to questions about the future: what they would like to be and where they would like to live. Discontent and ambivalence toward one's own neighborhood or barrio are symptomatic of personal social discomfort and desire for social mobility. Satisfaction with one's social standing and social identity, on the other hand, correlates with the desire to maintain the status quo.

The lower-class boys wanted to become football players, mechanics, carpenters, military officers, and radio announcers; the girls wished to become nurses, singers, sewing teachers, and primary school teachers. All of the children were satisfied to reside in their barrio at the outskirts of the city. In the future, six wanted to live in Paraná, while the rest preferred Buenos Aires, Córdoba, or Santa Fé. The standard explanation for the choices was: "I'd like to go there because I'd just like it."

In the middle-class group, ten students wanted to continue through university training (medicine, engineering, law); twelve wished to undertake secondary training with specialization in business administration; and seven were interested in music, painting, or sports. All of the children reside in the transitional social area of the city between the center and the low-class neighborhoods. All except two wanted to change their place of residence, particularly to move toward the center of the city or into the sophisticated residential area facing the Paraná River. The cities of Córdoba, Buenos Aires, and Mendoza were selected as desirable places, but only after one had obtained semiprofessional degrees. Relatives who reside in these cities were mentioned as the reason for the desire to change.

The ambition of the upper-class girls was to become professional at the university level. Ten would like to study medicine, psychology, architecture, or economics; eleven wanted to become primary school teachers, and then to continue studies in the Instituto de Profesorado for a specialization in languages first, history second, and mathematics third. Two would like to become actresses or fashion models, and one made no declaration of her intentions.

All of the girls were happy to reside in the downtown section of the city, although they would prefer to live in the new residential area of Parque Urquiza. The areas of the country known for attracting tourists—San Carlos de Bariloche, Córdoba, and Mendoza—were selected as desirable to visit and perhaps to reside in, followed by Paraná and Buenos Aires.

The children's answers clearly show that the lower class and the elite are satisfied with their present residential location; it correlates with their ambitions in life. In other words, for the upper-class child who wants to become a doctor or a lawyer, his present place of residence is suitable and matches his aspiration. Highly ambitious *clase media* children, however, most strongly express the desire to move toward the center of the city. The lower class and the upper class express their present stability by the concept of tranquillity. This theme is not brought out in the essays of the *clase media*.

The middle-class children, like the middle-class adults in the city, experience the turmoil and hardship of unrealistic ambition. According to their teacher, eighteen children overestimated their intellectual and economic ability to pursue secondary education and to become doctors, lawyers, and engineers. Although in any particular case the possibility for continuing education may be very remote, still everyone in the sixth grade talks about plans and aspirations.

One girl of criollo background wanted to become a national accountant. She was, however, uninformed about the procedure and the nature of the program. Another girl wanted to become a lawyer, but she also considered studying languages. She reported that her father constantly said, "If you think that you would like to become a lawyer, we might be able to sacrifice and together the family might finance your career. But if you are not certain, how can you make us spend the money on books and clothes if you eventually abandon everything?" The girl was not sure what she would do. One realistic student stated that he would like to do something exciting but did not want to decide exactly what type of work since it is impossible to know what the future would bring. One has to wait for luck and opportunity.

Children in the sixth grade are at a major juncture of their lives when, with their parents, they have to decide their social future. Children from the most modest social and economic backgrounds verbalize their aspirations with a sense of resignation, well aware that only luck can allow them to fulfill their objectives. This group seems to have borrowed the aspirations of those who are better informed and will be able at least to begin higher education. In all cases there was insufficient concern about one's intellectual capacity. At this point the alternatives were: (*a*) to bypass ambitions; (*b*) for parents to correct their children's aspirations; or (*c*) to encourage the children to follow the road to success regardless of the obstacles before them.

Parents do not consult with teachers on career planning, nor do the teachers volunteer information. Children face an unknown unless their parents have received higher training and know the programs in secondary schools and universities. Teachers do not talk with the children about careers or their own training; this is something very personal, and the obscurity in the background constitutes the very element that separates teachers from children and parents. In planning a program for life, only parents and relatives have a right to be involved.

The privileges that parents of the middle class have not been able to enjoy, the economic shortcomings during the time they were growing up, the nearness to immigrant ancestors, all are translated into one single phrase: with education, everything will be different for our children. Regardless of the economic possibilities, parents hope that their children might become professionals. They are willing to make any sacrifices so their child can go through secondary school and perhaps university. Children also speak about these dreams as if they were a reality, even though the economic means may prohibit even secondary education. Only economic limitations, however, may stand in the way of achieving higher education; it is assumed that everyone is capable intellectually of going on.

Many children believe that their parents will have sufficient pull through acquaintances to arrange entrance into secondary school, even though the child's performance in primary school may not warrant admission. The limited number of secondary schools compared to the number of primary schools significantly reduces the possibility for continuing education. It seems that the lower the economic potential of the middle-class family, the higher the ambitions for education, which is viewed as a means to economic salvation.

The oldest son of an independent small tailor with a very modest shop was finishing the sixth grade, and this was the time for a decision. He spoke as follows:

My father has a small tailor shop, but I do not want to be a tailor. I will continue my studies. I like to study, and my father wants me to continue in secondary school. Perhaps I will study to be a teacher, because one can do it here in this city and it is easy. This can be done in the Normal School.

We are also thinking that I can finish the third year and then I could go to another town with some relatives to study agronomy in a university. I heard about these studies from a boy in my neighborhood who tried to get into the school, but he was not lucky. About 120 students wanted to enter, and he did not have enough pull and his grades were not very good. He was not lucky, but perhaps I will be. Agronomy is nice because you can get a degree in two years, and the studies are not very difficult. For law or medicine one must go to another city, particularly Buenos Aires, but I am not very well informed about these things and we have no means.

The student and his father realized that there were advantages in the facilities in their own city for secondary education, and economically this was feasible for the family. Higher education for one son eventually could improve the economy of the household. For a few years the son could be spared from the household economy to become a teacher. It would be an economic sacrifice, but the father expected returns from his son in later years. It remained, however, that this student was hardly able to graduate from primary school; he had no proper facilities in his own home to study. Even if he could be accepted into the Normal School, it was unlikely that he could go past the first year. His parents, like most middle-class parents, assume that each child has the innate capacity to finish secondary school, and the teachers must help in the process of the child's development. There was the case of a young man who became a pilot in his teens. But after a few years of flying, his mother declared that she could not go on living with the constant worry about the hazards to which her son was exposing himself. The mother reported: "I was in such a state of nerves that I became sick. The cause for my physical condition was the career of my only son. I was not about to lose him in an accident." The household situation grew more and more strained as the mother pressured her son to abandon his career. Finally he succumbed to her demands. Temporarily he "accommodated" himself in a government job that would last as long as the political administration remained in power. He had no economic worries, since his parents owned a lucrative business and plan to pass it on to their son. Both parents were born in southern Europe and raised in Argentine urban centers. Others explained this situation in terms of the parents' ethnic background, but no one found it unusual that a son should abandon his ambition at the request of his mother. "A mother comes first, and that is destiny."

Secondary Education

Many children finishing the sixth grade in institutions of the *primera categoría* will manage to continue into secondary school. The greatest dropout at the termination of the sixth grade comes from the schools of the barrios and neighborhoods. This does not mean that the students' aspirations have dropped at this point but that they now realize that implementing their ambitions may be impossible. Children of skilled laborers may enter the Escuela Industrial de la Nación, where technical skills are taught at a professional level. These institutions are intended for people of the barrios and neighborhoods and are staffed by individuals of lesser intellectual capacity.

Students from low-income families of the *clase media* attend institutions of the second category, such as night schools or the business school, the latter being the more popular. Students attending the business school are classified in the same way as those in the Escuela Industrial. They combine working with education, and not many of them are likely to finish the program.

The Normal School may accept students from a lower social category, but informants find it exceptional that parents with limited economic resources would seek space for their child in the Normal School. In theory, all institutions are open to everyone, but if the gap between the reputation of the institution and one's social and economic standing is sufficiently broad, there is general recognition that personal discomfort both for the parents and the child may result. Such a situation is therefore avoided.

The association of masculinity with the *bachiller* degree has always been strong, just as femininity has been associated with the Normal School for teachers. When individuals reach this level of formal training, the social class differences projected by the category of the primary school tend to disappear. A natural selection of students from the higher social classes occurs. The elite of the primary schools, those with good academic standing, a steady income, and good social position, appear in higher concentration in the secondary schools, particularly toward the end of the secondary cycle.

It is well known that the secondary schools of the city that function during the day attract the best group of students. Here one finds individuals from the higher levels of the *clase media* and from the upper class. It has been estimated that 31.7 percent of the student-age population in Paraná were in secondary training in 1962.[1]

The programs described for primary schools do not change for this higher level of education. To some extent secondary education can be specialized, but it still constitutes a general liberal education, particu-

---

[1] IPRUL sample.

larly as preparation for university. Only large towns can maintain secondary institutions, and rural families send their children to stay with relatives while attending secondary school.

On account of the large dropout, a *bachiller* degree has its social merits. An informant reported that a few years ago forty-five students were accepted into the first year of secondary school. By the second year only thirty continued, and twenty finally received a degree after five years. Many students left after the third year.

In school the students are expected to perform orally in every class. Professors dictate material or adopt a textbook from which students memorize to recite in class when called on by the professor. Students are frequently examined in written tests. Grades are reported four times a year, and if the average is above seven, the student is exempt from a final oral examination with a board of three professors. (Grades from zero to three are failing, four is very low passing, seven is a good grade, and ten is distinguished.) Perfect presentation means recitation close to the paragraphs in the books and notes. Those with a good memory succeed in obtaining the highest honor.

The programs are relatively heavy; every day the students attend four or five classes with different professors during the half-day between eight and twelve. A typical secondary school program would include:

First year: Spanish, history, geography, English or French, botany, mathematics, democratic education, drawing, physical education.

Second year: Spanish literature, modern history, European geography, English or French, zoology, mathematics, democratic education, music, drawing, physical education.

Third year: the same, except Argentine history, anatomy instead of zoology, and physics and accounting are added.

Fourth year: Spanish literature, history, geography, French, Italian or Latin, philosophy, physiology, physics, and organic chemistry, mathematics and trigonometry, music, and physical education.

Fifth year: American history, geography and history of Argentina, French, Italian, or Latin, logic, organic chemistry, mathematics and geometry, hygiene, and civic instruction.

Students and their parents are constantly preoccupied with the matter of grades. A letter to the editor of the local newspaper expressed well the emotional position of the parents: "One must not overlook the fact that the parents are the ones who ultimately suffer most with the frustration and fall of those who fail the class; these are, after all, their own sons. What other pain can be compared to this?"[2] They feel that students are on trial daily; those who succeed for four or five years have truly accomplished a great deal. Again it is the *conquista*.

Within the rigid and rigorous system students experience much anxiety, particularly when they are not well prepared and must "save" themselves. The assistance of colleagues is expected to obtain at least a passing grade. Many also prepare or borrow hideable notes for a possible examination. The general school situation has its implications for interpersonal relationships. As in primary school, the fear of public punishment continues and creates a significant distance between professor and students. Professors feel that there is a lack of proper respect toward their authority and leadership. Some of them believe that the impertinence of students has increased greatly during the last decade.

Not all teachers in secondary schools are professors; medical doctors may teach anatomy, hygiene, physiology, or chemistry; lawyers may teach history or literature. Students remember the years of secondary education as a true life drama. Vacation is indeed a much needed relief. The following account typifies a student's view of life within a secondary school.

We created disciplinary problems with the purpose of annoying the professors. Some professors inspired fear and rebellion in us. We divided professors into good and bad. Those who liked to talk about general topics outside the subject matters were good. They showed some *compañerismo*; they were like fathers and would frequently exhort us that some day we would be sorry for not applying ourselves to work.

We felt close to some teachers, and we could feel that they had an interest in us. These were very few, however, and with them there were few disciplinary problems. One history professor made us like the subject; he never gave an exam, and we felt comfortable like his children. He had a traditional gaucho manner and was *muy simpático*. He always wore a bow tie,

[2] *El Diario* 1965.

and one day all the boys came to class with bow ties, and he took the joke graciously.

There was a chemistry professor who made us really like the subject. Through the five years he was among the few who stimulated our curiosity and interest. He never raised his voice. He was very exact and worked hard for his class, and he was responsible for many students from this town who went to study chemistry at the university. During one of the student strikes, he took our side. I did not know much about his private life in the city. I only knew that he lived in an excellent house in the city and had an excellent library.

I and most of my colleagues best remember class with a lab. We made jokes when the experiment did not come out right, especially if the teacher was modeling. And of course there was that professor who made jokes that were not funny, and we laughed hard anyway. But we were afraid of him and laughed with some fear, I believe. In general, it is difficult to remember a professor who did not raise his voice to us frequently. There were occasions when a professor would tell us that he was looking forward to retirement so he could lead a peaceful life.

Many of the professors received nicknames, and among ourselves we referred to them by the nicknames. The worst ones went to those professors we hated most. One professor that stands out in my mind is the one who made it known each year that there was someone he hated, and certainly this person felt that he just didn't have any chance. Each professor acquired a reputation, and, like a myth, it would be transmitted from generation to generation.

We had rules among ourselves. For instance, we copied and cheated, and we all knew it and cooperated with each other. But no one would think of mentioning such things to a professor. It would have been unforgivable if someone would complain to a professor about a low grade and accuse another with a high grade of cheating. Most of us copied examinations and prepared *machetes*: a ribbon of paper rolled at each end and held together with a rubber band. This could be easily concealed in one's hand, and as you rolled it between the fingers notes would appear.

We gave nicknames to students who did very well without copying or assistance from others. And in this way we put pressure on them. During finals we would try to get their assistance. There were studious persons who were not very bright, and bright ones who were not studious. The latter did not want to become the very best students. There was no value in that. As a matter of fact, sometimes the person with the lowest grades was the most *simpático* in class and enjoyed a lively reputation. Those doing very well used to have a difficult time; we expected them to be unselfish. Otherwise we looked upon them as *carneros* [male sheep].

We did not think of examinations as something for which to think and learn. Primarily we tried to obtain good grades. One felt pressured to learn material with immediate application, constantly thinking that one must stay in school to get a degree so he will be able to make a living.

The status of secondary school students appears to be that of individuals without much voice, both at home and in school. Many incidents observed reflect the rigid, rigorous, and formal attitude of the staff. Each professor is very much concerned with keeping discipline. One professor in a private Catholic institution illustrated his attitude by describing the following incident.

I came to class, my fifth year class, and we professors are entitled to give a small speech about life or any other comment for spiritual uplifting before beginning lessons. It may be something related to morality. When I enter a class, everyone stands up; if I decide to talk, I command them to sit down and listen. But yesterday I decided to pray. There was one student who had predicted that I was going to do something else and remained seated when I entered. When I started to pray, he got up. I stopped and asked him to sit down. He said, "No, professor," and I commanded him to sit down and continued with the prayer. When I finished I asked him to stand up while the class sat down. I admonished him that here no one is forced to pray, and if he didn't want to pray, he could wait for me outside to let me know. This student, I noticed, did not know what to do the rest of the hour. He was very embarrassed. After class he came to me to apologize that he had not seen me coming in, but I did not pay attention to his excuse. I told him that I had been teaching for fifteen years and I knew that he didn't want to pray, and he finally agreed.[3]

Specialized Training

The pattern of education and the quality of relationships between students and staff members (teachers) continues past the secondary level. In a way, this continuity perpetuates the system. The following

---

[3] The reason for the student's not getting up is not relevant in this instance. The professor is bound to reject whatever excuse the student tries to make. The only course for the student is to agree with the professor's explanation.

are excerpts from many hours of interviews with an outstanding student at the institute for teachers. The informant's evaluation of his own experiences and career gives us valuable insights toward understanding this level of education in the city.

The Instituto de Profesorado does not form part of the university system. The minister of education of the nation directly controls it. This organization makes it very difficult to affect reforms. The students feel that the consequences of a centralized program are mostly negative, inasmuch as the programs are antiquated and structured with the mentality of the last century. We feel that the ministry of education is something like a police bureau. Adult students are strictly supervised, even though some have a degree for teaching in primary school. But the system does not take these things into account; I cannot share this attitude myself.

The centralized system also allows staff members to be poorly prepared in their major subject. But the fear that we may be put out of the institution forces us to attend all classes instead of studying at home or in the library. The students cannot complain, and we cannot form a center of students with legal rights; the minister prohibits it.

Therefore, though we are adults, we feel as if we are still in secondary school. Eventually it all becomes part of a way of looking at things: the role of the student is to come to class, to listen, and to memorize. In the system there is a lot of feedback, and finally it is all preserved without much change. Students feel that it is aristocratic to remain inactive, receiving, and being entertained. Change would be interference, and the majority of students accept the system and all of its implications for society. Students seem to feel more comfortable with the prefabricated knowledge. There is hardly any independence of thought.

Students with aspirations and desires to change become known as rebels. This has serious consequences in a place like ours. Attempts at reform are never successful; many of us who are known to be reformers face many difficulties, become less enthusiastic, and finally withdraw from the program. But the fear of defrauding parents who support our studies weighs heavily in each one's mind.

The intention of many people in my class has been to test the freedom of thought and the degree of personal responsibility in decision making. But evidently tradition still plays a very important part. The conservative definition of what a student is supposed to be is perpetuated. The pattern, which began in primary school, continues through secondary education and lasts even through the Instituto, which is directly involved in forming professors for secondary schools. A separation has been made between instruction and education. Professors must give instruction and must also educate. They must learn to be on their own, analyzing issues and participating in the fight for noble ideas. To educate, in this sense, means to produce free men.

Censuses seem to show that students at our level still behave in fear instead of being guided by their own consciences and reasoning. We do not act decisively for fear, and through the years the apathy seems to increase. When students want to meet and discuss problems of the institution, a large majority do not attend and provide tactful excuses, although much that happened during the students' childhood in the neighborhood, at home, and in primary and secondary school seems to promote this attitude. The feeling seems to exist that it is the duty of every good citizen not to become involved in radical issues. This is not the pattern for everyone, but a large majority show the desire to take the line of least resistance.

Within the institution itself there seems to be much peace and *compañerismo*. This, however, is a tranquillity of awaiting the last hour of class and the return home, a tranquillity resulting from intellectual weariness. The Instituto is a place to acquire some knowledge and particularly a degree; it is something without a soul. To separate socially the institution preparing professors for secondary schools from a university is to stop progess. One cannot hope to continue university education and eventually acquire a higher degree under this system. We had been requesting a change to be allowed to continue from the Instituto to a university for a doctor's degree, but we have not succeeded.

This account adequately illustrates the generational and social conflicts in the context of a well-established tradition in the city and also in the culture of Argentina.

A Rite of Passage: The Army

At the age of twenty the young man comes to a hurdle that weighs heavily on his mind and on the minds of his parents. He spends one or two years (depending on the branch of service) in the military. Although students enjoy some privileges, it still constitutes an uncertain moment for them. It means a break in studies and professional career. Unless the family can supply its son with cash, he suffers much poverty. The military provides food, transportation, and a token pay insufficient even for a month's supply of cigarettes. For many, this is the first time they have been separated from their households. The upper class considers it something of the lower class and thus below their dignity.

Families, and particularly mothers, view this situation with sadness. Having a son in the army brings sympathy from other mothers. Mothers believe that in the army their sons suffer personal deprivation, get no understanding, and undergo much injustice in the name of discipline. In the military an individual cannot be himself; his dignity and that of his family are no longer important. The first three months of army life are the most rigorous, and everyone is most sympathetic toward the boys. But still there is the feeling that the "army makes men."

The intent of this section is to unfold some of the social ramifications related to this situation as a rite of passage for the men. Women do not serve in the army, but as those very close to the men—mothers, sisters, wives, or future wives—they vicariously experience this rite with the men. Informants readily expressed views similar to the following:

> For the boys, the military service is a difficult step in life, particularly for those who are students. For boys who are not in school, the army may not represent too much of a loss. Often they cannot find a job until after military service, so they are doing something temporarily and waiting until they are twenty to pass this first turning point in their lives. Some in the lower class may even look forward to the army with the hope of staying or learning a skill that would help them economically later on. The upper class feels that this is simply a waste of time in one's life.

> Boys finishing primary or secondary school have to wait quite long. It is difficult to find a job; no one likes to employ pre-army people. This implies obligations for the employer who must provide part of the salary while the boy is serving in the army. Sometimes employers make the arrangement because they would like to have the person after the completion of his army duties. Those aiming for professional careers view the year in the army as a demoralizing time.

> Life in the army is very different from anything else one has experienced, and all of us in the service feel very sad. Boys coming from other provinces resign themselves rather quickly because they have no alternatives. But the

ones near home find it very difficult to stand the prison type of existence. One feels a sense of desperation, and it takes a long time to adjust. In the army one learns to appreciate and love his own family, particularly his mother. After many weeks of seclusion, the first weekend leave comes. Soldiers are advised about the reputation of each section of the city. Areas of prostitution are pointed out, and the usual contraceptive is advised. Soldiers begin to ask for extra money from their families or withdraw from their savings in order to take advantage of some of the city's recreational facilities.

The first few months are very strenuous; soldiers fear corporals and sergeants, who use fear to inculcate proper behavior. The fear here is much more rigorous than that experienced in school. Nevertheless, there is continuity from having been a student to being a soldier. In both cases one remains in an inferior role. During training, corporals and superiors use ethnic or rural stereotypes and other means of public embarrassment. In addition, stereotypes about army life reinforce the feeling that in the service one faces something hostile, unpredictable, and almost inhuman. On national festive days the army parades in the streets and joins the public celebration. Many hours of drilling and much physical endurance are required to appear most proper in each of the public events.

After finishing the year in the service, all face financial uncertainty. The father may have been searching for a position for his son through acquaintances, but most view the situation with discouragement. A primary school teacher or a person who graduated from the national college cannot expect much. Many women receive degrees before they are twenty and fill most vacancies while the men are in the service. One cannot be very choosy about jobs and is happy with any kind of honorable occupation. It is always difficult to find work appropriate to one's social image; many of us prefer to wait and continue to live with our family until something may open up.

The reaction toward class and regional differences constitutes an interesting social aspect in the setting of the army. Individuals of European descent mix with the very poor, illiterate *humildes*. During the first few months all are brought under one roof. For many this is truly an unforgettable experience. In the course of the year, however, each soldier is assigned a specific task in terms of his ability and background. Those with secondary education usually pass to administrative posts, while the rest continue in regular duty. The social differences soon emerge, and again the basic principle of social stratification is used to organize individuals.

Entering Adulthood

Already in secondary schools, Paranaenses begin to enter into the social network of the city. A great majority of students in secondary schools belong or wish to belong to clubs of the city. Many withdraw from the barrio and neighborhood clubs. They use the facilities of the clubs of the city and the more prestigious neighborhood clubs. By association with secondary school and certain clubs, they qualify as persons of the city. They become oriented toward the center and the main plaza, away from their place of residence.

Higher education offers social rewards and constitutes a social symbol. In many cases schooling is viewed not so much in terms of knowledge and education as for the social benefits of a degree. A person with education and degrees can become socially haughty (*una persona orgullosa*). Occasionally a child of the neighborhood becomes a doctor. When he returns and remains friendly, people point out with a sense of surprise that, with all the degrees and training, he still remains a humble and friendly person. When a person from the upper category witnesses such social mixing, however, he will judge the action as showing a lack of social style, an absence of *cultura*; he will comment that the other "still shows his old social background."

Upward mobility is generally an individual undertaking. If a person attempts to improve his social standing, this causes social imbalance within the family. The father may be a skilled worker, oriented toward his neighborhood and active in a neighborhood club; one son is attending secondary school, and another the Escuela Industrial. In situations like that, a natural social distance emerges; there may be some embarrassment when the persons are socially sensitive. Families with one son working while another is enjoying the life of a student have more acute problems. One solution is that the son who has been working and helping the family finally chooses to move to another town or province.

The family not only constrains individuals in their upward climb, but also affects career selection. Although many young people feel that they are free to choose a career, it is very likely that through the years they have been conditioned to think as their parents wish. Many cases are known where parents, particularly mothers, have not allowed youngsters to follow an ambition in life. Parents may argue that the profession is physically hazardous or not sufficiently lucrative.

The premise of social stratification and mobility underlies the organization of the educational system in Paraná, and the system perpetuates the fundamental social principle. Already in the sixth grade, children begin to manipulate the system by selecting the appropriate friends and adopting the dress and speech style of the group to which they aspire to belong. This trend continues through later education and preparation for a career. Thus the social arena of childhood and adolescence prepares young Paranaenses to live in their class-structured society.

V. Images of the City

11. THE DIVERSITY OF SOCIAL IMAGES: AN INVENTORY OF PARANAENSE VIEWS

> Our individuality is, after all, our characteristic. Everyone likes to think that each individual must hold his own viewpoint. To be different has been and still is a strong social theme. This makes life interesting and brings out discussions and public arguments. (a Paranaense informant)

Previous chapters have been based on abundant historical and ethnographic data. This chapter is personal: it presents statements and interpretations made by Paranaenses about Argentine society, about life in their own city, and about other Paranaenses. Each individual freely portrays his own views. The subtleties of each model, the informants felt, are complex and frequently "beyond the meaning of words." To incorporate all of the diverse views is an overwhelming task. Therefore each informant chose to represent only personal profiles that were derived from his social standing and ethnic background. Their views and interpretations are valuable not only as a rich source of data, but also as manifestations of basic elements of the world view. By watching each Paranaense explore his own social world, the reader should be able to penetrate into the social situation created and maintained by people of European descent with their own Argentine historical experiences.

Two Overall Views

The following account is an interpretation of Paraná society by a retired teacher, a first-generation Argentine. He married into a traditional elite Spanish family that had been in Argentina since the early 1800s. The case takes us from an immigrant father (southern European) with limited means, to a son who succeeded through education and participation in the upper social circles. However, he prefers to remain socially aloof from the superficiality of the Club Social. He is one of the few who has earned his social place through both marriage and personal achievement. The style and tone of the conversation, as well as the selection of terms, are significant. The problems of the present day challenge an intellectually active man as he attempts to describe the sources of evil.

The true *gente criolla* are rapidly disappearing in this country. One finds poor criollos in the outside barrios of the city; they are known to be lazy and to have low aspirations. They are *los humildes*. The elite criollos, however, value tranquil existence, but keep their aspirations high. They feel they are social monuments to the Argentine past. They are an elite, and busy in a social orbit. As criollos, they emphasize less the things that modern life requires of us such as punctuality and a rushed existence. The criollos are similar to the Andalusians and are not very eager to work. For many people, especially the poor, Perón accentuated the criollo style of life; he went along with the theme of "canvas shoes, yes—books, no." This was not grasped by the elite criollo who associated progress with books. Pure criollos, or criollos *de tradición*, are well off, cultivate their social position, stress their ancestry, and so differ from the large number of European immigrants. *Criollismo* is associated with people of darker skin who lead a slower style of life inherited from the Indians.

Paraná has a magnificent *tradición cultural*, and much of it was centered in the Normal School. The participation in the Normal School of a North American principal before 1900 left a significant mark. Scalabrini, Peret, and other European teachers came to Paraná, and they were responsible for the liberal positivism imparted in our training. In the setting of the educational institution the aristocrat, the Indian, and the mestizo came together.

The Diversity of Social Images

That man [Perón] brought social anarchism and provoked distrust among us. All associations with cultural interest became less active. One could no longer trust friends and acquaintances. At one time a well-wisher warned me to take care because a *vecino*, my childhood friend (now pro-Perón), knowing that I opposed the regime, had accused me. In Perón's days, those of us with democratic views felt one step removed from prison. All that came with Perón cannot be blamed on him. Without a doubt he saw the situation and took advantage by exaggerating our basic weaknesses. Materialism was advancing before Perón, but the struggle for things associated with social distinction increased.

The *gente conocida*, or the elite group, has individuals of high intellectual caliber. The traditional families of Entre Ríos have members with university degrees (primarily law and medicine). In the past these families could place their children in secondary schools and universities. In these institutions professors were of, or identified with, the *clase alta*. As oligarchs, the elite did not maintain a democratic attitude toward the people. They were liberals in legislation and in their position toward the Church and doctrine, but the upper class was against the participation of the people in high levels of government. The *gente de tradición* did not influence the people directly, although they arranged for primary schools to reach all the people. Primary school teachers were of the *clase media*, deficient in their backgrounds, and so social and intellectual progress has been slow. During the Perón period again much was disarranged. One year we had only 120 half-days of classes. Much disorder took place, based on the issue of social class differences. Libraries were not well taken care of and received little or no help from the elite group. This indicates our intellectual interest. Nowadays mostly the middle-class students, rather than the *clase alta* ones, use the libraries. Especially, the young Jewish people constantly use the public library.

Intellectual life among the traditional class has not been properly cultivated. No doubt this group is always better informed, but it is difficult to invite anyone to a friendly argument. The Club Social is like a social clearing house; it is not an intellectual center.

The greatest value of the present government is its effort to pacify the people, since we continue in a trend toward spiritual anarchy. The old generation of intellectuals came to an end during Perón; those who were in formation during that period were corrupted; the present generation is the product of an anarchic situation. The process of *argentinización* and the creation of a nationality based upon elements accepted by all has been crushed.

We now have social chaos instead. We need tranquillity and peace to live in freedom. Our students of the *clase media* are impertinent and no longer trust their professor. I believe that we exist in a negative social atmosphere with professors who lack the force to generate intellectual curiosity.

Another of our problems is the fact that parents have limited formal education. Their educated children face difficult problems. This is especially acute in a society like ours, where so much emphasis is placed on social class differences and everyone's ambition is to move upward socially. The generational disagreement disrupts smooth domestic relations. Many *clase media* students are socially ashamed of their parents. The difference between parents and children is a type of social punishment. . . .

Social differences affect personal relations among young people. When a young man begins a romance with a girl of a socially distinguished family, the family will first be interested in his social background and the status of his family. The phrase "Who is his family" asks for more than mere demographic information. A humble social background may be a stumbling block. The family might not consent to the relationship and advise the girl to discontinue it.

In our city people tend to observe rules; the stress on being appropriate in all dealings gives life an artificial shade. People avoid showing their true selves. Certainly this may not be so in Buenos Aires, but in small cities like ours, formality as a means to guard one's social position is most evident.

The present hopefully will come to an end. Unfortunately, our society suffers from a lack of good models for young people. Nowadays there are too many individuals with unsound answers to serious social problems. This situation in a sense is a threat to the society itself and to the government.

The following material has been excerpted from extensive conversations with a semiprofessional, upper-class informant. The social forces derived from his own family background and standards prevent him from adopting the way of life he most desires. His views and interpretations of his own society differ considerably from those of the previous informant.

People of the city generally believe that people of the *ranchos* are bad people. It does not mean that all of them are poor and bad, but one thinks of them this way. Mostly they are laborers and do not want to abandon their way of life or to leave their straw huts. They have another mentality

The Diversity of Social Images

altogether. One refers to them as *los negros*; this term has a great deal more to do with occupation than the color of the skin.

We are very sensitive to the proper place for people and elements. It is a social scandal for the son of an important doctor to open his business in a third-rate place. In the public image, physical labor is something of *los negros* and, therefore, of those residing in ranchos. In general anything that tends toward the native things or *criollismo* and rural existence is considered low in the social concept. It is interesting that the father may be a *negro*, but not the son if he has advanced socially and becomes a white-collar worker or a skilled laborer. For a long time he will be known as the son of *un negro*. Of course there are some wealthy persons, even professionals, who behave like *negros*, and one refers to them as such. The top social layers know that the *negro* is not to be trusted but to be used. One also feels that the socially *negro* person is by nature a sad person and expresses his values in sadness. One must differentiate this group of socially classified *negros* (servants, washwomen, sweepers, peons) from others in the low class who live in modest brick houses. Of course some people in this group, as well as in other groups, may have the mentality of *negros*. Here lies the most important point in our reaction to people: that the material appearance may not reflect the social being. Once one knows the background, however, the clothing—modern as it may be—does not change the image. Behavior and type of work usually give away a person's status. Therefore, anyone with a mentality of a *negro* must be avoided because he lacks loyalties.

The middle class forms the large bulk of the people, and I personally find them a boring group, narrow-minded, without much interest in accomplishing work well and meeting the best standards. A middle-class person is a dissatisfied individual, always searching for something beyond himself. In many ways the image is of an empty group without historical depth or interest. Generally they prefer to remain neutral rather than to take a strong position on social and political issues. These persons search for the safest social and political position and move with the prevalent current of opinion, neither hurting anyone nor participating in community life. There is apathy, and perhaps one can characterize them as "people who like strong claws."

People of the middle class are very much concerned with themselves. Among them much stimulation for social consumption predominates. Of course one must allow for variations within the group in a complex stratified city, but in general I see that people share these characteristics, although in differing amount and differing degrees of sophistication. Things change in the upper layers of the *clase media*, and many of the features outlined give way to traits of the upper class. The upper elements have a wider view of the social universe, while at the bottom of the same social group there is a narrow "vision of the world."

In order to qualify for a higher social category, one needs to cultivate his social manners. To start the "decantation" process, the person must show knowledge, act socially secure, and know how to shine socially. The natural force of gravity acts in the situation and purification occurs. It is most advantageous to be active in the social clubs of this city and, if possible, to enter the social power structure itself. This does not mean the political and economic power structure, since the three rings—political, social, economic —do not necessarily coincide in our modern days.

Of course outsiders consider the Club Social as the prime center of all the power in the city. Because of the club's historical position and general elegant image, all officials sooner or later visit it. Many social and political connections develop there, and so the view that the club promotes and concentrates power becomes widespread.

If the governor does not join in the celebration at the Club Social on a national holiday, people will comment; the middle class will speculate that the governor does not get along well with the people of importance.

It is my personal impression that we are not a happy group of people; we lack internal happiness and gaiety. But we all must pretend, and early in life we learn to do this. We expect the municipal authority to solve all our problems. A movement to create an independent *municipio* may evoke some public concern, but it is indeed needed. A revolution could be initiated from below. When the *pueblo* become directly concerned and try political maneuvers, they will realize that there are ways to avoid further problems. The habitual situation is to let things happen from above, and the result may be mediocre because the people do not really participate in the community development.

From the beginning of our independence, we have continuously been searching for a savior—somebody to come from Mount Sinai to bring salvation. In our streets we frequently hear the phrase "We are facing a crisis in our leadership," but there it all stops, and the same problems continue through the years. The same issues repeat themselves even after severe political changes, and we remain an amorphous mass of people seeking for a savior.

Everyone is constantly analyzing the meaning of change. Some of the leaders may go from left to right, or vice versa, or they may linger at any

Social Classes in Paraná

A Woman of the *Clase Tradicional*

ntry People at the City Bus Terminal

Vecinos One Generation Removed from Europe

A Paraná River Fisherman and His Family

La Tradición Criolla

La Curandera (the Curer)

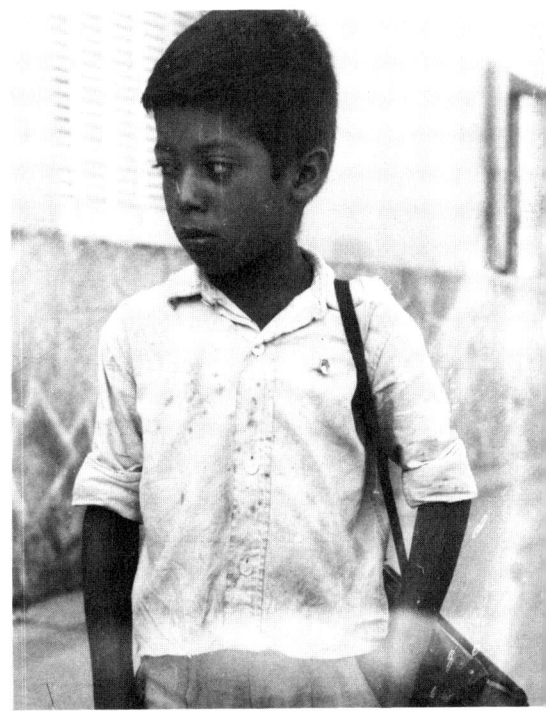

Shoeshine Boy in the Plaza

Private and Public Schools

The Traditional Public-School White Uniform

Private-School Boys in a National Holiday Parade

Public-School Football Team

Burial by Social Class

The Cemetery

Individual Mausoleums (*Panteones*) of Upper-Class Families

Mausoleum for Members of the Italian Society

Graves in the Walls of the Cemetery (*Nichos*)

Individual Tombs

Modest Graves

Grave Marker

point in between. In 1939 everyone thought that Hitler would win; when the war ended, the same individuals became fierce *democráticos*. Later, and temporarily, they were democrats against Perón; after Perón won, they became Peronistas. Political people shift positions, no doubt for economic reasons. In Paraná there were so many Peronistas, from the most upper level to the poorest, that when the revolution triumphed, the Peronist archives were burned. In this way many people saved themselves.

It was tragic indeed to see members of *familias tradicionales*, with a specific obligation toward the people, participating in Eva Perón's functions only for convenience. This was done in the name of social etiquette for the first lady, but there were also economic motives for participation. It is difficult to understand this nation and this people. We have everything that is necessary to be an excellent nation, but I believe we lack spiritual fortitude, though we say that we are more spiritual and less materialistic than the North Americans.

Young people appear in public now to ask questions. They ask good things now that they are young, but what will they ask when they are parents with responsibility? Will they continue to ask when they are old? Each one is always waiting for something, for someone to associate with and for benefit from the relationship. Much of the internal political trend emanates from this pattern, and the result lacks the intellectual vigor that it could have. The pattern is repeated in clubs. Recently, a benefit program was held at one of the prestigious local clubs. The members who made most use of the club did not attend, but they are always first in line to be interviewed by reporters, to request help from governors and *intendentes*. They are not willing to work for a good community cause. Some assistance always comes from government sources, but the problem is not solved from within.

All upper- and middle-class individuals seem to wish a change in government. On the street corners, in the coffee shops, in the factories, planes, buses, and trains, everyone speaks about the fall of the government. Each one speculates about the means, the hour, and the day. Nothing happens, and the daily exercise continues. The majority agrees that it is necessary to live in a democracy, but they do not understand this deeply, I think. This is similar to the attitude to social classes. People say that here is the ideal place where there are no social classes and a democratic society exists; this is not so, but it may be wishful thinking. We want a democratic tyrant who will take us on the road to salvation. It is all very amorphous nowadays. We have a constitution copied from democratic nations, but it seems strange to our mentality and does not function well here. Our local government undertakes projects, but we seem only to get more lost in the branches of a very complex tree.

The Middle Class Talks

From an upper-class intellectual we come to a first-generation Argentine, less educated, who for many years has been a small entrepreneur. Born in the Argentine to Russian-German parents, he was raised in a small "European" village near Paraná. He has lived in Paraná for the last twenty years. Socially he still finds life in the village very rewarding, and he preserves a heavy accent. He shares his views about Argentine people and society with many people of a similar background. A strong European image contrasts with Argentinismo and colors his interpretation of the people and of the nation. While the previous informants presented more or less total pictures of Paraná as each saw it, this informant operates from a narrower perspective and dwells on what he most intimately knows.

Los negros are the humble people who live in straw huts around the city. They do manual labor. They are all pure Argentine people. Their style of life is characterized by laziness; if they earn fifty, they spend sixty. Their children may beg for bread in the streets when parents are too lazy to work. They live from day to day and they do not seem to worry. Very seldom will these people copy European ways. They are not interested in religion; they are not consistent in any of their habits, and so this way of life has become customary. In the country these same people live better and are trustworthy. Those here are thieves, although not all of them, but enough.

When the harvest fails, they run to the city and the government may help them, but it does not discipline them. There is a school to help them; some of them have improved, others have not. The city itself offers little employment, and the city has no industry. A large number of them are on their own looking for jobs from day to day. But I will say that those of us who try can make it, although it is hard work and we worry.

People in general trust the European descendants, and they see that some people who have come to this city from the Russian-German villages have become professionals. While the Europeans like us work hard, the criollos become Peronistas.

We Germans save money and never create mutual societies like the Ital-

The Diversity of Social Images

ians and the Swiss. In general Europeans are disciplined and productive people. The criollos are responsible for our problems; they do not work hard and are not punctual like Germans and Swiss.

I remember Paraná as a very small town when the municipal officials worked willingly for the city. Now they receive large salaries and press us to pay more taxes on our properties. But now the people have revolted, and this year we will not pay the increase demanded of us. The *pueblo* are constantly fooled by the many promises made by the local politicians seeking offices and votes.

I have a house of my own and a retirement pension of thirty dollars a month to support four members of my family. This is now impossible, and I must continue to work independently selling farm products. The rise in the property tax will certainly ruin me. The people suffer, and this year with the dryness of the season, everything continues to go up.

For someone to belong to the *clase alta*, he must belong to the Club Social, but the Club Social is not a good *ambiente*. Many of them have ruined themselves, and now they are poorer than the *clase media* people, but they are still people of society. At one time there was more social discrimination, and even today the *clase media* does not know the *clase alta* intimately. Things are changing, and my own children are now leaning more to the criollo in some ways, but they remain decent workers, thrifty, and particularly honest. They also have a spirit of progress. There are those of the *clase media* without good ancestry and race. I know, for instance, an Italian tailor, relatively poor, but now all his daughters have teaching degrees and the three sons are doctors. Now they are all in the *clase alta*.

The following sketch was made through time by a young man of a rather humble *clase media*: second-generation Italian on one side and criollo on the other. Both parents lacked formal secondary education and were born and raised in rural areas of the province. His attempt to become professional has not met with success, and his economic future will be as a government office employee. His views of society guide his interpretation and define his social standing. He exists as if he were in a classless society. This informant is concerned with people's relationships, and individual traits are more relevant in his statement than in the others.

Italians, Russian-Germans, "Turcos," and Jews are not distinguishable in the city. People are not very concerned with your background. There are enough of each group, and all have been mixing with the criollos. There are, however, many ideas about each group. For instance, an Italian is known for being stingy. Of all the groups, the Jews can be separated, and there is a large number of them in the city. Although the parents are in business, the children become professionals, particularly medical doctors. They are very enterprising people, losing no opportunity to make profit.

The typical distinction in our city is that of *clases baja*, *media*, and *alta*, but there are other characteristics. They are related to the style of life in each family. In neighborhoods there are cliques in which certain families feel closer than others, although they do not necessarily interact frequently. In general, the people of the *clase media* constitute the nexus between the families of very low standing and those of the upper brackets, particularly in the life of a neighborhood.

The schools, primary and secondary, are socially differentiated. The better-off families send their children to the schools that provide a better education. For all young men there is the military service—a difficult step because it affects one's career. No one can get a job before going through the military. Thus a young person can hardly expect to earn a living before he is twenty-one or twenty-two. The country does not offer an encouraging panorama to a young person with a secondary degree who wants to continue his studies. In the city there are a few open positions for teachers, but to make a living and maintain a family are most difficult. If one wants to teach, he must go to the interior; but this is a temporary arrangement since one likes to return to his own town and province. Many of us seek a combination of two jobs, one in the morning and one in the afternoon, in order to keep up our standing.

Gossip stands at the roots of many aspects of people's relationships. One is aware that gossip can develop in a neighborhood. The gossip begins with individuals who are not interested in searching for the truth. They simply talk about something without the proper knowledge and without measuring the consequences; there is no guilt feeling.

We also differ from people in other Argentine provinces and particularly from the Porteños of Buenos Aires. They always want to be superior, important, and value themselves above everyone else. We consider the Porteño as not too much of a man and not worthy of much respect. We like to criticize them and their city because they exploit the interior for their own benefit. This is true economically as well as politically. The Porteños are ready to accommodate themselves but are not willing to give help; their selfishness is obvious. While the *clase baja* finds it exciting and prestigious to go to Buenos Aires, those of us in the typical *clase media* do not see this as so important. In the past it was more so but not now. I dislike the artificiality of life there, and I prefer my city above all.

As to politics, in each political campaign the strength is with the people and the party in power. Government money is used for campaigns, and many people appear at this time in order to accommodate themselves with jobs.

Most of the people belong to the Catholic religion. Perhaps more than half, however, do not participate in the Church. To be Catholic does not mean to support the clergy. They believe in the basic things of the Church but disregard and criticize the priests for having an excellent life without working. There is an antipathy toward supporting the wealth of the Church while its charity appears limited. Thus many people of the Catholic religion do not attend church services, although they partake of the basic sacraments of the Church.

The following is an account of another young person, university educated, working in the field of applied social sciences. She is a second-generation Italian-Swiss Argentine. Rather than describing the situation, this informant attempts to analyze and explain the problems of friendships and groups in the *clase media*.

From an overall point of view, a lack of solidarity characterizes the middle-class people. Of course each person has his own personal group in the clubs or in the schools. Teamwork has become very fashionable. Many decisions are made by groups, and the responsibility is thus collective; a person's mistake is never evident. This type of work in groups is most difficult when there is so little confidence in the individual. It is difficult to form groups, particularly with the rural migrants into the city. In sociological terms, the transition from a purely primary association to a secondary group is not easy. In our society there is a vein of strong individualism manifested in many aspects of barrio life. To have neighbors is important and necessary, and a great deal of people's thinking and organization is based on neighborhood experiences. The concept of neighborliness, however, has not been translated into social reality. There is a strong anomie in the situation. It is difficult for the *clase media* to form groups of a secondary nature. This may have something to do with the way people judge each other. There are always two opposite poles: left or right, good or bad, for or against. People look at each other in these terms and react to such distinctions. When it is not possible to find a niche and the person is neutral, then relations are also neutral. But when a relationship between two persons becomes intense, any kind of doubt hurts the basic dignity of the people involved.

In the *clase media* secondary education separates a great many friends. Under these circumstances one is left very much alone within his own family circle. Relationships between individuals constantly fluctuate. There is a lack of demarcation and a lack of group social consciousness. In this framework, one cannot help but form individual—often seriously deformed —images about politics, the power structure, and society.

The problem of generational conflict adds to these individualistic images. The young people are alert but are receiving a very poor formal education. They face their parents' generation with practical know-how and with limited education. One of the present problems for young people of the *clase media* is finding one's own position in relation to political and social issues. The rule seems to be that dyadic relationships, friendships, or convenience decide the position in many issues. There are, therefore, innumerable changes in the personal level, and the social dislocation of individuals is most evident today. Society is not ready to cope with this serious problem.

In clubs, the *clase media* people learn to be socially superficial and negatively critical of others and of themselves. The fear of what people will say demands much concern with one's outward appearance. There are a few organizations whose members feel challenged by intellectual interest. For themselves and for those who feel qualified, they sponsor programs to expand the horizons of *cultura*. They invite speakers who are not radical and who agree with the position of the group. Some of these groups are well read; they contrast with the general *clase media*, who read popular journals and whose households contain few books. There are differences in the objectives of, let us say, the Rotary Club and the Jockey Club. The first aims for *cultura*, while the members of the latter are interested in the economic world. Both clubs are composed largely of well-established, middle-class businessmen.

Another attitude of the *clase media* seems to be fear of assuming responsibility for errors. The fear of admitting mistakes seems to be very prevalent among us. This attitude contrasts with the security assumed by individuals of the *clase alta*. The general impression is that the present generation is living through a period of negative values and attitudes. It is indeed analogous to a negative of a photograph. The positive of the negative is only an ideal at this point. There is a lack of frankness resulting in social isolation and loneliness; to find another person whom one can trust is a great emotional experience. Learning to trust is our major task these days.

The Upper-Class Outsiders

The next sketch is of a first-generation Argentine of Iberian descent, a professional who is wealthy and linked by marriage to *familias tradicionales*. His present condition stands in direct contrast to the *ambiente* provided by his immigrant parents. He is a man of determination, intellectually very capable, successful economically, professionally, and socially. His mother's past is hardly mentioned. People recognize his social and economic career as spectacular, but the middle-class professionals sometimes criticize him. The interior of his home reflects the European tradition of the nineteenth century; after trips to Europe his own *cultura* and general identification became tightly linked to the continent. He has participated in key positions in the local, provincial, and national governments; his interest is in helping to generate *cultura* in the city with Europe as his model: "If Europe has it, why not us, after all?"

Ethnic background and class affiliation structured the concerns of the middle-class informants in the preceding section; this professional begins with distinctions internal to the upper class. He describes the social setting, with some remarks about friendship and personal associations.

Patrician families do not really exist nowadays. Their descendants are left over, but most of them are in a different position from their ancestors in the past. Those who participated in the formative years of Paraná have disappeared, and only families that have become prominent in the last twenty years remain active. We must face the fact that most of the families of the city are the children of immigrants; some of them have succeeded economically. Many of the early families that had large landholdings have lost their fortunes, some through gambling in the social clubs. In some cases the administration of the estates was poor, and some men married women who spent lavishly to acquire material luxuries.

The Club Social is an institution of great importance in the history of the city. Members believe themselves to be of superior extraction. I like to attend only the formal celebrations; other times I stay out. A large group of the members interact daily and a complex maze of communication exists; within this class everyone knows a great deal about everyone else. I see this pessimistically. Nowadays the middle-class man with drive can join the Club Social; there are professionals of the *clase media* whose ambition is to become members of the club. As soon as they are accepted, they acquire the social sensitivity of this class and usually experience so much anxiety that it can lead to social paralysis.

Paraná has a style of its own; we lack spontaneity in interaction. This is a personal observation, but as far back as 1930 I remember being surprised when I met people from other Argentine cities who were more open than those in this city. In our city, boys used to walk around the plaza in one direction, the girls in another, and we could not talk to each other. At the same time in other Argentine cities the girls had a different attitude, and interaction across sex lines was socially correct.

Much from our past continues, and the present results in boring social gatherings, even in the important Club Social. One must always have his own little group; on formal occasions one must never go alone. One goes with family friends and relatives. People who know each other well occupy neighboring tables, but act toward each other as strangers. People know the stories of each other's lives, so perhaps avoidance acts as social protection. In that surrounding acquaintances behave like total strangers.

One time I was traveling by boat on the Paraná River. A passenger commented to me about a group of young ladies who were very happy and outgoing. I answered him, "You must wait until we dock. The same girls will not speak to you and they will be different." And so it was. People know each other, they greet each other, but still they always keep a significant social distance. I like this city and these people, but I have the authority to say that life here is boring, because everyone of us lives with the great fear of what people will say. It is a people in apathy; in public office it is most difficult to generate enthusiasm among the people. Even the artists remark about this when they compare us with people in other provinces. People shield themselves from each other with elegant etiquette even when they have been interacting closely for fifty years.

To expect full cooperation even among members of the ethnic clubs is wishful thinking. As president of one of them, I requested twenty young fellows to whom I could talk about the objectives of the club and delegate some of the responsibility, because they were children of Europeans the club represented. Only two boys came, and I had to give up my plans. Class differences and social egotism undermined the program.

There is much social sensitivity related to our class consciousness; in some cases individuals' ancestors sold clothes in the street, so to speak, and even though they made a fortune, the present generation does not want to be socially disqualified on account of the activity of someone in the past. This, I think, is a Spanish characteristic. In general, there is much egotism and resentment, which makes community work difficult, and it is not possible to work in teams.

The predominance of the Russian-Germans and the Jewish people has a great deal to do with our situation. One should only compare us with the other provinces where Italians and Swiss constitute the bulk of the population. The village style of life of the Russian-Germans stands as an example of lack of progress. The settlement of the Jewish people in the rural areas has not worked out because they are urban oriented and given to business. Paraná has received many of them from the rural areas, but the Jew keeps to himself. Their participation in public life of the city is very limited.

A young intellectual who has been accepted and, in essence, adopted into the upper class because of his professional achievement offers the following remarks. He again deals with the social environment and its effects on interpersonal relationships. He has extensive contacts among the traditional families and also among the elite of the middle class. He is not very wealthy, but his taste coincides with that of the most traditional or European-oriented individuals. Intellectually he surpasses many traditional members of the Club Social.

It would appear that the society we have is very rigid and severe. It would seem that individuals of the upper social bracket, particularly of the upper middle class, are constantly sanctioning behavior. The sanctions come most frequently from the older generation. The older men and particularly women are most preoccupied with evaluating people's behavior and judging their *cultura*. A person without the support of his family or a group can rapidly fall into disrepute. There are members in the Club Social who worry a great deal about the future of their families. There is a real social fear.

Many of the people in the upper bracket entertain opinions about the reputation of others, but the information is usually not firsthand. If a reputation fits well because of a situation of animosity or jealousy, then its validity is further tested. People are disinterested, however, in information that may prove the opposite.

Life in a small city is indeed traumatic for a lot of people, particularly the young sensitive ones who are struggling for social independence. They explode when they leave for other towns to attend universities. In general, Paraná is progressive and has its problems. But we lack a cooperative social life in our neighborhoods because of our peculiar mentality. We are not interested in the lives of others for the benefit of the whole, but we are extremely curious on the individual basis. Neighbors do not enter into each other's lives, but they are well-informed about and constantly in touch with each other, although it is all at a distance.

Clubs in Paraná whose names are associated with ethnic groups are no longer ethnic in character. In general there is very little ethnic consciousness among people in Paraná. People are aware, to a greater or lesser degree, of the ethnic background of their families, but they do not segregate themselves on this basis. The tendency is toward *argentinización*. Those who have been in Argentina for a long time are very proud of being criollos.

The Paraná society is divided horizontally, with people from all ethnic groups in each category, including criollos on each level. In the upper class, however, age of the family in Argentina constitutes a requirement that excludes a large percentage of people.

Another young professional outsider describes the dynamics of interaction in the upper class. This man, born in another city of the republic, has arrived recently in Paraná. He is at present trying to become integrated into the society, and in his conversations he focuses on that process.

Social adoption in this city seems to be accomplished by a series of social chains of people publicly known in the city and in the city clubs, especially the Club Social. The clubs and associations are in the center of the web of social relationships; through them one can establish contact with individuals of different social reputations.

In the streets of the city, one encounters the same individuals; as they see each other again and again, they may begin to exchange very brief and formal greetings even though they have not been properly introduced. Usually through the grapevine they know of each other's social identity and professional activities. A stranger in the city is soon spotted, and one knows that people are trying to gather information about him, particularly if he is trying to establish himself socially. Of course this applies especially to the people in the downtown area—*la gente de la ciudad*. Many sectors of the city population seldom appear in the plaza area.

Paraná has not yet developed the style of life of a large city; it is still a large town. People know each other's habits of life; socially they like to ignore this knowledge, but it is not always possible. This is primarily the style of the *clase media*. The upper class interacts with the people of the *clase media* only during public events or perhaps at work. Therefore, it is more difficult to know them on a personal level. The *gente superior* attend certain restaurants or *confiterías* at times when the bulk of the *clase media* has retired. From time to time young people from the upper levels of the *clase media* and the *clase alta* use the same places for recreation. But the people of the *clase alta* can be easily recognized. The economic situation certainly is not the important criterion for the distinction; more important is the way in which they conduct themselves. The people of the *clase alta* display a social power that derives from their family name.

The style of life in the city proper is not one of impersonality and anomie; strangely enough, however, people behave with an air of anomie and social distance. One sees people in the city and cannot help but learn a great deal about their social rhythm simply by observation. One feels controlled on account of this observation, and rarely does one act with a sense of freedom. This social sensitivity constitutes a concern that absorbs people's time and energies. With this preoccupation people forget about other aspects of *cultura*. In particular the socially active persons with a strong desire to move upward socially waste a great deal of time worrying about what people will say and trying to counteract the public opinion.

The *clase tradicional* maintains a personal relationship among themselves, particularly the very traditional families. However, the old city families do not have the means to separate themselves thoroughly and cannot leave the well-off members of the *clase media* in complete social isolation. The new elements are causing much discomfort to the traditional levels; and the traditionals understand that they cannot withstand the pressures of our modern time. They are obliged to give up some aspects of their traditional public role.

In addition, the city is not free from ethnic discrimination. In general conversations people make remarks about Jews, Arabs, and Turks—people known for their mercantile activities. The images people entertain nowadays respond to long-established stereotypes. For instance, there is the general impression that the Russian-German in the surrounding areas will not achieve progress.

In this society an outsider begins associations at work, then in public places, and finally in clubs. To be successful, one must not move too quickly. People constantly observe, and within their own group they share information about new professionals in the city. The bars, the coffee shops, and the plaza are places for exchanging information. One's social personality is soon designed. Your own case is presently a very interesting social item; people of *cultura* are speculating on your research work and on you as a social person. The high social sector of the city wants to be informed about the trends of life.

The Traditional Upper Class

The following informant is a young professional man who conforms to all the mores and etiquette of his patrician group. The image of his ancestors considerably influences his world view. Although some Paranaenses may argue that he is not a typical representative of the *clase alta* at large, he nevertheless often represents his class on public occasions.

There are many families in this city who possessed a great deal of land. You have the great-grandchildren of governors who owned easily many hundreds of leagues of land. Of course some of them have sold or lost practically everything, and the only thing that they cannot lose is their name. People like this now have to change in some ways and have to accommodate themselves to work in offices along with the *clase media*. However, they do not lose their standing; they maintain their aristocratic mentality. The important thing is to continue to be a person with distinction and *cultura* and an interesting person from the social point of view.

A long time ago, when Paraná became the capital of the confederation, my family came from another province, and I am the descendant of an outstanding provincial governor. To be surrounded with antique symbols of my family is my personal destiny. My house is indeed a true museum. It is sometimes depressing, but it is our mentality. My family also has a *panteón* in the cemetery. I find it hard to believe that there are families who do not think of preparing a place for their final rest where the whole family may remain together.

The Diversity of Social Images

In Paraná there is a very powerful *clase media*, powerful in number, and they are interested in a high level of *cultura*. Many people of the *clase media* would like to join the Club Social. Many of them are already members, but although we let them in, afterward they receive the treatment. One knows when a person has been raised to belong to this class; the children receive an education and *cultura* that then reflects what they are. The child must be educated and polite to an extreme. The demands may cause a psychological trauma, but this is the way with the *gentes tradicionales*.

In the club some racial differences may be made. There are a few professional Jews of the high economic level of the *clase media* in the Club Social. These people do not make themselves *simpáticos*. It is a tragedy for them when a daughter marries a non-Jew, so they themselves are really race conscious. In the club there have been attempts to preserve social purity. Social reception and relations are spontaneous among families of the very old group; the people with old roots feel spiritually very close.

In our level, socially the women are the most conservative; men are progressive and think of themselves as more advanced. Women are highly sensitive socially and act in their relations very formally. Men are more pliable and have opportunities to mix a great deal with the people. The "spirit" of social caste is in the women. For myself, I can say that there are times when I feel no different from the other classes; women, however, retain the sense of being very different. The women of society feel that they should help the low-class people, and therefore they are active in the charitable institutions.

When I think of dividing society, the matter of classes becomes critical —the only way to divide society is by classes. Our high class has a role to help the people, to raise those from below and to erase some of the differences. Our mission is to help day by day. My own work takes me to talk with laborer and professional. I maintain voluntary and business relationships with many people in the streets. The high class and those below interact mostly by the nature of their work. It must be understood, however, that the contacts of *peón* and *patrón* carry very little human interest. The paternalistic orientation no longer exists. Now the people from below demand legal rights and do not respect the *patrón* as they did in the past.

Perhaps some of the oldest family names are losing their distinction and importance as new families emerge to social prominence through the years. An individual who knows how to behave with social finesse, cultivates things in life related to *cultura*, seeks out the proper company, and proves that he has fine qualities—he may enter into the upper circles and become socially accepted. By his style of public behavior, he differentiates himself from those in the *clase humilde*.

The following is an interview with another informant deeply rooted in history. His ancestors were prominent in the political formation of the province. Socially, his is a patrician family, but their economic situation has deteriorated in the last few years. His views represent those of families *venidas a menos*. The elements expressed in this interview constitute a profile of their self-image and the image they hold of their society.

In this city the common people are noticeable for their speech. Among them there is a definite lack of security. There can be no mistake in placing people since everyone, and particularly the women, tends to project in conversation what he is. I, myself, as a person who belongs to an upper social class, economically displaced, must continue to show through my conduct what I really am. Namely, I must show that I am not of the common run of the mill, although today I stand at the same economic level as the rest of the people. It is a must, and not pedantry, because one owes this respect to those who made our past, our style, and our role in society. And I have inherited all these things. We differ from those who are trying to become upper class. In our modern style of buildings and modern world we do not need to search for old and antique symbols for house decoration. We have it. For them this is fashionable; for us it is our own history. We are not with the fashion, we are with what is historically ours. Fashion is to search for what one does not possess; we have it by right of birth.

There is nowadays a deliberate desire to climb socially, but those people are anchored in the present and have a vision of the future. I behave in a specific manner because I know that behind me there is a series of events, things, and people who oblige me to be what I am. It is my destiny to think in those terms before deciding and carrying out an assignment. In this sense the people in the middle class possess more freedom since they can act as they wish. I feel that in our group we must be always careful and very proper in our actions because we have been entrusted with the past. It is not to be used with ostentation but with distinction as something very personal. One cannot help but notice in the majority of people, even in the new elite, the lack of aristocratic manner and of the spiritual quality. This group of people lives without a vivid past for anchorage.

As a teacher in a reputable state institution, I have given the same to all students of all classes. I have practiced my manners and have been a model for them. I have presented them with the refinements necessary for a life in society. I have offered them not only the formal instruction, but also *educación* and *cultura* [manner and refinement]. In classes I have tried to give the students *cultura* by practicing good manners, exercising my rights, and accentuating my values and views. Many people value these aspects of *cultura*; several socially aspiring families have asked me to tutor their children outside of class.

Our city and our situations emphasize the tradition of classes. There are indeed qualitative differences among people. Some of us cling to the past and use it regardless of our economic condition. But that is the element that nobody can take away from us. There is no doubt that in other cities the class system is not so open as ours. In our own history we know that, although the class structure remains important, the human element has changed. Because of economic changes, new people have been incorporated. As patrician families become less powerful from the economic standpoint, they prefer to remain in the background without directly intervening in social affairs. The leading classes have incorporated new elements that sometimes have qualified for the elite group. But this process has weakened the old patrician group.

One must realize with regard to the Club Social that it no longer represents a symbol of society, which it was a hundred years ago. It represents the situation of today. In the nineteenth and twentieth centuries, the European immigrants came and displaced the old families. It seems a logical development as a society continues its evolutionary trend with an open class system at its base. The Club Social now does not represent the past of the truly traditional families; instead, it has become a place where the elite of the town gather. Many of us no longer like to be active except on the most exceptional occasions. Many public places are available to everyone, but I feel comfortable in places of another social category. When I do not find internal tranquillity in the social atmosphere to fit my standards and my position, I would rather avoid such places.

The intimacy of life nowadays centers primarily in the household. To visit, to bring friends and *compañeros* to one's house, is not a prevalent custom. To keep the door of one's house open to acquaintances is not customary. Of course one encounters friends and acquaintances in the streets, converses with them, and drinks coffee; one may call on the telephone. So the communication continues, but the social gatherings of the past in different households about which my grandparents told me no longer exist. No doubt the economic situation has affected many of these traditions.

Distrust derives from a lack of knowledge about each other; it would seem that communication breaks down rapidly. The fact that *desconocimiento* [lack of knowledge] exists among *vecinos* explains the distant relationship among them. It is usually based on social differences. Areas of the city with deeper roots, where descendants of patrician families live, still maintain a striking difference in the social atmosphere and the daily existence from the newly developed neighborhoods. One woman of the elite with a tradition of her own attempted to preserve the distinction of her family name and history. She assisted neighbors and became a godmother for some of them. Because of her past and her social position she could be accepted among *vecinos* as an authority on social and moral issues. But this has passed, and seldom does one find parallel cases. It is a tradition of half a century ago. I had an aunt like that, and although she died, she left our family with a reputation and distinction among our *vecinos* that we still enjoy; we inherited social authority from her. But there are changes, and as new people take residence among us, traditions and sentiments change.

A Final Overview

The final informant, a young teacher of the *clase media* of traditional origin (with a criollo speech style), presents another overall view of his society. He grew up surrounded by some thirty relatives older than his own generation. In his background there is a strong identification with the events of independence, and other Argentines classify him as an Argentine *puro*. His personality was formed under the strict vigilance of three spinsters—his maternal grandmother's sisters. This was the household of his social orientation. All members depended on the opinion of the three sisters—the oldest had the power of the household. Through the years the young man learned a great deal about life in the city, colored by the political and social opinion of the older members of the household.

In the informant's generation there are twenty first cousins, all of whom acknowledge and properly act out this relationship still. The informant finds that now it is difficult to know each other since the three great aunts have died. In the city they were individuals *muy tradicionales*, mentally linked to the traditional upper-class families.

In this family all married other Argentines, in some cases first cousins. The relationships were further strengthened by having aunts and uncles as godparents at baptisms. This informant, however, was an exception, since he married a second-generation Russian-German. Her parents migrated to Paraná from one of the European-type villages just a few miles from the city.

During many hours of conversation, the informant assumed the role of a teacher. He freely expressed his views and oriented the author to the social complexity of Paraná. He knew the city very well. In childhood he developed a keen curiosity for history. He learned general history from books, but the three spinsters made local and provincial history a reality for him.

We are a land of immigrants, and we possess little in common with each other. There is today little to which we can point as traditionally or typically Argentine. On our hands we have the problem of tradition and *cultura*. Partly this is because many people who came from the Old World have not adapted to Argentina .Therefore, it has been difficult to form a national type.

Sometimes I wonder if this people could be one with true horizons. It seems that thinkers have become very inactive in our midst. The masses have become obstinate and undisciplined, and this stands in the way of defining ourselves as a group. By contrast to other nations of the world, I think we are still in the stage of formation. In the turbulent democracy of the Americas surprising events may occur, and who knows, tomorrow a nobody may become a minister or something else. What happens then in our interpersonal relations? Well, one has learned to be constantly on social guard; the rule is not to antagonize anyone because one never knows what the future might bring.

Politically, the people believe that the Constitution of 1853 is wise and not to be changed. Now, after Perón, we are saying that we must respect the Constitution, but only a few do so. Our problem is the lack of proper education, especially among the half-literate people who are always ready with strong opinions on all subjects. I see the population of the *clase media* without the historical roots of my own case as something very dangerous to a young nation. The danger rests on the fact that we are aging rapidly, accepting problems as if they were a normal aspect of our own society.

The *caudillo* of the past still exists. Individuals of the upper class are behind the actions of the provincial and local government. Some of the *caudillos* of Paraná have become national figures, and thus they can easily influence the decisions of the city government. Mayors of humble origin with insufficient preparation to govern are supported by the stronger leaders. Thus a clique forms a tightly knit network across social class. These people constantly consult with each other, bound not by friendship, but by convenience. Those in a higher office exploit, and are in turn exploited. Leaders of some cliques have no scruples, and then it follows that politics becomes a muddled thing—*politequería*. Much goes on at the verbal level in our situation—talk and always a lot of planning—but this can end only when a nation attains a well-established tradition and much *cultura*, as in the case of Europe. So far, ours is a country of favoritism—*gauchadas*. We all feel linked by this attitude. As the folkloristic advice of Martín Fierro says, you must become the friend of the judge and not cause him discomforts because it is desirable to have a post [*palenque*] on which to scratch. Such notions guide our wisdom; the soul of the Argentine nationality must be understood through the poems of gauchos like Martín Fierro.

During the Perón time, many things changed. The traditional social affairs guided by class differences were disarranged. The *clase humilde* became very active during Perón's time; they used Perón. Although I grew up in Paraná, I never knew the lower-class barrios very well. During the school census I had the opportunity to visit them. After I returned home, I could not eat; I had not known their social conditions. I grew up in the center of the city. I have had students from those sections of the town in night school, but by their appearance, I thought of their home life differently. Among them there seems to be an indolence that I cannot explain too well, and, of course, that was Perón's preoccupation and problem.

The humble people are not able to distinguish between those of the *clase media* who may only own a little home and those who are truly rich. For them, we in the city proper are all rich; we all are an oligarchy. For the poor there are two groups: the submerged people and those in power. I do not find that they have an incentive to improve themselves through practical education. So long as the government does not reach them with definite programs, this low class of people will not progress. And therefore this country cannot progress. The lower-class people are noted for their feeling of resentment. They train their children with the assumption that this rich country could provide a good life for everyone if the *clase alta* were not exploiting it. They always picture the *patrón* as someone who exploits the poor; a *patrón* is without *vergüenza*. Parents blame the *patrón* for their economic shortcomings and for the fact that they cannot provide the necessary things in life for their children.

The *clase humilde* is not prepared to take a position in the *clase media*. In the *clase media* one finds small businessmen who did not make their fortune; small landlords who rent a few houses but are not rich; professional people who expect to be well-to-do; moneylenders, etc. However, one must see this matter of *clase alta* and *clase media* as something relative. There are middle-class individuals who are not in the Club Social, but by their level of *cultura*, they could easily qualify for the *clase alta*.

The strong sense of social classes in our city cannot be denied. Parents who have made some money help their sons to achieve a professional career. Let us suppose that a son becomes a lawyer. Then he certainly will try to climb to a higher class level. The motive for ostentation [*figuración*] may become an obsession. At times these people may fall into ridicule, particularly during family events like weddings. These are occasions to show what one is, or what he wants to be or wants to become. There is much desire for social *figuración*. You people [North Americans] do not seem so interested in the superficialities of life as we are; Italians, Spaniards, Argentines are indeed very sensitive about their social standing. They spend much energy on the social game of *figuración*.

Some groups, like the Jewish people, are something apart; they remain separate and concerned with their own way of life and religion. Social differences are not so important to them as to us. Turcos are even less involved. But a small entrepreneur will not oppose the marriage of an attractive daughter with a professional man, and so eventually they all become involved in the social game.

Most people in Paraná entertain climbing aspirations. The association of barrios with social classes is evident. Some families face serious problems; they want to *figurar* and to progress socially. They must leave the barrio, which is known to be of a low class. Even if their home is good, they feel discomfort and a desire to move toward the center of the city or to the residential area along the river. While the country people and the pueblo people with some savings want to come to the city, the city people invest in promoting their social standing. We are all involved in this game.

People in the higher classes will go out of their way to marry a daughter to a highly placed military man. This is an obsession among them. The family derives great pleasure from having an officer as a member of the family. Officers, of course, carry much prestige because they are in the highest social spheres of government. Any officer stationed in the city has an obligation to become a member of the Club Social. Local girls from the *clase alta* compete to find husbands from among them.

Our people like to *figurar* [show off], and the credit system fosters this psychological attitude. People can afford many more material things if they buy on credit. While we think a great deal about our own self, the *cultura* of Paraná has been impoverished. We are lacking universities in our city, and many excellent professors have been fired because of their political views. Nowadays many teachers come from humble homes. The encyclopedic men are rapidly disappearing. Many of us, and especially our children, wonder why one should study hard if any brute can become a governor.

In our religious thinking there is a feeling of egalitarianism. In the past the Cathedral was for the rich people only; now mixing takes place in the church. Perhaps in church one may find less emphasis on social distinction, but our people still manage to express social differences. The church is a public place and a place to *figurar*.

Our present economic situation is very difficult; the government depends on taxes but is not creating new resources. There is little faith in the government. People in government come from the lower strata and do not have the preparation, the imagination, or the proper historical background to govern. What is done is based on improvisation. But we do not lose faith; we hope for better times to come. Anxious people are skeptical about promises made by politicians, but many of us want to believe that there is some truth in them. One looks for improvement, and the people of the *clase humilde* hope that some day a savior will come and solve all of their social and economic problems. In a way we all do the same—expect the savior while we sit and wait.

No doubt we are in a state of formation, and we are not yet a definite type. When the doors of this nation were open in the past, people from all corners of the world came to our shore. Through time we have not developed our own style and tradition; people in Mexico seem to have had more success. Perhaps we are still sentimentally tied to the past historical models of many European nations. We cannot free ourselves from these models and thus cannot proceed independently toward our own ways. The modern generation is trying to change, but many assumptions of the past remain in the present and we are very conscious of them.

A Paranaense Summary

Each case in this sample of informants stands at a strategic point where class, ethnic, economic, and political variables intersect. Other

The Diversity of Social Images   365

individuals at the same nexus may interpret things differently according to their own views and personal experiences in life. Therefore, these are only illustrative models. In each case the ethnic identity is specified, although this theme is not of much consequence in the *clase media*. The large majority of people in Paraná share a foreign background and are attuned to the differences and their implications. The distinction is occasionally made when the ethnic stereotypes are used.

In the course of the investigation innumerable comments were made that coincide with the views expressed in these cases. The versions varied, but still Paranaenses share some basic models to guide their public actions. Each of the above spokesmen was well grounded in the social past and present of the city. The images, therefore, are not those of passive observers. Each informant has been exposed to and affected by the local, provincial, and national processes. One Paranaense reacted to these interpretations by offering his own:

> The country has been formed by heterogeneous European migrations and is still in the stage of formation. Argentinismo is something poetic and of the gaucho literature. Some ethnic groups have been assimilated into the general social matrix, but this social matrix has not been sufficiently stable and strong to stamp everyone with a general orientation and tradition. Some groups still remain as separate ethnic entities.
>
> This situation, almost like a frontier, seems to elicit a strong individualism, a self-centered attitude, and the resulting absence of smooth interpersonal relationships.
>
> People are grouped not only by ethnic background, but also as part of a three class system. The class system is considered open by the *clase media* but not so open by the upper class. Therefore, there are discomforts and social discrimination. The social consciousness of the elite manifests itself in the constant search for avenues to social success. While the lower class feels isolated, the others share some of the feelings but have various means available to improve their social position. There is a manifest lack of group action in the city to cope with the social problems and a high degree of disunity and intentional anomie.
>
> The country has been constantly moving from one political crisis to another. This results in a country with a constitution that is not respected. Many people assume that the local and national situations are in the hands

of individuals who conduct political business by improvisation and lack the ability to govern.

Individuals, especially the young ones, are socially and politically dislocated. They soon learn to become involved in *gauchada*, using each other for mutual advancement.

All this leads to a decadence of *cultura* and a loss of personal tranquillity. People want to believe something and all are waiting for solutions and for a savior to lead them to the next historical stage. People see education as a solution to all problems; the total eradication of ignorance should bring society to a good level of *cultura* and social equality.

EPILOGUE

Man, I concluded, may have come to the end of that wild being who had mastered the fire and the lightning. He can create the web but not hold it together, not save himself except by transcending his own image. For at the last, before the ultimate master, it is himself he shapes. (Loren C. Eiseley, *The Unexpected Universe*, p. 66)

The Anthropologist's View

Basic to the understanding of Paraná, its people and its physical and social development, stands the concept of *city*. Paranaenses define the city as the type of human organization that contains and accommodates "the basic accessories of civilization." A true city must differentiate its population socially; and this is done through social classes. A place without a rigorous social breakdown can only be considered less socially developed, incomplete, and therefore not a city but a pueblo (town).

A city, furthermore, is a place where extremes or opposites are expected to appear and coexist; the rich and the poor, the good and the bad, the modern and the old, the intellectual and the illiterate, the native and the foreign are among the many opposites that are most evident. The city, to Paranaenses who in the past formulated policies, was a unit where all sorts of people met and mingled. The need to order diversity was an inescapable consequence of such a situation. Ideally, classification of individuals should be in terms of their capacity and quality. Social classification was their choice for a large heterogeneous population so people could understand one another and predict behavior.

Furthermore, development and progess are linked to the city's dynamics. Paranaenses are proud of their achievements. To have passed from village to city in a few years has been their first and most outstanding accomplishment. This implies that the community has moved from a partial social structure to a full one, from simple to complex, from rural to urban. Paraná stands at the apex of a regional economic and political network, and as a city Paraná has a unique history. Paraná was the capital of Argentina for over a decade, but it has not become an industrial center. It continues as an administrative city with civil servants, small entrepreneurs, and a few powerful landowners. Consequently, the pace of life is not that of a large metropolis, and many outsiders judge Paraná as conservative and even antiquated when compared to a city like Buenos Aires or the recently industrialized city of Córdoba. (Twenty years ago Córdoba was similar to Paraná, but today it is an important industrial center in the interior of the republic.)

In contrast, Paranaenses view the order in Paraná as an organization able to support a style of life proper to a dignified city. Important is the fact that Paraná has completed its basic cycle; the social and the physical organization constitutes a monument to the past. The very upper and the lower classes readily accept the cultural forces of the past. They attempt to understand their social position in terms of the past; the middle group struggles against it. It is difficult for the middle-class man to accept that the basic structure has been cemented; he cannot identify with the city as a product of the past nor accept such an organization as final. Modernization and change stand as the nearest solutions to his basic social and economic problems.

In reviewing the total situation of Paraná, the fundamental overall cultural style that prevails is based on an upper-class tradition. Eliteness as a concept behind people's orientation and social behavior remains basic and is endowed with the legacy of the past. There may be a radical entrepreneur who claims to oppose a class-stratified society and supports liberal political ideas. Yet when the time comes to select a burial lot in the cemetery for himself and his family, he prefers a place near the entrance where *panteones* of well-to-do and socially outstanding families cluster. The do's and don't's appear clearly in an elite-oriented society. Generally everyone strives to reach a higher social position. Mobility is an important aspect of the dynamics of this society. *Cultura* is represented best at the highest social level, and this is where the educated and socially aspiring individual wishes to be.

Although Paraná is a unique product of Argentine history, it shares fundamental social features with other Latin American cities. Social class, in particular, "gives an apt and useful sorting of ideas, behavior, possessions, and institutions."[1] Many Latin Americans recognize and admit that their society is socially stratified and that the class system is their social reality.

If to be a Paranaense is the first order of identity, to be Argentine is not a separate feeling; the first constitutes an integral part of the second. So long as Paranaenses maintain this view, all national moods, crises, and changes are going to be intimately felt in the city. An editorial in the city's newspaper comments on the national situation, but it reflects and applies to the local just as well. The editor writes:

> Nobody can deny that our country is living through tense and difficult hours filled with drama and danger. We suffer the effect of those groups that are purposely engaged in creating disturbances in the political life and preventing spiritual peace, economic recuperation, and faith in the institution of a republican form of government as well as faith in those men who embody it.[2]

This editorial continues to advise that there is need to restore trust in order to achieve a level of mental unity, patriotism, good judgment, peaceful conviviality, and respect toward men—all of which are essential traits for a civilized way of life.

Because of the political and economic links with the nation, Paranaenses keep themselves well informed. They constantly discuss national news, but feel unable to participate in or to influence decisions

---

[1] Hawthorne 1948:21.
[2] *La Capital* 1964.

at a level beyond their immediate surroundings. One informant explained:

> Our nerves must adjust to insecurities; otherwise we would indeed have a nervous breakdown [*enfermo de los nervios*]. Serious as these national issues are, we end up believing that they are things in the course of life. We are in the hands of professional politicians. They are operators, and after all, if I were a politician, I would do the same; that is to get rich if possible.

The local newspaper constantly provides reports of cases that negate the political principles for which the republic should stand.

During the period of field work, the atmosphere was heavy with pessimism toward an uncertain future; one informant confessed that "it all seems like a dead-end street." The *picardía criolla del acomodo* (personal pull) and lack of vision and responsibility were constant topics for discussion, particularly among the upper middle social group. Many people felt that a strong hand in the government—a savior or messiah—was needed. "We are waiting for another overthrow of the government." "Revolution, however," observed another informant, "is only a temporary relief and not a permanent solution to our problems."

The local newspaper of September 30, 1965, pictures the existing situation in an editorial entitled "The Country of the Never-Ever." Argentina is

> a country where the elements of power have not been consolidated in favor of general progress and have not reached stability, equilibrium, and harmony in the main centers of the nation. It is, then, the country of the never-ever, the country of the going and coming, of violent changes, of crucial alternatives. Destinies are characterized by the absurd and the paradoxical. . . . Champion bulls worth millions of pesos next to poverty . . . highly priced bread in the midst of wheat fields. . . . a nation full of schools with the memory of Sarmiento, yet where illiteracy is a tremendous problem.

The contemporary situation undoubtedly has roots in the past. After a visit to Argentina, José Ortega y Gasset, the Spanish philosopher, wrote:

> The pueblo criollo . . . have known how to make of their nation a body perfectly porous, with men of all races, all languages, all religions, and all

customs. . . . But that facility to receive the stranger, the porosity of society, brings the danger that it will all produce a lack of cohesion. The life of a pueblo such as this will be disorderly, uneasy, turbulent, brutal, and without solidarity, decreasing and preventing the great task of bringing unity and common spirit. . . . The Argentine . . . feels deeply in his life . . . sadness, desolation, discontent, estrangement from satisfaction.[3]

Similar points of view are expressed in other recent works. Mafud calls attention to the Argentine uprootedness: "The man here does not behave as if he loved his society, instead he behaves by reacting against it. . . . Each time the Argentine society reaches a crisis there emerges in the social and political life the spirit of a factory rather than the spirit of a community."[4]

In each of these subjective works, the author attempts to present an emotive interpretation of the national character. All of the writers are products of the society that Ortega y Gasset characterized by its lack of cohesion. In Argentina and in Paraná, quiet disbelief, social dissatisfaction, individual apathy, and psychological uprootedness underlie the way of life and affect interpersonal relationships. In addition, improvisation and imitation constitute prevailing characteristics in Argentina according to some upper-class informants. These provide means to adapt to a changing world and to keep up with technological development. The national objective is to push forward with industrialization and modernization; these trends are centered in a handful of cities.

In contrast to other situations of the New World, corporate social systems do not characterize Argentine communities. Most of the Argentine towns are—and to a large extent feel—part of the national network. The degree of social and cultural sophistication varies from one community to another, but all of them share a significant number of common social and cultural elements. It is indisputable that the more important and more populous centers of the interior feel closer to the design and the destiny of the nation than the less developed areas. The cities activate the economic and political components of the national social network. There is, however, a quiet struggle between

[3] Ortega y Gasset, *Obras completas*, vol. 8, pp. 366–367.
[4] Mafud 1965:84. See also Giusti 1954; Scalabrini Ortiz 1941; and the generalizations of T. R. Filliol 1961:16–18.

Buenos Aires and the cities of the interior. The latter are involved in a common effort to consolidate their position in the nation. The struggle with Buenos Aires is an old one, and it does not seem to be coming to an end.

The local, provincial, and national levels are plagued with the notion of change, but the leaders at each level hold a different idea of change. A complex network of channels of information feeds into the individual's mind and frequently produces confusion. The individual feels entangled as he strives to sort out the information in answer to his questions about society. What is society? What should it be? What will it become? The individual's social position may be relatively fixed in the stratification system of his own community, but the society around him is inducing changes. The task, frequently psychologically exhausting for the individual, is to adjust to the social world around him.

Discovering the City's Social Order

Culture is defined in the introduction as the accumulation of human events through time directly experienced by members of a specific group from which living members derive assumptions and create principles to guide their thinking and behavior. Essentially, this point of view guided our examination of Paraná, its social system, and its people's actions. In the abstract, culture is the product of people, particularly of those from previous generations who set the social machine in motion. The living stand then as administrators of the inherited past—culture; the sense of freedom to innovate or create is in a way defined by the very phenomenon one is administering. Paranaenses are within the web of time and cannot escape the legacy of their own history. If the social and cultural web created through time within the boundaries of Paraná alone is in itself an intricate phenomenon, its study becomes overwhelming. Time hides many significant events and features; present-day Paranaenses cannot be expected to be fully conscious of all their acts in life. Much is simply explained as "tradition" —a shortcut to a complex philosophical explanation.

Paranaenses know their past, and when they use the past to prepare for the future, the social phenomenon of Paraná seems to open up.

Epilogue

When the anthropologist looks for a starting point and tries to discover for himself the nature of the social phenomenon contained in the city, he faces a problem of significant magnitude.

As a city Paraná contains all the elements of a folk-model city, but it is a dignified city with predictable regularities. Behind the drama of city-community life, there is order. This special character of the city, I assume, should respond to a clear and forceful viewpoint on personal relationships; and if a specific point of view is apparent in the present, its beginning should be perceptible in the past history. The problem was therefore to isolate that central viewpoint as a principle or a set of principles that underlie the organization of Paranaenses, guard the dynamics of city-community culture, and can be ethnographically and historically validated. Living in the city and examining its past pointed to social *class* as central in the dynamics of the society. The social division is a sociological phenomenon of unique dimension extending also into the psychological and cultural levels.

An unplanned visit to the city cemetery at the outset of the field work threw the best light upon the basic principle underlying the social organization of the city. This inactive document of life is the most dynamic social testament among Paranaenses. Each tomb dramatically preserves the social past and present of families. The cemetery is a site of considerable social interest; it stands as a symbol of the past, the present, and the future. In subtle ways, the arrangement of the cemetery portrays what one's ancestors were, what one is, and what one would like to become. The life of the cemetery clearly disclosed to me the crucial and fundamental concern of the people. And the effort to perpetuate, eradicate, or blur social distinctions is a revealing dynamic process. Organizing people by social class was and is an active principle in the social organization of the city and it affects the city ecology and the material world as well. The organization in the cemetery reflects the high sensitivity and consciousness of what one is or desires to be, vividly portrayed in funerals and tombs. Having recognized their basic viewpoint, the problem of working ethnographically among 100,000 people, most of them descendants of those who lie in one of the specific social areas of the cemetery, became less overwhelming.

One way to understand the dynamics in the life of a class-organized city society is to analyze actions, thought patterns, rules of interaction, sentiments, formation of groups, economic and political networks, and leadership. In the spirit of this work, not all aspects of individuals' behavior need to be reached. Individuals' actions become relevant at the very instant when one steps out of the household and enters the streets of the city. Individuals in the public domain are in the full setting of the culture created through the course of the years.

Paranaenses refer to the organized web of their behavior as "our way of being" (*nuestra manera de ser*). Since it is something woven in the past and handed down, can its continuity be broken? Should its impact upon the present become less decisive? Should one continue to live with it? Many similar questions were raised, and, while some social levels are devoted to the status quo, other sectors are dedicated to the concept of modernity and change. Change, with its deep psychological meaning, continues to puzzle Paranaenses. It appears that class organization is predicated on the assumption of change by renovation, while the value system, particularly that held by the *clase media*, calls for change by the substitution of new elements. To administer a society thus put together constitutes a very complex problem indeed. The people see their social system as something transplanted from across the sea, the property of an older civilization. The social system is a copy that helped to organize Paraná society in the early stage of its development; the value system derived later from the Argentine experience. Here one was born amidst rapid and continuous change, and change has become an intricate part of the world view. There is an anachronism in the social reality that hides in its dynamics an inexplicable human reality. The social structure is more deeply rooted in history than the value system. Perhaps the existing gap between the two causes *desarraigo* (uprootedness) and apathy. If this is the case, Paranaenses at present need to interlock the assumptions behind the dynamics of the values and social structure into a single system.

Immigrants of the past century conceived and expected an existence in the New World based on "change" and wide social opportunities. But the search for change sometimes was in vain. The dynamics of the social matrix did not coincide with the immigrants' aspirations. Existing in a city such as Paraná is predicated on the concept of social mobility; it is precisely on the individual level that changes should take place. Achievement may not seem difficult; however, in reality it is. Social advancement must be accompanied by a constellation of changes in behavior, attitudes, physical appearance, language style, club membership, etc. In the process of mobility, the individual, perhaps unaware, helps to strengthen the organizational principle of his society and helps to perpetuate the status quo of a social class. From above, the mobile person now is less interested in the value of change. A static conservative orientation accompanies his change of social role.

How long the present organization of the city of Paraná will last must remain an open question. It has been documented that whenever industrialization, modernization, and demographic expansion take place, social changes occur; but how Paranaenses will react and accommodate the past cultural heritage to the new technological development remains to be seen. The choices in theory are many and yet the decision is not of the Paranaenses alone but of Argentines at large. Argentines, regardless of social background and locale, share the destiny of their society. Past generations may have set the design of the social structure, but the present generation must decide how to continue the everlasting social building.

To conclude, this book should give an idea of what it is like to be an Argentine living in Paraná. The work focuses on the people. To think of Paranaenses without the central plaza, the cathedral, the national and local historical names for streets, the schools, the social classes, the barrios and neighborhoods with *almacenes* and clubs, is to take away all that is most Argentine and typical of Argentina. These institutions constitute pivots of the social network that characterize the social structure of the city and give coherence to people's behavior.

The social story of Paraná is and will remain here inconclusive. How Paranaenses will emerge is a decision that lies with them. They, like people everywhere, continue to search for their own selves.

WORKS CITED

Ashton-Warner, Sylvia. 1963. *Teacher.* New York: Simon and Schuster.
La Capital. 1964–1965. Local newspaper, Rosario, Argentina.
Cervera, Manuel M. 1907. *Historia de la ciudad y provincia de Santa Fé, 1573–1853,* vols. 1, 2. Santa Fé: Librería, Imprenta, y Encuardernación La Unión.
Cochran, Thomas C. 1959. *The Puerto Rican Businessman.* Philadelphia: University of Pennsylvania Press.
———, and Ruben E. Reina. 1962. *Entrepreneurship in Argentine Culture.* Philadelphia: University of Pennsylvania Press.
De Laguna, Frederica, ed. 1960. *Selected Papers from the "American Anthropologist," 1888–1920.* Evanston: Row, Peterson.
El Diario. 1964–1965. Local newspaper, Paraná, Argentina.
Eiseley, Loren C. 1969. *The Unexpected Universe.* New York: Harcourt, Brace and World.
Eisenstadt, S. N. 1961. "Anthropological Studies of Complex Societies." *Current Anthropology* 2, no. 3:201–222.
Erasmus, Charles. 1953. *Las dimensiones de la cultura.* Bogotá: Editorial Iqueima.
Ferrer, Aldo. 1967. *The Argentine Economy.* Berkeley: University of California Press.
Filliol, Tomás Roberto. 1961. "Social Factors in Economic Development: The Argentine Case." M.A. thesis, Massachusetts Institute of Technology.
Foster, George M. 1960. *Culture and Conquest: America's Spanish Heritage.* New York: Wenner-Gren Foundation for Anthropological Research.
Germani, Gino. 1962. *Política y sociedad en una época de transición de la sociedad tradicional a la sociedad de masas.* Buenos Aires: Editoria Paidos.
Gibson, Charles. 1964. *The Aztecs under Spanish Rule: A History of the Indians of the Valley of Mexico, 1619–1800.* Stanford: Stanford University Press.

Gillin, John. 1949. "Methodological Problems in the Anthropological Study of Modern Cultures." *American Anthropologist* 51:392–399.

———. 1955. "Ethos Components in Modern Latin American Culture." *American Anthropologist* 57:491–494.

Giusti, Roberto F. 1954. *Momentos y aspectos de la cultura argentina.* Buenos Aires. Editorial Raigal.

Hallowell, A. Irving. 1955. *Culture and Experience.* Philadelphia: University of Pennsylvania Press.

———. 1960. "The Beginnings of Anthropology in America." In *Selected Papers from the "American Anthropologist," 1888–1920*, edited by F. de Laguna, pp. 1–90. Evanston: Row, Peterson and Company.

Hardoy, Jorge E. et al. 1967. "Conclusions and Evaluation of the Symposium on 'The Process of Urbanization in America since Its Origins to the Present Time.'" *Latin American Research Review* 2:76–90.

Hawthorne, Harry Bertram, and A. E. Hawthorne. 1948. "Stratification in a Latin American City." *Social Forces* 27:19–29.

Hernández, José. 1962. *El Gaucho Martín Fierro.* Buenos Aires: EUDEBA.

Homans, George. 1950. *The Human Group.* New York: Harcourt, Brace.

Honigmann, John. 1967. *Personality in Culture.* New York: Harper and Row.

Hymes, Dell. 1966. "On Anthropological Linguistics and Congeners." *American Anthropologist* 68:143–153.

———. 1967. "Why Linguistics Needs the Sociologist." *Social Research* 34:632–647.

Instituto de Planeamiento Regional y Urbano. 1963. *Plan Director de Paraná*, vol. 1. Rosario: Universidad Nacional del Litoral.

Instituto de Planeamiento Regional y Urbano. 1963. *Plan Director de Paraná*, vol. 2. Rosario: Universidad Nacional del Litoral.

Keesing, Felix M. 1953. *Culture Change: An Analysis and Bibliography of Anthropological Sources to 1952.* Stanford: Stanford University Press.

Kroeber, A. L., and Clyde Kluckhohn. 1952. "Culture: A Critical Review of Concepts and Definitions." *Papers of the Peabody Museum of American Archaeology and Ethnology* 47, no. 1. Cambridge.

Labov, Eric E. 1965. "American Historians and the Story of Urbanization." In *Social Dialects and Language Learning*, edited by Roger Shuy, pp. 77–103. Champaign, Ill.: National Council of Teachers of English.

Lampard, Eric E. 1961. "American Historians and the Story of Urbanization." *American Historical Review* 67, no. 1:49–61.

López, Lucio V. 1928. *La gran aldea.* Buenos Aires: El Ateneo.

Works Cited

Lowie, Robert H. 1937. *This History of Ethnological Theory.* New York: Farrar and Rinehart.

Lynch, Kevin. 1960. *The Image of the City.* Cambridge: Technological Press.

Mafud, Julio. 1961. *Contenido social del Martín Fierro.* Buenos Aires: Américalee.

———. 1965. *Psicología de la viveza criolla.* Buenos Aires: Américalee.

Mallea, Eduardo. 1966. *All Green Shall Perish and Other Novels and Stories.* New York: Knopf.

McGann, Thomas F. 1957. *Argentina, the United States and the Inter-American System, 1880–1914.* Cambridge: Harvard University Press.

Mead, Margaret. 1953. *Growing Up in New Guinea.* New York: New American Library.

———, and R. Bunzel. 1960. *The Golden Age of American Anthropology.* New York: G. Braziller.

Michelena, J. A. Silva. 1963. Review of "Entrepreneurship in Argentine Culture," *Revista de Ciencias Sociales* 7, no. 3:307–311.

Miner, Horace. 1939. *St. Denis: A French-Canadian Parish.* Chicago: University of Chicago Press.

Morse, Richard. 1965. "Urbanization in Latin America." *Latin American Research Review* 1, no. 1:35–75.

Municipalidad de Paraná. *Actas Municipales 1873–1900.* Libro de Actas Municipales. Entre Ríos, Argentina.

Nadel, S. F. 1951. *The Foundations of Social Anthropology.* Glencoe: Free Press.

Oddone, Jacinto. 1956. *La burguesía terrateniente argentina.* Buenos Aires: Ediciones Populares Argentinas.

Ortega y Gasset, José. 1937. *Invertebrate Spain.* New York: W. W. Norton.

———. 1965. *Obras Completas.* Madrid: Ediciones Castella.

Parsons, Talcott; Edward Shils; Kaspar D. Naegele; and Jesse R. Pitts. 1961. *Theories of Society: Foundations of Modern Sociological Theory,* vols. 1, 2. New York: The Free Press of Glencoe.

Paz, Octavio. 1961. *The Labyrinth of Solitude: Life and Thought in Mexico.* New York: Grove Press.

Penniman, Thomas Kenneth. 1952. *A Hundred Years of Anthropology.* London: G. Duckworth.

Pérez-Colman, César B. 1946. *La parroquia y la ciudad de Paraná en su centenario 1730–1930.* Rosario: Emilio Fennter, S.R.L.

Pitt-Rivers, Julian A. 1954. *The People of the Sierra*. London: Weidenfeld and Nicolson.

Powdermaker, Hortense. 1966. *Stranger and Friends: The Way of an Anthropologist*. New York: W. W. Norton.

Redfield, Robert. 1958. *The Little Community: Viewpoints for the Study of a Human Whole*. Chicago: University of Chicago.

———. 1962. "Anthropological Understanding of Man." In *Human Nature and the Study of Society: The Papers of Robert Redfield*, edited by Margaret Park Redfield. Chicago: University of Chicago Press.

Reglamentos del Club Social. n.d. Club Social de Paraná. Paraná, Argentina.

Reina, Rubén E. 1964. "The Urban World View of a Tropical Forest Community in the Absence of a City: Petén, Guatemala." *Human Organization* 23, no. 4:265–277.

———. 1966. *The Law of the Saints: A Pokomam Pueblo and Its Community Culture*. Indianapolis: Bobbs-Merrill.

Reula, Filberto. 1963. *Historia de Entre Ríos*, vol. I. Santa Fé: Librería y Editorial Castellvi.

Rojas, Ricardo. 1927. *Las provincias*. Buenos Aires: J. Roldán.

Ruiz Moreno, M. *Leyes sobre tierras de Entre Ríos*. n.d.

Sabrelli, Juan José. 1965. *Buenos Aires vide cotidiana alineación*. Buenos Aires: El Gráfico.

Scalabrini Ortiz, Raúl. 1941. *El Hombre que está solo y espera*. Buenos Aires: Editorial Reconquista.

Scobie, James R. 1964a. *Argentina: A City and a Nation*. New York: Oxford University Press.

———. 1964b. *Revolution on the Pampas: A Social History of Argentine Wheat, 1860–1910*. Austin: University of Texas Press.

Solari, Aldo E. 1964. *Estudios sobre la sociedad uruguaya*. Uruguay.

Strickson, Arnold. 1962. "Class and Kinship in Argentina." *Ethnology* 1, no. 4:500–515.

Taylor, Carl C. 1948. *Rural Life in Argentina*. Baton Rouge: Louisiana State University Press.

UNESCO. 1963. *Social Aspects of Economic Development in Latin America*. Edited by Egbert de Vries, José M. Echavarría, et al. Paris: UNESCO.

Wagley, Charles. 1963. *An Introduction to Brazil*. New York: Columbia University Press.

Wallace, A. F. C. 1961. *Culture and Personality*. New York: Random House.
Weber, Max. 1958. *The City*. Glencoe: Free Press.
Whiteford, Andrew H. 1960. *Two Cities of Latin America: A Comparative Description of Social Classes*. Beloit College, Bulletin no. 9. Beloit, Wis.: The Logan Museum of Anthropology.
Wirth, Louis. 1938. "Urbanism as a Way of Life." *American Journal of Sociology* 44:1–24.
Wolf, Eric R. 1964. *Anthropology*. Englewood Cliffs: Prentice-Hall.
———. 1966. "Kinship, Friendship, and Patron-Client Relations in Complex Societies." In *The Social Anthropology of Complex Societies*, edited by Michael Banton, pp. 1–20. London: Tavistock Publications.
Zanio, Alfio. 1926. *Páginas de oro de la ciudad de Paraná*. Paraná.

INDEX

Adams, Brooks: on nature of society, 168
adults: concern of, with children's behavior, 265–266; and disciplining of children, 266–269; relationship of, with children, 274–276
agriculture: importance of, to economy, 20–21
alfalfa: as important crop, 20
Alianza Francesa: 146
almacenero: in social network, 112, 113, 114, 115, 116, 117; on lying technique, 267
almacenes: serves neighborhood clientele, 112–113; business practices of, 113–114; and credit, 114–115; place of, in community, 115–117
ambientes: descriptions of, 48, 50–53; distribution of, throughout city, 49
Amigos de Calle San Martin: 149
Amigos de la Casa del Periodista: 151
Amigos de la Facultad de Ingeniería de Paraná: 151
Amigos de la Música: 151
Amigos del Museo Histórico: 151
anthropology: and study of modern civilization, xv
apariencia: in the upper class, 210; and social class, 215–216
Argentina: city life in, xv; colonization of, 3–10; Europeanization of, 250–252, 351; as society in formation, 361–362, 364, 365; as rootless society, 369–372
Arias de Saavedra, don Hernando: 8
Arias de Saavedra, Francisco: 8
army, the: in the socialization process, 261; attitudes toward, 331–332; effect of, on career plans, 332, 333; life in, 332–333; and social stratification, 333–334
Ashton-Warner, Sylvia: on freedom in education, 311
Asociación Argentina de Cultura Inglesa: 146
Asociación Argentina Israelita Sefardi Religiosa y Cultural: 146
Asociación Cívica Mayo-Caseros: 152

Asociación Croata: 146
Asociación Croata "Rey Tomislav": 152
Asociación Docentes Nacionales: 151
Asociación Israelita: 146
Asociación Juvenil John F. Kennedy: 152
Asociación Pro-Patria: 152
Asociación Sirio-Libanesa: 146
Asociación Verdiana: 152
Asunción del Paraguay: established, 3
Austrians: and settlement of Argentina, 70

Bank of the Province of Entre Ríos: 43
barley: as important crop, 20
Barrio Antoñico: 42
barrio clubs: and social strata, 154–155; objections to, 155–156
barrios: description of, 64–65, 172–173; children's view of, 313–315
Barrio San Agustín: 42, 64
Barrio Sarmiento: 42
Basques: arrive in Paraná, 29; place of residence of, 52; stereotype of, 100–101
begging: regulation of, 31
behavior: classification of people by, 106–108, 184
British: and settlement of Paraná, xvi; arrive in Paraná, 29; and settlement of Argentina, 70; cultural identification of, 71; death notices for, 228
Buenos Aires: and Argentine culture, xvi; attempted settlement of, 3; sets styles for Argentina, 250–252; criticism of, 348–349; and modernity, 368, 371
Bunzel, Ruth: on history of anthropology, xv n.
burial: relation of, to social standing, 217–219; history of, 219; types of, 219–224. SEE ALSO cemetery, the; funerals

cabildo: composition of, 10
careers: planning of, 322–324; selection of, 334–335
Carnaval: as political issue, 32–33; bene-

fits masses, 123; description of, 123–125; and social taboos, 125; mentioned, 60
Casa Rosa: 43
Catedral de la Ciudad, La: 43
cemetery, the: location of, 62; as sacred land, 224; reflects social distinctions, 373. SEE ALSO burial; funerals
Centro Amigos del Ciego de Entre Ríos: activities of, 150
Centro Asturiano: 144
Centro Commercial e Industrial: activities of, 150–151
centros gremiales: flourish, 158
Centro Vasco: 144
charitable institutions: and social role playing, 158
children: run household errands, 263–265; public behavior of, 265–266; disciplining of, 266–269; hostility to, in *vecindad*, 269–270; recreational activities of, 270–271; formation of friendships among, 272–274; relationship of, with adults, 274–276; formation of social perceptions by, 276–277
Chinautla: author's study of, xxii
churches: in Cuartel 2, 59–61; as club-substitute, 156–157; lower-class membership in, 181; middle-class participation in, 194–195; upper-class participation in, 211; popular response to, 349
Círculo de Maestros: 151
Círculo de Oficiales: 151
Círculo de Suboficiales: 151
Círculo Médio Obreros: 151
círculos: activities of, 151
Cisneros, Viceroy: 9
city, the: as social organism, xvii, 367–369; inhabitants' perception of, 40–41; and social change, 369, 371–372
city clubs: vs. *clubes de vecindad*, 121, 122; membership of, 138–140; activities of, 140–142; and social standing, 142–143; decline of, 157; needs filled by, 159–160; internal structure of, 160–161
city ecology: definition of, 39–40
ciudad. SEE city, the
clase alta: view of middle class of, 196; substrata of, 198–200; acceptance in, 200–203; family life among, 203–205; and interaction with other classes, 205–207; importance of the past to, 207–209, 213–214, 215, 358, 359; importance of decorum to, 209–211; religious-philosophical orientation of, 211–212; group identity among, 212–213; importance of *cultura* to, 214–215; cultural orientation of, 245–249; claims inherent right to rule, 249–250; changes in, with immigration, 252; worldview of children of, 317–319; ambitions for future among children of, 321; social requirements of, 344; middle class's image of, 347; decline of, 351; social interaction within, 352–353, 359–360; social consciousness of, 356, 357–358; and social ostentation, 363–364. SEE ALSO *clase aristocrática*; *familias conocidas*; *familias tradicionales*
clase aristocrática: and makeup of society, xx. SEE ALSO *clase alta*
clase baja: stereotype of, 102, 173; environment of, 172–173; and social advancement, 177; view of other classes by, 178; and political organization, 178–179; view of social structures of, 179–181; religious orientation of, 181; belief of, in natural signs, 181–184; interpersonal relations within, 184–186; cultural orientation of, 240–242; effect of immigration upon, 254; worldview of children of, 313–315; ambitions for future among children of, 320, 321. SEE ALSO *clase humilde*; *negros, los*
clase humilde: and makeup of society, xx; attitude of, toward higher classes, 362; aspirations of, 364. SEE ALSO *clase baja*
clase media: and makeup of society, xix, xx; growth of, 38; defined, 59 n.; stereotypes of, 102–103; diversity of, 186–187; social consciousness of, 187–191, 196–197; generational conflict within, 191–193; religious-philosophical orientation of, 194–195, 349; as figurative concept, 195–196; political orientation of, 197–198; cultural orientation of, 242–245; formation of, 254, 255; worldview of children of, 316–317; ambitions for future among children of, 320–324; blandness of, 343–344; self-image of, 346–347; social interaction within, 349–350; anxiety of, 350–351; interaction of, with upper classes, 355; as social climbers, 357, 358; and social ostentation, 363, 364
Club Belgrano: 142
Club de Estudiantes: 142, 153, 154
Club Echagüe: 142
clubes de vecindad: activities sponsored by, 117–119; conscious of public image, 119–120; perceived as disrepu-

table, 120–121; and social standing, 121–123; internal structure of, 161–162; survey of, 162–163
Club Paraná: 142
Club Progreso: 154
clubs: and social climbing, 163–164; social usefulness of, 164–165; as a means to social contacts, 164, 166; and social atomization, 166–167, 168; effect of, on social interaction, 350. SEE ALSO barrio clubs; *circulos*; city clubs; *clubes de vecindad*; ethnic associations; service organizations
Club Social: as scene of upper-class hijinks, 125; serves social elite, 140–141, 153–154, 199, 201; admission of new members to, 202; and *cultura*, 214–215; superficiality of, 340, 341; contempt for, among middle class, 347; social interaction in, 352, 353–355, 356, 357; and social fear, 353; reflects on modern society, 359; mentioned, 43, 96, 97
Club Urquiza: celebrates anniversary, 119
Cofradía del Niño: 211
colonos: defined, 30 n.
comisiones de vecinos: activities of, 148, 149
Comisión Intervecinal: 148
commerce: distinguishes urban from rural life, 21, 23; in Cuartel 1, 56; in Cuartel 2, 59–61; in Cuartel 3, 62; in the barrios, 64
Committee of Public Morality: activities regulated by, 32
compañerismo: in student life, 295–296
Concepción del Uruguay: as seat of government, 10
confiterías: social importance of, 45, 46
Congress of Americanists, 1966: and urbanization, xxiii
Congress of Tucumán: drafts constitution, 10
conquista: in courtship, 45; and the acculturation of children, 259, 260; and children's social perceptions, 276–277
consejo deliberante: authority of, 25
Constitution of 1853: popular attitudes toward, 361
Cooperadora Enrique Berduc: activities of, 149–150
cooperadoras: activities of, 149–150
Córdoba: and Argentine culture, xvi; founded, 3; and Indian attacks, 8; industrialization of, 368
corn: as important crop, 20
corso, the: celebration of, 60
courtship: and the plaza, 45; in the *vecindad*, 91; restrictions on, 94–95; conduct of, as reflection on social standing, 127
creencias: among the lower class, 181–182; among the middle class, 195; among the upper class, 211, 212
criollo(s): defined, 4 n., 255 n.; relations of, with Spanish conquerors, 8; in provincial structure of Entre Ríos, 10; and urban growth, 24
Cuartel 1: description of, 56–59
Cuartel 2: description of, 59–61
Cuartel 3: description of, 62
Cuartel 4: description of, 62–64
cuarteles: in city planning, 25–26, 53, 56
cultura: defined, 33 n.; importance of, to middle class, 188–189; importance of, to upper class, 214–215; identified with upper class, 368
cultural orientation: explanation of, 239–240; variation of, by social class, 240–249
culture: definition of, xviii–xix; heterogeneity vs. integration in, 81–82; provides analytical perspective, 372
curanderos: role of, 182–183; belief in, among the middle class, 195; belief in, among upper classes, 211–212

Damas Católicas: 211
Defensa Vecinal: encourages tax resistance, 148
delinquency: regulations against, 31
development: institutionalization of, 27–28; and financial crisis, 28
Durkheim, Émile: contribution of, on social classes, 257 n.

economy: main features of, 20–23
education: facilities for, in Cuartel 1, 58–59; importance of, to middle class, 189–190, 191–193; resistance to reform in, 330–331; as status symbol, 334; perpetuates social structure, 335; as viewed by retired teacher, 340–342. SEE ALSO schools
1824 census: results of, 11–20
El Argentino: attacks municipal government, 28 n.
El Centro: as political center of city, 42
English. SEE British
Entre Ríos: ownership of, 8; changes in political status of, 10; economy of, 20–21
Escuela Industrial de la Nación: serves lower-class students, 324–325; mentioned, 334
Escuela Normal. SEE Normal School

ethnic associations: significance of, 73–74; and neighborhood life, 96–97; formation of, 143–144; effect of, on members, 144–145; activities of, 146–147; decline of, 156–157, 354; burial plans of, 221–222; apathy in, 352–353
ethnic diversity: and social relations, 85–86
ethnic stereotypes: use of, 97–98; and social relations, 101–102, 104–106; held by middle class, 347–348; prevalance of, 355–356
Eva Perón Foundation: 179
extranjero: defined, 30 n.; enculturation of, 254–255

familia, la: activities of, 205
familias conocidas: 198, 199, 205, 213, 215
familias tradicionales: 199, 210, 212, 213, 214–215
family, nuclear: in upper-class life, 204–205
Federación Entrerriana Agricolas de la Provincia, La: and development, 20–21
field work: and preparation of present volume, xxii–xxiii
Fierro, Martin: observations of, on Argentine society, 362
fisherman: profile of, 173–177
Five Corners: activities at, 60–61
flax: as important crop, 20
French: arrive in Paraná, 29; and settlement of Argentina, 70; death notices for, 228; in primary school, 281
French Association: activities of, 145, 146
Friends of Children: 150
Friends of the Blind: 150
Friends of the Needy People: 150
funerals: relation of, to social standing, 224–228; and ethnic background, 228. SEE ALSO burial; cemetery, the

gambling: regulation of, 31
Garay, Juan de: 7
Gath and Chaves: 43
gaucho: tradition of, 20 n.; and urban growth, 24
gente: as behavioral classification, 106, 107, 184
Germans: and settlement of Paraná, xvi; opportunities for, opened, 29; and settlement of Argentina, 70; cultural identification of, 71; stereotype of, 98–99; death notices for, 228; accommodation of, to social structure, 256; live in ethnically mixed surroundings, 263; in primary school, 281
Gillin, John: on social position, 261
Golf Club: 153, 154, 155
golondrina: defined, 71 n.
grocer. SEE *almacenero*
Guatemala: author's study in, xxii–xxiii
Guipur: 43

hacendados: in early class structure, 252
Hernández, José: portrays gaucho tradition, 20 n.
household: composition of, 16–17
houses: of upper-class families, 56–58; of the *nouveaux riches*, 62–63; cleaning of, in daily routine, 86–87. SEE ALSO *ranchitos*; *ranchos*
Hymes, Dell: and linguistic terminology, 231 n.

immigrants: and neighborhood relations, 96–97; and ethnic associations, 143, 144; acculturation of, 254–256
immigration: and settlement of Paraná, xvi; and municipal development, 29; reaction to, 29–30; effect of, on Argentine society, 70–71; effect of, on class structure, 252, 254
Indians: and Spanish colonization, 4; relations of, with Spanish conquerors, 7–9; in provincial structure of Entre Ríos, 10; distribution of, by age and sex, 13; and urban growth, 24
informants: point of view of, xxi; anthropologist's debt to, 152, 152 n.–153 n.; as mirror on social situation, 339–340; diversity of, 364–365
Instituto de Profesorado: resistance to reform in, 330–331; mentioned, 321
intendente-mayor: in governmental structure, 25
IPRUL sample: results of, 276 n.
Irish: arrive in Paraná, 29
Israeli Association: 149, 156
Italia libre movement: opposes totalitarianism, 145
Italiani Meridionale: 143
Italiani Uniti: 144
Italians: and settlement of Paraná, xvi; arrive in Paraná, 29; place of residence of, 52, 59, 60, 64; and settlement of Argentina, 70; cultural identification of, 71; stereotype of, 98; accommodation of, to social structure, 256; live in ethnically mixed surroundings, 263
Italian Society: 143

Jesuits: attempts of, to placate Indians, 8
Jewish Center: 147
Jews: opportunities for, opened, 29; place of residence of, 60, 64; cultural identification of, 71; stereotype of, 99–100; death notices for, 228; accommodation of, to social structure, 256; live in ethnically mixed surroundings, 263; in primary schools, 281; separateness of, 363
Jockey Club: 142, 154, 350
Juyjuy: founded, 3

Katz, Stanley: analyzes sociometric data, 296 n.; on popularity, 299 n.
Kerawalla, Sandra: gathers material on private school, 307 n.
Kroeber, Alfred L.: contribution of, on social class, 257 n.

La Bajada de Paraná: founded, 8; growth of, 8–9; achieves *villa* status, 9–10; experiences political change, 23
labor unions: lack of concern with, 167 n.
Labov, Eric E.: linguistic terminology of, 231 n.
La Gran Aldea: 250
Lampard, Eric: contribution of, to literature on urbanization, xxi n.
land use: proportional analysis of, 22
language: variation of, by locale, 229–230; variation of, by social class, 230–239
La Rioja: founded, 3
Lawn Tennis Club: 142
Libanés Sport Club: celebrates anniversary, 119
Liga de Inquilinos: 151
Liga de Jubilados: 151
Liga de Madres: 151
Liga Social Pro-Comportamiento Humano: 152
Lions Club: 149
livestock: importance of, to economy, 21
López, Lucio V.: on Buenos Aires elite, 250
lower class. SEE *clase baja*; *clase humilde*; *negros, los*

McGann, Thomas F.: on the Europeanizing of Argentina, 250
Madrinas del Ampero Maternal: 150
Mafud, Julio: on rootlessness of Argentine society, 371
manzanas: in city planning, 25–26, 53

marriage: mixed vs. unmixed, 14, 74; in upper class, 202–203, 208, 209
Marx, Karl: contribution of, on social class, 257 n.
Maya: author's study of, xxii–xxiii
Mead, Margaret: on history of anthropology, xv n.
Mendoza: founded, 4
mestizos: relations of, with Spanish conquerors, 8
method. SEE study approach
Mexico: develops national style, 364
middle class. SEE *clase media*
Middle Easterners: and settlement of Paraná, xvi
Morse, Richard: contribution of, to literature on modernization, xxi n.
municipalidad: authority of, 24–25
municipio: xxi
My Son the Doctor: 193

names: cultural significance of, 66, 69–70
National Bank: 43
national holidays: celebration of, 63–64
National Ministry of Education: 279
Negroes: in provincial structure of Entre Ríos, 10; distribution of, by age and sex, 13; and urban growth, 24
negros, los: characteristics of, 343; middle-class image of, 346
neighborhood. SEE *vecindad*
neighborhood clubs. SEE *clubes de vecindad*
newspapers: publicize club activities, 119, 120; image of clubs created by, 157; coverage of funerals by, 225–228
New Year's celebration: social relations reflected in, 130–132
Normal School: and teacher training, 301, 302, 303; social position of students of, 325; as center of cultural tradition, 340; mentioned, 58, 280, 282, 323, 324

occupations: distribution of, by ethnic group, 17, 18–19
Operai Italiani: 143
Ortega y Gasset, José: on Spanish colonization, 6–7; on Argentine lifestyles, 251; on rootlessness of Argentine society, 370, 371

Paraná River: 3
Paraná Soccer League: 120
Pardo(s): distribution of, by age and sex, 12; definition of, 15
Parque Urquiza: as symbol of progress,

52-53; uses employed for, 63; as preferred residential area, 321
Patriotica XX Settembre: 144
Peña: preserve criollo folkways, 152
Peñarol: celebrates anniversary, 119
Peret, ———: 340
Perón, Eva: 65, 105
Perón, Juan: appeal of, to lower classes, 64–65, 180; ethnic stereotypes under regime of, 105; scrutiny of clubs under, 161; distrust of, 340, 341; effect of, on social order, 362
Peru: access to, sought, 3
planning: and urban growth, 25–27
play: in the *vecindad*, 90
Plaza Primero de Mayo: as social center of city, 42–46; origin of name of, 66; mentioned, 63
plazas: cultural significance of, 43–47; origin of names for, 66, 68
Poles: accommodation of, to social structure, 256
politics: and clubs, 167 n.; lack of popular involvement in, 344–346; distrust of, 347, 361–362, 364; money and power in, 349; popular attitudes toward, 361; instability of, 365–366; and anxiety, 369–370
population: distribution of, by age and sex, 11–13, 15; growth in, 24; distribution of, by cuartel, 35; ethnic configuration of, 71–75
Porteños: criticism of, 348–349
prostitution: regulation of, 32
Provincial Board of Education: 279
Provincial Ministry of Education: 279
public morals: regulation of, 30–33
public performances: regulation of, 31–32
pueblo: and settlement of frontier, 8

racial classification: determination of, 14–15
ranchitos: as home of fishermen, 173
ranchos: description of, 51–52; in Cuartel 1, 58
Redfield, Robert: on anthropological description, 39, 40
reducciones: organized, 8
Río de la Plata: discovery of, 3
Rocamora, don Tomás de: 9
Rosas, Juan Manuel de: 63
Rotary Club: 149, 350
Rowing Club: 142
Rusos: stereotype of, 99. SEE ALSO Russian-Germans
Russian-Germans: colonization by, 29; place of residence of, 59, 64; active in churches, 156–157; accommodation of, to social structure, 256. SEE ALSO Rusos
Russians: and settlement of Paraná, xvi; and settlement of Argentina, 70

Sabrelli, Juan José: on the middle class, 196–197
Salta: founded, 3
Sanchez, Florenzio: 193
San Juan: founded, 4
San Luis: founded, 4
San Martín, José de: statue of, 66
San Martín primary school: background of students of, 280–281; further education of students of, 281–282
Santa Fé: as important settlement, 7–8; and founding of Paraná, 8–9
Santiago del Estero: founded, 3
Sarmiento, Domingo Faustino: 24
Scalabrini Ortiz, Raúl: 340
schools: and the socialization process, 260–261; city vs. *vecindad*, 301–302
—, primary: progress through grades in, 279–280; curriculum of, 282; presentation of lessons in, 282, 283–285, 304, 305, 307–308; facilities of, 282–283; maintenance of students' performance in, 285–287; sex orientation in, 290; enrollment in, 303–304; vocational training in, 305; variations in, by social class, 306–307, 308–309; promote conformity, 309–312
—, secondary: background of students of, 325–326; prestige of, 326; curriculum of, 326; presentation of lessons in, 326; importance of success in, 326–327; discipline in, 327, 329; student's recollection of, 327–329. SEE ALSO education
school system: structure of, 278–279
Schwartz, Henry, III: gathers data on *clase baja*, 186 n.; compares schools, 303 n., 306–307
service organizations: activities of, 147–152
Sherzer, Joel: linguistic analysis of, 230 n.
shopping: in daily routine, 87; by children, 263–265
simpático: in student life, 295
Soccores Mutuos: 143
social areas: descriptions of, 75–81
social class(es): and anthropological study, xix–xxi; in early Paraná, 16, 19–20; historical roots of, 33, 35–37, 256–257; descriptions of, 48, 50–53; distribution of, throughout city, 49; distribution of, in concentric rings, 53, 56; stereotypes of, 102–104; and so-

Index

cial relations, 104–106; as analytical tool, 171, 373–374; and educational differences, 306–309; effect of, on orientation toward *vecindad*, 319; as viewed by retired teacher, 341, 342; as viewed by middle class, 348; cuts across ethnic lines, 354; identifiability of, 358, 359; as integral part of city life, 367–369. SEE ALSO *clase alta*; *clase aristocrática*; *clase baja*; *clase humilde*; *clase media*; *hacendados*; *negros, los*
social distance: prevalence of, within neighborhoods, 132–137
social institutions: distribution of, 54–55
socialization: in the *vecindad*, 260, 276–277; in the schools, 260–261; in the army, 261
social mobility: desirability of, 37–38; Latin American view of, 261; and the educational system, 334, 335; and support of status quo, 374–375
social structure: movement within, xx–xxi; ideal model of, modified, 35; immigrants' accommodation to, 256; vs. value system, 374; future of, 374–375
Sociedad Damas Vicentinas: 150
Sociedad Dante Alighiere: 150
Sociedad de Socorros Mutuos: 150
Sociedad Española de Socorros Mutuos: 144
Sociedad Friulana: 146
Sociedad Hermanas de los Pobres: 150
Sociedad Italiana: 146
Sociedad Mutuos Unión Suiza: 150
Sociedad Unión Arabe: 146
Sociedad Vendedores de Diarios: 151
Société Français de Secours Mutuel: 143, 146
Sorokin, Pitirin: contribution of, on social classes, 257 n.
Spaniards: colonization by, 3–10; place of residence of, 60, 64; and settlement of Argentina, 70; cultural identification of, 71; stereotype of, 100; accommodation of, to social structure, 256; live in ethnically mixed surroundings, 263; in primary school, 281
Spanish Association: activities of, 145, 146–147
streets: origin of names for, 66–69
students: on note taking, 287; perceptions of teachers by, 287–289; background of, 291, 292; social interaction among, 291, 293–301; selection of school for, 302; social orientation of, by social class, 313–320; ambitions of, for future, 320–324; entry of, into social network, 334–335
study approach: explanation of, xvii–xxi; and participation, xxi–xxiv
superstitions. SEE *creencias*
Swiss: and settlement of Paraná, xvi, 29; and settlement of Argentina, 70; cultural identification of, 71; in primary school, 281
Syrians: and settlement of Argentina, 70; in primary school, 281

Taylor, Carl C.: on class in Argentine society, xx
Teacher: 311
teachers: background of, 282; presentation of lessons by, 282, 283–285, 307–308; maintenance of students' performance by, 285–287; students' perceptions of, 287–289; identified with feminine terminology, 289–290; class consciousness among, 302–303; relationship of, with students, 304–305; as guardians of discipline, 309–312
Tucumán: founded, 3
Turcos: stereotype of, 100; uninvolved in social games, 363
XX Settembre de Mutuos Soccorso: 144

Unione a Beneficenza: 143
uniones vecinales: activities of, 148–149
Unión Residente Paraguayas: 146
Unión Suiza: 146
upper class. SEE *clase alta*; *clase aristocrática*
urban growth: and city planning, 25–27; and city finances, 27–28; and social divisions, 33, 35–37; stages in, 36; retards social intimacy, 136–137
urbanism: as way of life, xvii
Urquiza, Justo José de: 63
Urquiza Park. SEE Parque Urquiza

value system: vs. social structure, 374
vecindad: importance of, as concept, 85; profile of life in, 85–92; social exclusiveness in, 104–106; power structure of, 108; social consciousness in, 108–110; points of reference in, 111–112; ingredients of social standing in, 125–130; and social atomization, 167–168; place of, in socialization, 260, 276–277; as viewed by lower-class children, 313–315; as viewed by middle-class children, 316–317; as viewed by upper-class children, 317–319; effect of, on children's social views, 319–320; gossip in, 348
vecino(s): importance of, as concept, 85; perceptions of, by each other, 92–

93; curiosity of, about each other, 125–130
verdulero: daily rounds of, 87–88; social function of, 117
vergüenza: effect of, on social relations, 127–129
vocational training: in a barrio school, 305

Weber, Max: contribution of, on social classes, 257 n.
wheat: as important crop, 20
Whiteford, Andrew H.: treats problem of social equilibrium, 256 n.
whites: distribution of, by age and sex, 12
Wirth, Louis: on urbanism, xvii

Yeager, Malcah: assists in linguistic analysis, 230 n.
youth: accommodation of, to society, 259–261
Yugoslavs: in primary school, 281

zona activa nueva: description of, 79–80, 81
zona central: description of, 76, 78, 80–81
zona de charas: in city planning, 25–26
zona de ciudad: in city planning, 25
zona de los barrios: in city layout, 42
zona de quinta: in city planning, 25–26
zona desconocida: description of, 80, 81
zona dormida: description of, 78–79, 81

DATE DUE

5/17/90	6020562		
Messiah College Library			